Berlin
and Potsdam

N. Hautemanière

★★★ Ägyptisches Mus
Museumsinsel > Pergamum Mus
Kulturforum > Gemaldegalerie
Zoo

D1041928

Travel Publications

38 Clarendon Road – WATFORD Herts WD1 1 SX - U.K.
☎ (01923) 415 000
www.michelin-travel.com
TheGreenGuide-uk@uk.michelin.com

Manufacture française des pneumatiques Michelin
Société en commandite par actions au capital de 2 000 000 000 de francs
Place des Carmes-Déchaux – 63 Clermont-Ferrand (France)
R.C.S. Clermont-Fd B 855 200 507

Typesetting: NORD COMPO à Villeneuve d'Ascq
Printing and Binding: I.F.C. à St-Germain-du-Puy

Cover design: Carré Noir, Paris 17ᵉ arr.

THE GREEN GUIDE:
The Spirit of Discovery

The exhilaration of new horizons,
the fun of seeing the world ,
the excitement of discovery: this is
what we seek to share with you.
To help you make the most of your
travel experience, we offer first-hand
knowledge and turn a discerning eye
on places to visit.
This wealth of information gives
you the expertise to plan your own
enriching adventure. With THE
GREEN GUIDE showing you the way,
you can explore new destinations
with confidence or rediscover old
ones.
Leisure time spent with THE GREEN
GUIDE is also a time for refreshing
your spirit and enjoying yourself.
So turn the page and open a window
on the world. Join THE GREEN
GUIDE in the spirit of discovery.

Contents

Sanssouci: Teahouse statue

Y. Travert/DIAF

Berlin beer house

Zoological gardens

Pratt-Pries/DIAF

Philharmonic

R. Janke/Focus/COSMOS

Maps

MAPS AND ROAD ATLASES FOR USE WITH THE GUIDE

Berlin plan no. 33

This plan shows all majors roads, one-way streets, main car parks, main public buildings post offices, useful information and an alphabetical street index.

... and to get to Berlin:

Europe road and tourist atlases 136 et 130

– no 136: spiral-bound atlas (Western Europe, scale 1:1 000 000, Eastern Europe, scale 1:3 000 000) containing road information, a mileage chart, 74 town and urban districts, a climate map, with an index of towns and other place names indicated for easy location.
– no 130: bound atlas.

In addition to these maps and atlases, there is a web site – www.michelin-travel.com (certain services available on subscription only) – which enables you to calculate detailed itineraries with travelling times, and offers a number of other services.

The Berlin boroughs

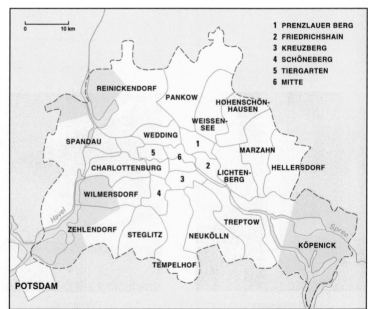

1 PRENZLAUER BERG
2 FRIEDRICHSHAIN
3 KREUZBERG
4 SCHÖNEBERG
5 TIERGARTEN
6 MITTE

Michelin Map no. 987 Germany, Benelux, Austria, Czech Republic

Michelin Map no. 415 to 420

Six regional maps cover the main regions of the country (scale 1:300 000).

Thematic maps

Town maps

Grounds plans

Using this guide

The Green Guide is a faithful travelling companion. **In it, you will find:**

● **maps of the centre of Berlin and Greater Berlin**, with a list of the streets and the sites of the main sights; thematic maps on the city's history, natural environment leisure facilities; maps of the city of Potsdam and its environs.

● an **introduction** containing a host of information about the capital city of Germany: this outlines its geographical features, the historical events which have marked the city and its artistic, literary and musical heritage, as well as its shows and singers.

● the chapter on **Berlin life**, with a wide range of practical tips and addresses: excursions by boat, swimming baths and beaches, theatres and concert halls, cafés and tea rooms, shops and markets.

● the sights, devoted to the principal attractions in Berlin, describing the **various districts** of Berlin and Potsdam in alphabetical order.

● **practical information** which will be very helpful in preparing your trip: useful addresses and information, opening hours and visiting conditions of the sights and attractions as indicated by the symbol ⊙.

● a detailed **alphabetical index** allowing you to find a given sight, person or subject quickly.

Despite all the care taken in producing this guide and verifying the information, a few errors or typing mistakes may have crept in. This is why we ask you kindly to send any corrections and criticisms, as well as your suggestions and comments, to Michelin Travel Publications, 38 Clarendon Road, Watford Herts WD1 1SX, Internet: www.michelin-travel.com or to the e-mail address:

Friedrichstraße: "Quartier 206"

Key

★★★ **Highly recommended**

★★ **Recommended**

★ **Interesting**

Tourism

⊙	Admission Times and Charges listed at the end of the guide	►►	Visit if time permits
	Sightseeing route with departure point indicated	AZ B	Map co-ordinates locating sights
	Ecclesiastical building	ⓘ	Tourist information
	Synagogue – Mosque		Historic house, castle – Ruins
	Building (with main entrance)		Dam – Factory or power station
■	Statue, small building		Fort – Cave
†	Wayside cross	⊤	Prehistoric site
◎	Fountain		Viewing table – View
	Fortified walls – Tower – Gate	▲	Miscellaneous sight

Recreation

	Racecourse		Waymarked footpath
	Skating rink	◆	Outdoor leisure park/centre
	Outdoor, indoor swimming pool		Theme/Amusement park
	Marina, moorings		Wildlife/Safari park, zoo
	Mountain refuge hut		Gardens, park, arboretum
	Overhead cable-car		Aviary, bird sanctuary
	Tourist or steam railway		

Additional symbols

	Motorway (unclassified)		Post office – Telephone centre
❶ ❶	Junction: complete, limited		Covered market
	Pedestrian street		Barracks
	Unsuitable for traffic, street subject to restrictions	△	Swing bridge
	Steps – Footpath	∪ ✕	Quarry – Mine
	Railway – Coach station	Ⓑ Ⓕ	Ferry (river and lake crossings)
	Funicular – Rack-railway		Ferry services: Passengers and cars
	Tram – Metro, Underground		Foot passengers only
Bert (R.)...	Main shopping street	③	Access route number common to MICHELIN maps and town plans

Abbreviations and special symbols

J	Law courts (Justizgebäude)	U	University (Universität)
L	Provincial government (Landesregierung)	ⓐ	Hotel
M	Museum (Museum)		Park and Ride
POL.	Police (Polizei)		Covered parking
R	Town hall (Rathaus)	19	Federal road (Bundesstraße)
T	Theatre (Theater)	Ⓢ	S-Bahn station
		Ⓤ	U-Bahn station
8 EX	Page number and grid reference indicating the position of the sight on the map of Berlin		

NB: The German letter ß (eszett) has been used throughout this guide.

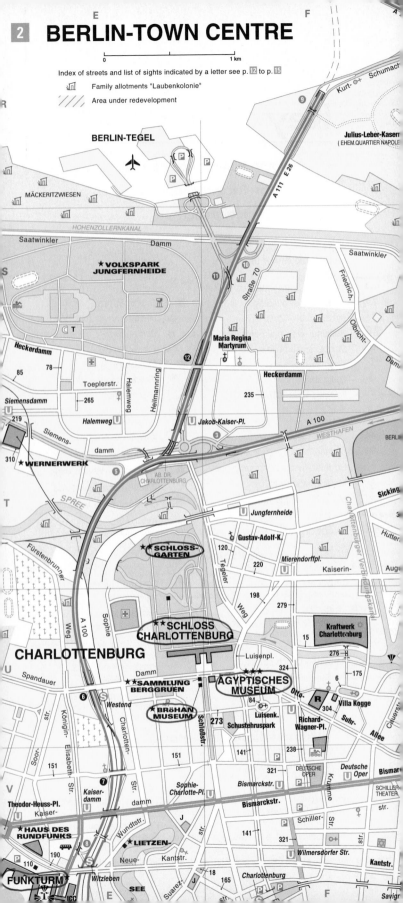

2 BERLIN-TOWN CENTRE

0   1 km

Index of streets and list of sights indicated by a letter see p. 12 to p. 15

Family allotments "Laubenkolonie"

Area under redevelopment

BERLIN-TEGEL

Julius-Leber-Kaserne
(EHEM.QUARTIER NAPOLE

Kurt- Schumac

MÄCKERITZWIESEN

HOHENZOLLERNKANAL

Saatwinkler Damm

Saatwinkler

★ VOLKSPARK
JUNGFERNHEIDE

Friedrich-

Straße 70

Dam

T

Maria Regina
Martyrum

Heckerdamm

Heckerdamm

85 78

Toeplerstr.

Halemweg

Heilmannring

265

235

Siemensdamm
219

Halemweg

Jakob-Kaiser-Pl.

A 100

WESTHAFEN

BERLI

310 ★ WERNERWERK

Siemens-
damm

AB. DR.
CHARLOTTENBURG

SPREE

Sicking

Hutter

Augu

Fürstenbrunner

Jungfernheide

Gustav-Adolf-K.

120

Tegeler

Mierendorffpl.

Kaiserin-

★ SCHLOSS-
GARTEN

220

Weg

198

279

15

Kraftwerk
Charlottenburg

CHARLOTTENBURG

Sophie

A 100

Weg

★★ SCHLOSS
CHARLOTTENBURG

Luisenpl.

276

175

6

Damm

324

Spandauer

★ SAMMLUNG
BERGGRUEN

★★★ ÄGYPTISCHES
MUSEUM

Otto-

Villa Kogge
304

R

Westend

84

Luisenk.

Richard-
Wagner-Pl.

Suhr-

Allee

Charlotten-

★ BRÖHAN
MUSEUM

273

Schlossstr.

Schustehruspark

Königin-

Elisabeth- Str.

Soor-

151

151

141

238

321

DEUTSCHE
OPER

Deutsche
Oper

Bismar

Kaiser-
damm

Sophie-
Charlotte-Pl.

Bismarckstr.

SCHILLER
THEATER

Theodor-Heuss-Pl.

Str.

Bismarckstr.

Schiller-

Str.

str.

★ HAUS DES
RUNDFUNKS

Wundtstr.

★ LIETZEN-

141

321

110

190

Neue-

Kantstr.

Wilmersdorfer Str.

Kantstr.

FUNKTURM

Witzleben

SEE

Suarez-

18

165

Charlottenburg

Savign

ICC

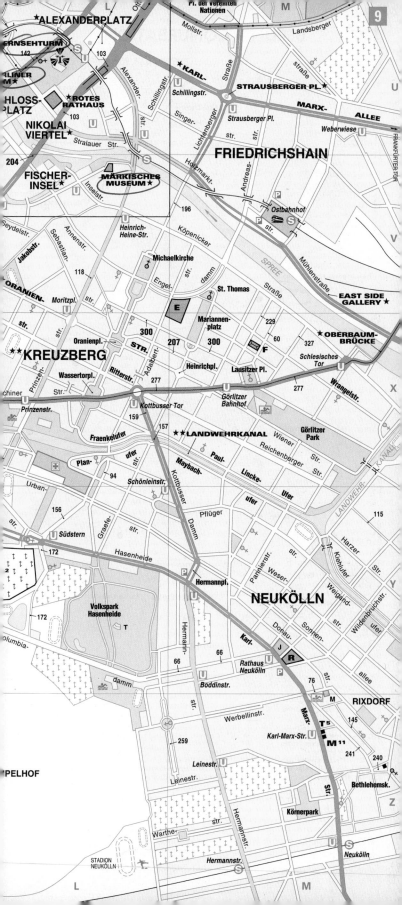

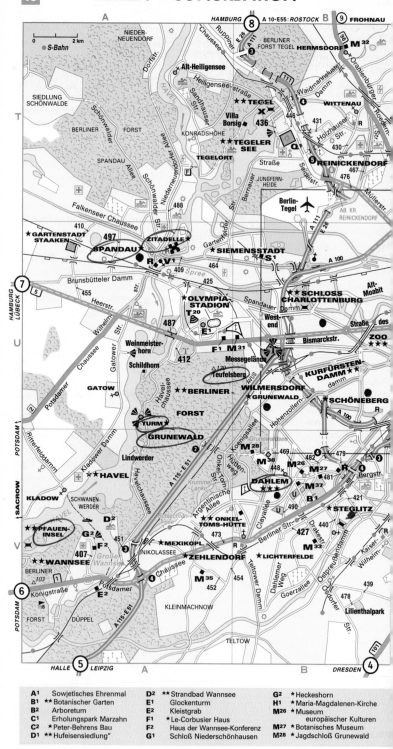

A1	Sowjetisches Ehrenmal	D2	** Strandbad Wannsee	G2	* Heckeshorn
B1	** Botanischer Garten	E1	Glockenturm	H1	* Maria-Magdalenen-Kirche
B2	Arboretum	E2	Kleistgrab	M26	* Museum
C1	Erholungspark Marzahn	F1	* Le-Corbusier Haus		europäischer Kulturen
C2	* Peter-Behrens-Bau	F2	Haus der Wannsee-Konferenz	M27	* Botanisches Museum
D1	** Hufeisensiedlung"	G1	Schloß Niederschönhausen	M28	* Jagdschloß Grunewald

Street index **12** to **15**

Roads leading into and through the town
are indicated in red or yellow on our local maps.

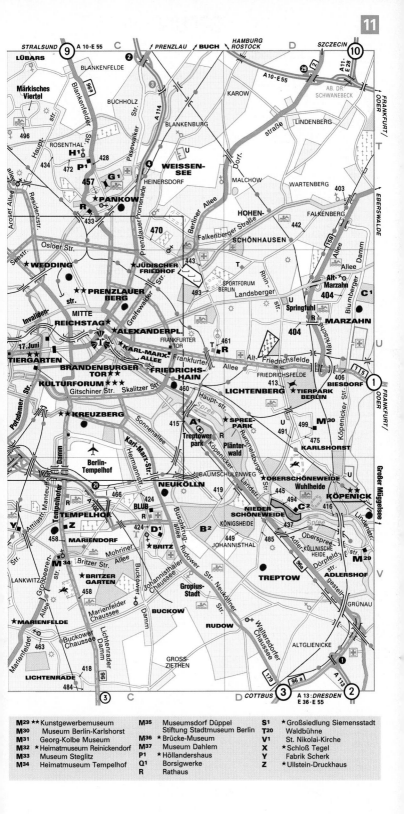

M29 ★★Kunstgewerbemuseum	**M35** Museumsdorf Düppel	**S1**	★Großsiedlung Siemensstadt
M30 Museum Berlin-Karlshorst	Stiftung Stadtmuseum Berlin	**T20**	Waldbühne
M31 Georg-Kolbe Museum	**M36** ★Brücke-Museum	**V1**	St. Nikolai-Kirche
M32 ★Heimatmuseum Reinickendorf	**M37** Museum Dahlem	**X**	★Schloß Tegel
M33 Museum Steglitz	**P1** ★Holländerhaus	**Y**	Fabrik Scherk
M34 Heimatmuseum Tempelhof	**Q1** Borsigwerke	**Z**	★Ullstein-Druckhaus
	R Rathaus		

Sights are indicated in orange on our town plans.
Either the name or a letter appear on the plan.
The letters are identified in the green box.

Sights indicated by a letter on plan 2 to 9

A	Charlottenburger Tor	M11		Puppentheatermuseum
B	Reste des Anhalter Bahnhofs	M12	★	Berliner Post- und Fernmeldemuseum (closed)
C	Mossehaus	M13		Polizeihistorische Sammlung
D	St. Bonifatius	M14		Zuckermuseum
E	Kunstamt Kreuzberg Bethanien	M15		Heimatmuseum Wedding
	(ehem. Krankenhaus Bethanien)	M38		Jüdisches Museum
F	Eisenbahnmarkthalle	P		Abgeordnetenhaus von Berlin
H	Villa Von-der-Heydt			(ehem. Preußischer Landtag)
	"Stiftung Preußischer Kulturbesitz"	Q		Akademie der Künste
J	Gerichtsgebäude	R		Rathaus
K1, K2★	Kirchhöfe	S		Prinz-Albrecht-Gelände - „Topographie des
M1	Museum für Kommunikation Berlin			Terrors"
M2	Haus am Checkpoint Charlie	T1		Renaissance-Theater
M3	Berlin-Museum (closed)	T2		Hebbeltheater
M4 ★	Musikinstrumenten-Museum	T3	★★	Philharmonie, Kammermusiksaal
M5 ★★	Kunstgewerbemuseum	T5		Neuköllner Oper
M6 ★★★	Gemäldegalerie	T6		Metropol
M7 ★	Neue Nationalgalerie	T7		Musical Theater Berlin
M8 ★	Staatsbibliothek Preußischer Kulturbesitz	T8		Theater des Westens
M9	Gedenkstätte Deutscher Widerstand	V	★	Haus der Kulturen der Welt
M10 ★	Käthe-Kollwitz-Museum			(ehem. Kongreßhalle)
		W		Abspannwerk Scharnhorst

Street index for the plans 2 to 11

Join us in our constant task of keeping up-to-date.
Please send us your comments and suggestions.

Michelin Tyre PLC
Tourism Department

The Edward Hyde Building
38 Clarendon Road
WATFORD - Herts WD1 1SX
Fax: 01923 415250

The sculpture "Berlin", situated near the Memorial Church

J. Raga/EXPLORER

Introduction

Berlin, City of open spaces

Lying in the great North-German plain, 35m above sea level, Berlin boasts a unique natural setting.

AN UNPROMISING ENVIRONMENT

The site on which Berlin developed consisted originally of forest, sandy heath and marshland. The landscape of Brandenburg and the Berlin region took on its present form at the end of the last Ice Age, some 20 000 years ago.

The valley of the Spree is flanked by two plateaux of marl and clay: the **Barnim** (50-60m) to the northeast, and the **Teltow** (45-55m) to the southwest. As the city grew, it spread out onto these plateaux, absorbing the existing villages. The underlying structure of the terrain is still apparent in the rise and fall of the streets, explaining the difference in level between the Hauptstraße and Schöneberg, Humboldthain and Wedding, Spandauer Damm and Spandau, Schönhauser Allee or Prenzlauer Allee and Prenzlauer Berg. As well as the man-made Teufelsberg, which rises to 115m, Berlin has a number of natural areas of high ground: the Havelsberg (97m) and Schäferberg (103m) to the west, the protuberant Kreuzberg (66m) and the Müggelberge (114.7m) to the east. A more characteristic feature of the area, however, is its complex of lakes: the Müggelsee to the east and the Havel lakes to the west, the biggest fluvial lakes in Germany.

The Havel

LAKES AND RIVERS

The name "Berlin" derives from the root *bri*, meaning a wet place. Three river valleys, including that of the Spree, run east to west, effectively linking Berlin to Warsaw. These valleys are interconnected by a dense network of secondary valleys. The deeper channels have given rise to the **Havel** and **Dahme** lakes, while the more modest have resulted in the extended belt of lakes bordering the Grunewald Forest (Schlachtensee, Krumme Lanke, Grunewald See, Halensee, Lietzensee). The **round lakes** to the north-east of Berlin (Malchower See, Weisser See, Fauler See, Orankesee, Obersee) were formed at a later date by the melting of large masses of ice.

The slow-running **Spree** flows through the **Müggelsee**, Berlin's biggest lake (740ha, with an average depth of 8m), receives the waters of the Dahme and Wuhle rivers at Köpenick, is swelled by the Panke near the Friedrichstraße station, then flows into the Havel, a tributary of the Elbe, at Spandau. The Barnim and Teltow plateaux are watered by many smaller streams, such as the **Panke**, which has been canalised, and the **Tegeler Fleiß**, whose wild banks are now a nature reserve. Potsdam was once an island separated from neighbouring areas by marshland, a lake and a canal to the north.

For a quiet place to stay
*Consult the annual **Michelin Red Guide France** (hotels and restaurants)*
*and the **Michelin Guide Camping Caravaning France***
which offer a choice of pleasant hotels and quiet campsites
in convenient locations.

Berlin's canals

Initiated in the 16C (the first lock was built on the Spree in 1550), a remarkable canal network was engineered in the 17C and 18C. The Frederick-William canal, completed in 1669, joined the Elbe to the Oder, following the course of the Spree. A link with the railway was established in 1830, the work of English engineers. The Spandau canal *(Spandauer Schiffahrtskanal)* was created in 1859. The Westhafen *(see MOABIT)* was the most important of Berlin's 14 commercial and industrial ports and, right up to the Second World War, ranked as Germany's second river port, after Duisburg. The city now has 197km of navigable waterways, and much of the heavy goods traffic with Poland still goes by canal. The Osthafen, opposite the mouth of the Landwehrkanal in Kreuzberg, is the city's second port. A new port is to be built on the Neukölln canal in the South of Berlin.

BERLIN'S OPEN SPACES POLICY

Open spaces account for almost a third (28.4%) of the area of Greater Berlin, 17.5% of which is forested. The original forest cover was long ago replaced by pines and broad-leaved species.

Endless possibilities for walks – Berlin's open spaces come in many shapes and sizes: forest areas (Düppel, Grunewald, Spandau and Tegel to the west; the Müggelberge and Wuhlheide to the east); parks big and small, traditional in the city centre (Tiergarten, Friedrichshain, Humboldthain, Hasenheide), modern (Jungfernheide, Rehberge) and contemporary (Britzer Garten); the banks of lakes and canals, for instance the Fraenkelufer in the Görlitz park at Kreuzberg; nature reserves along rivers (Tegeler Fließ) or depressions formed by moraines (the Obersee and Fauler See at Höhenschönhausen and the Weissensee). It is also worth mentioning the many "colonies" of family allotments, small village squares overlooked by ancient churches and the royal gardens all along the route to Potsdam. Köpenick and Spandau are reincarnations of the old Brandenburg landscape with its fields, lakes and woods. The village of Lübars in the northeast of Reinickendorf, on the slopes of the Barnim, and the corresponding area of Pankow (Blankenfelde) have managed to preserve their rural character, and many farms surrounded by meadows continue to exist within the city limits (5.7% of the urban area is in fact farmland). These open spaces are a great asset to the city.

Berlin's open spaces policy – Until the end of the 19C, it was illegal to fell trees on the banks of the Havel. Karl Friedrich Schinkel and **Peter Josef Lenné** created a new form of landscape art in their picturesque layout of the parks of New Garden, Babelsberg, Klein-Glienicke, Sacrow and Peacock Island, giving unity to a number of separate sites. The Havel is free of industrial development until it approaches Spandau, then quickly regains its verdant character on the banks of the Tegeler See.

Rudolf Virchow, a doctor and member of the Berlin city council, had trees planted along the streets to improve the quality of the air. Today, some 400 000 trees line almost all of Berlin's streets. Impressed by the idyllic aspect of Berlin's suburbs, Jean Giraudoux observed that: "Berlin is not so much a garden city as one big garden". Problems began to arise around the turn of the century, when wooded areas fell foul of building speculation. The liberal and social-democrat elements in the Prussian Chamber called for a debate on woodland conservation. Under the influence of **Martin Wagner**, the assembly elected by the inter-communal grouping of Greater Berlin showed concern for Berlin's woodland heritage and managed to save the Grunewald, Tegel, Potsdam and Köpenick forests from the prevailing development fever.

A city of allotment holders

Industrialisation and the disastrous conditions suffered by the working classes led to the development of "family allotments" *(Kleingärten)*, where the inhabitants of tiny tenements could stretch their cramped limbs. Bismarck understood the social importance of these small squares of green as a way of keeping the masses from rioting. 80 000 lovingly-tended individual plots *(Grundstücke)* are now grouped into 900 **Laubenkolonien**: areas of varying size, sometimes forming labyrinths of greenery and fragrant walkways. Altogether, they cover some 6 000ha. Even the smallest plots of unused land, in some cases lying beside the tracks of the S-Bahn, have been pressed into service. The names of the various *Kolonien* sometimes reflect contemporary events (Kolonie Port Arthur, for instance), but more often they are endowed with bucolic names: *Gemütlichkeit* ("Intimacy"), *Sonnenheim* ("Home in the sun"), *Grüne Wiese* ("Green meadows") or *Treue Seele* ("Faithful soul"). After the First World War, they formed enclaves, almost states within the State, with legislation of their own. In times of economic crisis, the little huts were often used as a final refuge and, during and after both World Wars, the little gardens were transformed into vegetable plots to meet the needs of a famished city.

Carrying on the tradition, the Grünes Berlin association is now active in seeking to bring new life to areas of waste land in the heart of the city, the environs of the Friedrichshain and the banks of the Spree (featured in the films of Wim Wenders), to create leafy walkways along the old city walls and to restore the Panke river to the light of day. The post-unification development of the city is being carried out with respect for the environment and includes a cautious increase in the density of existing residential areas (the green belt is to be completed with additional city parks).

THE PHYSICAL ASPECT OF THE CITY

A metropolis at the heart of Europe – Covering an area of 889km² (8 times that of Paris), with over 3.6 million inhabitants and stretching 45km from west to east, 38km from north to south, Berlin is Germany's second biggest urban area after the Ruhr, though it does not yet enjoy quite the same advantages. Before the War, accused of draining the vital forces of the nation, Berlin ruled over a hinterland conquered from the East. It is now a relatively isolated city lying just 70km from the Polish border and, as the capital of a highly decentralised country, its influence is balanced by other centres wielding considerable power.

"An archipelago of little towns" *(Franz Hessel, Stroll in Berlin)* – The fascination of Berlin can be ascribed partly to its many lesser centres, differing one from another yet forming a recognisable unity. This gives the city an inexhaustible quality, as if one could never finish exploring it. The visitor moves from the Alexanderplatz to the Friedrichstraße, from the Potsdamer Platz to the Zoologischer Garten station, caught up by the changing scene. Berlin has grown by absorbing villages which themselves have become towns. The modern city is roughly **star-shaped**. The outlying districts are either residential quarters (Dahlem, Grunewald, Pankow) or industrial suburbs (Charlottenburg/Spandau, Köpenick, Tempelhof), where workers live in model housing developments. The integration of the districts of **Marzahn** (1979), Höhenschönhausen (1985) and Hellersdorf (1986), where new towns were erected in the days of the GDR, is the last stage in the growth of a city that was unable to develop to the west. Unification has resulted in many major changes: peripheral districts have become central (Kreuzberg); the Potsdamer Platz and the Leipziger Platz again form the connection between the old city centre and West Berlin. There are still plenty of open spaces within the city boundaries. The continuing policy of preserving the multi-polar structure of the city whilst respecting the environment, depends on joint development of the **Berlin/Brandenburg** region. The growth of new settlements on the city outskirts is creating a regional ring of secondary centres (Königs-Wusterhausen, Oranienburg), connected to Berlin itself by high-speed train services.

TRANSPORTATION

Early forms of public transport – Sedan chairs (of which Berlin boasted 18 in 1688) were introduced by the Huguenots. The **berline** was the invention of another Frenchman, albeit of Piedmontese origin, Philippe de la Chieze *(see POTSDAM)*. The first horse-drawn cabs appeared fifty years later. In 1839, the Potsdam station was linked to the Alexanderplatz by an omnibus service, and the first omnibus company was founded in 1846. Berlin became an important railway junction, with monumental stations such as the Anhalt, but public transport really came into its own in the 1870s, to serve the rapidly expanding periphery, where the middle and wealthy classes were settling in large numbers.

S-Bahn and U-Bahn – The **Ringbahn**, which currently forms part of the S-Bahn system, linked Berlin's terminal railway stations. The first east-west link was established when the **Stadtbahn** was inaugurated in 1882. The S-Bahn tunnel between Yorkstraße and Nordbahnhof stations in 1939 meant the opening of the north-south line. Work on the metro, overground and underground, began in 1902 on the section linking the Stralauer Tor to the Potsdamer Platz. The six lines built by 1914 tended to serve the more fashionable districts and residential suburbs. Because fares were expensive, the **Untergrundbahn** (U-Bahn) was used mainly by the better-off. The electrification of the S-Bahn, in 1922, was a very costly undertaking. Trams, metro and buses were merged in 1929 into a **single transport company** (the "Berliner Verkehrs-Gesellschaft" or BVG), the world's biggest municipal enterprise. The managing director was **Ernst Reuter** *(see ERNST-REUTER-PLATZ)*.

A united city, time for a rethink – By 1989, 100km of S-Bahn had been abandoned and some metro stations walled up. The track was in poor condition and many bridges had deteriorated. After the reunification, enormous sums were invested to bring old lines back into service, replace rolling stock, restore the elevated sections and rehabilitate stations.

The city authorities gave priority to public transport (which was supposed to carry 80% of the traffic) and to railways over roads. A regional transport interchange system between Berlin and Brandenburg came into service on 1 January 1997. The new **Potsdamer Platz station**, directly accessible from the offices of big companies and intended to handle 50 000 passengers a day, will serve as a major communications hub for U-Bahn and S-Bahn lines and the regional (R-Bahn) network.

Berlin is now served by intercity and ICE trains. The development model used is the so-called "mushroom concept" *(Pilzkonzept)*, adopted in order to link the east-west line between the Zoo and Ostbahnhof stations with the new north-south tunnel. High-speed trains, the metro and the motor routes will be linked with the new Berliner Zentralbahnhof via several loops of the **Tiergartentunnel** beneath the Spree and the Großer Tiergarten. This new rail intersection is to be constructed on the site of the present Lehrter Stadtbahnhof in Moabit/Tiergarten.

Around 2010, most of the activity of the three existing airports should have been transferred to a new **Berlin-Brandenburg airport** built on the site of East Berlin's old airport at Schönefeld.

ECONOMIC ACTIVITY

Two separate economies – West Berlin managed to retain its position as the FRG's foremost industrial centre in the traditional fields of electrical engineering, automobile manufacture (Daimler-Benz) and mechanical engineering. However, after the erection of the Wall, businesses preferred to transfer their administrative offices to the FRG proper (to Munich in the case of Siemens). The loss of industrial jobs has now been offset by newly-arrived federal government departments, trade fairs and exhibitions and processing industries. The aim of economic policy in the 1980s was to transform the city into a centre of hi-tech industry: bio-technology, micro-electronics and IT (Siemens-Nixdorf), but the "miracle" was impossible to achieve without massive aid from the FRG and a heavy reliance on immigrant labour. Today, the city's major earners are the food processing and tobacco industries, while most jobs are in electrical engineering (Siemens is Berlin's biggest employer), precision engineering and chemicals. The economy of East Berlin, industrial capital of the GDR and formerly home to 18 major state enterprises, was thrown into total disarray by the reunification.

Ph. Cajic/MICHELIN

The Mexikoplatz metro station

The transition to a market economy – Monetary union and the East German economy's brutal exposure to competition precipitated a painful structural crisis. A body known as the **Treuhand** was given the task of privatising state industry. In 80% of cases, a "buyer" was found, but restructuring resulted in massive redundancies (with women first affected) and protest strikes. Of East Berlin's 187 000 industrial jobs, just 32 000 were saved. The collapse of the former East German economy was aggravated by the disappearance of traditional COMECON outlets for goods (Eastern Europe's common market). 40 000 jobs were also lost in West Berlin, where businesses lagged behind the rest of the FRG in terms of infrastructure and employee training. The recession also coincided with the phasing out of tax relief and federal subsidies, which came to an end in 1995 (West Berlin formerly covered only a quarter of its expenditure).

Renewal and future prospects – The economic reconstruction of East Berlin has been facilitated by financial transfers from the western *Länder*. The first task to be performed was an invisible one: recombining the sewage systems, re-establishing the water and electricity supply networks and joining up dead-end streets. The next was to renew public facilities (schools, government departments, universities, hospitals), which were very much below par in the East. Coal was abolished as a fuel for heating. Tax rises did not cover all the investment spending; the authorities also had to resort to raising loans, privatisations, sales of land and a general policy of austerity. These measures resulted in redundancies in the public sector, increased fares for public transport, the postponement of investment in infrastructure and the running down or closure of cultural and social facilities.

The industry-related tertiary sector, a network of some 100 000 small and medium enterprises, and the construction industry (Berlin is the biggest building site in Europe) have nevertheless remained dynamic. 150 000 people have found employment in 300 major investment projects. Foreign companies such as Samsung and BICC are setting up at Oberschönweide (Köpenick) and Coca-Cola at Höhenschönhausen, in the former East, while ABB, Sony and Daimler-Benz (Potsdamer Platz) have staked their claim in the western part of the city, closely followed by IBM-Germany, Deutsche Bahn AG and Siemens's railway engineering division.

INSTITUTIONS

On **3 October 1990**, the day Germany was reunited, Berlin regained its legal status as the capital city. This was confirmed on 20 June 1991, when the supporters of Berlin in the Bundestag prevailed by a small majority (17 votes) over the supporters of Bonn. However, the ministries of Education, the Environment, Health, Agriculture and Economic Cooperation are to remain in the former federal capital.

Three central institutions, the Bundestag (lower house of Parliament), the Bundeskanzleramt (Chancellery) and the Bundespräsidialamt (Presidency), which will stand close to the Siegessäule, will be housed in new premises in the **government district** in the sharp bend of the Spree known as the Spreebogen (the Bundesrat – upper house of Parliament – will take over the former Preußisches Herrenhaus). Many government departments will be accommodated in existing buildings in the Mitte district. Six ministries will have only their secondary administrative offices in Berlin.

The Berlin Senate – As one of the 16 States *(Länder)* of the FRG, Berlin has its own regional parliament, whose 150 members are elected for a 4-year term, and a government represented by the **Senate**. The members elect the **Burgomaster** *(Regierender Bürgermeister)*, who acts as mayor of the city and prime-minister of the Land, and the senators he proposes. As head of the Senate, the Burgomaster ensures that the general thrust of government policy is respected. The administration of the 23 **districts** *(Bezirke)* is overseen by the Senate, but each forms its own municipal council and appoints a mayor. They enjoy a degree of political and administrative autonomy and, since 1995, control over their own budgets, but are due to be reduced in number.

It is not difficult to become a Berliner....

The early population of Berlin was a mixture of immigrants from Lower Saxony, the Netherlands, Belgium, the Alpine countries and Bohemia. For two centuries, up until 1945, the city's growth was fuelled by immigration from Silesia and East Prussia. In the days of the GDR, new settlers arrived from Thuringia and Saxony. Nowadays, the city's population of 3.6 million (2.4 living in the former West; 1.2 in the East) includes 250 000 foreigners. The biggest ethnic minority are the Turks – numbering 150 000 – living mainly in Kreuzberg, where they account for 25% of the population, Wedding and Neukölln. They are followed by Yugoslavs, Poles, Russians, Italians, Greeks, Vietnamese and Chinese. More than half of these people were born or grew up on the banks of the Spree. The mass arrival of "economic refugees" and *Aussiedler* (groups of German origin) from Eastern Europe has sometimes created tension. The most densely populated part of the city is Neukölln (312 000 inhabitants); the least populated district Weissensee (52 000). Berlin's population is expected to grow by a further million.

The arms of Berlin

Formerly hunted in the forests around Berlin, the bear first featured on the city's coat of arms in the 13C, together with the eagle of Brandenburg, and later of Prussia. From the time the Hohenzollern came to power until 1790, the eagle was shown grasping the bear in its talons. At the present time, the bear stands alone on a silver background. A version of the arms surmounted by a crown is the prerogative of the Senate.

THE BEST TIME TO VISIT

An in-between climate – Owing to its geographical position, the city enjoys a climate which is half maritime (500 to 600mm of rain per annum), half continental. The prevailing west wind brings variable weather, while the continental influence accounts for extremes of heat in summer and icy cold in winter. The average temperature hovers between 7.7 and 9°C. In recent years, summers have tended to be hot and dry, winters mild and devoid of snow. The northeast of the city is always slightly colder and more windy than the southwest. The temperature difference between the city centre and the periphery may be as much as 10°C at night. Because of the lie of the land, summer storms tend to occur in the valley (Charlottenburg, Tiergarten, Mitte, Treptow) and rainfall is heavier on the slopes of the plateaux (Neukölln) than on the heights themselves. In autumn and winter, it is not uncommon for the sphere of the Television tower to be obscured, whereas the Radio tower is fully visible.

"Die Berliner Luft, Luft, Luft: die hat einen schönen Duft, Duft, Duft" (Paul Lincke) – The quality of the air in Berlin is often mentioned in songs from the early part of the century. Whether it blows from east or west, the wind has tonic properties. Bitingly cold in winter, when it covers the city in an great icy mantle, it is amazingly pleasant in the hot summers. However, the cool breezes can result in sudden drops in temperature. As the centre of Berlin lies in a valley, pollution can be a problem, as in all big cities. People then parody the popular song by changing the words to *Berliner Dunst*: Berlin smog.

The "red town hall"

The Burden of history

THE EARLIEST PEOPLES AND SETTLEMENT BY THE GERMANS

6 – 8C – The Slavs (or Wends) settled in western Europe. They entered Brandenburg from Bohemia via the Elbe, by migration routes along the Panke and the Spree. Slav settlement was sparse: the Havellans *(Havellier)* settled around the Havel (the fortress of Brandibor was their capital), the Spreewans *(Spreewanen)* along the Spree. Slav settlement was divided into *Burgbezirke*. Castles built of wood and earth, with rounded walls, were raised on defensive sites – fords, islands, confluences. The two main *Burgen* were **Spandau** and Köpenick, but there was also Blankenburg (on the Panke) and Stralau. Life in the Slav villages was devoted to agriculture and stock-raising, and crafts prospered (weaving, pottery, forging, spinning and the working of wood and bone; fishing and hunting were of less importance). Silver weights *(Hacksiber)* were used in trade. A small group of Germans remained on the Teltow and merged with new flows of Slav migration: *Spree, Havel* and *Dahme* all have Germanic roots.

10C – The region between the Elbe and the Oder was coveted by German princes. The endless struggle carried on by Henry the Fowler, the founder of the Saxon dynasty (winter 928-29, conquest of the region around Branibor, which became **Brandenburg**) was continued, with the help of the church, by his son **Otto the Great**. Missionary centres became the focal points for the Christianisation and colonisation of "Germania Slavica". The archbishopric of Brandenburg was founded.

12 February 962 – Pope Jean XII crowned **Otto I** as the first emperor of the Holy Roman Empire. Magdeburg became an archbishopric.

991 – Reconquest of Brandenburg by the young Otto III, who offered his aunt, the abbess of Quedlinburg, the places known as "Potzupimi" (**Potsdam**) and "Geleti" (Geltow), with a view to converting the Havellan countryside. The first official document mentioning Potsdam was drawn up two years later. German authority became progressively established, but it was restricted by the Slav principalities and the newly emerging Polish state which seized Köpenick.

11 – 13C – Colonisation was to take three centuries. The Germans became permanently established in the 12C. after the military conquests of the early Middle Ages. Extensive migration went hand in hand with population growth. The region between the Elbe and the Oder, Christianised and incorporated into the Holy Roman Empire was far from the old centres of German civilisation in the Rhineland. The Ascanian dynasty was to give a political dimension to the economic importance of the North Mark, a transit route.

THE ASCANIAN DYNASTY

1108 – The Ascanian count (from the castle at Aschersleben, in Saxony), Albert I of Ballenstädt, nicknamed **"Albert the Bear"** was invested with the North Mark by the Duke of Saxony, and then by the Emperor. Albert tied close links with the Havellan prince Pribislav of Brandenburg, who made the Ascanians his heirs. Albert took the official title of Margrave of Brandenburg (1157). Köpenick fell into the hands of the Margrave of Meissen.

1180 – Foundation of the first Cistercian monastery in the Mark at Lehnin, between Brandenburg and Potsdam.

From 1220 – Second stage of colonisation, the plateaux of the Barnin and the Teltow became cultivated. The Knights Templars established a command post at **Templehof** one of the leading German settlements in the Teltow. Religious groups and major traders founded Treptow, Stralau, Boxhagen and Wedding. Brandenburg became urbanised with an extensive network of fortified towns, like Spandau, surrounding the Slav Kietze (the word *Kietz* subsequently came to mean the working-class district of a large town).

1237 – Cölln, on the island in the Spree, was mentioned for the first time in a contract. Cölln comes from the Latin *Colonia* or the Slav *Kolia* ("piles").

1240 – Capture of Köpenick. Slav power was broken, but the population was not entirely absorbed until the 14C. Some names are of Slav origin: Spandau, Köpenick, Steglitz, Gatow, Glienicke, Lübars, Britz, Stolpe, Marzahn and Berlin.

1244 – There is no charter recording the foundation of Berlin, which was mentioned for the first time in an act by the Margrave. The town (in fact the present St-Nicholas district) was mentioned as such in 1251. Cölln in 1261. The oldest seal of Berlin dates from 1253. The product of German colonisation, the twin town of Berlin and **Cölln** was a trading centre where wood and furs from Slav hunters were exchanged for the first German colonists' cereals. On either side of the Spree, the two towns controlled river traffic and the ford.

They took as the patron saints of their respective churches St Nicholas, the patron saint of merchants and sailors, and St Peter, the patron saint of fishermen. Flemings were working on the control of water, and produced good quality cloth.

13 – 14C – Leaving Köpenick to one side, the main route (joining the plain of Poland to the North Sea) henceforth passed through the twin town. A north-south axis linking Saxony and the Baltic was added to this in the 13C. These two arteries drew off most of the Elbe-Oder traffic. Trade in fish (herrings), cereals and wood gave rise to Berlin's waterborne trade. Through Hamburg (to which it exported its wood), Berlin came within the sphere of the Hanseatic League.

1295 – The presence of Jews, who had been driven out from a West imbued with the spirit of the Crusades, is attested in Brandenburg. They were subjected to restraints and lived in a ghetto *(Judenhof)* which was closed off by guarded railings. As moneylenders, an occupation prohibited to Christians, they brought substantial financial and fiscal resources. Spandau had a Jewish cemetery located outside the town enclosure.

1280-1300 – Berlin was a city of freemen of 3 000-4 000 inhabitants, and larger than Spandau, Köpenick and Cölln. Its economic importance is confirmed by the right to mint money (1280), the first town east of the Elbe to receive that right. Its markets spread out into Eastern Germany. The town owned several villages in its vicinity and began to manage its hinterland. Religious orders increased the number of their establishments: Benedictines at Lankwitz, Lübars, Tegel, Cistercians on the Teltow and at Zehlendorf, Franciscans, who founded the **"Greyfriars"** *(see NIKOLAIVIERTEL)*. This strong religious presence and the presence of the Ascanians encouraged cultural growth.

20 March 1307 – Union between Berlin and Cölln, which built a common town hall on the bridge between them around 1345. The merchants combined into a guild. But each town remained independent and kept its own council, its budget and its seal. The introduction of Brandenburg law, copied from that of Magdeburg, established a firm legal and municipal basis. The community was free of the power of the Margrave residing in Spandau; it had judicial and fiscal freedom.

1308 – Berlin-Cölln entered a defensive alliance with several towns in the Mark. Anarchy had reigned in Germany since 1254. Without an emperor (the "Great Interregnum") the country fragmented and the princes took royal powers upon themselves.

1319 – The towns strengthened their independence. On the 30 September Berlin and Cölln received new privileges, including that of raising a militia *(Landwehr)* which gave its name to the Landwehrkanal. There then followed a century of political troubles during which epidemics alternated with raids by robber-knights.

THE FREE COMMUNITY

In the 14C Berlin became the principal town in the Mark of Brandenburg and profited from the weakness of the central power. It had 8 000 inhabitants.

1321 – Berlin-Cölln suggested a new defensive alliance to deal with bands of pillagers, to resist the ambitions of the nobility and to protect commercial routes. This agreement preserved the unity of the Mark.

1323 – Louis I, the son of the king of Bavaria, was recognised by the towns as the new Margrave. The Wittlesbach, which included the Ghibellines (supporters of the Emperor) fought against the Luxemburgers for the imperial title and against the papacy (the Guelph party). Tension rose between the populace and the clergy – incidents occurred and an interdict was placed on the twin towns for twenty years, from 1325 to 1347.

1345-45 – The craftsmen, who were seeking involvement in the town's business refused to join the struggle against the Margrave. The municipal council had to give way. The prince's debts were cancelled. Louis considered building a palace on the banks of the Spree, but this project was not completed until a century later.

1348 – Brandenburg was less affected by the Black Death than other regions of Germany. An impostor claimed to be the last Ascanian margrave who had feigned death and made a pilgrimage to the Holy Land for 30 years. Playing the Messiah, he was recognised by the two towns who were seeking to throw off Louis' yoke. The usurper gave Berlin-Cölln back its privileges and granted others. The Jews were accused of all ills and were the victims of pogroms (1349).

6 January 1349 – 35 towns in Eastern Germany joined together against Louis. In 1355 the States succeeded in appointing a permanent adviser to the Margrave.

1359 – Berlin and Cölln joined the Hanseatic League.

1363-1373 – Occupation of Brandenburg by **Charles IV of Luxemburg**. The condition of his new possession was recorded in the Great Estates Book *(Landbuch Kaiser Karls IV, 1375)* which described Brandenburg as an "uncultivated and deserted land", ravaged by plague and bands of pillagers.

1376 and 1382 – Two fires ravaged both Cölln and Berlin. The disaster provided an opportunity for widening the roads and paving some. The Margrave Sigismund of Luxemburg put pressure on the Mark and alienated profits to the benefit of the feudal lords. Banditry by the nobility prospered. The towns entered into an alliance, without success, to resist pressure from the Margrave and the demands of the nobility, who were disturbing trade.

1402 – The New Mark *(Neumark)* was granted to the **Teutonic Order**. The remaining territories fell into the hands of robber-knights, in particular the clan of the **Quitzow** *(see TEGEL)*. Rather than be subjected to pillage, Berlin decided to make a treaty. A kind of territorial policing was entrusted to Dietrich von Quitzow. This action was to sound the death knell of the town's independence.

1410 – The towns were unable to defend themselves and the Quitzows turned against them.

1411 – Sigismund was elected emperor. The Margrave's seat remained vacant for four years. The Mark was administered by a nephew, **Frederick VI of Hohenzollern**, the burgrave of Nuremberg, who had helped Sigismund put on the imperial crown. Originally from the Swabian Jura, the Counts of Zollern had split up into several branches. The Hohenzollern of Franconia had ruled over the burgravate of Nuremberg since the end of the 13C. and over the margravate of **Ansbach** since 1397.

1412-1414 – Frederick was an energetic and courageous leader. He defeated the Pomeranian Knights, took part in the reconquest of **Köpenick**, and the capture of the Quitzow. The emperor Sigismund was also in debt to him, and could only repay his debts by granting titles and lands.

30 April 1415 – Sigismund granted the burgrave Frederick with the dual hereditary title of Margrave and Elector of Brandenburg. With **Frederick I of Brandenburg** the Hohenzollern dynasty became established for five centuries. An able politician, he did not challenge the privileges acquired by the towns, so as to restore unity to the principality.

THE RESIDENCE OF THE ELECTOR OF BRANDENBURG

The German princes, including John the Alchemist, Frederick's son, took things in hand again. The towns rejected the pressure of taxation and strengthened their internal cohesion.

1432 – Berlin and Cölln joined into a single council of 15 members to preserve the liberties of the burgesses. But the nobility fastened onto power to the detriment of the corporations, a ferment of division which served the interests of the prince. The first Hohenzollerns turned on the treaty of union. They put pressure on the minor local nobility binding the free peasants to them, a widespread development in central Europe which created enormous landholdings in the hands of aristocrats linked to the army, the *Junkers*.

1442 – After an urban revolt, **Frederick II the "Irontooth"** repealed the union between Berlin and Cölln. This was the end of municipal independence. The states were summoned on the 29th of August and compelled to swear fealty and obedience to the Margrave and his descendants. The Margrave kept for himself land to the north of Cölln island on which he intended to build a palace.

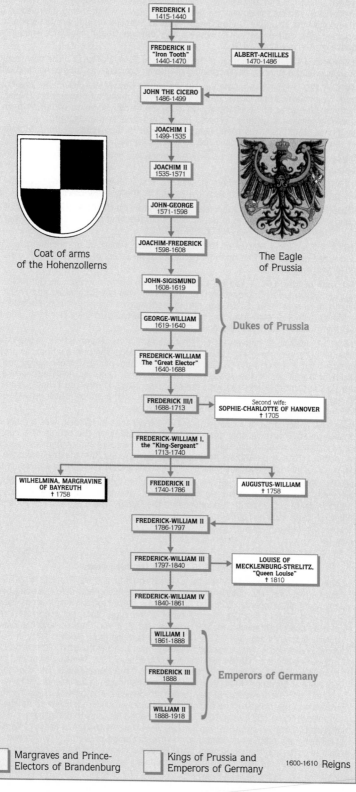

Reigning princes of the House of Hohenzollern

FREDERICK I
1415-1440

FREDERICK II
"Iron Tooth"
1440-1470

ALBERT-ACHILLES
1470-1486

JOHN THE CICERO
1486-1499

JOACHIM I
1499-1535

JOACHIM II
1535-1571

JOHN-GEORGE
1571-1598

JOACHIM-FREDERICK
1598-1608

JOHN-SIGISMUND
1608-1619

GEORGE-WILLIAM
1619-1640

FREDERICK-WILLIAM
The "Great Elector"
1640-1688

Dukes of Prussia

FREDERICK III/I
1688-1713

Second wife:
SOPHIE-CHARLOTTE OF HANOVER
† 1705

FREDERICK-WILLIAM I,
the "King-Sergeant"
1713-1740

**WILHELMINA, MARGRAVINE
OF BAYREUTH**
† 1758

FREDERICK II
1740-1786

AUGUSTUS-WILLIAM
† 1758

FREDERICK-WILLIAM II
1786-1797

FREDERICK-WILLIAM III
1797-1840

**LOUISE OF
MECKLENBURG-STRELITZ,**
"Queen Louise"
† 1810

FREDERICK-WILLIAM IV
1840-1861

WILLIAM I
1861-1888

FREDERICK III
1888

Emperors of Germany

WILLIAM II
1888-1918

Coat of arms
of the Hohenzollerns

The Eagle
of Prussia

Margraves and Prince-
Electors of Brandenburg

Kings of Prussia and
Emperors of Germany

1600-1610 Reigns

35

1443 – Berlin allied itself with other towns in the Hanseatic League to resist Frederick's policies. The latter waited and strengthened his power, authorising the Jews, whom he had thrown out, to re-establish themselves in the Mark on the strength of costly "letters of protection".

1448 – The "Berlin Discontent" *(Berliner Unwille)*. The entire town rose against Frederick II's thirst for power. He besieged the town, which, being deprived of help, abandoned the struggle. The burgesses went to Spandau for a final submission to the princely yoke and undertook to respect the "unequal treaty" of 1442. The independence of Berlin was at an end.

12 March 1451 – Inauguration of the palace *(see SCHLOSSPLATZ)*. The new municipal seal showed the princely eagle crushing the Berlin bear with its tongue hanging out.

1452-1470 – From 1454, the year in which the New Mark *(Neumark)* was bought back from the Teutonic Order, until 1470, the year in which he abdicated, Frederick II restored the unity of Brandenburg. In 1452 he forced Berlin to withdraw from the declining Hanseatic League, followed by all the towns in Brandenburg.
Economic stagnation was partly compensated for in the capital by the establishment of the Court, whose needs gave rise to new businesses.

1484 – An accidental fire in the town hall, which was demolished in 1514. The council became a tool of the prince.

1486 – John, the son of Albert III, was the first Hohenzollern to make Berlin-Cölln his permanent residence and thus the capital of the poorest Electorate in Germany.

1506 – The foundation of a university in Frankfurt-on-the-Oder through fear of creating a hostile cultured elite in Berlin. The main teaching establishment in Berlin was the "Greyfriars" school *(see NIKOLAIVIERTEL)*.

1511 – The Grand Master of the Teutonic Order, Albert of Brandenburg-Ansbach, converted over to the Reformation, secularised the assets of the order in Prussia and governed it as a lay prince.

1st half of the 16C – The 95 theses of Martin Luther, written in German, were quickly welcomed in Brandenburg, an area which was not Romanised and which had been late to become Christian. Joachim I fought against the new religion, but his wife, a Danish princess, converted to Protestantism. Refusing to deny her faith, she fled. Joachim I remained firm in his convictions.

1539 – **Joachim II** converted to Protestanism. The Reformation succeeded in Brandenburg because it was based on popular support. The prince's finances profited greatly from it through the secularisation of the assets of the Catholic clergy and distraint of the assets of the Jews, who were expelled. Other scandals also broke out during the century associated with the new personage of the "court Jew", promoted to high office, a zealous and often honest servant of the prince, but a power behind the throne hated by the populace and the nobility.

Late 16C – Berlin, with a population of one third that of Lübeck, was a quiet residential town. The town only grew by 1 000 inhabitants in the course of a century, mainly officers of the court, supplemented by Saxon traders and craftsmen. Joachim II attracted artists and scholars to his court, encouraged the theatre, enlarged the palace at Cölln and rebuilt the palaces at Köpenick and Grunewald *(see these names)*.

1618 – The Hohenzollerns patiently increased their lands. In 1569 Joachim bought the rights of succession to the Duchy of Prussia. As the second Duke of Prussia was mentally deranged, Joachim II administered the Duchy. The Electors of Brandenburg inherited it officially in 1618.

1618 – 1648 : Thirty troubled years

The 1555 compromise between the Catholic emperor and the Protestant nobility satisfied no one. The nobility of Bohemia, after revolting and defenestrating the envoys of the Emperor Ferdinand II, chose the Elector of the Palatinate as their new king. Victory first went to the camp of the imperialists, but the Protestant princes allied themselves with France, even though it was Catholic, and the Sweden of **Gustavus II Adolphus** (1594-1632), who had the most modern army in Europe. Brandenburg, lying between Swedish Pomerania and Austrian Silesia and Bohemia, became a battlefield, like the rest of Germany. The Swedes penetrated as far as Bavaria. The French ravaged the region of the Upper Rhine. The imperialists were at Stralsund. More than one third of the houses in Berlin and Cölln were abandoned. The town had to pay ransom to Sweden, and provide billets for its troops and the troops of the emperor; its economy foundered. It lost its function as a residence in 1627 when the Elector transferred his court to Königsberg, a less exposed capital. An armistice with Sweden was signed in 1641. The Peace of Westphalia, signed in Münster, confirmed the fragmentation of Germany, which was a field of ruins, and the weakening of the Emperor's power. Some regions had lost more than 60% of their population. Brandenburg had lost half.

The great coat of arms of the kingdom of Prussia graces the entrance to the Citadel in Spandau

THE ASCENDANCY OF PRUSSIA: 1648-1815

1643 – When he visited it for the first time, young prince Frederick-William found a town on the point of ruin.

1648 – Treaty of Westphalia. Brandenburg took in Western Pomerania and a few bishoprics. The Prince Elector worked to heal the wounds of the devastated Electorate and transform it into a powerful centralised state. The setting up of factories, the needs of the court, the building of a remarkable system of canals and the establishment of customs barriers helped to restore the economy under the supervision of the State, which called upon the services of many foreigners – Dutch craftsmen and merchants (Dutch influence was strong and the Crown Prince had been brought up in the Netherlands), some rich Viennese Jews and the first French Calvinists.

1650 – The first known map of Berlin. The town spread to the west: the avenue **Unter den Linden** was marked out and passed through the aristocratic district of **Dorotheenstadt** which obtained urban privileges in 1674. The Tiergarten (menagerie) was founded.

1658-83 – Berlin, a strong point and garrison town, was fortified. The inhabitants had to pay for it out of their own pockets, and they were themselves enrolled to wield picks and shovels. The new ramparts surrounded the marshy Island of Werder. Drained, this became a new district – the **Friedrichswerder**.

8 June 1675 – The Victory of Fehrbellin, a plain to the northwest of Berlin, over the Swedes. Frederick-William became the "Great Elector" and Brandenburg a respected power.

1685 – Revocation of the Edict of Nantes by Louis XIV, countered by the Edict of Potsdam. The Huguenots arrived in Brandenburg en masse. They accounted for one quarter of the population of Berlin and contributed to its growth in population (Berlin grew from 6 000 inhabitants to 55 000 between 1650 and 1709). The growth of the town made it necessary to create a new town: Friedrichstadt *(see GENDARMENMARKT)*.

1696 – Foundation of the Academy of Arts *(see Schloss CHARLOTTEN-BURG)*.

1701 – **Frederick III** supported the Emperor Leopold I in the War of the Spanish Succession and in exchange obtained the promotion of the Duchy of Prussia (located outside the Holy Roman Empire) into a kingdom. **Frederick I**, the king "in" Prussia, was crowned in Königsberg on 18 January.

Andreas Schlüter : Equestrian Statue of the "Great Elector"

1702 – Foundation of the Academy of Sciences *(see Schloss CHARLOTTENBURG)*.

Early 18C – Berlin had 56 000 inhabitants (with an additional garrison of 5 000 men) and spilled beyond its boundaries. The five communities of Berlin, Cölln, Friedrichswerder, Dorotheenstadt, Friedrichstadt merged together. The new constitution cancelled the last liberties and reduced the number of councillors in the *Magistrat* (municipal council). Berlin and Cölln were reunified by royal decree in 1710.

1713 – On the death of Frederick I, Prussia's debts were valued at 20 million thalers. The country was on the verge of ruin and an anonymous poster proclaimed that the palace was for hire and Berlin for sale.

1721 – Opening of the first "coffee house" in the Lustgarten.

1713-1740 – **Frederick-William I** wanted to consolidate the Prussian state. He attempted to balance the budget. The lifestyle of the court and the king were greatly cut back; the lions and tigers of the Charlottenburg menagerie were given to Saxony. Protectionist measures, the control of monopolies and corporations, and the encouragement of foreigners helped to diversify the economy: Protestants from Bohemia, valued workers in the first textile works, settled in Friedrichstadt and then Rixdorf *(see NEUKÖLLN)*. A wall serving as a toll barrier *(Akzisemauer, 1734-36)* replaced the "Great Elector's" enclosure and helped with the collection of tolls and the prevention of desertions. It was only destroyed in 1868. Berlin was a town which "contained many fields and gardens" and "districts in which no one was to be seen" (Count Guibert, 1771).

The "King-Sergeant"

During his reign the army was increased in strength to 81 000 men. The *Lustgarten* was converted into a parade ground. In 1750 soldiers represented a quarter of the population. Their lot was not enviable. Officers were trained in the Cadet School, founded in 1717. Rank and file soldiers were often recruited by force, only received their wages during the three months of exercises and hired themselves out as day labourers, apprentices, coachmen and lackeys for the rest of the year, or swelled the number of beggars, which explained the frequent desertions. In 1773 a French observer commented: "Berlin has the feel of the headquarters of a military metropolis". The army, the main customer for manufacturers of textiles and gold braid, and the armouries at Potsdam and Spandau, replaced the court as a factor of economic expansion.

1740-1742 – Start of the reign of **Frederick II**, who made bold use of the military instrument forged by his father to reduce Austrian influence in Germany. Profiting from the weakness of the young Empress **Maria-Theresa** (1717-1780), whose imperial title was challenged, he seized Silesia, the Habsburgs' richest province (which has belonged to Poland since 1945). The Second Silesian war (1748) gave him the name **"Frederick the Great"**. France, led by a war party and widespread prejudice against the "hereditary enemy", worked on behalf of the king of Prussia.

1746-56 – An enlightened despot, Frederick based relationships between the state and the individual on reason. But he remained an absolute monarch who felt himself close to the nobility. The scope of his social reforms was limited by this, but ten years of peace encouraged others. Forced labour was replaced by a fixed sum of money (but peasant soldiers of the armies of Frederick the Great continued to be subject to their lord's justice), compulsory schooling, accompanied by the foundation of many schools, simplification of the judicial system, the abolishment of torture (after 1742), the improvement of prison condi-

Antoine Pesne
The crown prince, the future Frederick II (1739)

Soldiers of the armies of Frederick the Great

Grenadier of the
6th Infantry Regiment

Standard-bearer
of the
7th Infantry
Regiment

Charging officer of the
Regiment of Hussars

Illustrations P. Boussard/MICHELIN

tions, and the codification of Prussian law, which was completed after the king's death. The king, who had published his conception of government in *Against Machiavelli* as early as 1739, written at the request of Voltaire and published through him, declared that a prince is "the first servant of the State", but "should only be guided by his own interests". All resources were directed to this end – the army was increased to 180 000 men, more than all the armies of Europe. The first barracks were built in 1753 (they appeared in Paris in 1770).

1756-1763 – France, Saxony and Austria eventually came to an agreement to counter Frederick's increase in power. Frederick turned to England. This was the **reversal of alliances**, the result of intrigues by the Prime Minister of Saxony, Brühl, the Abbot of Bernis, Louis XV's foreign affairs minister, and "Her Majesty Petticoat III", as Frederick called Madame de Pompadour. The result was the Seven Years War, the last and the fiercest of the wars which followed the taking of Silesia. Frederick invaded Saxony without warning, bombarded Dresden, defeated the French at Rochbach, but suffered a painful defeat at Künersdorf. Berlin was occupied by the Russians in 1760, but the Tsarina Elisabeth Petrovna, the mortal enemy of Frederick II, died suddenly and her son admired the King of Prussia. Peace was signed at Hubertusburg Castle. Prussia was a major power, economically exhausted, but whose rights over Silesia were finally recognised.

1765 – Foundation of the Royal Bank. The state took economic recovery in hand. Berlin started to become an industrial city. In 1784 it contained 5 000 looms, and its textile factories employed 6 000 workers. English machines arrived after 1781. This change took place at the expense of agriculture and crafts, and resulted in the emergence of an urban proletariat.

A court of luminaries

Frederick II attracted Voltaire to his court, as later Catherine II of Russia attracted Diderot. The Prussian king's opinions were influenced by French minds who liked to think themselves the "prince's advisors" and became the propagandists of absolute power.

The relaxation of censorship gave an impetus to the press (the young Lessing was the editor of the *Spener Journal*) and publishing. A new generation of writers appeared towards 1750.

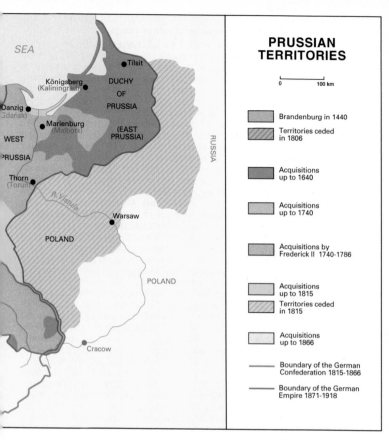

PRUSSIAN TERRITORIES

SEA

Tilsit

Königsberg
(Kaliningrad)

DUCHY
OF
PRUSSIA

Danzig
(Gdansk)

Marienburg
(Malbork)

WEST

(EAST
PRUSSIA)

PRUSSIA

RUSSIA

Thorn
(Toruń)

R. Vistula

Warsaw

POLAND

POLAND

Cracow

0   100 km

Brandenburg in 1440

Territories ceded
in 1806

Acquisitions
up to 1640

Acquisitions
up to 1740

Acquisitions by
Frederick II 1740-1786

Acquisitions
up to 1815

Territories ceded
in 1815

Acquisitions
up to 1866

Boundary of the German
Confederation 1815-1866

Boundary of the German
Empire 1871-1918

1772 – The first division of Poland on the initiative of Frederick II, with the help of Austria and Russia. The old rivalry between the Prussian state and the Kingdom of Poland dissolved with the disappearance of the latter. But the creation of a vast domain in the east, an old aspiration in the footsteps of the German colonisation of the Middle Ages, created a dangerous situation for Prussia. Prussia, Russia and Austria were directly at loggerheads. In the course of the 18C a European patchwork was established which was to be influential until 1945.

1775-1786 – The social situation deteriorated, with the population approaching 150 000 inhabitants. The Berlin "poor house" was built in 1774. The reign of Frederick II ended in uncertainty; Moses Mendelssohn died in the same year. The King was buried, against his wishes, alongside his father in the garrison church *(see POTSDAM)*.

1786-1797 – Frederick II's inheritance was squandered by his nephew and successor, **Frederick-William II**, who surrounded himself with favourites and mistresses. Despite a few improvements in the legal and financial field, the framework of Frederick's society burst under demographic and economic pressure. The capital's population doubled between 1750 and 1800, workers' and peasants' wages fell continually. In this adverse atmosphere social and cultural life blossomed. The first wave of Romanticism appeared. The king was a lover of music and promoted theatre in the German language. Militarily, Prussia came into conflict with revolutionary France.

1792 – The first paved road from Berlin to Potsdam. At 6 p.m. a "daily coach" set down passengers at the Octagon picked up in Potsdam at midday. The second paved road covered the route from Berlin to Charlottenburg. The services were provided by the royal mail.

"Old Fritz"

Scarred by his years of campaigning (he hardly saw Berlin at any time during the Seven Years War), Frederick II passed the last years of his life in military dress and became the miser "Old Fritz", a nickname given to him affectionately by his subjects. A strategist and an enlightened despot, a lover of the arts and music, the King, of whom Voltaire said that he lived in Sans-Souci Palace "without a court, without a council and without religion", passed a sad old age. He lost all his teeth and had to give up playing the flute. His hygiene left something to be desired and his room at Sans-Souci Palace was soiled by the many dogs which he kept with him, but he always conducted the affairs of state with ability.

Nationalism under a veil of charm

The story of Queen Louise (1776-1810), "the noble Muse" in the words of the Romantic poet Jean-Paul, began with a double marriage. On the 24 December 1793, while French troops camped on the Rhine, the young princess of Mecklenburg-Strelitz, aged just 17, wed the crown prince, the future Frederick-William III. Christian-Daniel Rauch had been her first tutor. She was already famous throughout all Europe for her beauty. Her sister, Friederike, married Prince Louis of Prussia two days later. Louise and Friederike were the subjects of the famous sculpture by **Johann Gottfried Schadow** which is kept in the Old National Gallery *(see MUSEUMSINSEL)*. The young princess was lively, vivacious and did not stand on ceremony. She adored dancing. Her generosity, and her easiness with her subjects, conquered Berlin for her. Her husband was considerate, but lacklustre. In November 1797 Louise was queen and personally supervised the education of her children. She was interested in avant-garde writers and poets, loved the tales which the Romantics were bringing back into fashion, and climbed the highest peak in the Mountains of the Giants *(Riesengebirge)* without hesitation. In 1802 she met the young Tsar **Alexander I**, with whom she fell in love. Understanding the danger represented by Napoleon after the victory of Austerlitz, she took the head of the war party. Prussia strengthened its links with Russia, but was defeated at Jena, Auerstädt, Eylau – Berlin was occupied. The Queen and the government took refuge at Königsberg and Memel. At the meeting between the Tsar and Napoleon I at Tilsit the King of Prussia was humiliated. She enjoined him: "All for one, one for all", the by-word of 1813 and the war of liberation. She met Napoleon on the 6 July 1807. He was impressed by the charm and determination of the Queen, who was not without self assurance. When at the end of a banquet he offered her a rose out of courtesy, the Queen replied, accepting it: "Only with Magdeburg", implicitly demanding that this town should stay Prussian. But Napoleon did not weaken – Prussia lost all its provinces to the west of the Elbe and a part of Poland which had been conquered following the division of the country at the end of the 18C The Queen appeared to submit, but driven by patriotic mysticism she surrounded herself with advisers who dreamt of making Prussia great again: Gneisenau, Scharnhorst, von Stein, Schill, Wilhelm von Humboldt. She read and reread Schiller's *The Maid of Orleans*, while her husband was nothing more than the "King of Königsberg". The couple returned to Berlin on Napoleon's orders on the 23 December 1809. The Queen died in her family home in the duchy of Mecklemburg-Strelitz on the 19 July 1810. Sixty years later to the day the France of Napoleon III, the nephew of the conqueror of Jena and Eylau, imprudently declared war against Prussia. William I, the youngest son of Queen Louise, would be proclaimed Emperor of Germany at Versailles.

Queen Louise
A portrait by Joseph Grassi

1797 – Accession of **Frederick-William III**, a lacklustre sovereign, but who formed an exemplary couple with the delightful Queen Louise.

Around 1800 – Berlin became industrialised. The Warehouse *(Königliches Lagerhaus)*, which employed 5 000 persons, was the largest cloth manufacture in Europe. Adult and child labour was abundant, working in the home or in workshops. The state controlled model enterprises: the Royal Porcelain works (KPM), which placed the second steam engine in service in 1800, and the Royal Foundry *(Königliche Eisengießerei, see CHARITE)*. Berlin was a young and dirty city (the citizens dumped their rubbish on the access roads), overpopulated, and the 6th largest in Europe. Misery and alcoholism were rife. Berlin's workers needed 3/4 of their income to buy bread. The average life expectancy of a wage earner's child was no more than 19 years; one baby out of four failed to reach its first birthday.

1797-1806 – The **years of silence** during which Prussia adopted a benevolent neutrality towards France were in fact a sign of weakness which Queen Louise, a devotee of confrontation, was loath to accept. Salons flourished.

1802 – The building of a new customs wall. Only three gates were decorated, one being the Brandenburg Gate.

1805 – The Tsar Alexander I, gave his name to the Alexanderplatz.

1805-6 – Prussia, which joined the coalition against **Napoleon**, was defeated at Jena and Auerstädt. Napoleon entered Berlin on the 27 October 1806 and remained for a month, living in Cölln Palace. It was there that he signed the decree for the Continental Blockade against England. The ragged state of the French soldiers was a surprise for Berliners.

1806-1808 – Napoleon's occupation hit hard. Works of art, like the four-horse chariot on the Brandenburg Gate, the *Quadriga*, were seized. Enormous levies, the billeting of French troops on the inhabitants, and the fall in industrial and commercial activity as a result of the blockade, brought Berlin to the verge of ruin. Loans made during this period were not finally paid off until 1861.

> ### "Calm is the first duty of the citizen..."
> A town militia was set up, but the richest members of the bourgeoisie evaded this duty by purchasing the right to do so. In an appeal for calm of the 17 October 1806 Count von Schulenburg declared: "The king has lost a battle. Calm is henceforth the first duty of the citizen...". The joke was then passed around to the extent that a member of the militia, who was found sleeping at his post, answered back to the officer reprimanding him: "Calm is the first duty of the citizen – I am only obeying orders". After the departure of the French in 1808, expansion of the town militia was one way of getting round the limitation imposed on numbers of troops.

1807 – Abolition of serfdom, which released considerable labour for the factories and marked the start of an extensive rural exodus, which explained the industrial flowering of Prussia and the unbridled urbanisation of Berlin.

1808 – Tension mounted rapidly, particularly over control of the press. From the spring onwards Berlin financed the building of the military camp of **Napoleonburg** *(see Schloss CHARLOTTENBURG)*. The town suffered from the absence of the king, who remained at Königsberg.

1809-10 – French occupation engendered a strong patriotic reaction accompanied by a desire to modernise the State and liberalise society (the absence of the king, who did not return until December 1809, encouraged reforming tendencies). This movement found literary, artistic and sporting expression. Prussia prepared for its recovery. The generals **Scharnhorst** and **Gneisenau** modernised the army. Minister **Von Stein** and the State Chancellor **Hardenberg** reformed the organisation of the state, and to help its reconstruction re-established a certain degree of municipal independence. In 1810 the edict on professional liberty suppressed the corporations. These liberalising measures encouraged the activity of Jewish entrepreneurs. The University, a hotbed of emerging nationalism and the crown of a renewed educational system, was founded in the same year through the work of **Wilhelm von Humboldt**.

10 July 1810 – The death of Queen Louise, to general dismay.

1813 – The retreat of the Grand Army led to an outbreak of enthusiasm. Aggression was widespread. The Russians entered Berlin on the 4th of March, inflicting heavy losses on Napoleon's rearguard. On the 17 March, Frederick-William III launched the campaign "of deliverance" at Breslau (*Wroclaw*, in Silesia), in a speech to German youth and his people, and declared war on France, after creating the **Iron Cross**, designed by Schinkel. The crusade against Napoleon I mobilised an army of volunteers (the free corps of the Berlin general von Lutzow) which drew upon all social classes. Napoleon's troops, attempting to return to Berlin, were beaten at the village of Grossbeeren.

1814 – Introduction of military service in Berlin. The *Quadriga*, brought back from Paris by General Blücher, was returned to its rightful place.

1815 – The unexpected arrival of Blücher reversed the course of the battle of Waterloo. Prussia emerged damaged from the **Congress of Vienna**. It did not recover the Polish territories gained in the partition of 1795, and did not conquer all Saxony, the ally of Napoleon, even though it took two thirds of its territory. However, with the Rhineland and Westphalia, to which it was granted to mount "a guard on the Rhine" and to prevent new French aggression, it held the richest lands in Germany, the base for its industrial expansion. The **German Confederation**, consisting of 39 states including Prussia, replaced the Holy Roman Empire. Austria was opposed to the creation of a unified Germany. Instead of establishing a modern constitutional monarchy as desired by the creators of national renewal, Frederick-William III restored the old order.

INDUSTRIALISATION AND THE MARCH TOWARDS UNITY

Unlike the east and south of Berlin, which remained agricultural zones, textile mills and the first steel mills (Borsig, Siemens & Halske) developed in the northern suburbs of Berlin (the suburb of Oranienburg or Rosenthal), along the Spree to the east (Luisenstadt, Stralau), and downstream from Charlottenburg (Moabit). The state continued to assist the start-up of pioneering ventures.

1816-1847 – The **Biedermeier** period was marked by formidable economic and population growth. Berlin's population increased from 197 000 to 409 000.

1830 – An echo of Paris's three glorious days, mass demonstrations on the palace square were dispersed. The rift between the king and his people widened. The press was muzzled, the university was under close surveillance, mail was censored. Associations and political meetings were prohibited. Another revolt erupted in 1833 on the king's birthday.

1831 – A cholera epidemic. Urban hygiene remained archaic until 1876.

1834 – Prussia favoured the *Zollverein*, a customs union of German States excluding Austria.

1838 – First Berlin-Potsdam railway. Stations were built at the gates of the capital, the area around them rapidly became urbanised. Berlin occupied a central position in the expanding railway network. **August Borsig's** locomotive company *(see CHARITÉ)* acquired a dominant position.

1844 – The first industrial exhibition for all the countries in the *Zollverein* was a triumph for Berlin's industry and received 260 000 visitors. The star of the exhibition was the locomotive *Beuth* which achieved the unimaginable speed of 35kph.

1844-47 – General recession in Europe. Prussia was the most affected of the German states as it was the most industrialised. A quarter of the population lived in misery. To subsidise the needy the municipality undertook major works such as the digging of the Landwehrkanal, between 1830 and 1850, but hunger riots broke out in April 1847.

1848 – The **Berlin revolution** *(Vormärz)* had above all an economic origin, and for the first time involved the workers, but it was also a stage on the road to unity. The citizens, meeting in the Tiergarten, drew up an address to the king claiming fundamental liberties. The latter hesitated between repression and concession. The mass demonstration around the palace was repressed by the army. The roads around Cölln town hall became filled with barricades *(see FISCHERINSEL)*. The troops retired but, divided, the revolutionary movement failed. General **Wrangel** entered Berlin on the 10 November without encountering any resistance, and declared a state of siege.

1848-1870 – With prosperity regained, Prussia caught up France's economic lead. On the eve of the creation of the Reich, 2/3 of Berliners were working in industry. Chemistry took off as a result of the pharmacist Schering's action *(see WEDDING)*. The army, a great consumer of medicines, disinfectants and substitute materials, stimulated this industry. With the bank and industry coming back together, large-scale capitalism was born. The *Deutsche Bank* was founded in 1862. The new neo-Renaissance stock exchange was built behind the cathedral in 1864.

1858-61 – Stricken by madness, Frederick-William IV had to leave the regency to his brother, who acceded to the throne three years later under the name of **William I**. He proved more conciliatory. The relaxation of censorship resulted in a flourishing of newspapers. Berlin entered the rank of major press towns. The liberal opposition regained its lost ground. The German Progress Party, an ardent defender of a constitution, obtained the majority of the seats in the Prussian Parliament in 1861.

1862 – Otto von Bismarck entered public life. The national question fired public opinion. A plan for rebuilding the capital, known as the Hobrecht Plan, named after a building advisor, was prepared. Building began on the *Mietskasernen*.

The "Iron Chancellor"

Born in Schönhausen, in the west of Brandenburg, Otto von Bismarck (1815-1898) was a Prussian through and through. It was in returning to manage his lands that he began his political career as a deputy in the *Landtag* convened by Frederick-William IV. A conservative, Bismarck disapproved of the 1848 revolution and the attempts to reform the German Confederation, but, representing Prussia in the Federal Diet in Frankfurt, and responsible for re-establishing good relationships with Austria after the "climb-down" of Ollmütz, he became convinced that "the policies of Vienna had made Germany too small for Prussia and Austria to live in it together". Ambassador to St Petersburg and, briefly, Paris, he was recalled by William I on the 22 September 1862. The Prussian state was in a crisis. The question of the military budget had placed the king, who considered resigning, and the *Landtag* at loggerheads. Bismarck declared from the podium: "It is not by talking and votes that most of the major questions of our era will be resolved, as was thought in 1848, but through blood and iron". Shortly afterwards he was appointed to the post of Minister-President (i.e. Prime Minister), a post which he occupied almost without interruption until 1890,

ROGER-VIOLLET

Bismarck

and Minister for Foreign Affairs. Governing by decree unconstitutionally amid general opposition, Bismarck counted on foreign victories to justify his policies. He built the unity of Germany around the Hohenzollern dynasty, using cunning and realism, but only actually really in the use of force.

1870-71 – The German empire was proclaimed on the 18 January 1871 in the Hall of Mirrors at Versailles. Through the treaty of Frankfurt, France lost Alsace and part of Lorraine, which became "Lands of the Empire" and had to pay an indemnity. The German Empire became the strongest power on the continent, but it was poorly unified. In Berlin a strong power imposed its views upon a hostile parliamentary opposition.

THE IMPERIAL CAPITAL: 1871-1920

In 1871 Berlin had a population of 871 000 and was still expanding. The bourgeoisie settled in the leafy districts of the West and South: Lichterfelde, Friedenau, Grunewald. The centre became depopulated.

1873 – The years following victory, known as the "Founding Years" *(Gründerjahre)* were years of opulence, financial scandals and wild speculation. Joint stock companies proliferated. The stock market crash which hit Vienna and then Berlin marked the beginning of a period of economic recession which persisted throughout Europe until 1890.

1876 – Public hygiene improved as a result of the drainage system designed by Hobrecht.

1878 – At the Congress of Berlin, Bismarck was the arbiter of Europe. To fight against his "inside enemies" and after taking up the "Fight for Civilisation" *(Kulturkampf)* against the Catholics, Bismarck tackled the socialist movement and ethnic minorities (Poles, Danes, Alsatians and Lorrainers) who in his opinion threatened the cohesion of the *Reich*.

1888 – The "Year of the Three Emperors" *(Dreikaiserjahr)*. Death of William I, the short 90 day reign of Frederick III, and the accession of **William II**. Manufacture of the first electric dynamos and motors in 1888 launched the electrical industry with Werner von Siemens and Emil Rathenau.

1890 – Bismarck, after a disagreement with the young William II, retired to his estate in Friedrichsruh.

1912 – The town had 2 million inhabitants. The intercommunity group was a precursor of "Greater Berlin".

August 1914 – The general mobilisation created enthusiasm. On the 4 August 1914 the Emperor asked all the party leaders to shake his hand as a sign of national solidarity. He left Berlin, to which he rarely returned, for the front line. The authorities hunted everything foreign.

Adolf von Menzel: *The Mill*

1915 – The unexpected continuation of the war sowed trouble. Deterioration in food supplies, as a consequence of the British sea blockade, led to rationing in 1915. Berlin was the first German town in which bread coupons were distributed. By 1916 all products were rationed: this was the "Winter of the Swedish turnips".

THE ROARING TWENTIES

Berlin woke up among the orphans, invalids and 300 000 unemployed whom the extremists attempted to win over to their side. Rationing continued. Misery, child malnutrition and epidemics of Spanish Influenza ravaged the population. But the cinemas and clandestine gambling dens were full, and the town "packed with the new rich and war profiteers". Until 1920 the streets temporarily had the upper hand over the authorities. Despite these difficult times, Berlin's civic officials accomplished great things.

9 November 1918 – Karl **Liebknecht** proclaimed the "Free Socialist Republic of Germany" from a balcony in the palace.

January 1919 – The recently elected National Assembly sat far away from the conflicts in Berlin, in Weimar, a small town in Thuringia where Goethe and Schiller are buried.

1920 – On the 13 March, free corps led by **Kapp** and General von Lüttwitz captured official buildings. The government fled, but the putsch came to nothing, because the Berlin working class decided on a general strike. No more gas, no more electricity, no more water! Those responsible for the putsch, who had no control over events, had to withdraw, leaving hundreds of victims in their wake. The law on the creation of "Greater Berlin" *(Gross-Berlin)* came into force on the 1 October.

1923 – In November one dollar was worth 4.2 billion Reichsmarks. An underground ticket cost 150 thousand million RM. The mayor of Berlin, **Gustav Boss**, published a brochure *Misery in Berlin* which described all the ills from which the capital was suffering.

1924 – Modernisation and rationalisation of the economy were accompanied by massive lay-offs, and unemployment became endemic. But between 1924 and 1929 the German economy stabilised as a result of American capital. Berlin became a city of pleasure. The leisure industry, broadly based on the American model, used new techniques such as the gramophone, radio and cinema.

1926 – Hitler appointed the young Rhinelander Joseph **Goebbels** head of the party cell in the capital. The Nazi Party had established itself in Berlin the year before. Goebbels launched into an assault on "Red Babylon" with strong words and subsequent violence. The first public meeting was held in February 1927 at Wedding. In 1928 "attack centres" representing "fortified positions in the combat zone" were established in proletarian districts. Intemperate and anti-Semitic propaganda was used in the newspaper *Der Angriff* ("The Attack") which castigated Berlin as a depraved city and called upon "true" Germans to denounce the "arrogance of the capital".

A native of Berlin

Born in Berlin on the 10 May 1878, Gustav Stresemann came to prominence as a member of the national-liberal party through his eloquence and his pugnacity. He entered the Reichstag in 1907; he was the youngest deputy and remained a member until his death (except between 1912 and 1914). He was a nationalist, a supporter of out-and-out submarine warfare, and convinced of the prime importance of the economy. He joined the Republic reluctantly and on the 22 November 1918 founded the German People's party (DVP, *Deutsche Volkspartei*). The DVP entered government in 1920. Stresemann, a dominant figure in the Reichstag, was appointed Chancellor of the Reich on the 13 August 1923. Together with the Minister of Finance he solved the problem of inflation. Between the 23 November 1923 until his death on the 3 October 1929 he was the Minister of Foreign Affairs, an exceptionally long tenure which explains Stresemann's importance. Seeking equality of rights *(Gleichberechtigung)* for his country, and using effective, discreet diplomacy, Stresemann achieved his greatest successes at the Locarno Conference and through obtaining a permanent seat in the **League of Nations** in 1926, and brought Germany back into the diplomatic game. But a letter to the Crown Prince disclosed the objectives of his policies: reducing reparations, a lasting peace for "Germany to regain its strength", "protection of Germans abroad", with, as an afterthought, the reattachment of Austria and adjustment of the frontiers in the East. This revisionism was accompanied by great prudence of tone so as not to provoke the Allies.

1929 – Berlin was the largest commercial city on the continent of Europe, the centre of industrial progress. It had 4.3 million inhabitants, with 840 000 white-collar workers and 1.7 million blue-collar workers. The **Sklarek Scandal** besmirched many personalities in the municipal administration and the SPD, which lost its image of integrity, but the conservative camp did not profit from it and the extremists gained in strength. The Nazi Party (**NSDAP**) entered the assembly with 5.8% of the seats. In October, following the Wall Street Crash, foreign banks required immediate payment of short-term loans invested in Berlin as part of long-term projects. This brought about a collapse, made out by the demagogues to be the result of social-democratic policy. Unpopular measures, increases in the price of water, gas, electricity, and public transport, a building programme which was revised downwards or suspended, and higher taxes only served to pay interest on the debt. The Communists and the Nazis vied in bringing help to the victims of the crisis.

1930-32 – The employment situation became dramatic. Unemployment in Berlin represented 10% of German unemployment. The spectacle of children running wild throughout the city, the needy haunting the bars in the poor districts, and the

Adolf von Menzel: *The Ball Supper*

unemployed workers was reminiscent of the immediate post-war period. The extremists profited from the chaos reigning in Germany and Berlin. The unemployed swelled the ranks of the paramilitary organisations. "The atmosphere in the city is feverish, stormy, unhealthy", said the new French ambassador, André **François-Poncet**, on his arrival.

Although the Nazis and the Communists were locked in a bitter struggle, they were sometimes in agreement, as in the transport strike, because the common target was the Social-Democrat government. The Sports Palace was the site of large meetings. The NSDAP made progress, particularly in middle-class districts, but the Communist bastions of Wedding, Friedrichshain, Neukölln, Weissensee and Lichtenberg were infiltrated. Everything took place in the streets, with fights, punitive raids and "clean-up" operations in the *Kneipen* (bars). After the legislative elections of 1930, the 107 Nazi deputies entered Parliament in overcoats, which they all took off together, revealing their brown uniforms. Outside, nationalist-socialist demonstrators attacked passers-by and broke the windows of the large Jewish owned Wertheim store.

1932 – Hitler obtained German nationality. The Nazis succeeded in obtaining a prohibition on the anti-military film *All Quiet on the Western Front*. A wave of violence broke out throughout Germany with the elections. Hindenberg dissolved the Social-Democrat government of Prussia and appointed the Chancellor, **Franz von Papen**, as commissioner. He proclaimed a state of emergency in Berlin and Brandenburg and the army took control of the capital. A few days after Von Papen's takeover by force, the Nazis outstripped all the other parties in the Reichstag, even though they obtained fewer votes in Berlin than in the rest of Germany. Apart from **Ernst Thälmann**, the head of the KPD (who died in Buchenwald in 1944), future East German personalities were to be found in the ranks of the Communists; Erich Mielke, who became head of the Stasi, and Walter Ülbricht, who masterminded the transport strike as the head of a union.

30 January 1933 – Hindenburg appointed Adolf Hitler to the post of Chancellor. Torchlight march of the Storm Troopers (SA) from the Brandenburg Gate to the Chancellery in the Wilhelmstraße.

THE THIRD REICH

The coming of the Nazis to power marked the triumph of provincialism over the spirit of the capital. Berlin was regarded by the Germans as a foreign body, a monstrous excrescence. The "hydrocephalic" capital *(Wasserkopf Berlin)*, the heartland of a "corrupt" culture, was a favourite theme of the extreme right movements. But, paradoxically, the Nazis strengthened centralisation: the States *(Länder)* disappeared, accentuating the supremacy of Berlin.

1933 – On the 27 February the Reichstag was burnt down by the Nazis. The left wing parties went into hiding. The inaugural session of the new Parliament was held in the garrison church in Potsdam. Two days later, the Reichstag, under heavy surveillance, granted full powers to **Hitler**. The totalitarian yoke was quickly applied. The municipal administration was purged, particularly in the working class districts, and the police became an instrument of repression. Goebbels became president of the government of the Reich's capital. The Gestapo was created in April, and set itself up in the Prinz-Albert-Straße. Himmler and Heidrich wove a vast web of espionage and informing based on "block guardians". The old Military School at the Tempelhof, the *Columbia-haus*, became a centre of torture for opponents. The SA and the SS launched punitive raids, as in Köpenick. The day after 1 May, declared the "Day of National Labour", the unions were suppressed. At Christmas the first concentration camp, Sachsenhausen, was set up in a brewery in Oranienburg, 30km to the north of Berlin. Its first inmates were 300 prisoners, members of the KPD and the SPD, and it became a laboratory for other concentration camps.

Bread and circuses

A calendar of ideological festivals governed the life of Berliners from 1936: celebrations of the rise to power, the foundation of the NSDAP, the cult of heroes, Hitler's birthday, the Festival of Labour, the summer solstice, the party congress, the harvest festival, a reminder of the Munich putsch. A desire to dragoon society and stir up national feeling was combined with the desire to make Germans forget about the difficulties of their daily lives. The apogee of this system was reached at the **Olympic Games of 1936**. The following year Goebbels invented the 700th anniversary of the town: a military parade traced the history of the capital of Brandenburg in a nationalist-socialist sense. Hitler, who did not like Berlin, was not present at the festivities.

30 June 1934 – "The Night of the Long Knives". Hitler eliminated internal rivals and in particular his long-standing companion, **Ernst Röhm**, a partisan of the "second revolution" who was executed in Bavaria. Large-scale executions took place in Berlin at the Lichterfelde barracks and the *Columbiahaus*.

1935 – The Nuremberg laws *(see WANNSEE)*.

9 November 1938 – "The Night of Broken Glass" *(see ORANIENBURGER STRASSE)*.

1936-39 – The march to war. Processions became more frequent, and increasingly military. The population of Berlin feared another conflict and relinquished all hope at the time of the invasion of Poland and the declaration of war by France and Great Britain.

1940 – The defeat of France did not give rise to any excitement. The inhabitants visited the Rethondes railway carriage, exhibited in the Lustgarten, until it was destroyed by a bomb. On the 26 August the RAF launched its first raid on Berlin in retaliation for a raid on London.

1941-42 – The bombardment continued. Working quarters were not as extensively evacuated as a result of an order from Goebbels: "Those who work stay here!". There were many foreign workers. Factories were relocated, but supplies became scarce and daily life deteriorated greatly, with the appearance of substitute products. The police hunted down Jews, gypsies and the members of various resistance networks.

1940-45 – The defeat at Stalingrad astonished Berliners. Goebbels announced "total war" at a meeting in the Sports Palace.

1944 – American raids took over, day and night, from British attacks. The citizens lived underground. The attempt by officers of the Wehrmacht to take Hitler's life failed on the 20 July.

Winter 45 – Cut off from the rest of the town, each district survived independently. The black market and crime blossomed. On the 1 February the Russians were on the Oder. Berlin became a stronghold divided into 3 concentric zones.

April-May 1945 – From the 20 April the armies of Zhukov and Koniev besieged the encircled and battered city. The ill-equipped and inexperienced battalions of the *Volkssturm* received the order to fight "to the last man, to the last bullet". The SS hung deserters with placards denouncing their crimes. Hitler and Goebbels committed suicide. On the evening of the 30 April the red flag was hoisted on the Reichstag. The Russians had lost 100 000 men. The Wehrmacht surrendered in Karlhorst, the headquarters of the Red Army.

THE COLD WAR

The Cold War started and finished in Berlin. The Potsdam Conference, which took place from 17 July to 2 August 1945 at the Cecilienhof Palace, ratified the plans for occupation. The State of Prussia disappeared. The occupied city, divided into four sectors of occupation, lived under permanent tension. A Control Council, consisting of the four commanders in chief responsible for governing the country, sat in Berlin.

1947 – Truman laid the basis of containment of Soviet influence. Germany was a bullwark consolidated economically by the **Marshall Plan**. Ernst Reuter was elected Burgomaster, an election invalidated by the Soviet representative. The two municipal administrations split (the Senate in the West, the Magistrat in the East) and were not to be reunited until 2 December 1991. But the links between the two parts of the city remained close. Shows were more accessible in the East, where Western goods could not be found. Controls prevented neither trade nor cross-frontier working.

4 June 1948 – 12 May 1949 – Eleven months of blockade *(see TEMPELHOF)*.

The 1950s – Berlin swarmed with secret agents. While the economic "miracle", accompanied by a great increase in standard of living, was taking place in West Berlin, a riot broke out in East Berlin, starting at a site in the Karl-Marx-Allee on the 16 and 17 June 1953. Soviet tanks intervened. The Paris Conference (October 1954) crowned the efforts of Chancellor Konrad **Adenauer** (1876-1967) to end the regime of occupation and include West Germany in NATO. In 1957, **Willy Brandt** (1913-1992), who headed a demonstration against Soviet intervention in Hungary, was elected Burgomaster of West Berlin. Krushchev wished to remove the "cancerous tumour" of West Berlin and achieve an overall settlement of the German question to his own advantage. Escapes to the West multiplied: 2.6 million people "voted with their feet" as Ernst Reuter put it, and fled before the building of the Wall.

1961 – During the night of 12 to 13 August, the various crossing points between the two parts of Berlin were closed. A wall was built, beginning on 15 August.

The murdering angels

On 3 June 1949, following a shoot-out in which two policemen were seriously wounded, a young man aged 18, Werner Gladow, was arrested at his home at Schreinerstraße 52 in the Friedrichshain district. Since 1948, and throughout the blockade, he had committed 127 crimes, including two murders, 15 attempted murders and 19 assaults, together with a band of 78 teenagers. His model was Al Capone. He profited from the lack of co-ordination between the police forces in the sectors of Berlin. The wearing of a white tie with blue spots was a sign of recognition. Gladow and two of his accomplices were judged in 1950, condemned to death and beheaded in Frankfurt-on-the-Oder.

BERLIN, A DIVIDED TOWN

- American Sector
- Soviet Sector
- British Sector
- French Sector
- —— Berlin Wall

0   10 km

REINICKENDORF   PANKOW

WEISSENSEE

WEDDING

STAAKEN

SPANDAU

CHARLOTTENBURG

LICHTENBERG

Brandenburg Gate

Detention Centre

Karlshorst

WILMERSDORF

Kommandantur

BERLIN-TEMPELHOF

ZEHLENDORF   STEGLITZ   NEUKÖLLN

TREPTOW

KÖPENICK

Glienicke Bridge

Havel

TEMPELHOF

BERLIN-SCHÖNEFELD

Spree

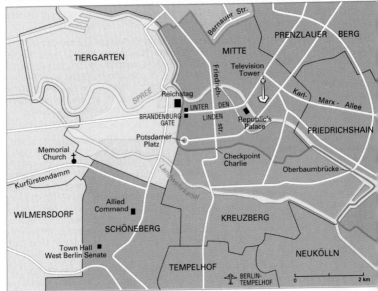

TIERGARTEN

Bernauer Str.

PRENZLAUER BERG

MITTE

Television Tower

SPREE

Reichstag

Friedrich str.

UNTER DEN LINDEN

BRANDENBURG GATE

Karl- Marx - Allee

Republic's Palace

FRIEDRICHSHAIN

Potsdamer Platz

Memorial Church

Checkpoint Charlie

Oberbaumbrücke

Kurfürstendamm

Landwehrkanal

WILMERSDORF

Allied Command

KREUZBERG

SCHÖNEBERG

Town Hall West Berlin Senate

NEUKÖLLN

TEMPELHOF

BERLIN-TEMPELHOF

0   2 km

1965-68 – A student uprising beginning at the free university of Dahlem, against social conformism in West Germany and the policy of the United States. Large demonstrations against the Vietnam war. East Germany took advantage of these disturbances to engage in food poisoning operations, infiltrating pacifist or leftist groups, helping the circulation of drugs, and providing a refuge for terrorists.

The early 70s – The Allies defined the status of West Berlin, which was not a *Land* and which was represented by deputies in the Bundestag who only had a consultative vote. This benefited detente. Berlin ceased to be a point of friction. A joint guard supervised the war criminal **Rudolf Hess**. The chancellor Willy Brandt engaged in an active **Ostpolitik**, founded on the mutual recognition of the two German states (Fundamental Treaty of the 21 December 1972), which became members of the UN.

East Germany attempted to obtain recognition of the fait accompli. The Wall became more "permeable" for West Berliners, but only pensioners in East Germany could visit their families in the Western sectors.

1975-1981 – The two parts of the German capital developed independently. East Berlin was the leading industrial town, political and cultural centre of East Germany. In the West the wall became covered with graffiti and attracted tourists, but the population fell, and included many old people and young people who had escaped military service.

1981-89 – In 1981 the Christian Democrat party (CDU) put an end to 35 years of Socialist rule. Richard von Weizsäcker was elected Burgomaster. The Alternative List (AL) entered the Chamber of Deputies. The Prussian heritage was the subject of discussion, marked by an exhibition at the Martin-Gropius-Bau in 1981, and in the East by an attempt at recovery which was accompanied by major restoration work on the occasion of the 750th anniversary of the city.

UNIFICATION

1987 – Coming to hear a rock concert organised in front of the Reichstag "on the other side" young people from East Germany chanted: "The wall must fall!" and were brutally dispersed by the police.

1989 – The SED ignored *Perestroika* which blew a new wind through the East. In West Germany the position of Chancellor **Helmut Kohl** appeared to be weak: his party had already lost the elections in West Berlin, where extremists were gaining strength. The Alternatives gained 11.8% of the vote, an unequalled score, and entered the Senate. The extreme right wing Republicans gained 7.5%.

Spring-Summer 1989 – The Kremlin invited the authorities in East Germany to liberalise the regime. 65 000 East Germans, particularly the young, fled through Hungary, whose frontier opened in May, and Czechoslovakia, or packed into the embassies of West Germany in Prague or Budapest.

5 September 1989 – First large demonstration organised by opposition groups (*New Forum, Democracy Now*) in Leipzig, a hotbed of opposition. East Berlin was placed under strict police surveillance.

7 October 1989 – On the 40th Anniversary of East Germany, as **Gorbachev** embraced **Honecker**, he withdrew his support: "Life punishes the man who reacts too slowly". The Soviet president was welcomed by the population as a "liberator". On the 9 October

Willy Brandt

ROGER-VIOLLET

On the wall on New Year's Eve 1989

100 000 demonstrators in Leipzig and other large towns in East Germany chanted: "We are the people!" Honecker resigned from power on the 18th. His successor, Egon Krenz, had no control over events.

4 November 1989 – A million people marched through the streets of East Berlin.

7 November 1989 – The government of East Germany resigned.

7 to 11 November 1989 – Günter Schabowski, the secretary in the central committee of the Sozialistische Einheitspartei Deutschlands who was responsible for information and a member of the Politbüro, announced that "final departure visas" would be issued the day after next. Rumour had it that the control point on the Bornholmer Straße would be open. Thousands of East Germans pressed around the Wall. The frontier guards, at a loss, ended up by opening the barriers. A human tide spread into West Berlin, to general rejoicing. At the **Brandenburg Gate** the Wall was taken by assault by a peaceful army of rejoicing youngsters. Giant traffic jams of backfiring Trabants, small polluting cars, paralysed the city. "Woodpeckers", armed with hammers and chisels, began to chip away at the Wall.

December 1989 – The East German state was in collapse. Unifying slogans appeared. The SED dissolved itself up in December. The Stasi was dissolved. The four occupying powers attempted to slow down an irreversible process. Pieces of the Wall were sold as souvenirs.

Winter-summer 1990 – Systematic destruction of the Wall. **Checkpoint Charlie** disappeared with the frontier. Monetary Union began on the 1 July. The Unification Treaty (31 August) established how the five just re-established *Länder* would join the Federal Republic of Germany, and attempted to deal with legal problems of ownership.

3 October 1990 – Occupation of the city ended. At midnight, Germany was unified again. The first Bundestag of United Germany met at the **Reichstag**. After the legislative elections in December, when Helmuth Kohl's party (CDU) triumphed, the latter became the first Chancellor of a unified Germany.

20 June 1991 – A close fight in the Bundestag to determine the location of government offices. Berlin gained the justice department. The capital received 11 ministries, the Chancellery and the Bundestag; Bonn kept 8 ministries. The Brandenburg Gate was restored 200 years after it had been built.

1992-93 – Public transport could again pass through the Brandenburg Gate. The trial of Erich Honecker was suspended. The former secretary general finished his days in Chile. Berliners could consult their files in the Stasi's archives. Integration made the market economy difficult, in a period of crisis and unemployment, and gave rise to profound dissatisfaction. Very major financial transfers were made to the new *Länder*. The advance of extremists (the PDS, the heir to the Communist Party, kept 1/3 of the votes in the East in the elections of 1992) was accompanied by xenophobic violence. A "human chain of light" against racism was formed by 200 000 Berliners at Christmas 1992. Willy Brandt, resistance worker and recipient of the Nobel Peace Prize, died in October. He was buried in Zehlendorf.

1994 – Final retreat of the Red Army. On the 8th, Chancellor Kohl took leave of the three protective powers. Start of work on the **Government district** (*Spreebogen*) and Potsdam and Leipzig squares.

1995 – Wrapping of the Reichstag by **Christo** and his wife Jeanne Claude.

Art

ABC OF ARCHITECTURE

Axial chapel: In churches which are not dedicated to the Virgin this chapel, in the main axis of the building, is often consecrated to the Virgin (Lady Chapel).

Ambulatory: in pilgrimage churches, the aisles were extended round the chancel to allow the faithful to file past the relics.

Chancel: nearly always facing east towards Jerusalem.

Arms of the transept, either projecting or not.

Bay: transverse section of the nave between two pillars.

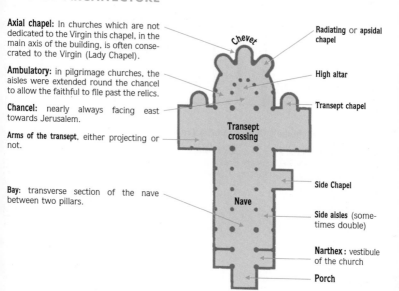

Chevet

Radiating or apsidal chapel

High altar

Transept chapel

Transept crossing

Side Chapel

Nave

Side aisles (sometimes double)

Narthex: vestibule of the church

Porch

Brandenburg March Museum (1899-1908, Ludwig Hoffmann)

This museum has certain features in common with famous monuments of the Brandenburg March such as the gable of the Holy Blood Chapel in St Catherine's Church in Brandenburg.

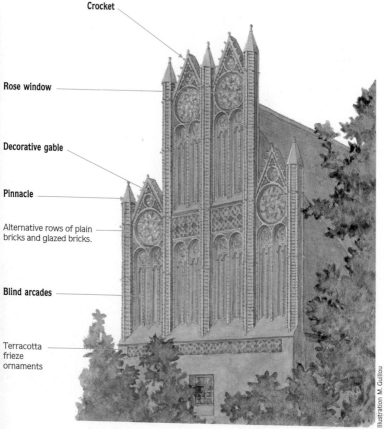

Crocket

Rose window

Decorative gable

Pinnacle

Alternative rows of plain bricks and glazed bricks.

Blind arcades

Terracotta frieze ornaments

Illustration M. Guillou

53

Hall-church

Unlike a basilica, a hall-church has aisles the same height as the central nave and covered with one roof: their windows let light inside the edifice.

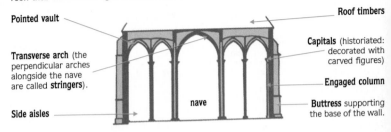

Pointed vault

Roof timbers

Transverse arch (the perpendicular arches alongside the nave are called **stringers**).

Capitals (historiated: decorated with carved figures)

Engaged column

nave

Buttress supporting the base of the wall.

Side aisles

St-Nicholas's Church, Berlin (end of 14C, 2nd half of 15C)

In the **brick-Gothic style**, which was used in northern Europe from the Netherlands to Finland, the southern shores of the Baltic and the Brandenburg March, decoration is either simplified or avoided, but polychromy applied on bricks can have striking effects (see above): the hall-church is the most common.

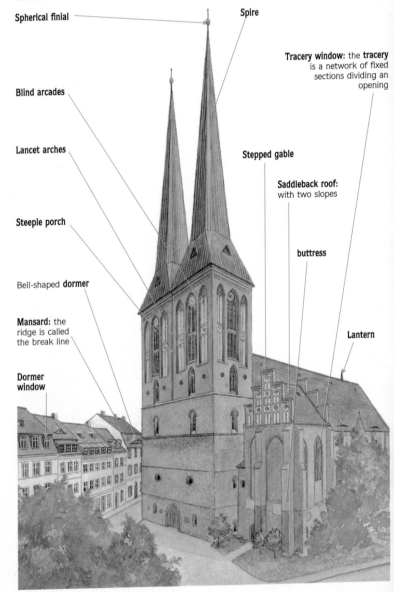

Spherical finial

Spire

Tracery window: the **tracery** is a network of fixed sections dividing an opening

Blind arcades

Lancet arches

Stepped gable

Saddleback roof: with two slopes

Steeple porch

buttress

Bell-shaped **dormer**

Mansard: the ridge is called the break line

Lantern

Dormer window

Arsenal (Johann Arnold Nering, Martin Grünberg, Andreas Schlüter, Jean de Bodt, 1695-1706)

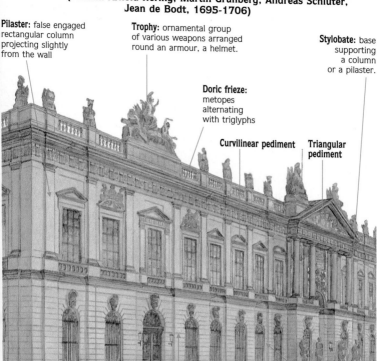

Pilaster: false engaged rectangular column projecting slightly from the wall

Trophy: ornamental group of various weapons arranged round an armour, a helmet.

Stylobate: base supporting a column or a pilaster.

Doric frieze: metopes alternating with triglyphs

Curvilinear pediment

Triangular pediment

Projecting cornice: Uninterrupted moulded projection round the salient part of a wall.

Boss (piece of ornamental stone carving): horizontal and continuous.

Grotesque mask: decorative carved masks

Pier: solid masonry between windows on the same level.

Potsdam, Sans-Souci Palace (Georg Wenzeslaus von Knobelsdorff and Frederick II, 1745-47)

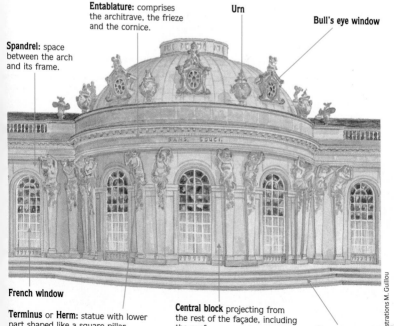

Entablature: comprises the architrave, the frieze and the cornice.

Urn

Bull's eye window

Spandrel: space between the arch and its frame.

French window

Terminus or **Herm:** statue with lower part shaped like a square pillar.

Central block projecting from the rest of the façade, including the roof.

Step arrangement

Illustrations M. Guillou

55

St Nicholas's Church in Potsdam (Karl Friedrich Schinkel, Ludwig Persius and Friedrich August Stüler, 1830-1849)

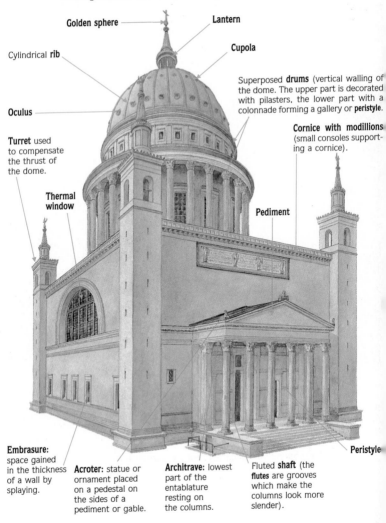

Golden sphere

Lantern

Cylindrical rib

Cupola

Oculus

Superposed **drums** (vertical walling of the dome. The upper part is decorated with pilasters, the lower part with a colonnade forming a gallery or **peristyle**.

Turret used to compensate the thrust of the dome.

Cornice with modillions (small consoles supporting a cornice).

Thermal window

Pediment

Embrasure: space gained in the thickness of a wall by splaying.

Acroter: statue or ornament placed on a pedestal on the sides of a pediment or gable.

Architrave: lowest part of the entablature resting on the columns.

Fluted **shaft** (the **flutes** are grooves which make the columns look more slender).

Peristyle

AEG electric turbine factory (Peter Behrens, 1908-1909)

As AEG's artistic adviser since 1907, **Behrens** designed the firm's trade mark, various objects and the buildings. Classical elements have disappeared: the structure is made of steel, glass and concrete.

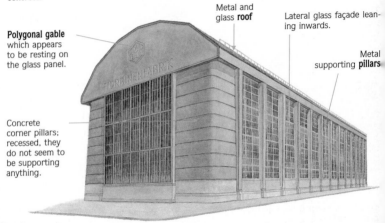

Polygonal gable which appears to be resting on the glass panel.

Metal and glass **roof**

Lateral glass façade leaning inwards.

Metal supporting **pillars**

Concrete corner pillars: recessed, they do not seem to be supporting anything.

"Uncle Tom's Cabin" estate (Bruno Taut, Hugo Häring, Otto Rudolf Salvisberg, 1926-32)

Designed to house 15 000 people, this estate built under the supervision of Martin Wagner, does not convey an impression of monotony. There is a U-Bahn Station in its centre as well as a shopping centre and a cinema.

All the buildings are of a moderate size

Terraced roof

The simplicity of the façades painted with bright colours, hence the nickname of **"parrot estate"**, is due to a rational building plan and the use of standard, relatively cheap, materials.

The natural surroundings are in keeping with the concept of **garden cities** at the beginning of the century.

Individual houses have re-entrant angles and tall windows characteristic of the style of Salvisberg who designed the buildings along Riemeisterstraße.

Philharmonie (Hans Scharoun, 1960-63) and Chamber Music Hall (Edgar Wisniewski, from a drawing by Scharoun, 1984-88)

In 1957, during a congress, H Scharoun expressed his wish to build "an adequately shaped hall for music making, where listening to music would be a common experience". The audience sits round the orchestra, which occupies the very heart of the arena.

Aluminium sheeting: perforated, it was only added in 1978-81. Before that time, the concrete roof was painted in an ochre colour.

The internal structure and the outside appearance are closely related. The place occupied by the orchestra determines the type of structure (three imbricated pentagons in the case of the Philharmonie, a hexagon in the case of the Chamber Music Hall): the tent-shaped roof provides good acoustics and adds a dynamic element to the visual aspect.

Philharmonie

Chamber Music Hall

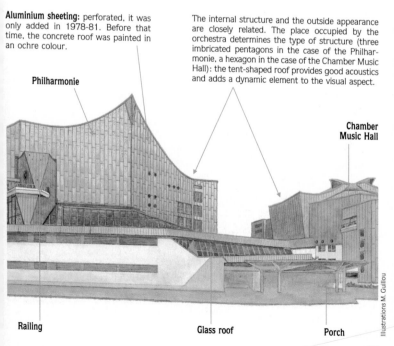

Railing

Glass roof

Porch

Illustrations M. Guillou

Architecture and city planning

A latecomer among the great cities of the world, "Berlin's only tradition is one of urban experimentation, in which the identity of the city is constantly being recast" (*Berlin, Portrait of a City*, DATAR report, 1992). Berlin is often compared to Chicago on account of its pioneering, can-do spirit. From the beginning, discontinuity has been a recurring theme in the life of the city. The latest reincarnation of Berlin and Cölln is a combination of poverty-stricken industrial East and residential, middle-class West.

THE GERMANIC COLONISATION

Little is left of medieval Berlin after the ravages of the industrial revolution, the 1930s and the Second World War. 1931 saw the demolition of the **Krögel**, an area of small workshops and half-timbered houses behind Heinrich Zille's town hall.

Angerdorf – Overflow settlements grew up around the double town of Berlin and Cölln. Variants of the single-street village, they are known as Angerdorf, from the name of the long, almond-shaped square *(Dorfanger)* formed by the two arms of the main street. In the middle stood the granite church surrounded by a cemetery and grazing for poultry and small livestock, and at either end was a duck-pond *(Entenpfuhle)*. This layout is still recognisable at the heart of Berlin's peripheral districts, some of which have managed to retain their rural atmosphere (Lübars, Marienfelde).

Berlin and Cölln – The ground plan of Berlin and Cölln, like those of other German colony towns between the Elbe and the Oder, is a more or less regular grid pattern of streets running northwest/southeast, in which the churches are set at an angle. An austere Gothic style is apparent in the massive brick structures of the **Churches of Our Lady (Marienkirche)** and **St Nicholas (Nikolaikirche)**, which underwent various transformations between the 15C and 19C. **St Peter's Church** in Cölln no longer exists. Around 1300, Berlin grew, gaining a new market *(Neuer Markt)* and its first paved street. The houses were in the Flemish style. The first city wall was a joint effort by the two towns. Enlarged by architect Caspar Theyss, the **Hohenzollern Castle** *(see SCHLOSSPLATZ)*, on the northern part of the island in the Spree, is of more Renaissance inspiration.

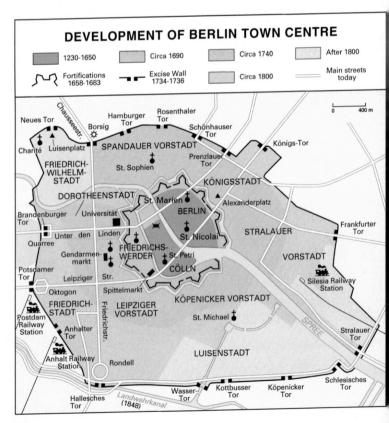

DEVELOPMENT OF BERLIN TOWN CENTRE

Small village churches

Lübars

Schöneberg

Wittenau

Marienfelde

Hermsdorf

Dahlem

A CITY OF RELATIVELY RECENT ORIGIN

Andreas Schlüter, sculptor and architect – As part of the reconstruction and defence of Brandenburg willed by the **Great Elector**, new, Italian-style fortifications were undertaken in 1658 by **Gregor Memhardt**. They also served to prevent soldiers from deserting. The line of the former bastions is still apparent in the irregular layout of the Rosentaler Straße, the Hausvogteiplatz and the Spittelmarkt.

Benefiting from Frederick III's liking for pomp and circumstance, **Andreas Schlüter** (c1660-1714) became the major artist of the late 17C. Director of the newly-founded Academy of Arts, his plans for the Castle Square and city centre remained on the drawing board, as did Schinkel's after him. But he rebuilt the Castle in a powerful baroque style and with a galaxy of other architects (including the Dutchman **Johann Arnold Nehring**, 1659-1695), took part in the construction of the Arsenal, for the courtyard of which he and his pupils sculpted masks of dying warriors. He was also responsible for the equestrian statue of the Great Elector and the tombs of Frederick and his consort Sophie-Charlotte. He fell into disgrace in 1706 and was replaced by the Swede **Johann Friedrich Eosander von Göthe** (1669-1728), who undertook to enlarge the small castle of Lützenburg (which became Charlottenburg) in 1695.

The influx of Huguenots was also favourable to architecture: the military engineer **Jean de Bodt** (1670-1745) was involved in the building of the Arsenal, while Potsdam's Town Castle was built by a Frenchman of Piedmontese origin, **Philippe de Chieze**.

With the accession of the more thrifty Frederick-William I, the emphasis shifted from new buildings to town planning. Worthy of note, however, are the Star hunting lodge *(Jagdschloß Stern)* near Potsdam and the Excise Wall *(Akzismauer,* 1734-36). The new district of **Friedrichstadt**, where the French immigrants settled, was based on a grid of "well-formed wide, straight streets" (count Guibert). Limits were set in 1734 by the building of three geometrical squares at the intersection of the main streets and the Excise Wall: the **Rondell** or Belle-Alliance Platz (now the Mehringplatz), from which radiated the Wilhelmstraße, Friedrichstraße and Lindenstraße; the Oktogon, now the Leipzigerplatz, which gave access to the Potsdam gate; and the **Quarré**, today's Pariserplatz.

The rococo style – The term "rococo" derives from "rocaille", a type of decoration characterised by ornate rock- and shell-work. In 1734, Frederick-William I bought **Rheinsberg** for his son, the future Frederick II, and gave him the means to transform the existing 16C palace. At Rheinsberg, the young Frederick and his small court emulated the world of Watteau's *Fêtes galantes*. Frederick asked his architect and friend **Georg Wenzeslaus von Knobelsdorff** (1699-1753), the painter **Antoine Pesne** and the sculptor Friedrich Christian Giume (1714-1752) to create a new style, which attained its fullest expression, soon after, in the **gilded gallery** of the palace of Charlottenburg and the **music room** of the palace of Sans-Souci. The latter, designed by Knobelsdorff with the active involvement of the king, is, with its terraces, one of the finest creations of the German rococo style. The decoration is ethereal, graceful and at the same time ostentatious, resplendent with gilding and combinations of pastel colours – an extravagant feast for the eyes. Frederick II was so fond of it that he used it again, pushed to extremes, for the decoration of the **Neues Palais**. Designed by four architects, Johann Gottfried Büring, Heinrich Ludwig Manger (1728-1790), Karl von Gontard and Jean Laurent Legeay (1710-1786), this building expresses the new-found power of Prussia. Frederick also wanted to build a Gothic-style inn and a mosque in the park at Potsdam, beside the

Gilded gallery in the palace of Charlottenburg

Neues Palais. The vogue for eclecticism in architecture, of which the **Nauen Gate** *(Nauener Tor)* is a good example, was beginning to spread throughout Europe, and Frederick II was an enthusiastic disciple.

The Neoclassical city – The close of Frederick II's reign, in the 1770s, coincided with a return to classical models. The classical layout of the young, rapidly-expanding city can be seen in the **Forum Fridericianum**, left unfinished beside the Unter den Linden, the palace of Prince Henry, later to become the Humboldt University and the **Gendarmenmarkt** designed by Karl **von Gontard** (1731-1791), the favourite architect of the ageing monarch.

The reign of the more extravagant Frederick-William II was favourable to the arts. A great lover of picturesque gardens, the king was familiar with the landscaped park at **Wörlitz**, near Dessau (his mistress, the future countess of Lichtenau, was a native of the town), one of the first manifestations of the Neoclassical style in Germany. A new style of public architecture began to appear at the end of the century. **David Gilly** (1748-1808) and his son Friedrich, and **Johann Heinrich Gentz** (1766-1811) adopted the architectural style of the French Revolution, with a predilection for baseless Doric columns. Gentz's Mint, which houses the Mineralogical collection and the Academy of Architecture, founded in 1799, was Berlin's first museum.

The elegance of Neoclassicism is particularly evident in sculpture: **Johann Gottfried Schadow** (1764-1850) was responsible for the *Quadriga* which surmounts the Brandenburg Gate, built by **Carl Gotthard Langhans** (1732-1808), and the double portrait of *The Princesses Louise and Frederika of Prussia*; **Christian Daniel Rauch** (1777-1857) sculpted the statues of generals from the Wars of Liberation (1819-22) at the New Guardhouse, the tomb of Queen Louise (1816) and the equestrian statue of Frederick the Great (1822-51) on Unter den Linden.

But Berlin remained essentially a country town. Around 1800, according to one observer, "thatched cottages were hidden away behind the fine facades", the houses "were too low for such wide streets", and "vile and noble were inextricably mixed" (General Fantin des Odoards), while Mme de Staël compared the city to a "huge barracks".

KARL FRIEDRICH SCHINKEL AND HIS SCHOOL

Prussian identity was strengthened by victory over Napoleon and found expression in the Neoclassical style. Frederick-William III (1797-1840) was a great admirer of the Parisian church of St-Philippe-du-Roule by Chalgrin. During his reign, **Karl Friedrich Schinkel** (1781-1841) erected a large number of buildings: palaces, bridges, churches, theatres, schools, gates and museums around the Unter den Linden avenue, in the suburbs (parish churches, between 1829 and 1833) and in Potsdam, spanning a period of twenty-five years.

An official in the service of Prussia – Born at Neuruppin, north of Berlin, and trained as a draughtsman, Schinkel became aware of his vocation when he visited an exhibition of plans for a monument to Frederick the Great in 1797. He became apprenticed to the Gillys, father and son, who had a strong influence on his development. From 1803 to 1805, he travelled in Italy, visiting Sicily and staying for a long time in Rome. He returned to Berlin via Paris and kept body and soul together by painting dioramas and stage scenery. He was appointed in 1810, on the recommendation of Wilhelm von Humboldt, to the Department of Building and Public Works *(Oberbaudeputation)*, where he eventually rose to the position of director *(Oberlandesbaudirektor)* and supervised plans for all restoration and new building development in Prussia.

An original genius – Although, in his attachment to purity of line and attention to detail, Schinkel belongs to the Neoclassical stream, he moved away from this movement to open the way for the eclecticism and industrial architecture of the 19C. On a mission to England with Christian Beuth *(see ERNST-REUTER-PLATZ)*, he studied the first metal bridges and noted in his diary: "it is a terrible and frightening thing to see these disproportionate masses built from necessity alone, in red brick, without any feeling for architecture". But economic constraints led him to adopt less costly materials: brick, which he used for a wide range of applications; cast iron, zinc and terracotta for architectural detail. His buildings were elegant, simple to the point of austerity and increasingly functional in design. Gifted with a lively imagination, Schinkel practised a mixture of styles and tended towards the ideals of **Viollet-le-Duc**, whilst treating Greek temple, Gothic church, Umbrian basilica and English manor house all with the same rational rigour *(see SCHLOSSPLATZ, Friedrichswerdersche Kirche)*. From his Italian journey, he derived an enthusiasm for integrating architecture into the natural environment. All his plans for palaces and family mansions included features tending to combine architecture and landscape: trellis-covered pergolas, porticos and grandiose staircases. In this respect, his ideas were akin to those of Lenné, who sought to embellish landscape with architecture.

The first interior designer – Interested in fields allied to architecture, Schinkel was also highly influential in the development of interior design and the decorative arts. He aimed to "go into as much detail as possible in all aspects of art" and particularly applied his mind to designing two types of furnishing: chairs and light fittings (candelabra, girandoles, chandeliers), which served as models for the craftsmen and manufacturers of Berlin. He rarely used gilding, preferring materials suited to industrial manufacture.

Schinkel and posterity – Schinkel left theoretical works and designs for projects both realised and unrealised (like his monument to Frederick II). However, unlike his Munich colleague **Leo von Klenze**, who went on to work in St Petersburg, Schinkel and his school remained rooted in Berlin. His followers included Georg Heinrich Hitzig (1811-1881), **Ludwig Persius** (1803-1845), **Friedrich August Stüler** (1800-1865), and also **Walter Knoblauch** (1861-1865?), architect of the new synagogue in the Oranienburger Straße, and **Martin Gropius** (1824-1880) of the former School of Applied Arts (Martin-Gropius-Bau). In 1841 another great artist, the landscape painter **Peter Josef Lenné** *(see WANNSEE, Klein-Glienicke Park)*, proposed a plan to lay out the Luisenstadt district, in Kreuzberg, to an orthogonal plan. A canal (filled in in the 1920s) was dug to bring in building materials for the project, which included the church of St Michael *(Michaelkirche)* and the Oranienplatz. After 1871, neo-Greek rationalism was superseded by a Beaux-Arts style, with representation considered more important than the quest for a coherent building system.

THE TRIUMPH OF ECLECTICISM

During the *Biedermeier* period, Berlin was still a small town compared with other European capitals. The drift away from the land led to a rise in property prices and higher rents. Property speculation resulted in the construction of damp, unhealthy, overcrowded tenements, in contrast with the summer residences built by the nobility and wealthy merchants in the neighbouring villages of Charlottenburg, Pankow and Schönhausen. The new arrivals settled on the outskirts of the town, in suburbs which were still semi-rural or undergoing industrialisation. After the opening of the Berlin-Potsdam railway line (1838), the Potsdam and Hamburg stations were built just outside the Excise Wall. Only Stralau station (now the *Hauptbahnhof*) was not located in a densely-populated quarter.

The dog tax

Between 1676 and 1679, on the orders of the Great Elector, street lighting and paving were introduced at the expense of the townspeople. Pigs were banned after a herd blocked the cortege of Princess Dorothea. The "street officer", whose job was to check that people cleaned their doorsteps, became a familiar figure. Barns were also prohibited, giving rise to a **"barn district"** outside the city walls *(see ORANIENBURGER STRASSE)*. In 1830, a royal decree required house owners to lay a stone slab in front of their door. When landlords complained of having to maintain the roadway, claiming that their income from rents was too low, the authorities decreed a tax on dogs, which remains in force to this day. The paving of streets speeded up after 1823. The first pavements were laid in 1828, two years after the introduction of gas lighting.

W. Otto/SUNSET

"The biggest city of rentable barracks in the world" (Werner Hegemann) – In 1862, engineer **James Hobrecht**'s plan to enlarge the city followed the example of Baron Haussmann's restructuring of Paris, but he also adopted some of the principles implemented in *Luisenstadt*: a grid street pattern, squares laid out around a church (Kollwitz-Platz, Savigny-Platz, Steinplatz), an outer ring of **boulevards** bearing the names of generals from the Wars of Liberation (Hardenberg, Yorck, Gneisenau). To bring light and air to the new districts, the plan included the first large public parks (Friedrichshain, Humboldthain, Alter Treptower Park), which were laid out by Gustav Meyer and Hermann Mächtig. It also made provision for four-storey buildings housing a mix of lower-income and better-off families, but this intention was thwarted by property speculation.

The network of major streets was never filled in, as planned, with private minor roads. The **"Riehmershofgarten"** block, in Kreuzberg, is the only existing example. Streets in the working-class quarters were lined with six or seven-storey brick buildings of poor quality. An Italian Renaissance style prevailed (1880-90), with some excursions into the picturesque and pseudo-medieval (1890-1905: *see WEDDING, Hussitenstraße 4-5*), but the uncorbelled facades gave Berlin a severe and monotonous appearance. In the eyes of an American diplomat, it was a "rather dreary" city, and Rosa Luxemburg, a native of Ruthenia, described everything as "cold, dull, massive".

The stucco ornamentation and opulent-looking facades concealed the poverty of crowded courtyards, deep shafts admitting limited light, just big enough (28.5m²) for a fire engine to manoeuvre in. The *Meyer's Hof* building in Wedding consisted of seven such units. Around these courtyards, with their ground-floor workshops *(Gewerbehöfe)*, a destitute population was packed into dark, unhygienic apartments. Many people lived in garrets or cellars until the 1920s, or simply rented a bed. On average, a tenement barracks of this kind accommodated 325 persons. One on the Ackerstraße, at the boundary of the Wedding and Mitte districts, was home to 1 000 people, living in extreme deprivation. These deplorable living conditions, aggravated by hunger, sickness and unemployment, inspired the work of **Käthe Kollwitz** *(see KURFÜRSTENDAM)* and **Heinrich Zille**, who concluded that: "You can kill a man with bad housing as effectively as with an axe!"

The growth of Berlin

Though now a city of many centres, Berlin first grew in concentric circles. The medieval towns of Berlin and Cölln were superseded by the princely grid-plan cities *(Fürstenstädte)* of **Dorotheenstadt** and **Friedrichstadt**. In the late 18C and early 19C, this nucleus was augmented by rapidly-growing suburbs: Spandauer Viertel (the "barn district"), Königstadt and Stralauer Viertel to the north, and Luisenstadt to the south. There were twenty access points in the Excise Wall *(Aksismauer, 1731-1869)*, including the famous Brandenburg Gate. In 1861, the area of Berlin increased by 70% with the incorporation of six new districts: Friedrichshain, Kreuzberg, Moabit, Prenzlauer Berg, Tiergarten and Wedding. Businesses began to move to the outer suburbs, to accessible, more affordable sites: **Borsig** to Tegel, the huge **Siemens** complex to the area between Charlottenburg and Spandau, Schering and **AEG** to Wedding. Breweries and textile works remained concentrated in the east of the city. People moved out of the city centre to live in the suburbs. By 1914, Berlin was surrounded by seven towns of over 100 000 inhabitants. These bloated settlements had completely lost their original structure, apart from their medieval church and area of common grazing land.

The Castle Square in 1903. Left to right:

Architecture under William II – For William II, architecture was to be "the symbolic expression of imperial power". He dotted his capital with monuments: the new cathedral beside the *Lustgarten*, the memorial church to Emperor William I on the Kurfürstendamm, the Reichstag. Gigantism and monumental historicism were rampant; Neoclassical buildings and the few vestiges of medieval architecture were demolished. The district **court houses** (Moabit, Wedding, Mitte), mostly designed in the same spirit by Rudolf Mönnich and Paul Thoemer, were remarkable for their magnificent flights of stairs. Together with the **town halls**, churches and high schools, they formed the monumental heart of the new residential quarters (Pankow, Wilmersdorf, Köpenick). The prolific **Ludwig Hoffman**, Berlin's chief architect from 1896 to 1924, experimented with every form of eclecticism. The Pergamon Museum was the last great imperial project in the field of culture. Even so, the powers that be did not like Berlin. Bismarck saw it as a "desert of bricks and newspapers" and, according to William II himself, there was "nothing to attract the foreign visitor apart from the odd museum, palaces and soldiers!"

THE BIRTH OF MODERN ARCHITECTURE

The city continued to have a dual personality. The baroque town, around the Friedrichstraße and Unter den Linden, was the traditional centre of banking *(Behrenensstraße)* and entertainment. Meanwhile, big department stores *(KaDeWe)* and fashionable cafés frequented by artists were opening around the Zoologischer Garten station and along the **Kurfürstendamm**. At the same time as the expressionist painters were celebrating the movement and lights of the big city, the aesthetic and social programmes of the 1920s were being born.

Urban renewal – At the turn of the century, the heavily populated areas lacked major road access; there was a shortage of housing for low-income families; green open spaces were being sacrificed. The Berlin Architects' Association redoubled its efforts and in 1905 published a new **city plan**. Daniel Burnham's plan for Chicago (1909) was presented at a general exhibition on town planning in May 1910. **Le Corbusier**, who at this time was working in the offices of Peter Behrens, visited the exhibition and expressed enthusiasm for the traffic schemes and allocation of green spaces which later became a feature of his work.

The "Deutscher Werkbund" – Around 1900, with the advent of *Jugendstil*, or Art Nouveau, there was increased cooperation between designers and engineers. This movement is sometimes confused with the "Teutonic Style" with its emphasis on pillars, heavy cornices and bow windows favoured by Bruno Schmitz (Friedrichstraße 167-168) and **Oskar Kaufmann** (Hebbeltheater). In seeking to "ennoble craftsmanship through collaboration between art, industry and manual labour", the **Deutscher Werkbund**, born in Munich in 1907, established an industrial aesthetic. **Alfred Messel** (1853-1909) and **Peter Behrens** (1868-1940) pioneered a functional style of architecture, foreshadowing the Bauhaus. In 1908, the Viennese Adolf Loos published *Ornament and Crime (Ornament und Verbrechen)*. The origins of the modern movement can be seen in such buildings as the overground metro, the transparent structure of the Wertheim department store (1904, Alfred Messel) on the Leipziger Platz (despite its neo-Gothic style) and the two machine shops (Huttenstraße, 1908-1909 and Voltastraße, 1909-1913) designed by Behrens for **AEG**.

the Old Museum, Cathedral and Castle

The "garden-city" movement – The crusade against tenement buildings (*Mietskasernen*) began before the First World War. The extension of the urban transport network into the suburbs, which encouraged the growth of middle-class residential areas (new S-Bahn stations in Dahlem and Zehlendorf), led to the first villa developments (*Villenkolonien*, 1860-70) in Friedenau, Wilmersdorf and Lichterfelde, built by the Hamburg entrepreneur J.A.W. Carstenn. At the turn of the century, country retreats on the lines of the English cottage were made fashionable among the aristocracy and in court circles by *House in the Sun*, a work by the Swedish Art Nouveau painter **Karl Larsson** (1853-1919). (The upper middle class preferred to imitate rococo palace architecture, for example Villa Borsig). **Hermann Muthessius** (1861-1927), a founding member of the *Deutscher Werkbund* who was sent to London as an embassy attaché, adapted this model to the Brandenburg setting. In 1902, the **German Garden-city Association** was set up. Berlin's first garden city was built in **Grünau-Flakenberg** (1913) by Bruno Taut and Heinrich Emmerich. The layout of the houses in the garden city of Zehlendorf (Mabes, Paul Emmerich, 1913-14) served as a model for the housing developments of the 1920s. During the First World War, the garden city of Staaken was designed by Paul Schmitthenner for armaments factory workers.

THE TWENTIES

The conflict between the ambitions and the economic capacities of the Weimar Republic meant that many projects remained unrealised, such as the glass and steel skyscraper Mies van der Rohe wanted to build on the Friedrichstraße, one of the symbols of modern architecture. But democratic principles were applied to the new urban developments and a concern for individual welfare was evident in the design of homes and facilities. The city continued to expand westward, towards Spandau. At the end of the east-west axis, Hans Poelzig built the Radio Headquarters (1929-39), and new residential areas were laid out, for instance in Neu-Westend.

"Greater Berlin" – In 1920, seven towns (Charlottenburg, Köpenick, Spandau, Lichtenberg, Neukölln, Schöneberg and Wilmersdorf), 59 local authority districts and 27 rural districts merged with the capital to form **"Greater Berlin" (Groß-Berlin)**. The new entity consisted of 20 districts, covered an area of 880km² (one more than New York) and had a population of 3.8 million.

All the Berliners elected an assembly, which in turn appointed a municipal council (the *Magistrat*) of thirty members led by a Burgomaster as executive head. From 1920 to 1929, Berlin was presided over by **Gustav Böss**, who implemented an imaginative social and cultural policy, but because of his involvement in the Sklarek scandal, he was forced to resign in 1929.

An aggressive modernity – Expressionist architecture, long on brick, but more decorative than functional, drew inspiration from the art of the ancient Near-East and tended to glorify electricity as a new source of energy. Its broken lines, pagoda-style porches and zigzags are equally evident in business premises, churches (Holy Cross Church in Wilmerdorf, St Mary Magdalene in Pankow), and places of entertainment such as Hans Poelzig's Grand Theatre (*Großes Schauspielhaus*, 1918-19), a vast "grotto" bristling with stalactites. After 1926, when the economic situation stabilised, a more "American" vision of the city came to the fore. Europe's first towers were built, such as those which grace the Borsig building in Tegel (1922-24) and the **Ullstein print works** in Tempelhof (1925-26). The style of a Manhattan skyscraper was adopted for the Karstadt department store on the Hermannplatz (1927-29). The **Avus** motor-racing circuit, which crossed the Grunewald Forest, was also the first section of urban motorway (1921).

Martin Wagner (1885-1957) – Engineer and architect, and a member of the Social-Democratic Party, **Martin Wagner** militated in favour of low-income housing. As town councillor in Schönberg before the War, he implemented his ideas as director of the "intercommunal group". In 1926, he was appointed Director of Town Planning for "Greater Berlin" and pursued an active building policy. The political crisis did not leave him time to complete his plans for the choked-up Alexanderplatz and Potsdamerplatz crossroads and for a satellite town for Spandau, nor Walter Gropius's project for a "cooperative housing development" to the south of the city. He was dismissed by the Nazis in 1933.

"Sunlight, fresh air and a home for all" – With Frankfurt-am-Main, Berlin spent more money on low-income housing than any other German town. Martin Wagner's ambition was to "concentrate housing in large developments offering a degree of unity and complying with modern building principles". He believed in a simple, inexpensive style of architecture based on standardised components, setting housing in a well-wooded environment and laying on collective services. Estates of this kind, such as Britz's **Hufeisensiedlung** (1925-27), designed in conjunction with Bruno Taut, began to go up on the periphery. 134 000 apartments were built in 9 years, almost 44 000 in 1930 alone. The buildings were generally flat-roofed, enclosing a garden, with large balconies and functional kitchens. In 1925, Martin Wagner first thought of organising a large architectural exhibition on the theme of "sunlight, fresh air and a home for all", which eventually took place in 1931 in the reorganised Exhibition Park. The exhibitors included the chief architects of the recently-finished model development of **Siemensstadt** and Mies van der Rohe, who presented his plans for a "contemporary house".

Functionalism and "publicity architecture" (Werner Hegemann) – In the mid-1920s, a new movement, less spectacular but more attuned to people's real needs, began to be influential: **New Objectivity**. Architects were concerned less with detail and more with plane surfaces, sharp outlines, and horizontal roof terraces. This abstract approach resulted in some of the finest housing developments (examples of the functional *Neues Bauen* architecture are Onkel-Toms-Hütte in Zehlendorf, the Haselhorst estate in Charlottenburg and Weiße Stadt in Reinickendorf) and was taken even further by the members of the *Bauhaus*. The increase in traffic in the city centre (Europe's first traffic lights were installed on the Potsdamer Platz in 1926) also influenced architecture, which began to conform to the circular flow of the vehicles, becoming more dynamic and horizontal. This is evident in the **Luckhardt brothers'** project for the Alexanderplatz, before Peter Behrens's twin office blocks and Emil Fahrenkamp's *Shell Haus* (1930-31) were eventually built. **Erich Mendelsohn (1887-1953)** was an architect much in demand. Using an industrial cast-concrete technique, his predilection was for simple shapes (*Universum* cinema, now the *Schaubühne*; *Mossehaus*; *Einsteinturm*) and large plate-glass windows. The *Columbus-Haus* (1931-32), on the Potsdamer Platz, introduced the idea of horizontal fascias as a setting for neon advertising signs.

Some interesting housing development projects:

14-26 Grabbeallee (Pankow) – 1908-09, by Paul Mebes. A good example of housing reform before the First World War.

Frohnau garden city (Gartenstadt Frohnau, Reinickendorf) – 1909-10, a villa development.

Staaken garden city (Gartenstadt Staaken, Spandau) – 1913-17, by Paul Schmitthenner. Built for munitions factory workers, its design was influenced by Hanseatic architecture.

Ceciliengärten (Schöneberg) – 1924-26, by Heinrich Lassen. The overall layout is by Schöneberg's town-planner in chief, Paul Wolf.

"Horse-shoe" development ("Hufeisensiedlung", Neukölln) – 1925-27, by Bruno Taut and Martin Wagner. Built in record time using pre-fabricated components.

"Uncle Tom's Cabin" development (Siedlung "Onkel-Toms-Hütte", Zehlendorf) – 1926-31, by Bruno Taut, Hugo Häring and Otto Rudolf Salvisberg. Built to a terraced-roof design on behalf of the Progressive Social Housing Association.

"Weiße Stadt" ("White Town", Reinickendorf) – 1929-31, by Bruno Ahrends, Wilhelm Büning and Otto Rudolf Salvisberg.

Siemensstadt development (Siedlung Siemensstadt, Charlottenburg/Spandau) – 1929-32, by Hans Scharoun, Walter Gropius, Hugo Häring, Fred Forbat, Paul Rudolf Henning and Otto Bartning. *See SIEMENSSTADT.*

The "Bauhaus" – Collaboration between architects, engineers and craftsmen was the *raison d'être* of this "great workshop", where all the arts were harnessed to the all-embracing task of building construction (literally *Bauhaus* means "house of building"). The Bauhaus invented the concept of design, the creation of objects for industrial manufacture. Among the people who taught there were the artists Lyonel Feininger, Paul Klee, Wassily Kandinsky and Laszlo Moholy-Nagy, and the two directors of the institution, architects **Walter Gropius** (1883-1969) and his successor **Mies van der Rohe** (1886-1969). The clear, abstract direction taken by architecture in Berlin was very much due to their efforts. In 1925, the *Bauhaus* was obliged to leave Weimar, where it had been founded in 1919, and settle in Dessau. Once again, however, it was the target of conservatives, who demanded its closure. In 1932, Mies van der Rohe transferred the institution to Berlin, to an unused factory building in Steglitz, but the Nazis banned it in April 1933. Teachers and pupils left Germany for the United States.

"GERMANIA" A GRANDIOSE URBAN VISION

Hitler never concealed his admiration for the *Ring* in Vienna and its sumptuous buildings. But he did not like the German capital, which he sought to transform into a display-case for the regime and a world metropolis of ten million people. These ambitions first resulted in demolition on a grand scale, which was of course completed by the War. His restructuring began in 1938 with the **New Chancellery**, built in twelve months using costly materials, and continued during the summer of 1940, after Hitler's visit to Paris. The plan was to inaugurate the new capital in 1950, as part of a universal exhibition, when Berlin would be renamed **"Germania"**. The building projects were self-glorifying, and not at all in line with the real needs of the population. There was in fact a sharp decline in the number of housing units built under the Third Reich. **Albert Speer** (1905-1981) was appointed Inspector General of Construction in 1937, and was directly answerable to the Führer.

The only remaining developments for which Speer was directly responsible are the street lights on what is now 17 June Avenue, but many buildings survive from this period: the **Fehrbelliner Platz** administrative centre; the former **Air Ministry building** (*Reichsluftfahrtministerium*, 1935-36), the first major construction programme of the Nazi era; **Tempelhof airport** (1936-41) by Ernst Sagebiel; and the **sports complex**, begun under the Weimar Republic, for the 1936 Olympic Games.

EAST/WEST: OPPOSING VISIONS

363 war-time air raids left 43% of Berlin's apartment blocks in ruins. The districts of Mitte, Tiergarten, Friedrichshain and Kreuzberg were the worst affected. The effects of reconstruction were similar in both East and West: a separation of residential accommodation and the workplace, new construction given priority over rehabilitation, and the demolition of much of the old urban fabric, in particular the surviving *Mietskasernen*. Buildings from the time of Emperor William II were not restored until the 1960s. Big housing complexes were built on the periphery, while the city, crisscrossed by expressways, bowed to the needs of motor traffic.

The construction industry – Women (*Trümmerfrauen*) played an important part in clearing the ruins, and reconstruction soon began under the leadership of **Hans Scharoun**, who was appointed head of city-planning services in 1946. During the 1950s, the area around the Zoologischer Garten station and the Kurfürstendam was rebuilt by private contractors, to become the "show-case of the West".

The historic districts of Berlin, located in the East, suffered from insensitive planning. Rather than repair and maintain old apartment blocks, it proved cheaper to demolish and rebuild. This process reached its height in the 1960s and 70s. Private contractors were replaced by a *Baukombinat*. Traditional materials were shunned in favour of factory-made prefabricated panels, giving rise to a sad grey townscape of dormitory complexes, which mushroomed in the areas of **Marzahn**, Hohenschönhausen and **Heilersdorf**. One third of the population was housed in this type of accommodation (known as "worker cupboards"). Building works in the city centre included the final section of the Karl-Marx-Straße, between the Strauberger Platz and the Alexanderplatz, and the buildings blocking off the Leipziger Straße (1972-82). In the West, the dormitory towns of **Gropiusstadt** (1962-72) and **Märkisches Viertel** (1963-74) rose in the open countryside. Wedding was the biggest urban redevelopment site in Europe in the early 1970s.

Berlin, architectural showcase – Successor to the international exhibitions of architecture held in 1910 and 1931, the *Interbau* (1957) was an opportunity to build a new residential district, **Hansaviertel**, illustrating the concept of integrating urban development and natural environment. The area chosen was on the edge of the Tiergarten, not far from the **Congress Hall** paid for by the Americans. A new housing development (1956-59) designed by **Le Corbusier** was built in the vicinity of the Olympic Stadium. These initiatives reflected political rivalry with the East, which launched a "competition for ideas on the socialist transformation of the centre of the capital of the Democratic Republic". A new Soviet embassy was erected on Unter den Linden avenue but, because the avenue itself was truncated by the Wall, the East-German authorities were obliged to create another prestigious thoroughfare. **Hermann Henselmann**, East Berlin's chief architect from 1953 to 1959, and his team of planners designed a series of ten-storey residential buildings which stretched for 1.5km along the former Frankfurter Allee, renamed **Stalinallee** and later **Karl-Marx-Allee** (1951-1956). He was also responsible for the new layout of the Alexanderplatz.

Reacting to the concrete jungle of the post-war period and wanting to restore the city centre as a residential area, the West Berlin Senate decided to organise a fourth architectural exhibition in 1978. The association of architects led by Walther Hämer, which inspired the international exhibition of architecture held in 1987 (**Internationale Bau-Ausstellung** or IBA), tried to bring to Berlin the imaginative vision of other Western-European architects (Grumbach of France, Siza of Portugal, Rossi of Italy) and encourage the new generation of local talent (Kolhoff and Kleihues). They carried through a programme of rehabilitation and new construction to provide fringe and immigrant groups with decent living conditions, whilst protecting the city's heritage. These projects were on a relatively modest scale. Until the early 1980s, Berlin was seen as the most sophisticated laboratory of contemporary architecture and town-planning "with a human face". Kreuzberg was renovated (Chamissoplatz) with the participation of its inhabitants, but in a climate of urban protest led by squatters.

City on a cultural drip – West Berlin acquired new landmarks in the shape of the **Europa Center** shopping precinct (1963-65), the restored Memorial Church, for which **Egon Eiermann** designed a modern bell-tower and sanctuary between 1957 and 1963, and the **International Congress Centre** (ICC, 1973-79). Federal subsidies and Allied initiatives, dictated by political circumstances and the need to keep the "island" of West Berlin alive, ensured the city of the cultural facilities it lacked: the Free University *(Freie Universität or FU)*, the Technical University *(Technische Universität or TU)*, the Dahlem museum complex and above all the **Kulturforum** buildings, erected close to the Wall in 1962. Hans Scharoun and his pupils designed the **Philharmonie** (1960-63), the National Library (1967-78) and the Chamber Music Concert Hall (1984-87), followed later by the Schiller Theatre and the opera house on the Bismarckstraße *(Deutsche Oper)*.

East Berlin, which inherited most of the historic core of the city, had more difficulty in clearing the ground. The authorities, led by **Walter Ullbricht**, made great efforts to remove all traces of the Prussian past, resulting in the destruction of the Castle and the centre of Potsdam. The redevelopment of the city centre left a sense of emptiness, presided over by the **Television Tower** after 1965. The Palace of the Republic was built on the Castle site in 1976. The nondescript State Council building and the Ministry of Foreign Affairs, which has since been demolished, were built alongside it. Fortunately, there was not enough money to fund the destruction of further districts to make way for new buildings, and although large parts of the Prenzlauer Berg and the Spandauer Vorstadt went into a slow decline, they have nevertheless survived.

Awareness of the city's past increased in the 1980s. The Prussian heritage was reconsidered on both sides of the Wall and the GDR attempted to lend the Communist regime historical legitimacy by restoring what remained. To mark the town's 750th anniversary, a programme was launched to reconstruct the Gendarmenmarkt and the medieval quarter around St Nicholas.

"Märkisches Viertel"

Schloßstraße 45-47

Fraenkelufer 38-44

Rönnestraße 17

Some noteworthy achievements

Charlottenburg
– Rönnestraße 17. Schloßstraße 45-47 and 56 (sports hall).

Kreuzberg
– South and east of the **Martin-Gropius-Bau**: Bernburger Straße 22-23 and 26. Dassauerstraße 9-10. corner of Kochstraße and Wilhelmstraße.
– In the old **press district**: Kochstraße. Charlottenstraße.
– Near the **Berlin Museum**: Ritterstraße and Alte Jakobstraße.
– Along the **Landwehrkanal**: Fraenkelufer 38-44.

Tegel
– Tegeler Hafen.

South of the Tiergarten
– Lützlowplatz and Lützlowstraße, Rauchstraße.

THE NEW FACE OF BERLIN

After reunification, Berlin became the biggest building site in Europe. Major projects – Lehrte station, the **government district** *(Spreebogen)*, Potsdamer Platz, Leipziger Platz – were undertaken to heal the fracture left by the 20 to 200-metre belt of no-man's-land on either side of the Wall.

A **"Stadtforum"** was set up by the Berlin Senate as a place where people could exchange ideas on the redevelopment of the city, and there, architects, town-planners and councillors expressed their views before a public free to speak from the floor. The debate was enriched by contributions from alternative groups, district associations and the daily newspapers, which published details of new projects. As a result of consultations attended by both German and foreign planners and architects (800 architects collaborated on the *Spreebogen* project), the new face of Berlin will be a striking patchwork: glass facades, buildings with square windows clad in noble materials and strictly aligned in the Prussian fashion, buildings painted in bright colours. To avoid the danger of "manhattanisation", architects must respect the "Berlin format", with a maximum height of 22 metres reminiscent of the Haussmann prescription for Paris. A few tower blocks were built on the **Potsdamer Platz** and the plans for the future **Alexanderplatz** development include some relatively high buildings. All these developments must include approximately 20% of residential accommodation.

The sad, grey **dormitory estates** of the former GDR, home to 700 000 people, are being renovated. Attention is also being given to the *Mietskasernen* of the older districts, which can be turned into attractive homes. At the same time, hundreds of thousands of new apartments need to be built (150 000 are planned each decade). There are also plans for completely new towns on derelict city sites and in open country, for instance the **Oberhavel city-on-the-water** *(Wasserstadt Oberhavel)* in Spandau, and Buch-Karow in the northeast part of Berlin.

MICHELIN GUIDES

The **Red Guides** *(hotels and restaurants)*
Benelux - Deutschland - España Portugal - Europe - France - Great Britain and Ireland - Italia - Switzerland

The **Green Guides** *(fine art, historical monuments, scenic routes)*
Austria - Belgium and Luxembourg - Brussels - California - Canada - Chicago - England: the West Country - Europe - Florida - France - Germany - Great Britain - Greece - Ireland - Italy - London - Mexico - Netherlands - New England - New York - Portugal - Quebec - Rome - San Francisco - Scandinavia-Finland - Scotland - Spain - Switzerland - Thailand - Tuscany - Venice - Wales - Washington DC
...and the collection of regional guides for France.

Painting

The first burgeoning of painting in Prussia – This dates from the 18C and the reign of Frederick the Great: **Antoine Pesne** (1683-1757), who was of Huguenot descent and the nephew of Charles de Lafosse, was appointed the first painter to the court of Prussia in 1711 under Frederick I and later under Frederick II. In 1722 he became the director of the Academy of Fine Arts. His portraits, especially of women (well represented in Schloß Charlottenburg), are finely executed, but people may prefer the realist vein of Daniel Chodowiecki (1726-1801), a sensitive draughtsman of Franco-Polish origin. The **Academy of Science and Literature**, re-established in 1744, organized its first art exhibition in 1786. The art-loving public admired the works of Lesueur, Chodowiecki and Charles Amédée Philippe Vanloo (1719-1795) who succeeded Pesne as court painter. Frederick the Great was always a passionate collector, using art to assert royal omnipotence; he had the idea of building one of the first painting galleries in Germany in the grounds of Sanssouci.

Daniel Chodowiecki: *Interior scene*

The Romantic period – The four leading names in Berlin painting of the Biedermeier period were the portraitist and genre painter **Franz Krüger** (1797-1857), the architectural painter **Eduard Gaertner** (1801-1877), the landscape painter **Carl Blechen** (1797-1840) and, first and foremost, **Caspar David Friedrich** who exhibited regularly at the Academy; his paintings were bought by the future Frederick William IV who was an influential and discerning purchaser of art from an early age. Frederick William II availed himself of Prussia's major talents in the field of the fine arts in the first half of the 19C.

Schinkel, the utopian – As a young graphic artist Schinkel sketched picturesque views, ruins, garden buildings and small monuments. In 1802 he started to plan decorative schemes for the **diorama**, a form of show invented in London which reached Berlin c1800: at Christmas time views of Italy or war scenes were displayed on ephemeral supports.

Schinkel was permanently in contact with the theatre and the opera. At the height of the Neoclassical period eclecticism was accepted for stage sets. Influenced by Piranesi's engravings and accounts of expeditions to Egypt he designed about 100 sets for some 40 plays between 1815 and 1829. As well as the famous sets for *The Magic Flute*, the whole history of architecture is unfolded: the interior of the Temple of Jerusalem in *Athalie* (1817); the temple of Diana at Ephesus in *Olympia* (1821). His imagination was kept under control in his architectural schemes. Those that were not carried out, like the Great Hall for the Acropolis and **Orianda**, designed to stand on a cliff overlooking the Black Sea in Crimea as a summer residence for Frederick William IV's sister, the Tsarina, combine a poetic dimension and rigour in the elegance of their decoration and the Greek style.

Caspar David Friedrich: *Village landscape in the morning light* (1822)

Caspar David Friedrich: *Monk by the sea* (1808-10)

Karl Friedrich Schinkel: *Banks of the Spree near Stralau* (1817)

Caspar David Friedrich: *Moonrise over the sea* (1822)

Karl Friedrich Schinkel: *Gothic church on a rock facing the sea* (1815)

Caspar David Friedrich: *Abbey in the oakwood* (1809-10)

The Berlin Secession – In 1898, 65 artists led by **Walter Leistikow** (1865-1908) and **Max Liebermann** (1847-1935) "seceded", choosing to show their works outside the official circuits. They advocated freedom and realism as opposed to the patriotic mediocrities produced by court artists. The exhibitions organized by the Secession artists were stunningly successful. Art galleries flourished, for example the gallery of Paul Cassirer who defended Impressionism in his magazine *Kunst und Künstler (Art and artists)* and brought the paintings of **Lovis Corinth** (1858-1925) and Max Slevogt to the public's attention. An exhibition of Hans von Marée's work was held in 1909. **Adolph von Menzel** was painting industrial scenes during the same period. But recognition was slow to

Max Liebermann: *Self-portrait* (1929)

come for these artists, and even more so for the French Impressionists. Hans von Tschudi *(see MUSEUMSINSEL)*, the director of the National Gallery, exhibited their work in dimly lit rooms, laying himself open to the hostility of William II who described it as "gutter painting".

Expressionism – The seed of the Twenties "miracle" had been sown well before the war. Before Munich where the **"Der blaue Reiter"** movement was founded in 1911, Dresden had been at the artistic forefront. The "Die Brücke" movement *(See GRUNEWALD, Brückemuseum)* had been founded there in 1905. The "Die Brücke" painters led by **Ernst Ludwig Kirchner** (1880-1938) and **Karl Schmidt Rottluff** (1884-1976) admired Van Gogh's and Gauguin's paintings and the engravings of the Norwegian artist Edvard Munch. They wanted to achieve fusion between man and nature and studied the nude with a total lack of inhibition, using their women friends as models. The female figure was very important in this movement. The "fifteen-minute" nudes forced the artists to get to the crux during their quarter-of-an-hour pose: the colours are violent and the eroticism provocative. The posters for the group's first exhibition were censored by the police. Kirchner and Schmidt-Rottluff visited the Cézanne exhibition in Berlin in 1909. A "New Secession" was founded there in 1911 centred on **Max Pechstein, Karl Schmidt-Rottluff** and **Emil Nolde**. The Expressionist movement took on an urban dimension which lay at the origin of the golden age in the Twenties. The hectic life of the city is captured in Kirchner's street scenes. Influential magazines such as **Der Sturm** (1910-1932) founded in 1910 by **Herwarth Walden** and **Die Aktion** (1911-1933) and run by the anarchist journalist Franz Pfemfert, ensured that all these avant-garde trends were well publicized. But from the end of the First World War, the moralizing attitude of the Expressionist artists was combatted by Carl von Ossietzky's *Die Weltbühne* and the Dadaists, supporters of the "American" artist, closer to the sportsman, manager and advertising executive than to the European poet.

Protest in the Dada movement – Trends cultivating derision and the negation of all values emerged at the end of World War I. The **Dada** movement, first started in Zurich in 1915, took on a political dimension in Berlin. **Georg Groß** (1893-1959) used the myth of the United States as a point of reference from 1916 on, decorating his Berlin flat with American trophies and posters and anglicizing his name to **George Grosz** as an act of provocation. Sent home from the front in 1917, he became the leader of a group of artists of protest then being formed: the painter and photographer Raoul Hausmann (1886-1971), the poet **Walther Mehring** (Walt Merin), the publisher **Wieland Herzfelde** who published Grosz's drawings and Herzfelde's brother Helmut who became **John Heartfield**. The Berlin Dadaists based their aesthetic on ugliness "to show the world it is ugly, sick and deceitful", as Grosz put it.

In their own manner the Dadaists took part in the revolution, founding a "Dada republic" in Nikolassee. **Richard Huelsenbeck** organized an evening meeting in April 1918 during which he launched the anti-militarist Dada manifesto. For two years Berlin was swayed by the movement. Its only show, the "International Dada Fair" at the *Burckart* gallery, was a huge success: objects of a trivial nature were displayed in a skilful disarray. Grosz was regularly condemned by the censors for his anti-clerical and anti-militarist collections such as *God with Us* (Gott mit uns, 1920) and *Ecce Homo* (1923).

A left-wing culture – In his novel tetralogy *November 1918* written between 1939 and 1950 **Alfred Döblin** conjured up the beginnings of the Weimar Republic. The great watchword of the period was **"take art to the people"**. The liquidation of the Spartacists by the Social Democratic party sealed the link between the avant-garde and the far left. Artists derived a pessimistic vision from the failure of the revolution, but they chose Bolshevism through the desire for emancipation with regard to the power of money and the middle-classes, to escape from the traditional channels whereby artists gained recognition. A plebeian, democratic way of life was preferred to art salons and painting galleries, symbols of the aristocratic concept of art peculiar to the Europeans. Culture became more political and more urban. Painters, associated in groups such as the Novembergruppe, founded at the end of 1918, linked through its name and pro-gramme to the revolution and in existence until 1932, exhibited at the *Große Berliner Kunstausstellung*, Berlin's annual art show established in 1919, Herwarth Walden's *Der Sturm* gallery or the Van Diemen gallery. Otto Dix and George Grosz resigned from the group in 1921 and it later opened its doors to musicians and writers.

The avant-garde from the East – Weimar Germany could be easily penetrated by avant-garde artists from the East and Europe discovered them in Berlin. Painters, writers and theatre directors from central and eastern Europe, from Russia in particular, came here to work, collaborating with German artists and taking advantage of the climate of freedom which for a short interval followed the October Revolution. Voluntary exiles started arriving in 1923, keen to spread Soviet culture in western Europe. The artists in question were known in Germany through the Suprematist painter **El Lissitzky** (1890-1941) who organized the first exhibition of Soviet art at the *Van Diemen* gallery on Unter den Linden avenue in October 1922; an exhibition of German art with the participation of the other East European artists was held in Moscow in 1924. **Wassily Kandinsky** became a teacher at the Bauhaus, Serge Charchoune devoted himself to Cubism, and the sculptor Alexander Archipenko rubbed shoulders with the Rumanian painter Arthur Segal and the Hungarian Làszlo Moholy-Nagy: it was impossible to "take ten steps without meeting someone famous" (Elias Canetti). Together with El Lissitzky, **Ilya Ehrenburg** founded the periodical *Gegenstand* which was supported by the Soviet state between 1922 and 1923. It disseminated the ideas of **Constructivism** which had a common concept of the artist, the engineer and the worker. During these few years of fruitful exchange, the Russians and East Europeans met in cafés and studios, e.g. the Kleiststraße studio of the young Russian painter **Ivan Pouni** who had taken up residence in Berlin in October 1920, which was a rallying point for more or less impecunious Modernists.

Neue Sachlichkeit – Up until 1923 culture reflected every upheaval: war, defeat, rev-olution and inflation. The five years of relative economic and political stability (1924-29) brought with them a distanced vision of reality: a kind of resignation followed the rev-olutionary lyricism in the movement known as **Neue Sachlichkeit** (New Objectivity). Paintings, stage sets and cinema screens were full of the city. Art and the reality of the modern world interpenetrated one another; for George Grosz who wielded his brush like a "gun", the city was nightmarish and chaotic, while for Max Beckman it was "a great human orchestra". **Otto Dix** stigmatized it, displaying its wounds. Urban realism full of protest and sensitivity was illustrated by **Käthe Kollwitz** *(see KURFÜRSTENDAMM)* and **Hans Baluschek** both of whom painted working-class poverty with keen observation. The Paul Cassirer, Flechtheim and Nierendorf art galleries became firmly established.

Rising danger – By the end of the 1920s the Moscow-Berlin connection was begin-ning to disintegrate. The Leninist leanings of the German Communist Party first became perceptible in 1925. Grosz distanced himself from it, while still calling on people to vote for the Communists as part of the anti-fascist struggle. Many artists rejected the aesthetic constraints imposed by the far left with its repudiation of cos-mopolitanism, once again turning to the wealthy middle classes for patronage. In 1927-28 Soviet avant-garde artists ceased to be tolerated in the USSR. Culture began to loosen its grip with the rise of Stalinist academicism. The final Soviet show, a ret-rospective of the work of the Suprematist **Kasimir Malevich**, was held in Lehrte station in 1927. Soon the rise of Nazism compelled Soviet artists to flee Berlin.

The painter and the war

Otto Dix, born in 1891 to a working-class family, was one of the few artists to have had a prolonged experience of fighting in the war. He enlisted as a volun-teer and spent three years on the front. Like George Grosz whom he got to know while they were both studying in Dresden, Dix was interested in individuals. He painted people whose bodies and faces had been mutilated by war with parti-cularly poignant perceptiveness. His paintings, inspired by early German masters such as Matthias Grünewald, are comparable in their social criticism to films like Karl Grüne's *Die Straße* (1923) in which a lower middle-class man covets pros-titutes whose faces change into death's heads. In 1927 Dix was appointed a professor at the Dresden Academy of Art. From 1928 to 1932 he painted the *War* triptych, kept in Dresden – *Flanders* could be one of its panels. In 1933 he was dismissed by the Nazis and took up residence near Lake Constance.

Otto Dix –
Flanders (1934-36)

George Grosz –
Pillars of society

Lyonel Feininger –
Teltow II (1918)

The audacity of the inventor of photomontage

Throughout his life Helmut Herzfelde, who changed his name to **John Heartfield** (1901-1968), drew inspiration from working in concert with his younger brother Wieland. He felt a boundless hatred for the orthodox middle classes. He started studying as a painter in Wiesbaden and Munich, moving to Berlin in 1913, where he immediately made contact with the Expressionist circles centred on the *Der Sturm* and *Die Aktion* periodicals. Invalided out of the army, he formed a pacifist group along with George Grosz. He produced book jackets using photomontage for his brother's publishing company **Malik Verlag**. Combining art and politics, John Heartfield sought to achieve a shock effect using the simplest of means. His collaboration with Kurt Tucholsky added Tucholsky's destructive abbreviations to the violence of the photographs. He realised the danger represented by the Nazis at a very early stage and they were his favourite target. The Nazis reciprocated with unrelenting hatred towards him, and John Heartfield had to go into exile in Prague, then London.

Nazi art – **George Grosz** who went into exile in the United States on 12 January 1933 was the first to be stripped of his nationality. He taught in New York, and did not return to Berlin until 1959 where he died a few weeks later. The Prussian Academy of Arts was purged. Heinrich Mann, the president of the literary section, and Käthe Kollwitz were dismissed, while Martin Wagner, Alfred Döblin and Thomas Mann resigned. Albert Speer, Arno Brecker and Werner March replaced Oskar Kokoschka, Erich Mendelsohn, Bruno Taut, Otto Dix, Ernst Ludwig Kirchner, Mies van der Rohe and Karl Schmidt-Rottluff. Very few artists compromised themselves: the poet Gottfried Benn, the philosopher Heidegger and the Expressionist painter Emil Nolde were exceptions. In July 1937 a House of German Art was opened in Munich, the "capital of the Nazi movement", a city to which Hitler was "more attached than to any other place in the world"; the intention was to give back to Munich the cultural prestige it had lost to Berlin, which had produced only "degenerate art". Between 1933 and 1939 almost 5 000 avant-garde paintings and sculptures were destroyed. At the Nuremberg party conference in 1934 Hitler stipulated that art should be based "on blood and the soil".

The "New Fauvists" – German post-war painting right up until the 1960s was characterised by abstraction, after which it turned again to representation with the painters Georg Baselitz and **Markus Lüpertz** (b 1941), who used motifs with symbolic expressive force. The painters in the "New Fauvists" school, which included Lüpertz and also Harl Horst Hödicke (b 1938), Bernd Zimmer (b 1948) and Helmut Middendorf (b 1953), created their inspired works in aggressive Expressionist colours. This movement, which came into being at the end of the 1970s, had many followers in Berlin and Cologne in particular.

Signatures, pseudonyms and tags, together with the first graffiti, appeared in the early 1970s. They appeared in all their glory on the walls of the New York subway and soon became familiar in Europe, especially following the publication in England in 1984 of the album Subway Art. The **Berlin Wall**, which was initially covered with slogans, mottoes and posters, proved an ideal medium for aerosol paintings. Famous painters such as Keith Haring, who produced a 100m long painting on the wall in 1986, together with countless unknown artists, found this opportunity irresistible, so that spontaneous folk art with freedom slogans and pictures in fluorescent colours appeared over a 130km stretch of the wall facing the west, whereas the side facing east remained a dull concrete grey. The most interesting aerosol paintings have been retained in the East Side Gallery along Mühlenstraße (see FRIEDRICHSHAHN).

The current edition of the annual **Michelin Red Guide Deutschland**
offers a selection of pleasant and quiet hotels in convenient locations.
Their amenities are included (swimming pools, tennis courts,
private beaches and gardens...)
as well as their dates of annual closure.

The selection also includes establishments which offer excellent cuisine: carefully
prepared meals at reasonable prices, Michelin stars for good cooking.

Babelsberg – cinema city

A favourable conjuncture between art and industry meant that the German cinema was able to achieve a kind of golden age in the Twenties. Berlin was its capital, with the largest studios in Europe and first-rate technical equipment. Film-makers used the camera with a hitherto unknown freedom. Expressionist (i.e. silent) actors played out their roles against carefully studied lighting effects in sets with angular geometry. Their jerky gestures matched the sets. Their success continued under the Nazi regime even though many directors and stars left Germany for Hollywood. The post-war period, notable for the foundation of the Berlin Festival whose main award, the Golden Bear, is highly regarded in the film world, produced mainly comedies and some very fine films relating to a city which continued to be the symbol of a tumultuous history.

Another inventor of motion pictures

Max Skladanowsky (1863-1939), the son of a travelling showman, was something of a jack of all trades: a painter on glass, a photographer, a builder of stage machinery and a pyrotechnist. With his brother he travelled all over Europe projecting still pictures and "nebulous images" *(Nebelbilder)*, paintings on glass that were mechanically animated, made in such a way as to produce a blurred image. Max Skladanowsky wanted his images to be alive. Using a Kodak camera and a spool of negative, he invented a box with a handle, an ancestor of the cine-camera, and asked his brother to act the clown. He took these shots in 1892 but they could not be projected. Max then invented the *Bioskop*, a type of double projector. The first public demonstration was given at the Winter Gardens in Friedrichstraße. But the **Lumière brothers** who showed their films at the *Grand Café* on the boulevard des Capucines in Paris on 28 December 1895 were quicker to promote their invention. The *Bioskop* continued to be featured in tours in the Netherlands and Scandinavia, and was used to produce films until 1930.

The early influence of the theatre – It was the theatre directors who laid the foundations for the success of the German cinema, which until World War I had been dominated by the Danish cinema. The work of the playwright **Frank Wedekind** (1864-1918), in the tradition of Strindberg, influenced the makers of silent films, but it was through their theatre contact with **Max Reinhardt** – who himself directed films – that a whole generation of actors, actresses and directors was trained. The list is long: Marlene Dietrich and Emil Jannings, future film stars, Murnau, **Paul Wegener** (1874-1948) – after acting in the film *The Student of Prague* (1913) by the Danish director Stellan Rye he went on to direct *The Golem* the following year – and first and foremost Ernst Lubitsch (1892-1947) who had learnt his trade treading the music hall boards. His sketches based on his observation of human oddities were transposed to the screen *c*1913-14. On a September evening in 1919 the *Palast am Zoo* cinema opened with a screening of *Madame Dubarry*, the first costume film; it and Robert Wiene's *The Cabinet of Dr Caligari* had an international audience (German products were then being boycotted by the victorious Allies). After Lubitsch had made *Die Puppe* (1919) and gone on his first trip to the United States, he took up permanent residence there in the autumn of 1922 where he was successful in the field of comedy. Up until 1924 the UFA produced an impressive number of adaptations of stage works for the screen.

"The UFA style" – In the summer of 1917 General Ludendorff asked for a film-making office to be set up, with the aim of filming military operations and countering British propaganda. The **UFA (Universum Film Aktiengesellschaft)** was founded in November of the same year, set in motion by the press baron Alfred Hugenberg and financed by the government and private industry. The UFA was a "dream factory" that successfully mounted some ambitious productions.

From 1923 to 1926 it was run by the Austrian **Erich Pommer**. After learning his trade from Léon Gaumont, he founded DECLA in Berlin in 1916, which made *The Cabinet of Dr Caligari* in association with Bioskop. In collaboration with the large American companies Erich Pommer produced *Die Nibelungen* (1923-24) and *Metropolis* (1925-26) directed by Fritz Lang, *The Last Laugh* (*Der Letzte Mann*, 1924) and *Faust* (1926) directed by Murnau, *Asphalt* (1928) directed by Joe May and Josef von Sternberg's *The Blue Angel* (1930). But these masterpieces did not bring in enough money. Faced with an acute financial crisis, the UFA had to form a provisional alliance with American companies, mainly producing films for entertainment; among the many made there are some successful examples from the early days of talkies, especially musical comedies and operettas. That was the period of **Lilian Harvey**, nicknamed the "blonde dream" (*Ein blonder Traum*, 1932), who appeared in *Die drei von der Tankstelle* (1930) and *Der Kongress tanzt* (1931). Four sound-recording studios, the most modern in Europe, were built in 1929. The "UFA style", a Berlin derivative of Hollywood sets, was perpetuated at the same time as the Hitler parades.

Friedrich Wilhelm Murnau – *Nosferatu*

Fritz Lang – *M or Eine Stadt sucht einen Mörder*

Robert Wiene – *The Cabinet of Dr Caligari*

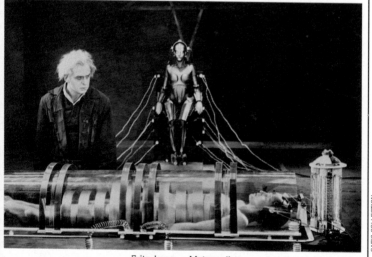

Fritz Lang – *Metropolis*

The anguish of the immediate post-war period – In Germany serial films, popular in Europe during and immediately after World War I, displayed "a liking for the super natural which foreshadowed the future" (Henri Langlois, *Images du cinéma allemand 1896-1956*). The Expressionist cinema had a metaphysical dimension, delving into Germany's past and the legends of Central Europe. *The Golem* (*Der Golem, wie er in die Welt kam*, 1914) by Paul Wegener, adapting a mediaeval Jewish legend about a creature made of clay, had blazed the trail. The war caused deep psychological trauma which can be felt in the dark, phantasmagoric inspiration of some films. The hidden role of the unconscious emerged in **The Cabinet of Dr Caligari (***Das Kabinett des Doktor. Caligari*, 1919) directed by **Robert Wiene** (1881-1938); **Friedrich Wilhelm Murnau** (1889- 1931) conjured up an old store of legends with his camera in *Nosferatu* (*Nosferatu, eine Symphonie des Grauens*, 1921) as did Fritz Lang in *Der müde Tod* (literally *"Tired Death"*), mixing exotic sets with the old Germanic tale. Murnau's *Faust* (Hindenburg and Stresemann attended its premiere) followed in 1926.

"Nosferatu"

The theme of vampirism which was an ingredient of Slav mediaeval folklore goes back to the figure of Vlad Tsepech Dracula, Prince of Wallachia and Moldavia, known as **Vlad the Impaler**, who had the unburied corpses of his Turkish enemies impaled. In his *Dracula* (1897) the Irish writer **Bram Stoker** transferred the action to London. The novel was adapted as a film in Germany in 1914 (with the same scriptwriter as *The Golem*). Dracula became Nosferatu. Murnau turned the actor **Max Scherck** who had played Count Orlock into the elongated silhouette of a bird of ill omen. Just as his dilapidated castle was in the depths of the country, the vampire's boat arrived silently against the realistic backdrop of a town with old houses, an everyday setting which accentuated the horror.

Metropolis – In all these films the city was perceived as a hostile, threatening environment, its underworld disturbed by secret struggles, haunted by crime. **Fritz Lang** and his wife Thea von Harbou (who elected to remain in Germany after 1933) perfected the plot of **Dr Mabuse** with its twists and turns in *Mabuse der Spieler*, followed in 1932 by the *Testament of Dr Mabuse* (and in the 1960s by a parodied sequel, *The Thousand Eyes of Dr Mabuse* or *The Diabolic Dr Mabuse*). In **Metropolis** (1926) a humanist message (and a happy ending that Fritz Lang never liked) attenuates the contrasts of a non-egalitarian, compartmented society. The city is shown as an American-style metropolis, the symbol of modernity but overwhelming, dominated by a gigantic tower. **M** or **Eine Stadt sucht einen Mörder** (1931), inspired by the misdeeds of the `Düsseldorf Vampire', was originally titled *Mörder unter uns* (Murderer in our midst). The inhabitants of the city set out to track down a child-killer at bay and the police are beaten to it by the underworld *(see FRIEDRICHSHAIN).* The street is a place of temptation and perdition: Karl Grüne's **Die Straße** (1923), Joe May's *Asphalt* (1928) – May like Lang was from Vienna – and Georg Wilhelm Pabst's *Die Freudlose Gasse* (1925) in which the still unknown Greta Garbo played alongside the Danish star **Asta Nielsen.** The underworld was the backdrop of *Berlin, Alexanderplatz* (1931), a "talkie" directed by Piel Jutzi and adapted from Alfred Döblin's novel.

From "Loulou" to "The Blue Angel" – A great many actresses at the start of their careers looked for walk-on parts in the cinema and theatre. Before she was well known **Marlene Dietrich** attracted attention through her outlandish way of dressing – she even wore a monocle – and her unusual musical instrument: a saw. **Georg Wilhelm Pabst** (1895-1967) came from Bohemia, and like Fritz Lang he enjoyed travelling. At the age of twenty he appeared on the Swiss stage, set off for the United States, then returned to France where he was interned during World War I. When he reached Berlin he was inspired by Freud's psychoanalysis (*Die Geheimnisse einer Seele*, 1926) and sociological observation (*Die Freudlose Gasse*, 1925). He was interested in women whose uncomprehended or stifled urges to rebel were indicative of society's troubles (*Begierde*, 1928). *Loulou*, a name derived from repeating the nickname of Lou Andréas Salomé, was played by **Louise Brooks**, a dancer from Hollywood born in 1900, who also starred in *Tagebuch einer Verlorenen* (1929). This film, which was the supreme achievement of critical realism, provoked a scandal.

Josef von Sternberg (1894-1969) was born in Vienna but emigrated to the United States at the age of seven; in 1925 he was Hollywood's most highly esteemed director. The film star **Emil Jannings** persuaded the head of the UFA to employ him to work in Germany. **The Blue Angel** (1930) was adapted from a novel by Heinrich Mann (Thomas Mann's brother), written in 1905, entitled *Professor Unrath*. A respectable teacher (his real name is *Rat*, meaning wise counsel, but his pupils give him the nickname *Unrath*, i.e. rubbish) has the misfortune to fall in love with the singer Lola-Lola at the Blue Angel cabaret. **Marlene Dietrich** (1901-1992), as an independent, self-assured woman singing "From head to toe... I'm made for love...", enjoyed a triumph with this film. She stole the show from Emil Jannings playing the deceived teacher made to look ridiculous. She accused him of attempted murder after the shooting of a scene in which he tries to strangle her! On the day of the premiere, 1 April 1930 at the Gloria Palast, she embarked for America, and did not return to Berlin until 1945. Marlene Dietrich, seductive but cold, was a very hard worker. Billy Wilder who used her in *A Foreign Affair* (1948) said of her: "At work she was a real trouper."

The cinema in the Nazi period – Fritz Lang fled to Paris on the very day that Goebbels offered to put him in charge of the German cinema (in spite of the fact that Lang was Jewish). He was one of the major

figures who preferred exile to compromise with the new regime, like **Marlene Dietrich** who refused to return from the United States although Goebbels invited her to do so. They were followed by a large number of extremely well-qualified technicians who continued their careers in Hollywood in the 1940s.

Leni Riefenstahl (b. 1902), who did not hesitate to appear in her own films about the high mountains, made a film about the Olympic Games in 1936: *Olympia*, made with the collaboration of Ruttmann, marked the zenith of her career. During the Third Reich the film-making industry was a centralized instrument for propaganda controlled by the state. The UFA was nationalized in 1937. The boroughs of Nowawes and Neu-Babelsberg were merged the following year, creating **Babelsberg** where the entire new German Academy of Cinema took up residence. A town-planning scheme including shopping streets, hotels, a station, offices and residential accommodation was developed to turn the town into a "cinema city". The first prize was awarded to **Emil Fahrenkamp**. Most of the films produced during the war were intended as entertainment; colour was introduced in 1941. In 1943 one masterpiece was filmed: Josef von Baky's *The Fantastic Adventures of Baron Münchhausen*.

The enduring myth – Berlin *has retained its mythic status* better in the cinema than in any other field. But relief from the Nazi regime did not give rise to a renewal that could be compared with Italian Neorealism, though Rossellini's *Germania, Year Zero* was set in the ruins of Berlin. The Allies preferred entertainment films shot by the pre-1945 directors. The **Berlinale** – Berlin's international film festival – was founded in 1950. DEFA (Deutsche Film AG), founded on 17 May 1946 in the Soviet-occupied zone, used the Babelsberg studios, but the Central Committee of the SED imposed strict censorship.

Marlene Dietrich in *The Blue Angel*

The story of the West German cinema was being written in new studios in Munich where the "young German cinema" was being born. The **German Cinematheque (Deutsch Kinemathek)** and the Association of the Friends of the German Cinematheque which organized screenings at the *Arsenal* cinema were founded in Berlin in the sixties. These two institutions will be housed in the Sony building on the Potsdamer Platz. Between 1979 and 1980 **Rainer Werner Fassbinder** adapted *Berlin Alexanderplatz* as a 14-part serial, and returned to the subject of *The Blue Angel*, transposing the story to the fifties, in *Lola* (1981). In the eighties several major directors took up residence in Berlin and worked there: **Wim Wenders, Volker Schlöndorff**, Helma Sander-Brahms and Jutta Brückner. Brandenburg and Berlin have joined forces and created a Film Bureau in Babelsberg where a new cinema and media city is currently being built.

Some films set in Berlin

Germania, Year Zero, *(Germania, anno Zero)*, Roberto Rossellini (Italy), 1948 – A young boy who is influenced by a Nazi schoolmaster ends up poisoning his invalid father.

A Foreign Affair, Billy Wilder (USA), 1948. – A commission arrives in the American sector to inquire into the morals of the occupying troops. Marlene Dietrich is superb as a music-hall star who turns out to be a dangerous Nazi.

One, Two, Three, Billy Wilder (USA), 1961 – The daughter of the chairman and managing director of Coca-Cola marries a young Communist; comedy laced with social satire.

Torn Curtain, Alfred Hitchcock (USA), 1966 – Paul Newman's presence does not make this vision of the German Democratic Republic any less despairing. Breathtaking suspense.

Cabaret, Bob Fosse (USA), 1972. An incomplete picture of the real world of cabaret.

Julia, Fred Zinnemann (USA), 1978 – Very moving account of a friendship between two women, a novelist and an anti-fascist militant from a wealthy background. Their final meeting takes place in Berlin.

Berlin Alexanderplatz, Rainer Werner Fassbinder (FRG), 1979 – Adaptation of Alfred Döblin's novel with Fassbinder's favourite actors: Günther Lamprecht, Barbara Sukowa, Hannah Schygulla.

Wings of Desire (Der Himmel über Berlin), Wim Wenders (FRG), 1986 – Damiel, an angel, falls in love with a trapeze artist and decides to become a man. His companion Cassiel comes back to a reunified Berlin in **In weiter Ferne** (1992).

Far from Berlin, Keith MacNally (France/FRG), 1993 – A worker from the former eastern sector of Berlin agrees to carry out a contract killing, paid for by a capitalist from the West.

Lola Runs, Tom Twyker (FRG), 1998 – In order to save her friend from a desperate situation, a young woman has to find DM 100 000 in 20 min. A fast-moving film, cut in a music video style, about Berlin in the 1990s.

Literature

THE RENAISSANCE AND THE BAROQUE PERIOD

The first poems, crude and popular in style, date from the 16C. The *Froschmäuselerkrieg* (1566) by **Gabriel Rollenhagen**, inspired by a parody of *The Iliad* and describing a war between frogs and mice, and the apprentice poems of Bartholomäus Ringwaldt, already reveal strong didactic demands. The first play was enacted in Berlin in 1540, since Margrave **Joachim II** (1535-1571) was fond of the theatre. Even though the Viadrina, Brandenburg's university, was founded in **Frankfurt an der Oder** in 1506, there were great scholars teaching in Berlin: **Johannes Trithemius** (1462-1516) from the Moselle area and the humanist **Leonhard Thurneisser** (1531-1596) from Basle, who set up his laboratory in a Franciscan monastery *(see NIKOLAIVIERTEL)*. Paul Gerhardt (1607-1676) and Michael Schirmer made a reputation for themselves in the Baroque period as writers of hymns. Frederick I (1688-1713) surrounded himself with court poets who recited their lines glorifying the sovereign at public ceremonies.

THE "AUFKLÄRUNG" AND THE EARLY ROMANTICS

The Enlightenment – The arrival of the Huguenots in Berlin had a lasting impact on the cultural climate. The playwright Lessing, whose play *Minna von Barnhelm* included a Huguenot refugee among its characters, speaks of a "French Berlin". The capital of Prussia was the German centre of the *Aufklärung* (Enlightenment) and liberal rationalism. Voltaire visited the court of Frederick II in 1750. The sometimes stormy relationship between the prince and the philosopher represents one of the aspects of enlightened despotism. **Gotthold Ephraim Lessing** (1729-1781), his cousin Mylius and the Jewish philosopher **Moses Mendelssohn** (1728-1786) belonged to the generation of playwrights and essayists who began publishing their works in 1750 thanks to publishers with liberal ideas like Christian Friedrich Voß and **Christoph Friedrich Nicolai** (1733-1811). The latter was the moving spirit behind a scientific and literary circle and his bookshop was the cultural centre of the kingdom *(see FISCHERINSEL)*.

Moses Mendelssohn and Jewish emancipation – In his youth Mendelssohn compensated for physical handicaps by his precocious intellectual gifts. He came to Berlin at the age of 14 with his father who was a rabbi, learnt German and gained a good grounding in philosophy. He became a tutor in 1750 and met the poet Lessing who became his best friend and introduced him to Nicolai and his circle. The publication of his essays established him as the major German philosopher of the Enlightenment. In 1763 he was accorded the status of a "protected Jew" (i.e. he was given a hereditary right of residence) through the good offices of the Marquis of Argens: "A philosopher who is a bad Catholic petitions a philosopher who is a bad Protestant to grant a Privilege to a philosopher who is a bad Jew. There is too much philosophy in all this for the request not to be justified."

Moses Mendelssohn,
portrait by Johann Christoph Frisch

PRUSSISCHER KULTURBESITZ

German literature becomes established – Salons and periodicals played a part in the emergence of German national feeling. The elite of the Berlin intelligentsia met at the **Monday Club** founded in 1749 at an elegant cafe. Nicolai became the advocate of the German language, meeting the aspirations of the enlightened middle classes. The first German theatre was founded in Berlin in 1764 in spite of the lack of interest shown by the Francophile king and court. It was only after the king's death (1786) that the **German National Theatre** was created on the Gendarmenmarkt in 1786. The last plays of Lessing, Goethe and Schiller were performed there, staged by its enterprising director, **Iffland** (1759-1814). Goethe who did not particularly like Berlin, stayed there only for brief periods, but shortly before his death in 1805 Schiller considered taking up residence: his play *Wilhelm Tell* had enjoyed huge success there. Frederick William II, a protector of the German-language theatre, commissioned Langhans to build the theatre in Schloß Charlottenburg (1788-1791). During the Napoleonic occupation starting in 1806 literary life turned more to the German tradition and became less open-minded. Aristocratic salons took over from the Jewish salons and were distinguished for their elitism and their patriotism: they were frequented by military men, civil servants and aristocrats such as **Heinrich von Kleist**.

Henriette Herz and Rahel Levin, the Egerias of Romanticism

The Jewish literary salons, promoting open-mindedness, tolerance and social mixing, played a major role in Berlin cultural life as the 18C gave way to the 19C.
The salon of **Henriette Herz** (1764-1847), a beautiful, cultured woman who spoke eight languages, is regarded as the birthplace of Berlin Romanticism. Ludwig Tieck, Jean Paul, Wilhelm von Humboldt, Friedrich Schleiermacher, Adalbert von Chamisso and Wilhelm Wackenroder – a passionate enthusiast for the Middle Ages which had been despised by the *Aufklärung* – met there. It was also frequented by Moses Mendelssohn's daughter Dorothea. At Henriette Herz's salon, affairs of the heart mingled with intellectual matters, and it was there that Bettina Brentano, the sister of the poet Clemens Brentano, met her future husband, Achim von Arnim.
Rahel Levin (1771-1834) had grown up in contact with the theatrical world whose members were her father's guests, and she in turn acted as hostess from 1790, receiving them in the attic of the family home where she tended to take refuge. This "attic" became a cosmopolitan salon which set the tone in the capital from 1801 to 1806. Madame de Staël – like Benjamin Constant, Thomas Young and the Prince de Ligne who were also among the foreign guests – speaks of a "happy mixture" bringing together "talented people of every class". Rahel Levin's circle included Jews and Christians, nobles and members of the middle classes, princes and philosophers: Prince Louis-Ferdinand of Prussia, the Schlegel brothers, Heinrich von Kleist. Her salons were discontinued in 1806 after Prussia's defeat in Jena. Ten years or so later Rahel, now Frau Varnhagen von Ense, opened another salon; it never achieved the same brilliancy, but it did count the young **Heinrich Heine** among its guests.

Johann Gottlieb Fichte (1762-1814), who advocated recasting the school system s as to forge a "strong, reliable German spirit", gave his *Speeches to the German Natic* in the winter of 1807-1808. The philosophers Schelling, Hegel Schleiermacher ar Fichte taught at the **University**, founded in 1810 with Fichte as its first Rector. Wit the lectures given by the Schlegel brothers, Romanticism became the most dominar element in literary life in Berlin.

THE BIEDERMEIER PERIOD AND REALISM

With the authorities waging an unrelenting war against all liberal ideas, many poet found the climate of the Restoration stifling after the Wars of Liberation, and with drew into private life. The second Romantic period devoted a cult to the ill-fated arti. personified by **Heinrich von Kleist** who committed suicide in 1811 on the shores of th Großer Wannsee. **E.T.A. Hoffmann** (1776-1822), the author of strange tales, withdre totally into a phantasmagorical world. However there were new developments afoc the young "Hegelian" philosopher **Karl Marx** met Friedrich Engels in Berlin and Heinric Heine came here in 1822. The irony of his *Letters from Berlin* (1824) gives a goc idea of the atmosphere of the city at this period when the taverns, tearooms – con centrated in Friedrichstadt – and the "reading cafes" which provided a wide selectic of German and foreign reading matter replaced the salons as centres of politic debate. With the golden age of the salons over, the journalist and writer **Moritz Gottlie Saphir** created a new setting for intellectual exchange with the poets' association *Tunn unter der Spree*; one of its first members was the young pharmacist's assistar Theodor Fontane, a descendant of Huguenot refugees, who was attracting attentic with his first poems.
While Berlin, along with Leipzig was the publishing capital of the German Empir Munich was its literary capital until 1914. Berlin realism was part of a European li erary trend, but it emerged after the disappointed hopes of the 1848 Revolution an the authorities' resumption of power. *Die Chronik der Sperlingsgasse* by Wilhel Raabe and the novels of **Theodor Fontane** (1819-1898), the first outstanding writer t devote a large body of work to Berlin and the Berlin area, are the best examples • this realism. The urban setting is still idyllic in his books.

THE WILHELMINE PERIOD

Berlin asserted its ambitions as a cultural capital, attracting an increasing number • young writers and artists. **Max Kretzner** (1854-1941), Berlin's answer to Zola, chron cles the social upheavals of the Wilhelmine era. Plays by Scandinavian writers like Ibse and Strindberg were enthusiastically received *(see CHARITÉ)*, influencing the formatic of German naturalism (*Irrungen Wirrungen*, Theodor Fontane; *Vor Sonnenaufgan* Gerhart Hauptmann). The Hart brothers, journalists wishing to promote "nationa modern writing", founded a **poets' colony (the Friedrichshagener Kreis)** in Friedrichshage near the Müggelsee; its main representative is **Gerhart Hauptmann** (1862-1946). His pla about the poverty of the Silesian weavers *(Die Weber)* provoked a scandal and le Emperor William II to cancel his private box at the theatre. Hauptmann was awarde the Nobel Prize for Literature in 1912, to the accompaniment of lively protests. Carl Sternheim *(Die Hose)* and Georg Kaiser who represents a link between naturalism and Expressionism were also among the leading playwrights of this period.

At the end of the 19C there were more than 400 theatres in Berlin. The Deutsches Theater was founded in 1883, and social democracy created the Volksbühne. A new theatre district sprang up along the Kurfürstendamm, and premieres were reviewed by fine critics such as **Alfred Kerr** (1867-1948) who worked for the *Berliner Tageblatt*.

THE TWENTIES

The Twenties were the most stimulating period in Berlin's literary history. The places where the Berlin intelligentsia foregathered were the *Adlon* hotel, the *Montmartre*, a "luxurious little restaurant", the *Schlichter* brasserie with its tables reserved for writers, the **"Romanisches Café"** and **"Café des Westens"** literary cafés, the *Schwanecke* for theatre and film circles, and the *Jaenicke* for journalists.

The **Malik Verlag** publishing company run by **Wieland Herzfelde** (1896-1988), brother of the photomontage artist John Heartfield, who surrounded himself with collaborators like the Communist theatre director Erwin Piscator and the poets Walther Mehring and Carl Einstein, was the main publisher of political books. Other important publishing companies (Ullstein, Samuel Fischer, Bruno Cassirer) were open to new literary trends.

Talented journalists – The existence of periodicals with high aspirations such as *Die Weltbühne*, a left-wing weekly edited by the pacifist **Carl von Ossietzky**, *Die literarische Welt* or *Das Tagebuch* gave rise to a new cross-fertilization between journalism and literature which unfortunately had little impact outside Berlin. The most famous of these "cross-over" writers were **Kurt Tucholsky**, Siegfried Kracauer, Franz Hessel, Theodor Wolf and Leopold Schwarzschild, as well as Joseph Roth and Alfred Döblin. The last two were novelists: Alfred Döblin wrote *Berlin Alexanderplatz* in 1929. A quarter of the national press was located in Berlin: 147 daily publications and 2 633 periodicals in 1927. The major publishing companies fought one another to gain a monopoly in that respect.

Max Reinhardt (1873-1943) – The supreme success of the Berlin theatre was encouraged by a keen public, exceptional actors, brilliant directors and discerning critics like **Alfred Kerr** and his rival, the polemicist **Herbert Jhering**, a defender of progressive plays. **Max Reinhardt**, whose real name was Maximilian Goldmann, was a native of the Viennese area and he had several theatres and halls including the *Deutsches Theater* on Schumannstraße; by 1905 he was the most important figure in the German theatre. He was unrivalled in his ability to direct the widest variety of plays, ranging from classical to avant-garde works and the popular repertory. His massive productions, distinguished for their striking use of light and shadow, sumptuous stage sets and costumes, were to have a great influence on silent movies. In March 1918 he founded an experimental theatre: *Young Germany*, followed in 1921 by *Young Stage*. Max Reinhardt was the moving spirit behind the **Großes Schauspielhaus**, a splendid theatre seating 3 000 people built by Hans Poelzig. The opening production, Aeschylus's *Oresteia*, was the first triumph to exploit the stage "in accordance with architectural principles" and "an art of acting based on rhythm". Reinhardt also knew how to manage crowd scenes and used the *Großes Schauspielhaus* for the performance of works by classical authors alongside plays about revolution (Büchner's *Dantons Tod* or *Danton* by Romain Rolland). He returned to Vienna in 1923.

The modern theatre – The *Schauspielhaus* on the Gendarmenmarkt, a theatre with a conventional repertory, became the foremost theatre in Germany under the young Socialist director **Leopold Jessner** (1878-1945) who ran it for ten years (1920-1930). His first production of Schiller's *Wilhelm Tell*, first performed on 1 December 1919, founded *Aktualitätstheater*, moving away from Reinhardt's ideas and bringing "modernity" into "a repertory ranging from Sophocles to authors not yet discovered,

Portrait of a pamphleteer

Kurt Tucholsky (1890-1935), a member of one of Berlin's middle-class Jewish families, was a poet, a song-writer, an essayist, a literary critic and a pamphleteer writing under a variety of pseudonyms – the literary counterpart of George Grosz. He worked for *Die Vossische Zeitung* (known as old "Tante Voss") and *Die Weltbühne*, serving as its Paris correspondent between 1924 and 1926. *Die Weltbühne* tackled the most sensitive problems head-on in a direct, polemical manner. Tucholsky was a clear-sighted observer of the Weimar Republic, publishing articles opposing the resurgent militarism and jingoism which followed the November revolution and commenting ironically on the supposed Germanic "values", which resulted in his incessant attack by the right-wing press. His books were burnt by the Nazis and he was one of the first militants to be stripped of his German nationality. He committed suicide in Sweden.

seen through the eyes of our times, felt with the nerves of our times, depicted with the means of our times" (Leopold Jessner, *Zeittheater*, *Berliner Tageblatt* of 6 April 1927); *Aktualitätstheater* lay behind a political concept of theatre which Erwin Piscator and Bertolt Brecht were to take up in the second half of the Twenties. Fritz Kortner was Jessner's favourite actor, playing all the main Shakespearean roles. **Carl Zuckmayer** (1896-1977) who came from the Rhineland serves as an illustration of high-quality popular theatre; his *Der Hauptmann von Köpenick* aroused the wrath of Goebbels.

"The street belongs to us" – The scenographer **Karl Hainz Martin** staged an Expressionist play at his "proletarian theatre". The idea was taken up by **Erwin Piscator** (1893-1966) who turned it into a propaganda instrument for the Communist party, in 1925 inventing **agitprop** theatre. He put on plays by Maxim Gorky, Upton Sinclair and Franz Jung with movable sets by John Heartfield. He ran the **Volksbühne** (*see ORANIENBURGER STRASSE*) between 1924 and 1927, then the *Metropol* on Nollendorfplatz. He set an example which was followed by a great many small Communist troupes.

Before the war **Bertolt Brecht** (1898-1950), born in Augsburg, learnt from the shows of the comedian Karl Valentin in Munich cabarets. In 1920 he went up to Berlin where he led such a poverty-stricken existence that he was admitted to the Charité hospital suffering from malnutrition. His play *Drums in the Night* (1922) is still strongly influenced by Expressionism, and he was criticized as much as Piscator. Elias Canetti made fun of this intellectual, playing at being a member of the proletariat, with his cap, his blue shirt and leather jerkin, yet having no scruples about signing an advertising contract with the *Steyr* car company. The premiere of *The Threepenny Opera*, inspired by John Gay's *The Beggar's Opera* and adapted for the screen by Pabst in 1931, took place in August 1928. Canetti saw it as a "sophisticated, coldly calculated production". Berlin's Marxist culture was a heightened expression of the individualism that can be found in *The Threepenny Opera*: "First you have to eat, morals come afterwards".

The Russian contribution – Literary life in Berlin attracted a fair number of foreign writers such as Julien Green, Christopher Isherwood (who wrote the novel on which *Cabaret* was based in Berlin), Stephen Spender and W.H. Auden. But the Russians formed by far the largest foreign contingent. During the 1920s there were 86 Russian publishing firms, three Russian daily papers and 20 Russian bookshops in Berlin. The Russian intelligentsia fled the Revolution in two waves (1918-20 and 1922): the ruined Russian aristocrats described by **Vladimir Nabokov** were joined by the intellectual avant-garde of Soviet Russia. Maxim Gorky (published by Wieland Herzfelde), Vladimir Mayakovsky, Sergei Essenin, Andrei Bely, Marc Aldanov, Alexey Tolstoy, Fedor Stepun and numerous journalists encountered one another in Berlin. The ideas of Vsevolod Meyerhold who advocated integrating the audience into the show had a powerful influence on Berlin stage directors. Writing in 1923 a French critic said: "The Berlin theatre is completely dominated by the Russians."

"America!!! The future!!!" (Grosz, *The Gold Prospector's Song*) – The group surrounding the Herzfelde brothers, George Grosz, Walter Mehring and Bertolt Brecht was one of the main debating centres for ideas about America. Faith in a world based on economics and technology was conveyed by an infatuation with all the symbols of the consumer society, particularly neon-lit advertisements, which affected even Marxist intellectuals.

Vladimir Nabokov (1899-1977)

Nabokov belonged to an old family of liberal aristocrats originating from St Petersburg. His father, who had a long-term involvement in Russian political life, took part in the provisional government of February 1917; he was assassinated, probably by mistake, at a meeting in Berlin in 1922. His extremely cultivated mother had come from the German nobility. The Nabokov family, forced to flee the Revolution, went to Crimea, then London and finally to Berlin once young Vladimir's studies had been completed (1923). He gave lessons in Russian, French, English, tennis and boxing to survive. He published articles in the anti-Soviet magazine *Rul* using the pseudonym **Sirin** because his father wrote for the same newspapers as he did.

His many short stories also appeared in newspapers. He left Berlin in 1937, long after the other émigrés, after writing *The Gift*, his last novel in Russian which sums up his whole literary experience in Berlin. As a representative of the old aristocracy Nabokov deals with the deceptiveness of appearances, describing with deadly irony the small world of St Petersburg which slaked its thirst on "tea, intrigues and readings of interminable poems", anxious to preserve its values and way of life. He felt a fascination for Berlin, a city of transit populated by people forever on the move, often seen through the windows of a tram or train.

As a country of gangsters and adventurers America remained a challenge. New values emerged: objectivity, rationality, precision, productivity. Speed became the keynote to the rhythm of city life. There was increased interest in sport, boxing and six-day cycle races. **Neue Sachlichkeit** opposed Expressionist sensibility with an approach that was cold, sometimes sarcastic and distant; it became the predominant trend in literature. **Erich Kästner** (1904-1974) with his ironic, distinctive poems about everyday life, can be regarded as its main representative.

THE THIRD REICH

Under an increasingly authoritarian government cultural life lost its vigour: the Nazis are featured in Alfred Döblin's *Berlin Alexanderplatz* (1929). In 1930 they managed to disrupt and finally to ban the showing of the film adaptation of Erich Maria Remarque's novel *All Quiet on the Western Front*. The first arrests (of Friedrich Wolf and Carl von Ossietzky, editors of the magazine *Die Weltbühne*) were followed by the first exiles (Erwin Piscator). The Nazis were to finish off the job.

On 10 May 1933 the infamous *auto-da-fé* took place on the square in front of the Opera *(see UNTER DEN LINDEN)*. Newspapers and institutions were brought to heel. The most celebrated writers of the Weimar Republic went into exile. Authors like Peter Huchel, Günther Eich, Oskar Loerke and Wolfgang Weyrauch who remained in Germany but did not collaborate with the Nazis withdrew into "internal exile", writing apolitical poems about nature. The cultivated Jewish middle classes who had contributed to the city's intellectual brilliance were wiped out.

THE POST-WAR PERIOD

The anti-militarist play *Draußen vor der Tür* by Wolfgang Borchert was performed in West Berlin in 1947. In East Berlin Brecht founded the **Berliner Ensemble** in 1949 (while Erwin Piscator returned to West Berlin in 1951). While East Berlin was the cultural centre of the GDR, only poets whose ideas matched those of the state (Brecht, Bredel) counted. Those who tried to jolt the conformity that governed the theatre were imprisoned, expelled and stripped of their nationality. Individual protests failed. Many authors crossed to the West, like **Uwe Johnson** (1934-1984) in 1959; his novel sequence *Jahrestage* deals with relations between the two Germanies. During the sixties the voices of a new generation were heard in the GDR. **Christa Wolf** succeeded the Communist novelist **Anna Seghers** (1900-1983) who had returned to East Berlin from exile in America, and poets like Volker Braun and Sarah Kirsch gave a new tone to lyric works.

In West Berlin, young politically committed writers came to the forefront in the wake of 1968: Peter Schneider, Hans-Christoph Buch, Friedrich Christian Delius. Günter Grass *(The Tin Drum)* had already moved to Berlin in the Fifties. In 1976 the poet and songwriter **Wolf Biermann** (1907-1986), a friend of Robert Havemann (1910-1982), a philosopher, opponent of the Nazis and dissident, was stripped of his East German nationality and expelled, as was his daughter-in-law, the rock singer Nina Hagen. Quite a few of his colleagues followed suit, leaving East Berlin voluntarily or after being imprisoned, e.g. Thomas Brasch, Jürgen Fuchs, Günther Kunert, Chaim Noll and Sarah Kirsch. They enriched the literary life of West Berlin which was in fierce competition with the main cities in West Germany, even though exiles from other countries like Antonio Skarmeta, Gaston Salvatore, Areas Ören, Herta Müller and Richard Wagner. **Peter Stein** ushered in a glorious period at the *Schaubühne*.

THE FALL OF THE WALL AND GERMAN UNIFICATION

The events which followed 1989 altered the literary climate in East Berlin in particular. Many poets belonging to the *Prenzlauer Berg-Szene*, a clandestine literary group that was half tolerated, were convicted of collaborating with the STASI, while the authors who had kept their distance from the GDR secret police are now among the most highly regarded writers: people like Elke Erb, Uwe Kolbe, the essayist and prose-writer Lutz Rathenow, and Durs Grünbein who was awarded the Georg Büchner prize – the FRG's main literary award – for his poems in 1955. Younger writers include Thomas Brussig *(Heroes like Us)*, Marko Martin *(By Taxi to Carthage)* and Ongo Schulze *(33 Instants of Happiness)*.

AKG PARIS

Christa Wolf

Cabaret, a Berlin tradition

Cabarets appeared on the scene at the beginning of the 20C, inspired by Montmartre. Das Überbrett (On Stage), run by Baron von Wolzogen, offered a two-hour variety show. Böse Mädchen (Naughty Girls) was created in 1903 as a response to Garnements (Rascals). But satire was still faint-hearted in Wilhelmine Berlin, and literary cabaret was a minority affair. Before World War I, the period when the future stars of the Weimar Republic were in gestation, the first writers of cabaret material, Otto Julius Bierbaum, Detlev von Liliencron, Frank Wedekind, the poet Christian Morgenstern (the author of *Palmström*), Richard Dehmel and Jakob van Hoddis, were delighting audiences in smoke-filled rooms. The composer Rudolf Nelson invented a catchy musical style. The cabaret **Schall und Rauch** (Noise and Smoke) on Am Schiffbauerdamm, founded by Max Reinhardt and several of his friends, combined satirical sketches and mime; Hans Hyan, Berlin's answer to Aristide Bruant, ran La Terrine de Punch en Argent (The Silver Punchbowl) where the middle classes came to mingle with the hoi polloi.

In the inter-war period Berlin had over 100 cabarets. The famous Schall und Rauch, a cabaret for intellectuals, was reopened by Reinhardt at the end of 1919, putting on songs and sketches – the best-known writer of these was **Walter Mehring** (1896-1981). Also in 1919 the Tribüne cabaret gained an international reputation as an avant-garde theatre. The poet **Erich Mühsam** (1878-1934) appeared at the Siebter Himmel (Seventh Heaven). The other main cabarets were Rosa Valetti's Kabarett Größenwahn (Delusions of Grandeur), Trude Hesterberg's Wilde Bühne (Wild Stage) where Bertolt Brecht appeared while he was still unknown, and the Nelson-Theater on the Kurfürstendamm where Marlene Dietrich and Hans Albers enjoyed their first successes. It was women, feminists loudly proclaiming their emancipatory ideas, who showed the most talent. The greatest star of that period was undoubtedly **Claire Waldoff** (*see SCHÖNEBERG*) who sang her saucy Berlin songs at the Die Linden cabaret. She brought in her friend **Gussy Holl** from Frankfurt, who parodied men and became the number one cabaret star during the Weimar Republic; the satirist Kurt Tucholsky wrote very beautiful songs for her. In a more sarcastic vein **Blandine Ebinger** was the darling of the Expressionist intelligentsia, singing songs with caustic lyrics.

This mixture of humour, irony and harsh social criticism upset the Nazis who drove most of the chansonniers, described as "Jewish street scribblers", off the stage and out of the country. Werner Finck's Katakombe was the only exception, continuing its criticisms until 1935.

In post-war West Berlin the cabaret stars were Günter Pfitzmann and Ralf Wolter who appeared at the Die Dachluke (Dormer Window). The fame of the radio cabaret show Die Insulaner (Islanders) which poked fun at the East German Communist officials and helped West Berlin regain its self-confidence extended beyond the boundaries of the city. The *porcupines* and the irreverent anarchist **Wolfgang Neuss**, the "man with the kettle-drum", are examples of 1960s cabaret. In East Berlin *Die Distel* (The Thistle) was cautiously critical of the state while other artists such as Wolf Biermann and – in the eighties – Stephan Krawczyk, were unable to appear anywhere, except in churches.

Attempts are being made to keep alive the old traditions of variety *(Wintergarten)*, revue *(Friedrichstadtpalast)* and cabaret *(Wühlmäuse)*.

The temple of music

Berlin is reputed more for the interpretation of music than for its creation. Most of the great composers came from central or southern Germany, or from Austria. But in the words of Beethoven "the Berlin audience [is] very cultivated".

Royal patronage – Frederick II was a talented flautist, librettist and composer whose works are still performed; he maintained a first-rate chamber music orchestra. The theatre at the Neues Palais in Potsdam which has never ceased to function was inaugurated on 18 July 1768 with a performance of an oratorio by Johann Adolf Hasse (1699-1783). Opera and French plays were performed there. The harpsichord player **Carl Philipp Emanuel Bach** (1714-1788), the son of Johann Sebastian, the official composer Johann Joachim Quantz (1697-1773) and the Kapellmeister Carl Heinrich Graun (1701-1759) – who officiated at the official opening of the Opera in 1742 *(see UNTER DEN LINDEN)* – were the founders of Berlin's musical tradition. The Opera orchestra, the **Staatskapelle**, is the oldest in Berlin and still enjoys a high reputation. **Frederick William II** was also a music-lover who played the cello in the orangery of the New Garden at Potsdam or in the banqueting room of his Schloß on Pfaueninsel. He had personal contacts with Haydn, Mozart (who in 1789 gave concerts of German music in the king's presence, but vainly awaited the offer of a post), Boccherini and at a later stage Beethoven. The **Singing Academy** *(Singakademie)* was founded in 1791.

The Romantic period – Between 1815 and 1835, in a repressive climate, the opera became an extremely political issue, compensating for the austerity of the *Biedermeier* period. The opera house on Unter den Linden could not compete with the new concert hall on the Gendarmenmarkt, the **Schauspielhaus**, rebuilt by Schinkel and inaugurated with a production of the Romantic opera *Der Freischütz* directed by **Carl Maria von Weber** (1786-1826). It was an immediate success but Frederick William III regarded Weber as "popular" hence "revolutionary". German music was put on the agenda in 1842 with Jakob Meyerbeer's *Les Huguenots*; Meyerbeer was appointed General Musical Director. The intensity of musical life in Berlin astonished Berlioz: "There are few capitals that can boast of harmonic treasures comparable to Berlin's. Music is in the air, you breathe it, you soak it up (...) Rich and poor, the clergy and the army, artists and art-lovers, the people and the king hold it in equal veneration." Paganini or Liszt could call on excellent choral and instrumental formations. Wagner's *Rienzi* was greeted with cat-calls in 1843, and his music provoked another scandal in 1870 as there was a reactionary wind blowing over the cultural scene after the 1848 revolution. A military man was in charge of the royal theatres until 1886, and musical life became "boring". A few oases of creativity like the Kroll grand opera welcomed modern composers.

The turn of the century – In reaction to this inertia, 50 or so musicians seceded in 1882 and formed the **Philharmonic Orchestra ("Berliner Philharmonisches Orchester" or simply the "Berliner Philharmoniker")**. Its first conductor was **Hans von Bülow** who issued invitations to the greatest composers: Brahms, Tchaikovsky, Grieg, Richard Strauss and Mahler. The Philharmonic which played a part in overturning the cultural dictatorship of the court rang out like an echo to the Berlin Secession and Expressionism. The Berlin conservatories were renowned. An opera house was built in Charlottenburg (1912, on the site of the present *Deutsche Oper*) which achieved fame under the baton of **Bruno Walter**. **Richard Strauss** (1864-1949) conducted the orchestra of the National Opera on Unter den Linden from 1898, later becoming its General Musical Director. The people preferred the sparkling operettas of **Paul Lincke**.

The "capital of the civilized world" – Those are the words the young virtuoso violinist **Yehudi Menuhin** used to describe Berlin when he played there at the age of thirteen. During the 1920s Berlin was the undisputed capital of modern music. The Prussian Ministry of Education and Culture and the municipal council recruited talented musicians. Those who came from the East like the cellist Gregor Piatigorsky and the pianist Horowitz also made their contribution.

At the end of 1920 the Italian pianist **Ferruccio Busoni** was director of the School of Music at the Prussian Academy of Fine Arts. From 1916 he had been called a "Futurist peril" by the defenders of traditional music, and he trained a whole new generation of German musicians (including Kurt Weill). The Austrian **Arnold Schönberg** (1874-1951) succeeded him from 1926 to 1933. In January 1933 his experiments in twelve-note music aroused the wrath of anti-Semitic Nationalists. Premieres at the national Opera sometimes caused a stir: Richard Strauss's *Die Frau ohne Schatten* in 1919; **Wozzeck** on 14 December 1925, an opera by **Alban Berg** which aroused fierce controversy, but Erich Kleiber, the General Musical Director, kept it in the repertory in defiance of everybody until 1929; and *Cardillac* by **Paul Hindemith** (1895-1963) in 1928. Eminent conductors were in charge at all three opera houses: Fritz Stiedry and Bruno Walter at the Municipal Opera in Charlottenburg, Leo Blech and Erich Kleiber at the National Opera, and Otto Klemperer and Alexander von Zemlinsky at the Opera Kroll.

Wilhelm Furtwängler conducting a concert, 1932

At the Philharmonic where **Wilhelm Furtwängler** (1886-1954) was conductor from 1923 there were exemplary performances of works by musicians from the generation that had founded it (Schönberg, Stravinsky, Bartok). These excellent concerts were heard only by a limited audience of specialists. But in January 1922 musicians from the school of Busoni and Schönberg joined the **November group** which organized musical soirées broadcast on radio from the room in the **Vox house** in Potsdamer Straße which became a centre for contemporary music.

Young composers of the second generation, Paul Hindemith, Ernst Krenek, Heinz Tietjen, Alois Haba and Eduard Erdmann, were supported by **Hermann Scherchen**, a conductor and founder of the periodical *Melos*. The works of Krenek, Hindemith and Weill, decried by the traditionalists, mixed elements from jazz with serious music. The score written by **Kurt Weill** (1900-1950) had quite a bit to do with the success of *The Threepenny Opera*.

Variety and revue – Establishments staging variety shows, serving as a cure for the accumulated anguish following on from the war, provided magnificent spectacles composed of songs, sketches and suggestive dances in sumptuous sets with showy costumes. La Scala which opened in 1920 was the prototype. The popularity of light-hearted shows did not decline. The American dream became reality through the *jazz bands* (and their German version, the *Comedian Harmonist*), tours by troupes from Broadway which inspired the shows put on by **Erik Charell**, the Hollywood-style revues whose greatest star, **Rudolf Nelson**, discovered Marlene Dietrich. Paul Lincke, Jean Gilbert, Walter Kollo, Richard Tauber and the delightful **Fritzi Massary** were the darlings of the Berlin public. The Viennese operetta, given a more caustic note by the city of Berlin, triumphed with the *White Horse Inn* which ran for two years at the Schauspielhaus. **Friedrich Holländer**, an old Berliner whose father had been the official musician at the Metropol theatre in William II's reign, composed the tunes of the "Red Melody" sung by Rosa Valetti and "I'm the dashing Lola" sung by Marlene Dietrich in Josef von Sternberg's *The Blue Angel*.

Getting through the war – The situation began to deteriorate in 1929. Censorship was reinforced, ending a period of freedom. *Das Berliner Requiem* by Kurt Weill, composed for the 10th anniversary of the crushing of the Spartacist uprising and intended to be broadcast on radio, was robbed of its essence. After leaving Germany for the United States in May 1933, Schönberg declared: "To be honest I've been prepared for what has just happened for fourteen years." The cultural scene sank into mediocrity. The people of Berlin chose sentimental comedies or light operettas. Wilhelm Furtwängler and Richard Strauss concentrated on their art and performed works written by Jewish composers.

Dance

Choreography attracted some fascinating interpreters: **Mary Wigman** (really called Marie Wiegmann, a member of a good Hanoverian family), **Valeska Gert**, a mime and clown who conjured up life's misfits on the stage, **Gret Palucca** and **Leni Riefenstahl** who stylized everyday gestures. Anita Berber invented a new style of choreography, but finally succumbed to a cocaine addiction. Dance is the liberating art par excellence. "Widows' balls" were an out-and-out success. The charleston, the shimmy and the foxtrot: booming business for shoe repairers!

Its prestige intact – Rehoused in a building designed by Hans Scharoun, the Berlin Philharmonic retained its international reputation with **Herbert von Karajan** as its conductor from 1955 to 1989, giving rise to the building's nickname, the "Zirkus Karajani", an allusion to the prewar Sarasani circus. Karajan was succeeded by the Italian conductor **Claudio Abbado**, but throughout the year the world's greatest conductors appear as guest conductors at the Philharmonic.

Berlin has eight other symphony orchestras, including the German Symphony Orchestra (Deutsches Symphonie-Orchester), founded by the Americans in 1946 as the Rias-Symphonie-Orchester. It has always been under eminent conductors such as Lorin Maazel. The Berlin Symphony Orchestra (Berliner Sinfonie Orchester), formerly based in East Berlin is currently conducted by the Dane Michael Schonwand, who will be handing over his composer's baton to Simon Rattle in 2002. During the GDR regime with Kurt Sanderling as its conductor, gained a high reputation for its interpretation of Russian music, particularly the music of Shostakovich. The Radio Symphony Orchestra (Rundfunk-Sinfonieorchester) is also highly regarded. Nor should we forget the three opera orchestras: those of the Staatsoper Unter den Linden (the **Staatskapelle**) with **Daniel Barenboim** as its General Musical Director, the Deutsche Oper Berlin and the Komische Oper.

Further reading

REFERENCE

Berlin (Prestel Guide) by Joachim Fait *(Munich, 1992)*

Berlin – The Rough Guide by Jack Holland and John Gawthrop *(London, 4th edition, 1995)*

Maverick Guide to Berlin by Jay Brunhouse *(Louisiana, USA, 1993)*

Odyssey Illustrated Guide to Berlin by Gordon McLachlan *(Hong Kong, 1995)*

Berlin *(Penguin Books, Harmondsworth, 1995)*

Germany and the Germans by John Ardagh *(Penguin Books, 1991)*

History

Gold and Iron. Bismack and Bleischröder, and the building of the German Empire by Fritz R. Stern *(Random House, 1979)*

Hitler : A Biography by Marlis Steinert *(Norton, 1997)*

Potsdam by Gert Streidt *(Knickerbocker, 1997)*

Literature

Berlin Alexanderplatz: The Story of Franz Biberkopf by Alfred Döblin *(Continum, 1984)*

Goodbye to Berlin by Christopher Isherwood *(Chatto Pocket Library, 1992)*

Mr Norris Changes Trains by Christopher Isherwood *(Minerva, 1996)*

Art

Karl Friedrich Schinkel: a Universal Man *(Yale UP, 1991)*

Schinkel's Berlin: A Study in Environmental Planning by Hermann G. Pundt

On the town

Sport and nature

PARKS AND FORESTS

A large area of Berlin is forested. It can be explored from the following S-Bahn stations:

Grunewald Forest (Berliner Forst Grunewald):

Ⓢ *3, 7 Grunewald. You can also go to* Ⓤ *2, 12 Theodor-Heuss-Platz, then take the bus which goes to the Olympic stadium and along the banks of the Havel shoreline (Havelchaussee) providing access to various attractions in the Forest of Grunewald such as the Grunewaldturm.*

Düppel Forests (Berliner Forst Düppel):

Ⓤ *3, 7 Wannsee, then the bus which takes you to Peacock Island (Pfaueninsel).*

Tegel Forest (Berliner Forst Tegel):

Ⓢ *6 Alt-Tegel, then bus.*

Forest covering the Müggelberge (Berliner Stadtforst):

Ⓢ *3 Köpenick, then bus.* Walk along the road to the Müggelturm. There are various walks you can take around the **Müggelsee** or along the **Langersee** to the south.

Further information:

Brandenburgische Exkursionen – *Müggelstraße 22;* ☎ (030) 291 25 02.
Parks are normally open at night too. Please do not leave litter. Keep to the paths in the royal gardens.

BOAT TRIPS

With its wealth of waterways and lakes, Berlin is perfect for boating. Boat trips can be taken from the beginning of April to the end of September along the Havel, a 14km trip from Spandau to Potsdam (the section called the Unterhavel which goes all the way to Werder) and an 8km stretch from Spandau to Heiligensee through the Tegeler See (**Oberhavel**: some boat trips go to Lehnitzsee, next to Oranienburg). The **Spree** and the Landwehrkanal (10km long), which links the port of Silesia (*Schlesiches Tor*) to Charlottenburg, will take you on a circular route through old Berlin during which you will discover surprising industrial, urban and water landscapes; boat trips take approximately 3hrs.

The **Müggelsee**, which crosses the Spree, is a very popular spot for boating. The **Dahme** extends along lakes, such as the **Langer See** and the Seddinsee, and is an idyllic natural setting. Leaflets on the boat companies are available at the Tourist Office. Most boats leave from Castle Bridge (*Schloßbrücke*, Charlottenburger Ufer), by the castle of Charlottenburg, by the Arsenal (*Zeughaus*) and by the **cathedral** (*Berliner Dom*) or after the "**Lange Brücke**" in Potsdam.

Some boat companies:

> **Some boating terms:**
>
> "Ausflug": excursion
> "Rundfahrt": cruise
> "Brücke": bridge
> "Abfahrt": departure
> "Kinder": children
> "Täglich": daily
> "2 stündige": 2 hours
> "Über Tegel-Ort": by Tegelort

City Schiffahrt H.G. Gabriel – *Tegeler Weg pier, at the corner of Bonhoeffer Ufer, in the park. 150m downstream from the Schloßbrücke;* ☎ (030) 345 77 83; fax (030) 345 99 33. Specializes in boat trips in Berlin, along the Spree, the Landwehrkanal and the Spandauer Schiffahrtskanal.

Reederei Bruno Winkler – *Schloßbrücke Piers (Charlottenburg), Reichstagsufer (Mitte), Lindenufer – Brücke 3 (Spandau), Tegeler Weg (Charlottenburg), Tegel Greenwichpromenade (Reinickendorf);* ☎ (030) 301 70 10, 391 70 70, 391 46 93; fax (030) 391 80 49.
Boat trip from Werder to Lehnitzsee and through Berlin; a wide choice of evening entertainment on board.

Reederei E. Schlenter – *Pier on the Spree from Tegeler Weg (Charlottenburg)*; Mierendorfplatz or Jungfernheide; Landgericht Charlottenburg from Zoo station; ☎ and fax (030) 416 27 32.
Day trip to the lakeside town of Werder, to the Müggelsee through Berlin, Königs Wusterhausen along the Spree and the Dahme, through the Brandenburg March.

Stern und Kreis Schiffahrt GmbH – *Puschkinallee 16-17 (Treptow)*; Ⓢ *6*, Ⓢ *8*, Ⓢ *9*, Ⓢ *10 Treptower Park*; ☎ *(030) 617 39 00; fax (030) 61 73 90 99*.
This company owns the "White fleet" (*Die Weiße Flotte*) which offers various boat trips along the Spree and the Dahme and on the surrounding lakes. The *Havel Queen* paddle boat and the *Moby Dick*, which is shaped like a whale, cruise on Tegel lake (Greenwich Promenade pier – Bridge 2; Tegeler Hafen, opposite the Humboldt library), to the Lehnitzsee, in the area of Oranienburg, and on the Havel between Wannsee and Cecilienhof.

Weiße Flotte Potsdam – *Customer service: Lange Brücke*; ☎ (0331) 29 15 27 or 280 00 31; fax (0331) 29 10 90.
A trip around the city, along the Havel to Brandenburg, to Peacock Island, Wannsee and Spandau, across Berlin.

SWIMMING

Havel

The banks of the Havel are perfect for swimming, but it is a good idea to bathe close to the supervised resorts:

Lieper Bucht – Lindwerder; opposite the island of Lindwerder.

Große Steinlanke – Großes Fenster.

Strandbad Wannsee - Ⓢ *1, 3, 7 Wannsee*. The biggest inland beach in Europe, which became a resort in the twenties.

Moorlake – *Moorlake*. A traditional resort very popular with Berliners. The creek is lined with inns.

Grunewald Lakes:

Krumme Lanke – *1 Krumme Lanke*. A wooded shoreline.

Schlachtensee – Ⓢ *1 Schlachtensee*. Swimming possible all around the lake, especially alongside the Paul-Ernst-Park.

BILDAGENTUR SCHUSTER

Boat trips are one of the delights of the Berlin summer

NATURE AND LEISURE ACTIVITIES IN BERLIN

⋈	Castle
✝	Church, chapel
☀	Tower, view

⚕	Animal sanctuary
🐘	Zoological gardens
⚘	Beach, bathing
🏊	Swimming pool

●	Planetarium
🎢	Theme/Amusement park
■	Theatre, concert hall

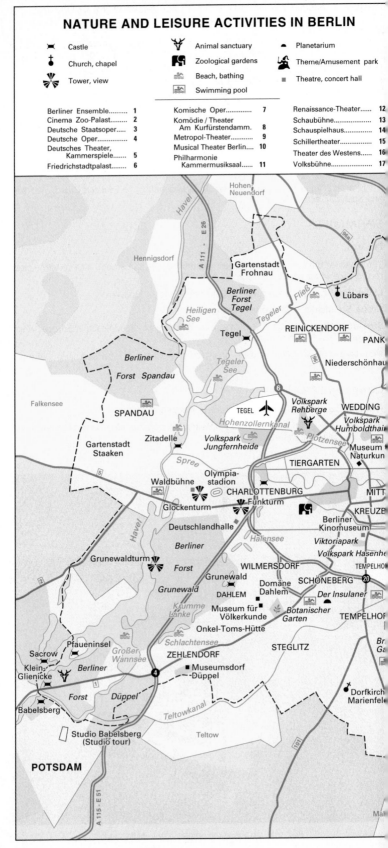

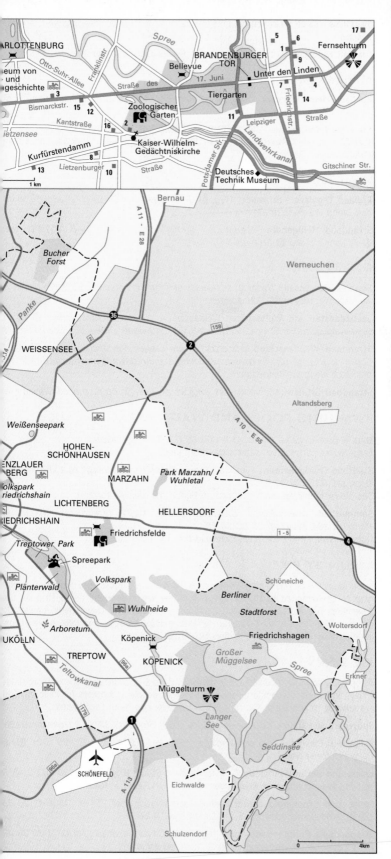

CHARLOTTENBURG

Spree

Otto-Suhr-Allee

Frankl.str.

eum von
und
geschichte

Straße des

Bellevue

BRANDENBURGER
TOR

17. Juni

Tiergarten

Unter den Linden

5
1
6
9
7
4
14

17

Fernsehturm

Bismarckstr. 15 12

Kantstraße

etzensee 16

Kurfürstendamm 8

13 Lietzenburger 10

Zoologischer
Garten

2

Kaiser-Wilhelm-
Gedächtniskirche

Straße

11

Leipziger

Potsdamer Str.

Landwehrkanal

Straße

Gitschiner Str.

Deutsches
Technik Museum

1 km

Bernau

A 11 - E 28

Bucher
Forst

Werneuchen

Panke

36

158

2

WEISSENSEE

2

Altandsberg

A 10 - E 55

Weißenseepark

HOHEN-
SCHÖNHAUSEN

ENZLAUER
BERG

MARZAHN

Park Marzahn/
Wuhletal

olkspark
riedrichshain

LICHTENBERG

HELLERSDORF

IEDRICHSHAIN

Friedrichsfelde

1 - 5

4

Treptower Park

Spreepark

Schöneiche

Plänterwald

Volkspark

Berliner

Stadtforst

Woltersdorf

Wuhlheide

Friedrichshagen

Arboretum

Köpenick

Großer
Müggelsee

Spree

Erkner

UKÖLLN

TREPTOW

969a

KÖPENICK

Teltowkanal

Müggelturm

Langer
See

179

Seddinsee

1

186d

SCHÖNEFELD

A 113

Eichwalde

0   4km

Schulzendorf

Teufelsee – Ⓢ *3, 7 Grunewald*; take the Neuer Schildhornweg heading west. A nudist beach.

Freibad Halensee – Ⓢ *9 Halensee* or 🚌 *Rathenauplatz*. A nudist resort.

Müggelsee:

Seebad Friedrichshagen – *Müggelseedamm 216*; Ⓢ *3 Friedrichshagen*, then 🚋 *60 Josef-Nawrocki-Straße*.

Strandbad Müggelsee – *Fürstenwalder Damm 838 (Rahnsdorf)*; Ⓢ *3 Rahnsdorf*, then 🚌 *Rahnsdorf/Waldschänke*; 🚋 *61 Strandbad Müggelsee or walk northwest along Fürstenwalder Damm.*

From Tegel:

Freibad Tegelsee – *Schwarzer Weg*; Ⓤ *6 Alt-Tegel*, then 🚌 *Spechtstraße*; go south-east along *Waldkauzstraße.*

Strandbad Heiligensee – *Sandhauser Straße/Alt-Heiligensee*; Ⓤ *6 Alt-Tegel*, then 🚌 *Falkenplatz* and 🚌 *Strandbad Heiligensee.*

Other lakes:

Freibad Plötzensee (Wedding) – *Nearest underground stations*; Ⓤ *9 Westhafen or Amrumer Straße; or* 🚌 *Dohnagestell.*

Seebadanstalt am WeissenSee (Weissensee) – *Nearest S-Bahn station*; Ⓢ *8, 10 Greifswalder Straße*; 🚌 *or* 🚋 *2, 3, 4, 13, 23, 24 Berliner Allee/Indira-Gandhi-Straße.*

Strandbad Wendenschloß (Köpenick) – *Am Langen See/Möllhausenufer 30*; Ⓢ *3 Köpenick*, then 🚋 *62 Wendenschloß; continue south down Wendenschloßstraße and then east along Möllhausenufer.*

Strandbad Grünau (Köpenick) – Ⓢ *3 Köpenick*, then 🚋 *68 Strandbad Grünau.*

SWIMMING POOLS AND WATER PARKS

Blub – *Bushkrugallee 64*; ☎ *(30) 606 60 60*; Ⓤ *7 Grenzallee.*
Large water park with a water slide 120m long.

Stadtbad Charlottenburg – *Krumme Straße 6a-8 (Charlottenburg)*; Ⓤ *2, 12 Deutsche Oper*; ☎ *(030) 34 30 32 41.*
The oldest municipal swimming pool in Berlin; the clientele tends to be elderly.

Sommerbad Kreuzberg – *Gitschiner Straße 18-31 (Kreuzberg)*; Ⓤ *1, 15 Prinzenstraße*; ☎ *(030) 25 88 54 16.*
Outdoor swimming pool, open from mid-May to September only.

BERLIN BY BIKE

In Germany the bicycle is king. Berlin has 800km of cycle tracks. The network is beginning to be extended to the eastern part. They are marked by a red strip on the pavement. You are advised to avoid walking or stopping on them; Berlin cyclists do not stop. Ask for the *ADFC Fahrradstadtplan* guide (DM 12.-) and look in the yellow pages (under *Fahrradverleih*) to find hire firms.

ICE RINKS

As opening hours vary considerably, generally 2- to 3-hour sessions one or more times a day, and some sessions are reserved for older people and others for children, you are advised to enquire at the rink. Some ice rinks also have discotheques.

Sportpark Neukölln – *Oderstraße 182*; ☎ *(030) 68 09 35 34*; Ⓤ *7 Hermannstraße.*

Erika-Heß-Eisstadion – *Müllerstraße 185*; ☎ *(030) 45 75 55 57*; Ⓤ *6 Reinickendorfer Straße.*

Eisstadion Berlin-Wilmersdorf – *Fritz-Wildung-Straße 9*; ☎ *(030) 823 40 60*; Ⓢ *9 Hohenzollerndamm and Heidelberger Platz.* Ⓤ *Heidelberger Platz.*

Sport- und Erholungszentrum Berlin – *Landsberger Allee 77*; ☎ *(030) 42 28 33 22*; Ⓢ *Landsberger Allee*; Ⓢ *8, 10 Landsberger Allee.*

Eissporthalle Berlin – *Jaffestraße (next to the Deutschlandhalle)*; ☎ *(030) 30 38 42 23*; Ⓢ *3, 7, 9, 75 Westkreuz* or Ⓤ *2, 12 Kaiserdamm.*

Entertainment

Listings for films, concerts, exhibitions and everything else going on in Berlin are published in the city magazines **Zitty** and **Tip**. The monthly publication **Berlin-Programm** provides information about events of all kinds. Berlin's daily newspapers publish a weekly events supplement. The publication **Führer durch die Konzertsälle Berlins** is available free of charge at theatre box offices. Tickets are available up to three weeks in advance from **Berlin Tourismus Marketing**: ☎ *25 00 25*.

Theatres

Berliner Ensemble – *Bertold-Brecht-Platz 1 (Mitte);* ☎ *282 31 60;* Ⓤ + Ⓢ *Friedrichstraße*
In 1928 Bertold Brecht set his successful Threepenny Opera in this building, (formerly known as the Theater am Schiffbauerdamm), which is over 100 years old. He founded the Berliner Ensemble, which has been staging plays here since 1954 and was later directed by Heiner Müller.

Deutsches Theater – *Schumannstraße 13a (Mitte);* ☎ *28 44 12 21;* Ⓤ + Ⓢ *Friedrichstraße*
The theatre gained international fame under the direction of Max Reinhardt. Extremely high quality productions can be seen on three stages under the direction of Thomas Langhoff, with a repertoire ranging from classical to modern plays.

Schaubühne am Lehniner Plaz – *Kurfürstendamm 153 (Wilmersdorf);* ☎ *89 00 23;* Ⓤ *Adenauerplatz;* Ⓢ *Charlottenburg*
The former Universumkino cinema dating from the 1920 s. has been used since 1981 by the Schaubühne Ensemble. The theatre, under the direction of Peter Stein, was hugely popular before reunification.

Volksbühne – *Rosa-Luxemburg-Platz (Mitte);* ☎ *247 76 94;* Ⓤ *Rosa-Luxemburg-Platz*
Provocative drama under the direction of Frank Castorf. Aside from theatrical productions, other events are also staged at the Volksbühne, in the **Roter & Grüner Salon**.

Kömodie/Theater am Kurfürstendamn – *Kurfürstendamm 206-209 (Charlottenburg);* ☎ *47 99 74 30/40;* Ⓤ *Uhlandstraße*
Very funny light theatrical productions often featuring well-known television actors.

Hebbel-Theater – *Stresemannstraße 29 (Kreuzberg);* ☎ *25 92 04 27/36;* Hallesches Tor; Ⓢ *Anhalter Bahnhof*
This Art Nouveau theatre which survived the war, has established a reputation for itself as "the" place for foreign theatre, dance and musical productions.

Ph. Gajic/MICHELIN

Schaubühne

Opera, ballet, operettas and musicals

Deutsche Oper Berlin – *Bismarckstraße 35 (Charlottenburg);* ☎ *343 84 01;* Ⓤ
.Deutsche Oper
The Opernhaus von Charlottenburg originally stood on this site. The building was
rebuilt after the war.

Staatsoper Unter den Linden – *Unter den Linden 5 (Mitte);* ☎ *20 35 45 55;* Ⓤ *+*
Ⓢ *Friedrichstraße;* Ⓤ *Französische Straße*
The oldest and most sumptuous opera house in Berlin, dating back to Friedrich II.

Komische Oper – *Behrenstraße 55-57 (Mitte);* ☎ *47 99 74 00;* Ⓢ *Unter den Linden;*
Ⓤ *Französische Straße*
This opera house was founded by Walther Felsenstein in 1947, and stages many inter-
esting productions by Kupfer.

Theater des Westens – *Kantstraße 12 (Charlottenburg);* ☎ *31 90 30;* Ⓤ *+* Ⓢ
Zoologischer Garten
Berlin's major musical productions are staged in this lavish building which dates from
the time of Emperor Wilhelm II.

Neuköllner Oper – *Karl-Marx-Straße 131-133 (Neukölln);* ☎ *68 89 07 77;* Ⓤ *Karl-
Marx-Straße*
Small theatre at which non-mainstream musicals can be experienced, ranging from
the contemporary avant-garde to the satirised delights of operetta.

Tanzfabrik (Theater am Halleschen Ufer) – *Möckernstraße 68 (Kreuzberg);* (*786
58 61;* Ⓤ *Möckernbrücke*
Experimental dance centre.

1995 "Cinema" Revue at the Friedrichstadtpalast

Variety shows, reviews and cabaret

Neuer Friedrichstadtpalast – *Friedrichstraße 107 (Mitte);* ☎ *23 26 23 26;* Ⓤ *+* Ⓢ
Friedrichstraße
A focal point of entertainment in the former GDR, this vast theatre stages outstanding
performances. The sumptuous productions, costumes and sets, and talented artists performing virtuoso numbers, all combine to make an evening at the Friedrichstadtpalast
an unforgettable experience. The Kinder Ensemble performs children's shows.

Chamäleon Variété – *Rosenthaler Straße 40-41 (Mitte);* ☎ *282 71 18;* Ⓢ *Hackescher
Markt*
This theatre in one of the finest buildings of the Hackesche Höfe presents sketches and
amusing acts by young artists. The audience sits at small tables, the host is humorous
and the atmosphere relaxed.

Wintergarten-Variété – *Potsdamer Str. 96 (Tiergarten)*; ☎ *230 88 20*; Ⓤ *Kurfürstenstraße*
Traditional variety shows featuring brilliant artistes.

Chez Nous – *Marburger Straße 14 (Charlottenburg)*; ☎ *213 18 10*; Ⓤ *Kurfürstendamm*
Show featuring transvestites.

Bar Jeder Vernunft – *Schaperstraße 24 (Wilmersdorf)*; ☎ *883 15 82*; Ⓤ *Spichernstraße*
Housed in a mirrored tent erected in the parking area of the former Freie Volksbühne; acts include Berlin songs and cabaret.

Die Distel – *Friedrichstraße 101 (Mitte)*; *204 47 04*; Ⓤ + Ⓢ *Friedrichstraße*
Political satire was performed at this venue in the Metropol-Theater even in GDR times.

Stachelschweine – *Europa-Center (Charlottenburg)*; ☎ *261 47 95*; Ⓤ *Kurfürstendamm*, Ⓤ + Ⓢ *Zoologischer Garten*
Traditional cabaret acts.

Classical Music

Concert halls

Konzerthaus Berlin (Schauspielhaus am Gendarmenmarkt) – *Gendarmenmarkt (Mitte)*; ☎ *203 09 21 01/02*; Ⓤ *Französische Straße*, Ⓤ *Stadtmitte*

Philharmonie and Kammermusiksaal – *Herbert-von-Karajan-Straße 1 (Tiergarten)*; ☎ *25 48 81 32*; Ⓤ + Ⓢ *Potsdamer Platz*

Sacred music

Berliner Dom – *Am Lustgarten (Mitte)*; ☎ *20 26 91 36*; Ⓢ *Hackescher Markt*

Kaiser-Wilhelm-Gedächtniskirche – *Breitscheidplatz (Charlottenburg)*; ☎ *218 50 23*; Ⓤ *Kurfürstendamm*; Ⓤ + Ⓢ *Zoologischer Garten*

Französischer Dom/Friedrichstadtkirche – *Gendarmenmarkt 6 (Mitte)*; ☎ *204 15 06*; Ⓤ *Französische Straße*

Concerts in the castles

Schloß Charlottenburg – *Luisenplatz (Charlottenburg)*; ☎ *32 09 11*; Ⓤ *Richard Wagner-Platz*

Schloss Britz – *Alt Britz 73 (Neukölln)*; ☎ *606 60 51*; Ⓤ *Blaschkoallee*

Schloß Friedrichsfelde – *Am Tierpark 125 (Lichtenberg)*; ☎ *513 81 41*; Ⓤ *Tierpark*

H. Maack/AKG PARIS

Concert at the Philharmonic

Rock, Pop Etc

Major events

Waldbühne – *Glockenturmstraße/Passenheimer Straße (Charlottenburg);* ☎ *30 06 33;* Ⓤ *Olympiastadion*

Columbiahalle – *Columbiadamm 13-21 (Tempelhof);* ☎ *698 09 08;* Ⓤ *Platz der Luftbrücke*

Arena – *Eichenstraße 4 (Treptow);* ☎ *533 73 33;* Ⓤ *Schlesisches Tor,* Ⓢ *Treptower Park*

Pink Floyd's concert *The Wall*

Bars and clubs featuring live music

Knaack Club – *Greifswalder Straße 224 (Prenzlauer Berg);* ☎ *442 70 60;* Ⓤ *Rosa-Luxemburg-Platz;* Ⓢ *Greifswalder Straße*

Oxymoron – *Rosenthaler Straße 40/41 (Hackesche Höfe-Mitte) ;* ☎ *283 91 885 ;* Ⓢ *Hackescher Markt*

Swing – *Nollendorfplatz 3-4 (Schöneberg);* ☎ *216 61 37;* Ⓤ *Nollendorfplatz*

Quasimodo – *Kantstraße 12a (Charlottenburg);* ☎ *213 80 86;* Ⓤ *+* Ⓢ *Zoologischer Garten*

Jazz

A-Trane – *Bleibtreustraße 1 (Charlottenburg);* ☎ *312 94 93;* Ⓢ *Savignyplatz*

B-Flat – *Rosenthaler Straße 13 (Mitte);* ☎ *280 62 49;* Ⓤ *Weinmeisterstraße*

Miles – *Greifswalder Straße 212-213 (Prenzlauer Berg);* ☎ *44 00 81 40;* Ⓤ *Rosa-Luxembourg-Platz;* Ⓢ *Greifswalder Straße*

Ballrooms

Clärchen's Ballhaus – *Auguststraße 24-25 (Mitte);* ☎ *282 92 95;* Ⓤ *Weinmeisterstraße*

Ballhaus Berlin – *Chauseestraße 102 (Mitte);* ☎ 282 75 75; Ⓤ *Zinnowitzer Straße*

Café Keese – *Bismarckstraße 108 (Charlottenburg);* ☎ *312 91 11;* Ⓤ *Ernst-Reuther-Platz*

Berlin on the Internet
http://www/berlin.de http://www.berlinonline.de http://www.zitty.de http://www.berlin-info.de http://www.d-berlin.de

For satire lovers: Bar Jeder Vernunft

CINEMA

Many of the large cinemas screening the Hollywood blockbusters are located around the Gedächtniskirche. The largest 19 screen multiplex *Cinemas* is situated on Potsdamer Platz. The **IMAX cinema** is also here. Arthouse cinemas, which screen auteur films, retrospectives and classics, are mainly located in the Kreuzberg, Schöneberg, Prenzlauer Berg and Mitte districts. The little guide *Theo's Tips* contains information about films for children.

Films shown with original soundtrack

Babylon – *Dresdener Straße 126 (Kreuzberg)*; ☎ 61 90 96 93; **U** *Kottbusser Tor*

UFA-Arthouse Kurbel – *Giesebrechtstraße 4 (Charlottenburg)*; ☎ 883 53 25; **U** *Adenauerplatz*

Odeon – *Hauptstraße 116 (Schöneberg)*; ☎ 78 70 40 19; **U** *Rathaus Schöneberg*; **S** *Schöneberg*

Olympia – *Kantstraße 162 (Charlottenburg)*; ☎ 881 19 78; **U** + **S** *Zoologischer Garten*

Open air cinemas

Freiluftkino Friedrichshain – *Volkspark Friedrichshain (Friedrichshain)*; ☎ 215 20 97; **U** *Strausberger Platz*

Freiluftkino Hasenheide – *Volkspark Hasenheide (Neukölln)*; ☎ 215 20 97; **U** *Herrmannplatz*

Waldbühne – (see MAJOR EVENTS)

Multiplex cinemas

Filmpalast Berlin – *Kurfürstendamm 225 (Charlottenburg)*; ☎ 883 85 51; **U** *Kurfürstendamm*

International – *Karl-Marx-Allee 33 (Mitte)*; ☎ 24 75 60 11; **U** *Schillingstraße*

Delphi – *Kantstraße 12a (Charlottenburg)*; ☎ 312 10 26; **U** + **S** *Zoologischer Garten*

Highbrow

Arsenal – *Welserstraße 25 (Schöneberg)*; ☎ 19 0010; **U** *Wittenbergplatz*

Filmkunsthaus Babylon – *Rosa-Luxemburg-Platz 30 (Mitte)*; ☎ 242 50 76; **U** *Rosa-Luxemburg-Platz*

Hackesche Höfe – *Rosenthaler Straße 40-41 (Mitte)*; ☎ 283 46 03; **S** *Hackescher Markt*

Classics

Berliner Kinomuseum – *Großbeerenstraße 57 (Kreuzberg)*; **U** *Mehringdamm*

Notausgang – *Vorarlbergstraße 1 (Schöneberg)*; ☎ 787 11 200; **U** *Kleistpark*

Cinemas with bars attached

Klick – *Windscheidstraße 19 (Charlottenburg);* ☎ *323 84 37;* Ⓢ *Charlottenburg*

Filmbühne am Steinplatz – *Hardenbergstraße 12 (Charlottenburg);* ☎ *312 90 12;* Ⓤ *+* Ⓢ *Zoologischer Garten*

Tilsiter Lichtspiele – *Richard-Sorge-Straße 25a (Friedrichshain);* ☎ *426 81 29;* Ⓤ *Weberwiese*

The Berlin scene

There is no "one" Berlin scene at "one" central location. Very many districts have plenty going on and offer a whole variety of different bars, cafés and taverns. There is something for everyone, the important feature being that no one will put a damper on your enjoyment by calling "time". A number of different publications, such as *030*, which provide information about all the latest trends and clubs, can be found in all the "in" shops.

BETWEEN ADENAUERPLATZ AND STUTTGARTER PLATZ (Charlottenburg-Wilmersdorf)

Voltaire – *Stuttgarter Platz 14;* Ⓢ *Charlottenburg*
The relaxing atmosphere here can be enjoyed equally by shopping-laden women and groups of men. The menu contains just the right tasty delights for any time of day or night.

Irish Harp Pub – *Giesebrechtstraße 15;* Ⓤ *Adenauerplatz*
The beer of choice here is Guinness, but an excellent range of whiskies is also available. The theme is of course "The Emerald Isle".

BETWEEN OLIVAER PLATZ AND LUDWIGKIRCHPLATZ (Charlottenburg-Wilmersdorf)

Jimmy's Diner – *Pariser Straße 41;* Ⓤ *Spichernstraße*
Along Pariser Straße there are about half a dozen American restaurants, with chrome and neon interiors and featuring US memorabilia on the walls.

Galerie Bremer – *Fasenenstraße 37;* Ⓤ *Uhlandstraße*
A cosy, dimly lit cocktail bar is hidden in the back room of the gallery.

Kahn – *Pariser Straße 20;* Ⓤ *Uhlandstraße*
This is a really "in" bar, which can get crowded in the evenings.

AROUND SAVIGNYPLATZ (Charlottenburg)

Schwarzes Café – *Kantstraße 148;* Ⓢ *Savignyplatz*
The *Schwarzes Café* only closes between 3am on Mondays and noon on Tuesdays. The ambience in this two storey cult café is reminiscent of the old West Berlin days, sometimes giving the impression that time has stood still.

Zillemarkt – *Bleibtreustraße 48a;* Ⓢ *Savignyplatz*
This bar is situated in one of the most beautiful corners of Charlottenburg in a former flea market. It is furnished in traditional style with small wooden tables and old lamps.

Café Hardenberg – *Hardenbergstraße 10;* Ⓤ *Ernst-Reuther-Platz*
Quite simply "the" meeting place for students from the Technical University and the Academy of Art, it is always busy and lively.

ALONG THE KU'DAMM (Charlottenburg)

Hardtke – *Meineckestraße 27;* Ⓤ *Kurfürstendamm*
Typical Berlin style café-bar with rustic wooden decor, serving traditional German food and Berlin and Brandenburg specialities.

Leysieffer – *Kurfürstendamm 118;* Ⓤ *Kurfürstendamm*
Ku'Damm flair in a traditional café offering a wide range of cakes.

Ranke 2 – *Rankestraße 2-3;* Ⓤ *Kurfürstendamm*
Ranke 2 is a tavern which plays host to the lovers of *Berliner Weisse*.

Café Kranzler – *Kurfürstendamm 18;* Ⓤ *Kurfürstendamm*
Once upon a time on Unter den Linden Avenue, there was a pastry-cook of Austrian origin who delighted Berlin High Society in the 1830s. The café, recognisable by its red and white façade is now much frequented by tourists.

AROUND WINTERFELDPLATZ (Schöneberg)

Café M – *Goltzstraße 33;* **U** *Nollendorfplatz*
"Being cool" is still the right expression in relation to this café, since it doesn't appear to have changed much since the 1980s.

Café Sidney – *Winterfeldplatz 40;* **U** *Nollendorfplatz*
Vast café in an excellent corner location, the tables on the terrace are ideal for observing what is going on in the market on Winterfeldplatz.

Slumberland – *Goltzstraße 24;* **U** *Nollendorfplatz*
Sand on the floor and reggae sounds from the speakers attract a colourful and cosmopolitan clientele.

AROUND LÜTZOWPLATZ (Tiergarten)

Café Einstein – *Kurfürstenstraße 58;* **U** *Nollendorfplatz*
One of the four large rooms on the ground floor of this big middle-class house has Rococo decor and a fine marble bar with wooden shelves. International reviews and newspapers are available to a chic, young clientele sampling the delights of Apfelstrudel. Turn-of-the-century Viennese-style charm.

Harry's New York Bar – *Lützowufer 15;* **U** *Nollendorfplatz*
This elegant bar is located in the Grand Hotel Esplanade. You may hear contracts being negotiated and stock market prices being discussed at the next table.

Bar am Lützowplatz – *Lützowplatz 7;* **U** *Nollendorfplatz*
Highly professional bartenders mix elegant cocktails at a very long bar in this famous cocktail bar.

AROUND CHAMISSOPLATZ (Kreuzberg)

Yorckschlösschen – *Yorckstraße 15;* **U** *Mehringdamm*
This bar, in its corner location, has a shady terrace and often features live music, mostly jazz.

Joe Peña's – *Marheineckeplatz 2;* **U** *Gneisenaustraße*
Café and restaurant with Spanish and Mexican flair. It features unusual leather seats and papier-mâché iguanas over the bar.

Oktobar – *Chamissoplatz 4;* **U** *Platz der Luftbrücke*
Comfortable bar on what must be the most beautiful square in Kreuzberg.

The "Ranke 3" - with its famous delicatessen

ALONG ORANIENSTRASSE
AND WIENER STRASSE (Kreuzberg)

Bierhimmel – *Oranienstraße 183;* Ⓤ *Kottbusser Tor*
Interior decor featuring mirrors of all shapes and sizes, gold walls and old chandeliers. Bierhimmel is a perfect example of the saying "Kreuzberger nights are long".

Madonna Bar – *Wiener Straße 22;* Ⓤ *Kottbusser Tor*
Bar which normally features extremely loud music. This Kreuzberg institution has been located here since the beginning of time.

Café am Ufer – *Paul-Lincke-Ufer 42-43;* Ⓤ *Kottbusser Tor*
A beautiful café on the banks of the Landwehrkanal, a pleasant place to meet friends.

CULTURAL CENTRES
(Music, literature, dancing, cinema, literature, art galleries)

Tacheles – *Oranienburger Straße 54-56 (Mitte);* Ⓢ *Oranienburger Straße,* Ⓤ *Oranienburger Tor*
The ruins of a shopping passage dating from the time of the German empire, became a centre for alternative culture after reunification. After years of uncertainty about its future, the existence of the Tacheles is now secure. Various (graffiti sprayed) entrances lead to workshops, a cinema, a café and to the gardens.

Haus der Kulturen der Welt – *John-Foster-Dulles-Allee 10 (Tiergarten);* Ⓢ *Unter den Linden;* Ⓢ *Lehrter Stadtbahnhof*
The former Congress Hall (see TIERGARTEN) is currently used for events relating to various non-European cultures. In the summer the Spree entices visitors from the terrace.

Künsterhaus Bethanien – *Mariannenplatz 2 (Kreuzberg);* Ⓤ *Kottbusser Tor*
The theme of this cultural centre located on a very beautiful square *(see KREUZBERG)* is Turkish culture.

Ufa-Fabrik – *Viktoriastraße 10-18 (Tempelhof);* Ⓤ *Ullsteinstraße*
Colourfully varied cultural programme on the site of the former UFA film studio. The complex, which includes a café, children's farm, bakery, circus and plenty more has an almost village-style character.

Kulturbrauerei – *Knaackstraße 97 (Prenzlauer Berg);* Ⓤ *Eberswalder Straße*
The range and variety of activities make this centre one of the culturally most interesting places in Prenzlauer Berg, on the site and in the buildings of a former brewery.

UNTER DEN LINDEN/FRIEDRICHSTRASSE (Mitte)

Opernpalais – *Unter den Linden 5;* Ⓤ + Ⓢ *Friedrichstraße, Französische Straße*
This café in a palace in the heart of old Berlin consists of two fine large rooms (in addition to the restaurant on the first floor). The Opern Café, a tearoom with decor typical of the old Prussian capital, serves marvellous cakes whereas the Opern Schänke is reminiscent of a 1920s cabaret. You can have brunch here or sip a glass of wine as you listen to the music amid the elegant clientele. The terrace opens onto a shady square. A Christmas market is held in front of the palace in the winter.

StäV – *Schiffbauerdamm 8;* Ⓤ + Ⓢ *Friedrichstraße*
This has to be the habitual haunt of the people who have moved to Berlin from Bonn. StäV stands for "Ständige Vertretung" (permanent representation), after the diplomatic representatives of the two German states in Bonn and Berlin.

Deponie – *Georgenstraße 3;* Ⓤ + Ⓢ *Friedrichstraße*
Extremely popular bar with a rustic ambience under the arches of the Stadtbahn.

AROUND HACKESCHE MARKT (Mitte)

Anna Koschke – *Krausnickstraße 11;* Ⓢ *Hackescher Markt*
These two rooms in a small street in the Barn district form a striking contrast with the large establishments of Oranienburger Straße. The old piano and many framed photographs (family portraits, wedding photos, etc) lend the decor an intimate, almost domestic turn-of-the-century charm. Young, local clientele.

Aedes – *Rosenthaler Straße 40-41;* Ⓢ *Hackescher Markt*
A café in one of the magnificently restored Hackesche Höfe courtyards with highly modern decor, including a double concrete and glass partition wall which diffuses the light and pale wooden designer furniture.

Berlin, techno capital

Those in the know don't talk about techno itself any more, and since the end of the 1990s, the scene has been made up of a number of independent styles. Techno originated from the House music in the clubs of Detroit and Chicago. After reunification, many techno clubs were set up in former bunkers, industrial hangars and ruins in the east of the city. These unusual locations, combined with the alienating effects brought about by the smoke and strobe lighting, were just right for this music, which is based only on synthetic noises, and is mixed live by the DJ. Berlin became a techno trendsetter, among other things due to the Love Parade, which is still held in July and which over 1 million people attend.

Since the legendary E-Werk no longer exists, the traditional locations in the Mitte district are the famous Tresor/Globus (Leipziger Straße 126a/corner of Wilhelmstraße) in the former strongroom of the Wertheim department store close to Potsdamer Platz, and the legendary WMF (it has moved into what are its fourth premises at Johannisstraße 19-21).

Hackbarths – *Auguststraße 49a;* Ⓤ *Rosenthaler Platz*
Hackbarths is on the corner of the street, as is the copper bar itself. With bronze lighting and black ceramics at the foot of the walls, it is a good place for a bite of quiche or other vegetarian dishes, with a good choice of wines by the glass. The young clientele is cosmopolitan and fairly bohemian.

NIKOLAIVIERTEL & ALEX (Mitte)

Telecafé – *Panoramastraße 1;* Ⓤ + Ⓢ *Alexanderplatz*
The café in the Television Tower revolves every 30 min (before reunification it revolved every 60 min). The view over the city is breathtaking.

Zum Nußbaum – *Am Nußbaum 3;* Ⓤ *Klosterstraße*
The Nußbaum, which has been in existence in Alt-Cölln since 1517, was the oldest restaurant in the city, until it fell victim to a bomb during the war. It was rebuilt in 1987 and is now well frequented.

Georgbräu – *Spree-Ufer;* Ⓤ *Klosterstraße*
Large, simply furnished bar in the Nikolai district right on the banks of the Spree and offering local cuisine. Its marvellous terrace is worth spending time on.

AROUND COLLWITZPLATZ (Prenzlauer Berg)

Anita Wronski – *Knaackstraße 26-28;* Ⓤ *Senefelder Platz*
Café situated directly opposite the Water tower, which is a protected building, an ideal place to sit and chat for hours.

Opern-Café in the Princesses' palace

Krähe – *Kollwitzstraße 84;* [U] *Eberswalder Straße*
Earthy locale in Prenzlauer Berg, a good starting point from which to get to know the neighbourhood.

Bla-Bla – *Sredzkistraße 19a;* [U] *Eberswalder Straße*
Original interior design, makes you feel you are in someone's living room. A good place to conduct an interesting social study of the Prenzlauer Berg night-life into the small hours.

ALONG KASTANIENALLEE (Prenzlauer Berg)

Entwederoder – *Oderberger Straße 15;* [U] *Eberswalder Straße*
Located right in the middle of the *Kiez*, extremely convivial, family setting, a good way to participate in the day-to-day life of the district.

Schwarz Sauer – *Kastanienallee 13;* [U] *Eberswalder Straße*
This is a café by day and a bar in the evening.

Kid Creole – *Lottumstraße 9/10;* [U] *Senefelder Platz*
Creole cuisine and southern states flair in this backyard building. The Kid Creole is an excellent place to sit out on warm summer nights.

OUT IN THE COUNTRY

Café am Neuen See – *Lichtensteinallee 1 (Tiergarten);* [U] + [S] *Zoologischer Garten*
A beer garden seating 1 000 right in the middle of the Tiergarten, very close to the authentic original Munich style.

Kastanie – *Schloßstraße 22 (Charlottenburg);* [U] *Sophie-Charlotte-Platz*
Small beer garden situated on the access road to Schloß Charlottenburg. Boule are played in summer on the grass opposite, where an aura of French flair may sometimes be experienced.

Golgatha – *in Viktoriapark along Katzbachstraße/Kreuzbergstraße (Kreuzberg);* [U] *Mehringdamm*
Beer garden in the Kreuzberg district beneath the national memorial. Things can get quite hectic here.

Ph. Gajic/MICHELIN

Sitting out in St. Nicholas

WITH MUSICAL ACCOMPANIMENT

Café Silberstein – *Oranienburger Straße 27 (Mitte);* Ⓢ *Hackescher Markt*
The decor here is characterised by chairs with outsized backs and metal sculptures, and the sound is techno.

Schnabelbar – *Oranienstraße 31 (Kreuzberg);* Ⓤ *Kottbusser Tor*
Very traditional bar hosted by a DJ in the heart of the Kreuzberg district.

The Pip's – *Auguststraße 84 (Mitte);* Ⓤ *Oranienburger Tor;* Ⓢ *Oranienburger Straße*
Highly colourful 1970s bar, good atmosphere with disco music and hits from the period.

AND IN THE POTSDAM AREA...

Babette – *Brandenburger Straße 71;* ☏ *(0331) 29 16 48.*
Very fine cakes to tempt the visitor as you enter this café and tea-room with its subdued, original decor, soft-coloured furniture and tapestry-covered seats. Engravings of old Potsdam adorn the walls. A fine outside seating area on the square which surrounds the port of Brandenburg.

Zum Fliegenden Holländer – In a Dutch-style brick house, this spacious café, decorated with fine pale-coloured woodwork, has a balcony decorated with house plants and a fine bar with a copper draught-beer pump.

Potsdamer Bierstänge – *Friedrich-Ebert-Straße 88;* ☏ *(0331) 23 170.*
In a pretty neo-Baroque house, this large café looks out over the street through picture windows. There is a quiet room on the first floor for those in search of peace.

Shopping

Shops are open from 9am to 8pm on weekdays and 9am to 4pm on Saturdays. Most Turkish shops in Kreuzberg and Neukölln are open on Saturday afternoons and from 1pm to 5pm on Sundays.

DEPARTMENT STORES

Galeries Lafayette – *Friedrichstraße 207;* Ⓢ *and* Ⓤ *Friedrichstraße; open Monday to Friday from 9.30am to 8pm and on Saturdays from 9.30am to 4pm.*
In one of the most extraordinary buildings of new Berlin, spacious departments present the latest Paris styles in clothes and accessories. Not to be missed.

KaDeWe – *Tauentzienstraße 21 (Schöneberg);* Ⓤ *1, 2, 12, 15; Wittenbergplatz; open Monday to Friday from 9.30am to 8pm and on Saturdays from 9.30am to 4pm.*
Luxurious interior serving a chic and conservative clientele.

Peek & Cloppenburg – *Tauentzienstraße 19;* ☎ *(030) 21 29 00;* Ⓤ *1, 2, 12, 15 Wittenbergplatz.*
Six floors around a central glassed-in area offering excellent quality fashions. You will find yourself easily tempted as you wander through the well laid-out departments of this very fine shop.

> ### Fashion on the Ku'Damm
> **Mey & Edlich**, at No. 217,
> **Kookai, at No.** 205,
> **Selbach**, at No. 195-196,
> **Budapester Schuhe**, at No. 199,
> **Jean-Paul Gaultier**, at No. 192,
> **Jill Sander** (on the corner of Wielandstraße)
> and **Gianni Versace**, at No. 185,
> **Escada**, at No. 186,
> **Kramberg**, at No. 56-57,
> **Yves-St-Laurent** and **Mentius**, at No. 53-52,
> **Hermès**, at No. 43,
> and in nearby Fasanenstraße:
> **Louis Vuitton**, at No. 27,
> **Cartier**, at No. 28,
> **Rena Lange**, at No. 29,
> **Chanel**, at No. 34,
> **Gucci**, at No. 73.

Hertie bei Wertheim – *Kurfürstendamm 231 (Charlottenburg);* Ⓤ *9, 15 Kurfürstendamm.*
Traditional department stores, a short way from the Memorial Church.

Galeria Kaufhof – *Alexanderplatz 9 (Mitte);* Ⓢ + Ⓤ *Alexanderplatz.*
Well located on Alexanderplatz. Comparable to Selfridges.

Leffers – *Wilmersdorfer Straße 53-54a;* ☎ *(030) 32 78 50;* Ⓤ *2, 7, 12.*
A traditional department store in a main shopping street.

PRESENTS

Da Driade – *Rosenthaler Straße 40-41;* ☎ *(030) 283 28 [?];* Ⓢ *3, 5, 7, 9 Hackescher Markt; open from 10am to 8pm Monday to Friday, until 4pm on Saturdays.*
Glassware shop at the entrance to the *Hackesche Höfe*. Well situated and well lit.

Fachgeschäft für Meissener Porzellan – *Unter den Linden 39 and Kurfürstendamm 214;* ☎ *(030) 881 91 58.*
The taste, a little more precious than Berlin porcelain, tends rather towards ornaments with bucolic subjects; the statuettes are delightful.

J. und M. Fäßler – *Tauentzienstraße; basement of the Europa-Center (Charlottenburg)* ☎ *(030) 261 48 07;* Ⓢ + Ⓤ *Zoologischer Garten; open Monday to Saturday from 10am to 6pm.*
A shop selling souvenirs and gadgets; figurines of people and animals, wooden, glass and crystal items; dolls, puppets, decorated plates, etc.

Keramik Galerie – *Kollwitzstraße 53;* ☎ *(030) 441 95 91;* Ⓤ *2 Senefelderplatz; open from 11am to 6pm Monday to Friday, until 2pm on Saturdays.*
A light, pleasant shop in an old district. Modern ceramics are displayed upstairs and you can view the kiln in the basement.

Königliche Porzellan Manufactur (KPM) – *Kurfürstendamm 26a (Charlottenburg);* ☎ *and fax (030) 886 72 10;* Ⓤ *15 Uhlandstraße.*
A delight. This shop displays the traditional qualities of Berlin porcelain; exquisite flower paintings, elegant Neoclassical decoration. Porcelain lovers (those with a large enough bank account) can choose between *Rocaille Neuosier, Kurland* or the more modern *Arkadia* and *Urbino*.

Rosenthal – *Kurfürstendamm 226;* ☎ *(030) 885 63 40;* Ⓤ *9,* Ⓤ *15 Kurfürstendamm.*
Very elegant porcelain and tableware shop just near the Memorial Church.

In Potsdam:

Kunsttruhe – *Mittelstraße 22; ☎ (0331) 28 03 209.*
Articles for interior decoration and old furniture. A very attractive display just before Christmas.

Mandy Hartung – *Mittelstraße 12; ☎ (0331) 270 11 71.*
An elegant Wedgwood ware shop in a good location on the main street of the Dutch quarter of Potsdam.

BOOK SHOPS

Artificium – *Rosenthaler Straße 40-41 (Die Hackeschen Höfe, courtyard II); ☎ (030) 30 87 22 80; Ⓢ 3, 5, 7, 9, 75 Savignyplatz; open from 10am to 9pm Monday to Thursday, until 11pm on Fridays and 1pm to midnight on Saturdays.*
Art bookshop (with fine publications on Berlin) in a beautifully restored courtyard.

Buchhandlung Kiepert – *Knesebeckstraße 20, corner of Hardenbergstraße (Charlottenburg); Ⓢ 3, 5, 7, 9, 75 Savignyplatz or Ⓤ 2 Ernst-Reuter-Platz; ☎ (030) 311 00 90.*
Enormous general bookshop.

Bücherbogen am Savigny Platz – *Stadtbahnbögen 593 (Charlottenburg); ☎ (030) 312 19 32; Ⓢ 3, 5, 7, 9, 75 Savignyplatz.*
Bookshop specialising in town planning, architecture, interior decoration and photography. Dealing with the same themes, other *Bücherbogen* bookshops have been set up under the S-Bahn arches at Friedrichstrasse station and Kochstraße 18, in the *Tageszeitung* building (particularly specialising in town planning).

FOR YOUNG PEOPLE:

Comics

Comics & More – *Oranienstraße 22; ☎ (030) 615 88 10; Ⓤ 1, 8, 12, 15 Kottbusser Tor.*
Comics, comic strips, scale models.

Großer Unfug – *Zossener Straße 32 and 33; ☎ (030) 69 40 14 90; Ⓤ 7 Gneisenaustraße; open Monday to Friday from 10am to 6.30pm, from 11am to 2pm on Saturdays.*
Three shops for comic strips, comics and scale models. A small gallery (upstairs) displays Star Trek and Star Wars spaceship models.

Peter Skodzik – *Goltzstraße 40; ☎ (030) 216 51 59; Ⓤ 7 Eisenacher Straße.*
Comics and comic strips.

Fashion

Gore-Tex – *Oranienstraße 3; ☎ (030) 785 04 35; Ⓤ 1, 8, 12, 15 Kottbusser Tor.*
Punk fashions in an atmosphere typical of the district.

Downstairs – *Goebenstraße 5; ☎ (030) 215 92 11; Ⓤ 7 Kleistpark.*
Specialising in spray paint.

Groopie deluxe – *Goltzstraße 39; ☎ (030) 217 20 38; Ⓤ 7 Eisenacher Straße; open from Monday to Friday from 11am to 6pm, on Thursdays until 8pm and on Saturdays from 11am until 4pm.*
Groove clothes; large range of *flyers* available.

Planet – *Schlüterstraße 35; ☎ (030) 885 27 17; Ⓤ 15 Uhlandstraße; open Thursday to Friday until 8pm, 4pm on Saturdays.*
Techno fashion.

Music

Bote & Bock – *Hardenbergstraße; ☎ (030) 31 10 03 12.*

Guitar Shop – *Goethestraße 49; ☎ (030) 312 56 07; Ⓤ 7 Wilmersdorfer Straße; open from 10am to 2pm and from 3pm to 6pm Monday to Friday, from 10am to 2pm on Saturdays.*
Large selection of classical and electric guitars.

Tema "City Music" – *In the "Ku'damm-Karree", Kurfürstendamm 207-208; ☎ (030) 89 68 87; Ⓤ 9, 15 Kurfürstendamm.*
Large CD and video department, but more interesting for Hi-Fi, audiovisual and photographic equipment.

Wom ("World of Music") – *Ausgsburger Straße 36-42 (behind the "Hertie" shop); ☎ (030) 885 72 40; Ⓤ 9, 15 Kurfürstendamm.*
Large department of contemporary music, from acid-jazz to techno; small classical department.

Christmas markets

A special tradition in Germany: delicacies, mulled wine, arts and crafts are sold in booths which sometimes mingle with fairground market stalls. The markets open in November and normally close just before Christmas. The main *Weihnachstmärkte* are to be found:

– Around the **Kaiser-Wilhem-Gedächtniskirche (Memorial Church)** (Breitscheidplatz); **S** + **U** *Zoologischer Garten* or **U** *15 Kurfürstendamm*.

– In Prenzlauer Berg, next to the **Planetarium Zeiss**; **S** *8, 10 Prenzlauer Allee*.

– On the **Schloßplatz**; **BUS** *100, Lustgarten*.

– **Opernpalais**, on the Unter den Linden avenue; **BUS** *100, Deutsche Staatsoper*.

– In the old town of **Spandau**; **U** *7 Rathaus Spandau*.

– On **Richardplatz** in Neukölln (Rixdorfer Weihnachtsmarkt); **S** *45* + **U** *7 Neukölln* or **U** *7 Karl-Marx-Straße*.

– Along the **Brandenburger Straße/Friedrich-Engel-Straße** and *Luisenplatz* in Potsdam; **S** *3, 7 Potsdam-Stadt*.

SHOPPING FOR CHILDREN

KaDeWe – *Tauentzienstraße 21 (Schöneberg); Wittenbergplatz (Charlottenburg);* **U** *1, 2, 12, 15 Wittenbergplatz.*
A very fine toy department, especially for cuddly toys and electronic games.

Klein-Holz – *Stuttgarter Platz 21 (Charlottenburg);* ☏ *(030) 323 86 81;* **S** *3, 5, 6, 9, 75 Charlottenburg.*
Part of a chain of stores; beautiful wooden toys for very small children.

Hennes & Mauritz – *Kurfürstendamm 234 (Charlottenburg);* **U** *9, 15 Kurfürstendamm.*
Classic fashion for children.

Miches Bahnhof – *Nürnberger Straße 21 (Schöneberg);* ☏ *(030) 218 66 11;* **U** *1 Augsburger Straße; open in the afternoon.*
Scale models of cars and trains.

Vom Winde Verweht – *Eisenacherstraße 81 (Schöneberg);* ☏ *(030) 784 77 69;* **U** *7 Eisenacher Straße.*
Kites for sale in every price range.

A FEW UNUSUAL SHOPS:

Hobbyshop – *Goltzstraße 37;* ☏ *(030) 216 55 87 or 215 48 89;* **U** *7 Eisenacher Straße.*
Three shops to satisfy the most demanding creative souls and to exhaust the possibilities of what you can build and make with your hands; there is a fantastic selection to provide you with a host of ideas.

Berliner Zinnfiguren – *Knesebeckstraße 88;* ☏ *(030) 313 08 02;* **S** *3, 5, 7, 9, 75 Savignyplatz; open from 10am to 6pm Monday to Friday, from 10am to 1pm on Saturdays.*
A vast selection of lead soldiers, from Roman legionnaires to the armies of Frederick II. Painted figures are displayed in the window of this little shop which has a good department on army books.

Metissage – *Dresdner Straße 119;* ☏ *(030) 615 10 95;* **U** *1, 8, 12, 15 Kottbusser Tor; open from 11am to 6pm Monday to Friday, from 10am to 2pm on Saturdays.*
All the beads and accessories needed to make the necklace of your choice.

Wiedenhoff – *Europa Center (basement level);* ☏ *(030) 261 27 30;* **U** *9, 15 Kurfürstendamm.*
Weapons shop, but also fine Solingen knives.

ANTIQUES

Antique dealers are concentrated in Eisenacher Straße, Kalckreuthstraße and Keithstraße as well as in Fasanenstraße; close to the Charlottenburg castle, Bleibtreustraße, Mommsenstraße, Schlüterstraße and Suarezstraße.

FLEA MARKETS

Antik- & Flohmarkt Mitte – *Bahnhof Friedrichstraße. S-Bahnbögen 190-203 (Mitte);* **S** + **U** *Friedrichstraße; open daily from 11am to 6pm except for Tuesdays.*

Berliner Kunst- und Nostalgie-markt – *Am Kupfergraben;* Ⓢ + Ⓤ *Friedrichstraße.* Opposite the Pergamonmuseum and the New Museum.

Flohmarkt Am Fehrbelliner Platz – *Fehrbelliner Platz (Wilmersdorf);* Ⓤ *1, 7 Fehrbelliner Platz; open Saturdays and Sundays from 8am to 4pm.*

Großer Berliner Trödel- und Kunstmarkt – *Straße des 17. Juni (Charlottenburg);* Ⓤ *2 Ernst-Reuter-Platz;* Ⓢ *3, 5, 6, 9, 75 Tiergarten open Saturdays and Sundays from 8am to 3pm.*

Kunst & Trödelmarkt – *Schönhauser Allee 36/38;* Ⓤ *2 Eberswalder Straße.*

Trödel-Flohmarkt Gustav-Meyer-Allee-Brunnenstraße – *Park Humboldthain (Wedding);* Ⓤ *8 Voltastraße et Gesundbrunnen; open Saturdays and Sundays from 8am to 4pm.*

In Potsdam:

Potsdamer Kunstmarkt – *Lindenstraße 53-56.*

GALLERIES

There are more than 300 of these in Berlin, mainly located around Savignyplatz and **Fasanenstraße** (Charlottenburg), not far from the Ku'damm, around the **Pariser Straße** (Wilmersdorf), between Nollendorfplatz and Winterfeldplatz (Schöneberg), around **Chamissoplatz** (West Kreuzberg), between Oranienstraße, Oranienplatz and Mariannenplatz (East Kreuzberg), in the old "**Scheunenviertel**" (Barn district), between Oranienburger **Straße** and Rosa-Luxemburg-Platz (Mitte), and in Prenzlauer Berg (along and around the **Schönhauser Allee**). Many cafés exhibit the work of local artists. For a list of the main galleries and their locations, consult the fortnightly *Berliner Kunstkalender* and the *Berliner Galerien* leaflet, which you will find in cafés everywhere.

Kupfergraben flea market

Fine food

Berlin cooking is simple and nourishing. It is served with a selection of vegetables: lettuce, sauerkraut or red cabbage and boiled potatoes. Cucumbers à la Spree forest (Spreewald), small Teltow beetroots *(Rübchen)*, and Werder cherries are all part of the Berlin culinary repertoire. Gherkins *(saure Gurken)* are also very popular.

Local specialities – Some restaurants offer authentic Berlin cuisine. Meat is included in all meals in the form of sausage, pork or cold meatballs *(Frikadellen)*. Pork is cooked in a number of ways: spare ribs *(Karbonade)* with a selection of vegetables, *Schweinekamm* Berlin-style, belly of pork with red cabbage and the famous **Eisbein**, knuckle of salt pork served with sauerkraut and puréed peas. Black pudding is known as *Frische Wurst*; it is served with fresh liver sausage *(Leberwurst)*, boiled pork and kidney, to form the *Berliner Schlachtplatte*.

The specialities *Eisbein* and *Wurstplatte*

Oxtail *(Ochsenschwanz)* is served with small Teltow beetroots *(Rübchen)*, and brisket with horseradish. Goose giblets *(Gänseklein grün)* and preserved goose *(Gänsepökel-keule)* are both popular.
Fish, which used to come from the Havel and the lakes around Berlin, now comes from further afield. Eels *(Aal grün)* and pike *(Hecht grün)* are served with a salad of cucumber à la Spree forest (**Spreewald**), grilled pike with a streaky bacon salad *(Brathecht mit Specksalat)*, carp (which come from the lakes around Peitz, near to Cottbus), roach, perch in beer, tench in dill sauce *(Schleie in Dillsoße)*, pikeperch from the Havel and, crayfish à la Berlinoise. Herrings *(Rollmöpse)* are served fried.

International cuisine – Eating in Berlin often means a snack at lunchtime or, to be honest, at any time of day, from one of the vans that park in the squares and in the busy streets. The selection of sausages is wide; *Bockwurst* (a short thick sausage, cooked in water), *Wiener Wurst* (a long sausage cooked in water), *Bratwurst* (grilled), *Currywurst* (served with a curry-ketchup mixture), *Frankfurter Würstchen* (small sausage "from Frankfurt"). All are eaten with a bread roll *(Semmel)* or chips. Many stalls also serve Vietnamese and Turkish food *(see below)*.
Meat lovers can get a good hamburger in the American-style restaurants, which are plentiful in Wilmersdorf, between Ludwigkirchplatz and Olivaer Platz, or in Mexican canteens. The best meat is served in the Argentinian grillrooms. There are also numerous Greek, Yugoslav and Chinese restaurants (well established in the east).
Berlin's pâtisserie comes from other regions of Germany. You can get a slice of cake practically anywhere, frequently cheap, shortcrust pastry covered with sugarlumps, flour and butter *(Streuselkuchen)* or with fruit *(Himbeerschnitte*, with raspberries; *Erdbeerschnitte*, with strawberries, etc.). Also popular is the log-shaped roll *(Baumkuchen)*, tarts in rich shortcrust pastry *(Sandtorte)*, small shortbread biscuits *(Spritzkuchen)* from Eberswalde, cream puffs *(Windbeutel)*, and fritters (**Berliner Pfannkuchen**), which are eaten throughout Germany on New Year's Eve and at Carnival.

SPECIALITIES

KaDeWe – *Wittenbergplatz (Schöneberg)*; ⓤ *1, 2, 12, 15 Wittenbergplatz.*
The largest catering department in continental Europe: a delight for gourmets, as the produce is of excellent quality. A selection of the best German and European special-ities. You can try a dish, sandwiches or cakes here, or eat your fill (if you have a well-lined wallet!) at the cafeteria on the top floor beneath the glass roof of the winter garden, which provides a view of west Berlin.

Berliner Weiße

In the Middle Ages, beer was made in the villages around Berlin-Cölln: Bernau (which had 143 breweries), Potsdam, and, Köpenick, whose speciality was wheat beer, the **Berliner Weiße**, drunk from a wide glass, with or without the addition *(Schuß)* of raspberry juice *(rot*: red) or woodruff *(Waldmeister*; *grün*, green). A glass of beer with a schnapps (grain brandy) is called *Strippe*.

Berlin white beers with raspberry or woodruff

Henkelm./ARCHIV

Leysieffer – *Kurfürstendamm 218 (Charlottenburg)*; Ⓤ *15 Uhlandstraße.*
A confectioner since 1809; in a good location.

Kaaswinkel – *Dunckerstraße 3;* ☎ *(030) 440 97 46;* Ⓤ *2 Eberswalder Straße.*
Fat Dutch cheeses sit on the shelves of this little shop which also sells produce from France and Allgäu (Bavaria).

The food department of the KaDeWe

Ph. Gajic/MICHELIN

A WEEKEND IN BERLIN

Berlin is a greatly spread out city (45km - 28 miles from east to west and 38km - 24 miles from north to south) and visitors don't just wander as they do in other more tightly compact European capitals such as London, Paris, Rome or Vienna.

Berlin is best explored district by district. This guide describes the districts in alphabetical order.

On arriving in Berlin it is a good idea to go to the nearest underground (U-Bahn) or railway (S-Bahn) station and buy a travel pass valid for 1, 2, 3 or 4 days on all public transport.

Two suggestions for walks in central Berlin:

Use the plan of the historic centre on pages 248-249

The first walk takes you from Brandenburger Tor to Alexanderplatz (about 6km - 4 miles including the detours) via the famous avenue Unter den Linden. Make a slight detour to see the handsome square, Gendarmenmarkt, before returning to Unter den Linden near Neue Wache and Zeughaus. If time is tight when crossing Museumsinsel, the Pergamonmuseum is a must. Turn right onto Spandauer Damm to reach Nikolaiviertel and discover the maze of narrow cobbled streets. Then make for the vast expanse of Alexanderplatz beyond the television tower, Fernsehturm.

The second walk takes in Friedrichstraße and its vicinity. The Friedrichstraße station is a good starting point. The northern part of this well-known thoroughfare is described under the district of Charité.

For the southern part follow the itinerary described under the heading Friedrichstraße. Finish with Martin Gropius Bau which is described under Potsdamer Platz.

Another alternative is to rent a bicycle in the Europa-Center. Cycle past that well-known landmark the truncated tower of Kaiser-Wilhelm-Gedächtnis-kirche to reach the Zoological Gardens, then continue across Tiergarten to reach Kulturforum. With woodland, animals, prestigious museums, including the new Gemäldesammlung, this itinerary has something for everyone.

CITY TOURS

There are many agencies offering bus and boat trips, or the two combined, throughout the city and towards Potsdam. You can take a trip in a horse-drawn carriage in the eastern part of Berlin, from **Pariser Platz** in front of the Brandenburg Gate.

BBS Berliner Bären Stadtrundfahrten ☏ (030) 214 87 90/247 58 70. Daily departures (trips take 1hr 30mins, 3hrs, 3hrs 30mins) in front of the Memorial Church, on the corner of Rankestraße and Kurfürstendamm at 10am, 11am, 12 noon, 12.30pm (Potsdam), 12.45pm, 2pm, 2.30pm, 4.30pm depending on the tour, and on Alexanderplatz, opposite the Forum Hotel at 10am, 11am, 11.45am, 1.30pm depending on the tour. DM 25.- to DM 39.- (DM 58.- for Potsdam).

Zille-Tour – Departure (1hr 20mins) on Breitscheidplatz, opposite the Memorial Church, every hour from 11am to 4pm; DM 25.- (DM 15.- for children).

Berolina-Stadtrundfahrt Meinekestraße 3. ☏ (030) 882 20 91, fax (030) 882 41 28. Leaves from Kurfürstendamm 220, on the corner of Meinekestraße: DM 25.- to DM 45.- (DM 54.- for Potsdam).

BVB-Stadtrundfahrt. ☏ (030) 885 98 80, fax (030) 881 35 08. Leaves from Kurfürstendamm 225, opposite the Kranzler Café. Special interest tours as well as traditional city tours; DM 25.- to DM 45.- (DM 45.- for Potsdam).

Severin & Kühn – Berliner Stadtrundfahrt, Kurfürstendamm 216, ☏ (030) 883 10 15. Leaves every day at 10.30am and 4.30pm in front of the agency, on the corner of Fasanenstraße; DM 39.- to DM 45.- (DM 54.- for Potsdam).

Tempelhofer Reisen – ☏ (030) 752 30 61/751 70 35. Leaves from Kurfürstendamm, on the corner of Joachimstaler Straße (Charlottenburg), Schloßstraße (on Bierpinsel, Steglitz), Unter den Linden (opposite the Humboldt University), DM 25.- to DM 40.- (tour combined with a boat trip).

Open air pipelines

Gateway and main courtyard of Charlottenburg Castle

Visiting Berlin

ALEXANDERPLATZ★

This vast square planned during the 60s was the heart of the socialist city. It opens out towards the southeast and is lined with modern buildings and towers. Its symbol is the **universal clock "Urania"**, which tells the time of day in the main cities of the world. The *Fountain of Friendship between Peoples* has replaced the *Berolina* statue, an allegory of the town which was for a long time the symbol of the square. This kind of town planning which uses the tower of the **Forum-Hotel Berlin** as its focal point and provides an opening to the south, in front of the **Teacher's House** (Haus des Lehrers, **A**), adorned with a mosaic inspired by the communist ideology, is not devoid of scope. As an important junction and commercial centre, the square always had a lively atmosphere and remains to this day the centre of the eastern part of town. Just as they do next to the Memorial Church, musicians and buskers perform in front of a mixed crowd including many punks who gather inside the S-Bahn station.

The Universal Clock "Urania"

HISTORICAL NOTES

Humble beginnings – A regular cattle and wool market took place in front of the former St-George's gate which became "Royal" (Königstor) as did the bridge spanning the moat (Königsbrücke) in 1701, when the very first king of Prussia, Frederick I, triumphantly returned from his coronation in Königsberg to his own capital in Brandenburg. The square was later named after Tsar Alexander I when he visited Berlin in November 1805, in order to seal an alliance against France with the king of Prussia.

Close to the "Barn District" – Until World War II, **Alexanderplatz** stood on the border between the official and pompous part of Berlin, full of museums and public buildings, and the somewhat shady world of the "Barn District" lying behind the scenes, an area where deals of all kinds took place and where immigrants from East European countries ended up, often stricken with poverty. This is the setting that the novelist **Alfred Döblin** chose for the characters and background noises of his *Berlin Alexanderplatz*.

In order to clear the district and make way for the public transport network, a competition was organised at the end of the 20s for the best town planning project. The most outstanding architects of the Weimar period took part and the first prize went to Alfons Anker and the Luckhardt brothers; however, the department in charge of rebuilding the square finally chose the plans submitted by **Peter Behrens**, the architect behind the AEG factories, who had come second in the competition. Work on the project began but, owing to the economic crisis, the funds allocated to it were reduced which in turn slowed the work down. The **Alexanderhaus** (to the south, **B**) and **Berolina building** (to the north, **C**) were eventually completed; their windows divided into squares denote the predilection of Berlin's New Objectivity architects for this shape which is also favoured by the new plans drawn up for Friedrichstraße and Alexanderplatz. Considerably damaged during the war, the two buildings have been restored and now house a banking group.

IN AND AROUND THE SQUARE

★Fernsehturm ⊘ – **Ⓢ** + **Ⓤ** *Alexanderplatz; No 100 Spandauer Straße* – Erected between 1965 and 1969, the 365m-high tower was the pride of the East Berlin authorities. The lifts are small, which explains the long queue. From the top, the exceptional **view★★★** extends across the Berlin conurbation with its historic centre, along the axis of Unter den Linden, whose monuments, as well as those of Museums Island, look like toys. The Brandenburg gate, which marked the boundary between East and West Berlin, appears to be quite close. In spite of large-scale wartime destruction, many districts have retained their specific character: the middle-class western and southwestern areas (the Europa-Center building, crowned with the Mercedes emblem, is the landmark of the Kurfürstendamm district), Kreuzberg, Prenzlauer Berg. The surface area occupied by green open spaces is impressive: Friedrichshain and Tiergarten parks, and Grunewald Forest. Tempelhof Airport can be seen to the south, and to the southeast the straight line of Karl-Marx-Allee and the industrialised Spree River flowing towards Lichtenberg and Neukölln.

There is also a good view of the "red town hall", the *Stadthaus* tower and the twin spires of St Nicholas's Church situated in the western corner, at the foot of the Television Tower.

Marienkirche ⊘ – **Ⓢ** + **Ⓤ** *Alexanderplatz or No 100,* 🚌 *Spandauer Straße* – Its steeple offers a striking contrast to the futuristic outline of the Television tower. The vaulted Gothic interior is plain and well-lit. The main works of art are the organ, the tomb of Marshall von Sparr and above all the **pulpit★** (1703), carved by Andreas Schlüter. The church was built of brick *c*1270, during a period of economic prosperity, and was one of the first examples of the Brandenburg Gothic style. It was only after the fire of 1380 that it became a hall church with three naves. It used to house the

cloth-manufacturers' altar, the other guilds having a preference for St Nicholas *(see NIKOLAIVIERTEL).* Behind the church which, in medieval times, was closely surrounded by houses, lay a shady district including a tax-paying brothel.

Heiliggeistkapelle (C¹) – *Spandauer Straße 1: No 100* 🚌 *Spandauer Straße.* This Gothic brick chapel is all that remains of the Holy Spirit Hospital *(Heiliggeistspital),* one of the three almshouses in Berlin; it was built in the 13C, near the Spandau gate, within the city, whereas the other two were built outside. In 1905-6, the chapel was incorporated into the buildings of the School of Commerce and is now used as a students' canteen.

Neptunbrunnen – This pompous neo-Baroque fountain, built by **Reinhold Begas** (1831-1911), used to stand in the Castle square, south of the palace of the kings of Prussia *(see SCHLOSSPLATZ).* It appears with children climbing on it, in the ruined setting of Rosselini's film, *Germania, Year Zero.* It is surrounded by a pleasant flower garden.

Berlin, a city of contrasts:
St Mary's Church and the Television Tower

ALEXANDERPLATZ

★Rotes Rathaus – *No 100* 🚌 *Spandauer Straße.*
The previous town hall was built in 1300 on the same site, halfway between Molkenmarkt *(see NIKOLAIVIERTEL)* and Neumarkt (New Market) which dates from 1250. The present building, erected between 1861 and 1869, is a fine specimen of the neo-Romanesque style and houses the Berlin senate. It has been nicknamed the "red town hall" because it is built of red brick. It represents the eclectic taste prevalent during the 19C in the field of architecture. Hollowed-out buttresses give a certain elegance to the outline of the belfry (97m) which is reminiscent of Giotto's campanile surmounting the cathedral in Florence. A frieze made up of thirty-six terracotta panels placed above the ground floor, relates the history of Berlin from the origins until the foundation of the Empire by Bismarck. The main doorway is also richly adorned with terracotta decorations.

Marx-Engels-Forum – Bronze statues, steel and marble stelae in honour of the founders of communism.

IN THE VICINITY

See **FRIEDRICHSHAIN, NIKOLAIVIERTEL★, PRENZLAUER BERG★★.**

CHARITÉ★

Mitte, Tiergarten
See map of Berlin Mitte p. 248-249 **NOXY**

Lying beyond Friedrichstraße, one of Berlin's main shopping streets, the district overlooked by the tower of the **Charité Hospital**, is today calm and peaceful. However, it enjoys a lively nightlife, for several streets offer a choice of shows and varied entertainment (theatres, music-halls, nightclubs). It is by no means certain that this provincial, slightly old-fashioned charm will survive. The district is very well situated in the centre of Berlin, a stone's throw from the future government district and from Lehrter Central Station.

HISTORICAL NOTES

From soldiers to medical students – During the reign of Frederick II, a large building, named **Invalidenhaus**, was set aside for the war-wounded. Soldiers occupied nearby barracks and trained on special ground close to vineyards, barns and windmills. The **Friedrich-Wilhelm-Stadt** suburb developed during the Biedermeier period (1830-1840). Its main artery is **Luisenstraße**, linked by a bridge to the suburb of Dorotheenstadt; Friedrichstraße has been extended as far as the Oranienburger gate making it the longest street in town.

"Feuerland" – This gate marks the birthplace of Berlin industry. The royal ironworks were the first to settle there, soon followed by Franz Egells's mechanical engineering factory and privately owned ironworks, the first of their kind. Noisy and full of smoke owing to the factories it attracted, the whole district was nicknamed "**Feuerland**". After **August Borsig**'s railway engine factory and **August Pflug**'s railway carriage factory settled there, the area became Germany's main rail engineering centre.

The "railway engine king" – A shy young man named **August Borsig**, trained as a carpenter, began working in the Egells factory in 1825. Thirteen years later, he opened the first railway engine works in Germany. His engines were faster than their English counterparts so that 120 engines came out of his factory during the first five years; more than half the railway engines used all over Prussia came from the Borsig works. He also built a machine which activated the Sans-Souci fountains and erected an iron bridge in Potsdam. In 1847, the works moved to Moabit into Germany's largest and most modern factory. The factory owner had an imposing house built for himself within botanical gardens designed by Lenné *(see TEGEL)*. His son Albert took over from him in 1854 and continued in his footsteps.

WALKING UP FRIEDRICHSTRASSE

Starting from Friedrichstraße station, go north along Friedrichstraße.

The first façade you see after the S-Bahn bridge is that of the **Admiralspalast**, decorated with *Jugendstil* reliefs. The SED *(Sozialistische Einheitspartei Deutschland)*, sole political party of the German Democratic Republic, was founded there on 21 April 1946, after a vote which sealed the union between the Social Democrats and the Communists from the Soviet sector. The *Metropol-Theater* (**T°**), which stages operettas and music-halls, is in the courtyard.

Weidendammer Brücke – The first bridge was built in 1685. The present one is decorated with lamp-posts and cast-iron imperial eagles. From the bridge, the view extends over a highly contrasting landscape typical of Berlin: the Bode museum, the Television Tower and Friedrichstraße station.

Schiffbauerdamm – Shipbuilders *(Schiffbau)* were allowed to settle there in 1738. *Go west along the Spree River until you reach Bertolt-Brecht-Platz.*

Since its foundation in 1949, the **Berliner Ensemble** or "**BE**" (**T**[10]) has been carrying on with the Brecht tradition since its foundation in 1949 by performing *Mother Courage (Mutter Courage)*. There is a vacant lot alongside it. Before World War II, the **Friedrichstadtpalast** stood there: it was a theatre with striking decorations imitating stalactites by Hans Poelzig, in which directors Max Reinhardt and Erwin Piscator staged some highly original productions.

Friedrichstraße – The new **Friedrichstadtpalast** (**T**[11]), a music-hall theatre with a seating capacity of 2 000 spectators, plated with concrete mouldings, was built in the so-called "improved" style, a characteristic feature of the architecture of the eighties in the German Democratic Republic. It is possible to get to the wasteland which extends behind the demolished Tacheles building *(see ORANIENBURGER-STRASSE and ON THE TOWN, the Berlin Scene)*.

U 6 Oranienburger Tor (underground station) – A painted wall on the corner of Friedrichstraße and Wilhelm-Pieck-Straße depicts the former **Oranienburger Gate**. It was here, in front of the gate, where a water-mill on the Panke River once stood, that the **Royal Ironworks** were founded in 1805; the State thus showed its intention to take an active part in the industrialisation of Prussia. During the wars of liberation, the works produced gunstocks, cannon-balls and 5 041 iron crosses. It was a model factory where technicians, craftsmen and artists such as Schadow and Schinkel worked together (many works decorating Schinkel's buildings were made there). However, competition from private ironworks forced it to close down in 1874. The view extends towards the new synagogue and the Television tower.

Chausseestraße – The street looks somewhat dull, but many celebrities lived or worked there: Brecht, Borsig, Liebnecht and, more recently, **Wolf Biermann**, a poet from the German Democratic Republic. The heaquarters of Borsig Industries at No 13 is in neo-Renaissance style.
Further up, on the left-hand pavement, a small green patch has replaced the building (located at No 121 Chausseestraße) destroyed during World War II *(Stela)*, where the lawyer **Karl Liebknecht** had his practice.

Dorotheenstädtischer und Französischer Friedhof (**K**[3]) – The Dorotheenstädtische Friedhof cemetery *Chausseestraße 126* which was opened in 1762 is one of Berlin's cemeteries for the famous. Very many artists (Schinkel, Schadow, Rauch), philosophers (Hegel, Fichte), authors (Berthold Brecht, Anna Seghers, Heinrich Mann, Arnold Zweig), composers (Eisler, Dessau) and many other personalities (August Borsig) are buried here. The adjacent Französischer Friedhof cemetery *Chausseestraße 127* was laid out in 1780 for the Berlin Huguenot community. The Classical antique style marble tomb for the Prussian princes' tutor Friedrich Ançillon, designed by Schinkel in 1840, is particularly noteworthy.

Brecht-Weigel-Gedenkstätte ⊙ – *Chausseestr. 15*
The front building houses the Brecht archives, a place for literary discussion, and a bookshop *(Buchhandlung Am Brecht-Haus)*. *Go to the end of the courtyard, where there is a pleasant café and go up to the first floor on the right.* The library, the living-room and the bedroom are relatively austere, light and airy; Chinese copperplate writing and portraits of Confucius hang on the walls. Helene's apartment, situated on the ground floor, level with the garden, contains more furniture and objects; blue and white earthenware crockery decorates the kitchen.

ALONG INVALIDENSTRASSE
Turn westwards along Invalidenstraße.

★**Museum für Naturkunde** ⊙ – **U** 6 *Zinnowitzer Straße. The ground floor is the only part open to the public.*
Erected between 1883 and 1889, the museum forms part of a group of neo-Renaissance buildings inaugurated by William II and dedicated to scientific research (Institute of Biology, which is under the control of the Berlin Technical University, and the Institute of Geology, which is to become the Ministry of Transport). The central hall, covered with a glass roof, houses the reconstructed skeletons of a **brachiosaurus** and a **diplodocus**. These give an excellent idea of the impressive size of these plant-eating dinosaurs. The head of the *brachiosaurus* is displayed in a small glass cabinet in front of the skeleton. It is actually quite large whereas it appears rather small perched on top of the animal's long neck. On the walls are displayed several fine specimens of aquatic reptiles as well as the reproduction of the skeleton of *archaeopteryx*, a flying reptile, a good example of genetic mutation. The theory of evolution leads to the classification of species, explained by means of many taxidermied animals, a reconstruction of a coral reef and excellent dioramas illustrating

Skeleton of a brachiosaurus

European fauna. An interesting section deals with taxidermy and the art of making reproductions: the models representing enlarged insects seem very real (mosquito, spider...). The museum also houses a collection of minerals.

Invalidenfriedhof – Part of the cemetery, which was laid out in 1748, fell victim when the Berlin Wall was built, so that very many noteworthy memorials were destroyed and tombs seriously damaged. The monumental tomb of the Prussian **General von Scharnhorst** (1755-1813) was completed in 1834 , based on a design by Schinkel. The reliefs are the work of Friedrich Tieck and the lion was cast in bronze from a design by Christian Daniel Rauch.

Sandkrugbrücke – This bridge marked the boundary between East and West Berlin. Just before reaching the bridge, the former hospital (1910) of the East German authorities can be seen; it is to become the headquarters of the Department of Trade and Industry.

★★ **Hamburger Bahnhof** – Museum für Gegenwart Berlin – Ⓢ *3, 5, 7, 9, 75 Lehrter Stadtbahnhof* – *SEE MOABIT.*

★**CHARITÉ**

Walk back towards Luisenstraße.

The tower of the surgical wing of the **Charité Hospital**, a prestigious building, erected between 1976 and 1982 and designed to accommodate 30 000 patients a year, overlooks **Luisenstraße**.

Akademie der Künste – *Luisenstraße 60.*
It houses temporary exhibitions.

Tierarzneischule (T¹²) – *Luisenstraße 56.*
Its Neoclassical style is similar to that of the New Stüler Museum *(see MUSEUMS-INSEL)*. The passageway situated to the left of the school leads to a garden in the middle of which stands an elegant **anatomy amphitheatre★** *(Altes Anatomiegebäude)* built by Langhans at the end of the 18C.

★**Schumannstraße** – Named after the soap-manufacturer, the street is lined with buildings in the *Biedermeier* style, painted with light colours; it leads to the **Deutsches Theater** *(at No 13, T¹³)* and to the **Kammerspiele (T¹⁴)**, two famous theatres standing side by side in a small square off the street. The former, which opened in 1883, began by staging Offenbach operettas, then competed with the Schauspielhaus *(see GENDARMENMARKT)* in presenting new plays by modern authors, in particular Ibsen and Strindberg. The Viennese director **Max Reinhardt** made a successful career here in the twenties and radically transformed the art of stage-setting with one guiding principle only: "realism at all costs".

Retrace your steps. The main entrance of the Charité Hospital centre is situated on the corner of Luisenstraße and Schumannstraße.

★**Charité** – Charité was founded when a lazaret (*Pesthaus*), outside the city walls in front of the Spandau gate was joined to the *Collegium medico-Chirurgicum* in 1710. The garrison lazaret (*Garnisonslazarett*) became a general hospital in 1726. At the beginning of the 19C, there were so many patients that

> ### Scandinavian artists
> During the Belle Époque period, Scandinavian writers were in fashion. Nordic artists met in Zum Schwarzen Ferkel Café. From 1890 onwards, the Norwegians **Ibsen** and **Edvard Munch** were among them. The Swedish playwright **August Strindberg** (who died in 1912) was considered immoral and outrageous; he had something in common with the Expressionists whose writings searched deeply into the human soul. His works were performed with success after World War I, at a time when German society found itself in complete disarray. After 1923-24, Strindberg and Expressionism were set aside and Ibsen made a comeback.

treatment could only be very basic, to the point that Frederick-William III went all the way to Paris to see a dentist. Schleiermacher, a native of Silesia who preached at Charité, attracted attention by advising unhappy wives to get a divorce. However, in 1810 Charité became an annex of the university and gained a reputation as a research centre. All the famous members of the medical profession practised there: Christoph Wilhelm Hufeland, Queen Louise's personal physician, Rudolf Virchow, Robert Koch and Ferdinand Sauerbruch, who specialised in chest surgery.

A walk among the **pavilions**★ topped with brick neo-Gothic gables, each dealing with its own speciality (there is a back view of it from the S-Bahn, between Lehrter Stadtbahnhof and Friedrichstraße), is interesting. This division of the hospital into several pavilions was initiated at the Charité and subsequently applied to R. Virchow's Hospital (*see WEDDING*).

Once through the entrance, continue straight on until you reach the last rectangular pavilion, on the left beyond the hothouse.

The **Institute of Pathology** or **"Rudolf-Virchow-Haus"** (**M**[16]), houses a collection (*on the ground-floor, to the right beyond the doorman*) of deformed skeletons, diseased organs and abnormal foetuses kept in formalin.

Karlplatz – Handicraft House (*Karlplatz 7*), situated behind Rudolf-Virchow's-Denkmal memorial, has interesting wrought-iron gates.

Reichstagsufer – *Take Marschallbrücke across the Spree River.*

An imposing brick building, marked with bullet holes, is situated on the corner of Bunsenstraße and Clara-Zetkin-Straße along the north pavement; it houses the Institute of Pharmacology and Toxicology, linked to Charité. A little further on, in the same building, the small **Robert-Koch Museum** (**M**[17]) is housed inside the Institute of Microbiology and Hygiene, next to the amphitheatre where, in 1882, the scientist revealed his discovery of the bacilli causing tuberculosis (one year later, he identified the cholera bacillus).

IN THE VICINITY

See **FRIEDRICHSTRASSE★, MOABIT★, ORANIENBURGER STRASSE★★, REICHSTAG★, UNTER DEN LINDEN★★, WEDDING★.**

Schloß und Museumsquartier CHARLOTTENBURG★★★

Charlottenburg

See map of Berlin Town Centre, **2**, **EFTU**

Charlottenburg Castle, together with the museums housed within it or next to it, is one of the main sights of Berlin. Some museums are due to be refurbished during the next few years, but the castle itself, including its Baroque and Rococo apartments and park, offers the opportunity of a very pleasant outing. Just like Potsdam, which later on also became the royal summer residence, the Charlottenburg estate is a blend of various influences: French-style decoration, Dutch gardens, a park landscaped in the English fashion with several features borrowed from Antiquity. The result is highly original but retains a human dimension which accounts for its appeal. The small town of Charlottenburg, founded in the 18C, has become a quiet residential district.

Portrait of Sophie-Charlotte by Friedrich Wilhelm Weldemann (1705)

J.P. Anders/SCHLOSS CHARLOTTENBURG - PREUSSISCHER KULTURBESITZ.

HISTORICAL NOTES

The Elector Frederick III (who became Frederick I of Prussia) was very fond of luxury pleasure boats. He gave his wife **Sophie-Charlotte** a plot of land situated near the village of **Lutzow** or **Lietze**, inside a meander of the Spree and therefore easily accessible overland or along the river, so that she could have a summer residence built. The Dutch architect **Johann-Arnold Nehring** designed it and supervised the construction during the five years it lasted.

A cultured princess – Second wife of Frederick III, **Sophie-Charlotte** (1668-1705) was an intelligent woman born into the House of Hanover. Her brother became George I of Great Britain. Her mastery of the harpsichord was very much admired in Versailles. Passionately fond of chamber music, she hired musicians and organised performances inside a small opera house. She had a particular inclination for Italian music but she did not stop there; she also welcomed at her court various artists and scientists, among them the philosopher **Gottfried Wilhelm Leibniz** (1646-1716) who had his own apartment in Lutzenburg. As a result of the royal couple's support and of the simultaneous massive arrival of French Huguenots who contributed to the cultural development of Berlin, the **Academy of Arts** was founded with Andreas Schlüter as its first director, together with the **Academy of Sciences** presided by Leibniz. The latter, which took its London and Paris counterparts as its models, was divided into three sections: mathematics and physics; German language, with the aim of compiling a dictionary; and literature and history, in particular German history. For the first time Berlin could deserve the title of the "Athens of the Spree".

From Lutzenburg to Charlottenburg – **Lutzenburg Castle** was not very large. In 1701, when the Elector became king of Prussia, the castle proved to be too small to be the official residence of a monarch. The Swedish architect **Friedrich Eosander**, also called **Göthe** (1669-1729), flanked the main building with two wings which formed the main courtyard and another two wings on the garden side but, above all, he erected the dome which became the emblem of the castle. When Sophie-Charlotte died at the age of 37, King Frederick I ordered that the castle should be renamed "Charlottenburg". An orangery was also built on the west side of the façade, but no counterpart was added on the east side. The construction of the castle was suddenly interrupted in 1713 because the King-Sergeant preferred his army to his buildings. It is only during the reign of Frederick II, who lived for a long time in Charlottenburg, that **Wenzeslaus von Knobelsdorff** (1699-1753) built the **"new wing"**, containing several magnificent Rococo rooms, thus restoring the symmetry of the façade. Frederick II supervised the building from afar during the conquest of Silesia. He wrote to his architect: "I should like each part of the columns in Charlottenburg to be the subject of a four-page description. That would give me much pleasure". Frederick-William II, who was a keen patron of drama in the German language, commissioned **C.L. Langhans** to build a theatre (1788-90) on the west side, thus completing the edifice which extends over 505m. It now houses the Museum of Pre- and Proto-History.

Following plans drawn in 1719 and 1777, the town developed along the avenues converging towards the castle: **Schloßstraße**, Alte Berliner Straße and Neue Berliner Straße (now renamed **Otto-Suhr-Allee**).

The "French era" – After the battles of Jena and Auerstedt, Prussia was occupied by the French; Napoleon marched into Berlin on 27 October 1806 after having stayed in Charlottenburg. French troops, which at first had been stationed in several Berlin barracks and in private houses (the publisher C.F. Nicolai had to lodge 22 men and look after 12 horses!), had their quarters transferred outside town from the summer of 1808. A military camp for 7000 soldiers, called "**Napoleonsburg**" was established near Charlottenburg, on the site of the present "Westend" district *(see OLYMPIA-STADION)*. At that time, Charlottenburg had a population of only 3 500 inhabitants. The town was made to contribute to the upkeep of the troops by providing supplies, whereas other towns and villages, which had no troops quartered nearby, payed a special tax. The French occupation was strongly resented. In November 1808, the troops left for Spain.

A rich and independent municipality – During the 19C, until German unity became a reality, Charlottenburg was the ideal place to head for on an excursion from Berlin. Numerous villas were built and the first factories erected. The **Flora** (1871-74) was a sought-after place of entertainment, which provided concerts and receptions and which boasted a hothouse full of luxuriant vegetation.

During the Imperial era, Charlottenburg was a wealthy district. It was a time when the population expanded considerably (the municipality included 26 000 inhabitants in 1875, 189 000 in 1900, 335 000 in 1920) which led to intense building activity: public edifices such as the **town hall**, charity headquarters *(Cecilienhaus)*, schools, factories, research institutes, the **heat-engine-driven power station** *(see below)* and the famous **Memorial Church**, now in ruins, along Kurfürstendamm *(see under that name)*. In spite of many hesitations, the municipality finally merged into Greater Berlin in 1920; it subsequently welcomed many immigrants who fled from Russia soon after the Revolution.

★★SCHLOSS CHARLOTTENBURG ⊘

Ⓤ *7 Richard-Wagner-Platz.*

TOUR *Allow 3 hours for a complete tour of the apartments.*

The entrance gate, surmounted by a pair of gladiators, leads inside the **court of honour★**.

The central block is crowned by Eosander von Göthe's famous green copper dome which blends harmoniously with the yellow of the façades, a characteristic feature of Baroque buildings. The Statue of *Fortune*, placed at the top of the dome, is a modern work. The **equestrian statue of the Great Elector** by **Andreas Schlüter** (1696-1709) has been standing in the centre of the courtyard since 1952. It used to stand on the town hall bridge *(Rathausbrücke)*, near the castle, but it sank to the bottom of Lake Tegel while it was being moved to a safe place during the last war. According to legend, the statue came to life every New Year's Eve, on the first stroke of midnight, and caracoled through the town. Note the beautiful figures in lively Baroque style, depicting chained prisoners, which decorate the pedestal.

Turn your back to the castle to appreciate the beautiful sweeping view over the twin guards barracks, built by **Friedrich August Stüler** (1800-1865) in the middle of the 19C on either side of Schloßstraße.

★★Historische Räume – The historical rooms occupy the ground floor of the central block of the castle. The **guided tour** *(1 hr)* starts with a room (**1**) containing two models of the castle and gardens, in the 18C (French-style Baroque garden) and at the beginning of the 19C, after Lenné had redesigned the park in the English fashion. The three rooms which make up the **Mecklenburg Apartments** (in which some members of the House of Mecklenburg, related to the House of Prussia, lived during the 18C) are relatively small; brightly coloured drapes hang on the walls and the doors are surmounted by remarkable carved wood panels, reminiscent of early Louis XIV style. The ceilings are decorated with arabesques. Note the fireplace in the bedroom.

The **official rooms** (formerly the king's apartments) which extend along the façade overlooking the garden, forming an uninterrupted 140m-long row, have lost their ceiling paintings. The tour is quickly over; note, as you go by, the series of portraits of the Prussian and Hanoverian dynasties, several beautiful pieces of lacquered furniture, Sophie-Charlotte's white harpsichord (**2**) and the bathroom (**3**) next to the king's bedroom (**4**). The number of beautiful Chinese porcelain objects increases as one approaches the famous **Porcelain Room★★** (1706) which contains a magnificent collection brought together again after World War II and consisting of various porcelain objects either set into the walls or resting on cornices and stands. In order to make the illusion created by the paintings (for the most part mediocre) look even more real, reliefs representing fruit and a deer's head overlap from the ceiling onto the cornice.

Porcelain Room

Eosander's Chapel★ (Eosander Kapelle, 1706) has been remarkably well restored. A huge crown, carried by two allegorical figures symbolising Fame and surmounted by the Prussian eagle, rests above the royal box. In summer, concerts are given in the chapel. The tour ends with the west rooms which were Sophie-Charlotte's apartments. There used to be 66 paintings hanging in the bedroom (**5**). The beautiful overhanging **staircase** by Eosander von Göthe (1704) was the first of its kind built in Germany.

Go back upstairs in order to visit the first floor of the Central Block. A few rooms only are open to the public.

An elegant chandelier decorates the Neoclassical rotunda overlooking the main courtyard. Another rotunda, clad with mirrors and adorned with an equally beautiful chandelier (made of porcelain), offers a fine **view★** of the garden and, in the distance, to the right, a glimpse of the roof of the Belvedere.

The **former apartments of Frederick-William IV**, the last monarch of the House of Hohenzollern to have stayed regularly in Charlottenburg, have been deprived of their decorations and are now reduced to the role of being a museum of paintings, tapestries (*The War Exploits of the Great Elector*, 1690-1700), and collections of porcelain, glass, gold plate and medals. The most remarkable exhibit is the silverware collection of the House of Hohenzollern, originally kept in the Silver Room *(Silberkammer)* of Berlin Castle. The most interesting piece is the **Crown Prince's dinner service★★** (Kronprinzensilber).

The Kronprinz's silver

In 1904, 414 Prussian cities clubbed together to offer this masterpiece of 20C German silver plate to Crown Prince William, William II's son, on the occasion of his engagement to the Duchess Cecilia of Mecklenburg-Schwerin. Completed in 1914, the dinner service never belonged to the couple. After the abdication of the last reigning member of the House of Hohenzollern, it became the property of the Berlin Senate and is still used today for official receptions. It was taken to the USA for a short while at the end of World War II. It was then referred to as the "Hohenzollern silver". Displayed on an 8m-long table, the service now consists of 24 place settings. It originally comprised 2 600 pieces of silver, sufficient to serve 50 persons, for which a 16m-long table was needed. The napkins and glasses (of five different kinds, displayed in a glass case) have disappeared. The small statues are charming. Tureens, dishes and salad bowls are arranged to form a magnificent buffet at the back of the table. A team of six persons, consisting of architects, sculptors and the director of the Museum of Decorative Arts supervised the manufacture of the service which is in Neoclassical *Jugendstil*-style. The monumental figures representing elephants surmounted by an obelisk as well as equestrian statues and candelabra are traditional components of services used at court.

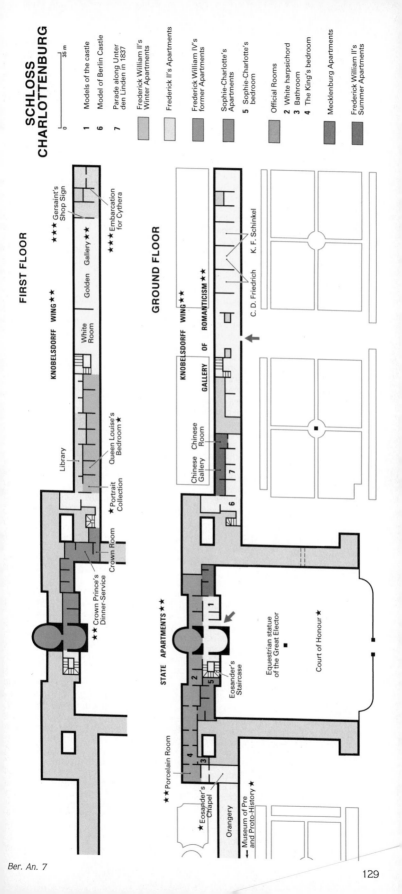

SCHLOSS CHARLOTTENBURG

0   35 m

1   Models of the castle
6   Model of Berlin Castle
7   Parade along Unter den Linden in 1837

Frederick II's Winter Apartments

Frederick II's Apartments

Frederick William IV's former Apartments

Sophie-Charlotte's Apartments

5   Sophie-Charlotte's bedroom

Official Rooms
2   White harpsichord
3   Bathroom
4   The King's bedroom

Mecklenburg Apartments

Frederick William II's Summer Apartments

FIRST FLOOR

★★★ Gersaint's Shop Sign

★★★ Embarcation for Cythera

KNOBELSDORFF WING ★★

White Room

Golden Gallery ★★

Library

Queen Louise's Bedroom ★

★ Portrait Collection

★★ Crown Prince's Dinner-Service

Crown Room

GROUND FLOOR

KNOBELSDORFF WING ★★

GALLERY OF ROMANTICISM ★★

C. D. Friedrich   K. F. Schinkel

Chinese Gallery

Chinese Room

7

6

STATE APARTMENTS ★★

2

5

Eosander's Staircase

Equestrian statue of the Great Elector

Court of Honour ★

1

★★ Porcelain Room

4

3

★ Eosander's Chapel

Orangery

Museum of Pre and Proto-History ★

Ber. An. 7

129

A series of goblets decorated with coins (*Münzhumpen*) is on show just before the small **Crown Room**, where the "crown jewels" of Prussia are exhibited: a special helmet (1688) topped by a tricoloured crest, used for the funeral of male members of the royal family; the Elector of Brandenburg's sword; the bejewelled sceptre (the eagle's body is made from a ruby given to Frederick I by Tsar Peter the Great); and the necklace of the order of the Black Eagle, founded in 1701 on the eve of the Königsberg coronation.

★★**Knobelsdorff-Flügel** – *It extends to the east of the Central Block. The historic apartments and the Gallery of Romanticism are visited separately.*
The staircase (*on the left*) leads to the **White Room**, used by Frederick II as a throne-room and banqueting hall. The ceiling frescoes are a modern work painted by Hans Trier to replace the original painting by Antoine Pesne, destroyed in 1943.
The **Golden Gallery**★★ (1746), a huge ballroom decorated in almond green, pink and gold, is one of the finest examples of the Rococo style at the time of Frederick II. Next come **Frederick II's apartments**, also in Rococo style with white and gold decorations; they contain masterpieces of 18C French painting greatly appreciated by the sovereign: **Gersaint's Shop Sign**★★★ (1720), hanging in its original place in the concert hall, and the **Embarcation for Cythera**★★★, both by Watteau, many paintings by Chardin (*The Supplier, The Letter Sealer*), by Boucher (*Mercury, Venus and Love*), by Nicolas Lancret and again by Watteau (*Love in the Country, The Shepherds*). Also worth noting is the Frederick-style furniture: chests of drawers and corner cabinets in cedar wood in the former bedroom. *Retrace your steps.*

★**"Winterkammer"** – They were the apartments used by Frederick II's successors, Frederick-William II and Frederick-William III, at the end of the 18C and at the beginning of the 19C. These south-facing rooms have the strict elegance of the Neoclassical style. Particularly remarkable are the warm colours of the Gobelin tapestries and of the fully restored inlaid parquet flooring.
Among the more attractive features are the original stoves in striking antique style, with complex frames decorated with Egyptian motifs, and some small delicate pieces of furniture. The unassuming yet attractive **bedroom of Queen Louise**★, clad with white veils enhanced by touches of pale lavender, was decorated by **Schinkel** in 1810, when he worked for the royal family for the first time. Note in particular a set of toilet accessories in gilt silver marked with an L, displayed in a small glass cabinet. The last two rooms contain a beautiful **collection**★ of ladies' portraits by **Antoine Pesne**: Frederick II's wife *(see PANKOW, Schloß Niederschönhausen)* and the very charming Countess of Voss, who acted as chaperone to the future Queen Louise, stand next to a dancer called Barberina, whom Frederick adored and whose portrait hung in his study in Berlin Castle. The three rooms overlooking the garden display a kind of ostentatious Rococo style, in particular the **library** decorated in pale green, white and silver; a glass cabinet contains a selection of Frederick II's collection of diamond-studded **snuffboxes**. The other rooms (note the beautiful gilt inlaid clock made circa 1740 by a Parisian cabinet-maker) are used as picture galleries.

Go down the stairs.

One (**6**) of the ground floor rooms houses a model of **Berlin Castle** demolished by the German Democratic Republic authorities in 1950-51. There are many paintings depicting the castle and the surrounding buildings. The next room contains several pieces of heavy and sumptuous neo-Baroque furniture ordered by William II for one of the rooms in the castle.
The **Chinese gallery and room**, which formed part of Frederick-William II's summer apartments, overlook the garden. The brightness of the colours (particularly in the study) makes up for the loss of some wallpapers decorated with Chinese landscapes. In one of the rooms hangs Franz Krüger's painting *Parade along Unter den Linden in 1837* (**7**) (*Parade Unter den Linden im Jahre 1837*), which depicts the main monuments along the famous avenue. In another room is displayed Jacques-Louis David's *Consul Bonaparte getting over the Great-St-Bernard Pass* (1800-1801), brought back to Germany as booty by Blücher after the battle of Waterloo.

★★**Galerie der Romantik** – *time: 1 1/2 hours* – **Caspar-David Friedrich**'s admirers will undoubtedly make a point of visiting Charlottenburg in order to see the most comprehensive collection of his works *(see the chapter on painting in the Introduction)*, including such famous paintings as **The Monk on the Shore**★★★ and **The Abbey in the Oak Forest**★★★, two canvases exhibited in Berlin in 1810 and admired by Goethe ("There is nothing to be seen!", exclaimed the wife of another painter), as well as imaginary dreamlike landscapes, represented at night, at dusk or in daylight but devoid of all human presence. **Karl-Friedrich Schinkel**'s visionary inspiration comes as a surprise; he depicts a kind of ideal architecture inspired by Gothic art, which was believed to be the essence of Germanic civilisation, but he also paints Greek art in Romantic landscapes: **Gothic Church on a Rock facing the Sea**★★ (1813), *Medieval City on a River* (1815), its cathedral being a manifesto in favour of the achievement of Cologne Cathedral, and *Antique City on a Mountain* (1805-1807). The other Romantic painters were greatly influenced by Italy, which all of them visited, and in particular by the art of Raphael; their pictures denote a kind of idealism which, in spite of being a little too finicky, is nevertheless fascinating: *Portrait of Mrs Clara*

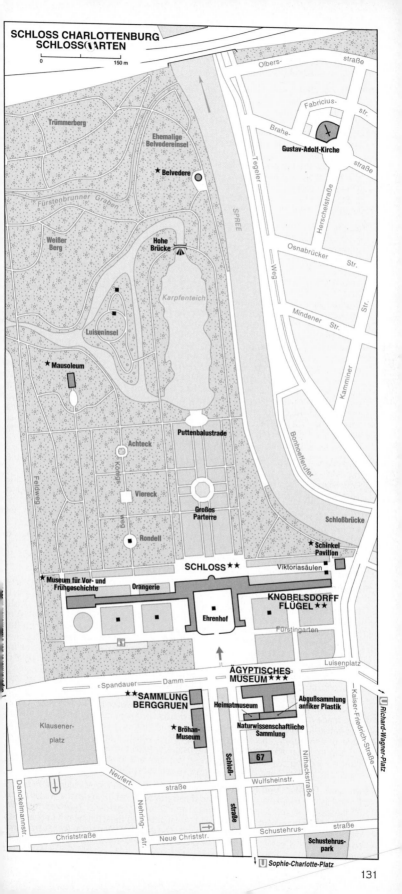

Bianca von Quandt (1820) by Julius Schnorr von Carolsfeld and *Portrait of the Artist Franz Pforr* (1818-1865), whose figure shows hermaphrodite characteristics, by Friedrich Overbeck.

★★Schloßgarten – With the help of her cousin, the famous "Princess Palatine" (*"Liselotte" von der Pfalz*), Duchess of Orleans, Sophie-Charlotte had been able to visit the remarkable gardens designed by Le Nôtre and she asked him to modifiy the plans which his pupil, Simion Godeau had drafted for the Charlottenburg estate. The result is a combination of the strict geometrical design of a French-style Baroque garden (or rather Dutch-style, since the terrain is flat and there are no terraces, ramps or staircases) and the free style of a park in the English fashion, laid out at the instigation of **Lenné** between 1819 and 1828. It is at that time that the banks of Carp Lake were given their curved shape.

The oval pavilion, which stands out in the middle of the façade, is reminiscent of those of Vaux-le-Vicomte and Raincy, two castles built by Louis Le Vau.

Scattered about the park, are three unobtrusive yet interesting buildings.

★Schinkel Pavilion – *Go round the Knöbelsdorff Wing.*
Frederick-William III liked to lead a typical middle-class life, surrounded by his numerous children; two of them, Charlotte, the future Tsarina Alexandra Feodorovna, and Charles, who built Glienicke Castle, were born in Charlottenburg. In 1824, he took as his morganatic wife the young countess **Auguste von Harrach**, who became Princess of Liegnitz, and he wished to acquire a summer residence. This was built according to drawings by Schinkel. The cube-shaped pavilion was inspired by a similarly-shaped Neapolitan villa the king had stayed in. The façades are quite plain. The interior, destroyed by fire on 23 November 1943, was faithfully reconstructed, except for the furniture which dates from the same period but came from elsewhere. The rooms denote simplicity and elegance; they are decorated with plain, brightly coloured wallpaper edged with a frieze; Pompeian grotesques are painted over the stairwell. The most attractive room overlooks the garden (**Gartensaal**); there is a pleasing sense of harmony between the star-dotted blue silk of the antique parlour, the white marble and the exquisitely chased bronze furniture. Following its refurbishing, the pavilion was turned into a museum of art of Frederick-William III's period, including, among others, many works by Schinkel (drawings, sketches of settings and a mysterious *Landscape with Gothic Arcading*, 1811), by Carl Blechen, as well as two panoramic views by Eduard Gärtner: *Panorama of Berlin* (1834), a wide circular view of the historic centre as seen from Friedrichswerdersche Kirche, and *Panorama of the Kremlin*.

★Belvedere – *Just before you reach the belvedere, turn left along a path leading to the lake.*
From the middle of the small redwood bridge, there is a lovely **view★★** of the castle. The **Belvedere** (1789-90) is a charming building designed by **Carl Gotthard Langhans** with both Baroque and Neoclassical features. Frederick-William II used it for his mystical Rosicrucian (*Rosenkreutzer*) meetings. The façade is almond-green and white, the attic windows are framed with termini while the ridge of the roof is decorated with golden cherubs holding a basket of flowers. The Belvedere houses a small **museum★** of the Berlin Royal Porcelain factory (*KPM, see ERNST-REUTER-PLATZ*) which includes some very delicate pieces; among them are Frederick II's dinner services, decorated with an enchanting floral pattern.

★Mausoleum – Queen Louise was so deeply attached to Charlottenburg that, after her death, her grief-stricken husband decided to build a mausoleum on the estate where he was later buried and which became the crypt of the Hohenzollern family. Originally, the mausoleum only consisted of a small Doric temple built in 1810 by **Heinrich Gentz**. The sandstone façade was replaced by another in polished granite (the original portico now stands on Peacock Island). A raised adjoining temple, designed by Schinkel and added later, somewhat spoils the harmonious proportions of the initial building. However, one cannot help being taken by surprise at the sight of this temple suddenly appearing at the end of a pathway, in romantic surroundings shrouded in mystery. **Queen Louise's funeral monument★★** (*see INTRODUCTION, The Burden of History*), which was completed in Rome, arrived in Charlottenburg in May 1815, after an eight-month sea voyage. **Christian-Daniel Rauch** (1777-1857), the artist who made the monument out of Carrara marble, acquired instant fame. The smooth and sensual curves of the marble figure, the natural and very unconventional attitude of the queen (the king himself specified which attitude he preferred), her crossed legs, her attractive hands, the beautiful folds of the cloth enhanced by the diffuse light and the kind expression on her face are in striking contrast with the rigidity of William I and his wife Augusta's recumbent effigies.

★Museum für Vor- und Frühgeschichte ⊙ – Since 1960, the Museum of Pre- and Proto-History has been housed in the theatre built by Langhans at the western end of the castle. A pleasant stroll through the Orangery gardens, reserved for temporary exhibitions, leads to this small but enlightening museum where only a small percentage of the collections are displayed. *The explanatory panels, which are numbered to make it easier to follow the order of the visit, have summaries in English and in French.*

The Belvedere

P. Broquet/EXPLORER

Ground floor – The cultural development of Europe, before writing was introduced, is compared to that of contemporary civilisations in the Middle East. Most of the exhibits come from the former Hohenzollern collection. The living conditions of cave men are cleverly reconstructed with the help of numerous dioramas. There is a gradual progression from the palaeolithic to the end of the ice age, from the time when Man finally became sedentary to the beginnings of agriculture and stock-farming, then to the invention of pottery and the establishment of the first towns in the Middle East. Some sections are illustrated by authentic works of art such as idols from Anatolia painted over with wavy lines, the "Snakes' Vase" ("Schlangenbecken"), a Mesopotamian work which remains difficult to explain, and small statues from ancient Iran, reminiscent of the Scarred Man in the Louvre.

First floor – Devoted to the Bronze Age, Troy and the Iron Age, this floor was reopened at the same time as the controversial exhibition "**The Trojan Gold**" took place in Moscow. The fabulous treasure discovered by **Heinrich Schliemann** on the site where Troy was supposed to have stood is still a subject of controversy. Taken by the Soviets at the end of World War II, this treasure consisting of 10 000 pieces, which was believed to have been destroyed, had been lying for half a century in the cellars of the Pouchkine Museum. Berlin still holds the greater part of the treasure, but the most precious items, reconstructed in gilt copper, are in Moscow. Ceramics, including a huge pithos, or earthenware jar used to store oil, cereals or wine, illustrate the different periods of a town with a very ancient history.

Gipsformerei der Staatlichen Museen ⓥ – *Follow Spandauerdamm and turn north into Sophie-Charlotten-Straße. The museum is situated at No 17-18.* The room shown to visitors has been specifically arranged as a shop offering a wide choice of reproductions of works of art from Ancient Egypt to pre-Columbian America. Founded in 1819, this rich collection of reproductions survived the war without too much damage.

Sammlung Berggruen Picasso and his time ⓥ – *Schloßstraße 1.*
The collection principally features works by **Picasso**, which demonstrate all the facets of his artistic creativity. The visitor is first captivated by the cubist bronze sculpture, the *Head of Fernande*, 1909, in the rotunda. Since the collection is entitled "Picasso and his time", visitors are also able to enjoy a few works by **Paul Cézanne** (*Young Girl with Doll*; *Mrs Cézanne*) and **Henri Matisse** (*Girl Skipping*) and the beautiful *Garden in Autumn* by **Van Gogh**, which the artist painted for Gauguin. A few African objets d'art are justifiably included, for example a remarkable bronze from Benin (c 1600) and the *Great Bird* (19C-20C), a wooden sculpture from the Ivory Coast.
The actual Picasso collection includes over 70 works – paintings, sculptures, gouaches and drawings – and covers the lengthy creative era and individual periods of the artist's life. One of the earliest works, *In the Coffee House*, was painted in 1902. The oil study which Picasso produced for his pioneering oeuvre, the *Demoiselles d'Avignon*, is of particular interest. The remarkable *Portrait of Georges Braque*, 1909-1910, is immediately adjacent to two works by the same artist (*Still life with glass*

Archaeologist or adventurer?

The son of a vicar from Mecklenburg, **Heinrich Schliemann** (1822-1890) owes his passion for Troy to an illustration in a children's book. He started as an apprentice in a grocery and left for Venezuela when he was only 14 but was shipwrecked off the Dutch coast. The young Heinrich then became a salesman in an import-export business in Amsterdam. He travelled the world, selling indigo in St Petersburg, lending money in San Francisco and made his fortune during the Crimean War. He was self-taught, learned to speak ten languages and began to study archeology in Paris in 1866.

Between 1871 and 1873, he thoroughly searched Hissarlik Hill, situated in Turkey, near the entrance of the Dardanelles Straits. Schliemann was so anxiously looking for treasure and glory that he made a botch of it ("I shall dig the treasure out myself with a big knife..."), destroying a thousand clues, including those relating to the town of Troy which he was looking for, since the first objects discovered, consisting of 250 gold jewels, are more than a thousand years older than the fall of Troy in Homer's epic (c 1250 BC). Schliemann promised the Turks he would give them the unearthed objects, but instead he smuggled them out of the country. He gave the Turkish goverment 40 000 gold francs above the 10 000 they were demanding and declared himself the sole owner of the treasure. His wife, Sophia Kastromenos, a young Athenian girl of 17 (their two children were called Andromache and Agamemnon!), wore some of the jewels for the purpose of a photograph. He proposed to donate the treasure to the Italians, the Russians, the French and the Greeks, sometimes to all of them, but the precious objetcs were exhibited in Berlin Museum in 1881. Schliemann did not stop there, but went on to search the funeral circle inside the citadel of **Mycenae**, discovering the large gold masks, which today are displayed in the Archaeological Museum in Athens.

and *Newspaper*, 1914). In the painting entitled *Guitar and Newspaper* which dated from 1916, Picasso has also used sand on the canvas. Other works are worthy of mention: *Seated Nude drying her Feet*, a pastel from 1921, *The Sailor*, 1938, *The Yellow Jumper*, an oil painting from 1939. The etching *Minotauromachie*, 1935, bears the dedication "For my friend Berggruen". The watercolour *The Artist and his Model*, painted in 1971 is also beautiful.

The small works by **Paul Klee**, whom Heinz Berggruen always greatly appreciated, are displayed to advantage on the second floor. They include *Urban Construction*, a tempera painting from 1917, *Adults*, an aquarelle from 1920, *Remote Landscape*, an oil painting from 1931. Sculptures by **Alberto Giacometti** (*The Cat*, 1951, *Woman for Venice IV*, 1956-1957) round off the collection.

★**Bröhan-Museum** ⊘ – Schloßstraße 1a.
This museum of decorative arts spans the period from 1889 to 1939, i.e. from the *Jugendstil* (and Art Nouveau, its French and Belgian equivalent) to the beginnings of modern design; based on **Karl H. Bröhan**'s collection, the exhibition is extremely well presented, the lighting being particularly remarkable. It is like taking

Art dealer and collector

Heinz Berggruen, a native of Berlin, studied literature (he is a graduate of the University of Toulouse) and began his career as a journalist for the *Frankfurter Zeitung*. His Jewish origins compelled him to leave Germany in 1936. He took up studying again at Berkeley, in California, where he made friends with the director of the San Francisco museum and became her assistant. Soon after the war, in which he took part as an American citizen, he was sent to Germany in order to contribute to a magazine intended to restore the tarnished image of "degenerate art" in the eyes of the Germans. His protector from San Francisco offered him the opportunity of working with her at the UNESCO headquarters in Paris. After discovering one of Toulouse Lautrec's sketch-books, he opened a gallery in place Dauphine on the main island in the Seine. André Breton, Paul Eluard and Tristan Tzara acted as a bridge of contact with the artists. Heinz Berggreuen became internationally acknowledged as an expert in the field of prints, engravings and lithographies, after he organized the first exhibition of Klee's prints in 1950 and of Matisse's "cutouts" in 1953. He exported art to Germany and the United States. He began buying Klee's works by the dozen, as well as a number of Picassos. He did not hesitate to barter, and once exchanged 13 Matisses for Van Gogh's *Autumn Landscape*.

a stroll through a series of drawing-rooms. One cannot help admiring the humorous bestiary, the women seated and the flower-shaped porcelain vases in *Jugendstil-style* (Danish porcelain in particular denotes originality and freshness), glassware from Bohemia, furniture signed by all the great cabinet-makers of the Art Nouveau (Guimard, Majorelle) and Art Deco (Dominique Chareau, Süe and Mare, Ruhlmann, Iribe) periods. The various pieces of furniture are displayed together with French and Danish contemporary porcelain and silverware, paintings by members of the Berlin Secession (Karl Hagemeister, Hans Baluschek), the New Objectivity (Willy Jaekel), and the cubist artist Jean Lambert-Rucki as well as a remarkable collection of works in metal: lights, candelabras and pewterware.

Take the lift or the main staircase to the third floor.

Two rooms are devoted to the youthful works of Belge Henry van de Velde and Josef Hoffmann, representatives of the Viennese Secession. In the great gallery and its well-lit mezzanine, porcelain from the 1930s (Sèvres and Berlin) is displayed.

★★★ÄGYPTISCHES MUSEUM ⊘

Schloßstraße 70. time: 2 1/2 hrs.

The Berlin collections of Egyptian antiquities rank among the finest in the world; however, because Berlin was split in two, some of them are at present housed in the Stüler Pavilion in Charlottenburg (*see MUSEUMSINSEL*). The Bode-Museum in Charlottenburg now displays objects representing antique Egyptian art, including works from Amarna. The two collections will be reunited in about ten years' time, when the rebuilding of the **New Museum (Neues Museum)**, situated next to the Bode-Museum, where they were displayed before World War II, has been completed. The main exhibits in the collection are the priceless objects found in **Amarna**, formerly called Akhetaten ("Land of the sun of Aten"), the capital city of the heretic Pharaoh **Amenophis IV-Akhenaten** (*see below*). German archaeologists, who excavated the site between 1911 and 1914, avoided the city centre, where temples and palaces had been used as quarries, and concentrated their efforts on individual houses containing a variety of objects, some of them religious. These underline the break which occurred in the history of ancient Egypt spread over several thousand years. This period, which was exceptional in every aspect, brings added interest to this collection of masterpieces; a selection of these is listed below.

Ground floor (Stüler-Pavilion)

★★★**Bust of Nefertiti** – Miraculously preserved, this bust was discovered in the workshop of one of the court sculptors. It was used as a model for the future effigies of the queen (which explains why one eye only was inlaid). There is not the slightest imperfection; the colours stress the enigmatic and hieratic expression of the sovereign. The next room gives explanations (in German) about the site and culture of Amarna.

★**Gold plate, pottery and glassware** – These different crafts reached their climax during the reigns of Amenophis III and Amenophis IV. Particularly remarkable are an alabaster vase engraved with black hieroglyphs, several perfume bottles, the blue turquoise cup of the heir to the Scheschonk throne and various pieces of jewelry.

Former stables:

A passageway situated right of the stables gives access to another room which houses temporary exhibitions.

★★**Doorway of the temple of Kalabsha** – The visitor is greeted by this gift from Egypt to the German Federal Republic in acknowledgement for its help in moving the temple out of the area flooded by construction of the Assouan dam. It dates from the Roman period of Egyptian history (20 BC) but it comes from a town situated at the southern extremity of the country, in Nubia where, as in Philae, traditional art had been preserved. A few years before, the emperor Augustus had

---

Amenophis IV-Akhenaten's revolution

As soon as he came to the throne, **Amenophis IV** (c 1375 – c 1354 BC), the son of Teje and Amenophis III, forced his subjects to believe in a single god. All other forms of divinity gave way to **Aten**, represented as the sun's disc; at the end of the sun's rays are human hands grasping the sign of life (*ankh*). Amenophis changed his name to **Akhenaten**, "he who serves Aten" and outlawed the cult, priests and temples of other gods, thus offending the rich and powerful clergy. The reign of his son, **Tutankhamun**, who left Amarna after two or three years, marked the return to tradition.

put an end to the Greek Ptolemaic dynasty ruling in Alexandria. The emperor is shown dressed as Pharaoh performing the ritual sacrifices to the traditional gods of Egypt.

Art of the reign of Amenophis III – Two **reliefs★★** (360 BC) depict Amenophis III; on one of them he is wearing the blue crown, worn at war (the same crown, part of a glazed statue, is displayed in another glass cabinet) and on the other he is wearing a diadem. The **head★** of an unknown person can be seen close by.

Shortly before the Amarnian revolution, the art of portraying people reached near perfection with the **head of Queen Teje★★** (1355 BC, *immediately to the left of the entrance*), carved in yew and originally of a light orange colour. The hostile facial expression of Amenophis III's great royal spouse, a commoner who became more powerful than a queen, shows a remarkable sense of realism. When it was made the head looked quite different; it was covered with a rich silver headdress decorated with *auraeus* (the sacred cobra). This can only be seen by means of X-rays; for a linen wig was stuck over it when Teje had to give up her title of royal spouse in favour of Nefertiti on the death of Amenophis III. The head was later completed by the addition of a crown of the goddess Hathor, which has been preserved and will be put back on the tenon used to keep it in place.

Art of the reign of Amenophis IV – The interest of this section lies in the collection of **royal effigies★★★**, heads and reliefs representing Akhenaten, Nefertiti, Tutankhamun and several princesses, all showing beautifully refined workmanship. In the case of Nefertiti, it is possible to compare the fragments of various statues of the queen with their famous model in painted limestone.

Official works of art dared to depict the sovereign's features with realism, particularly concerning his age, but the outlines were strict and virile. The Amarnian artistic trend went further, asserting a sense of caricature and accentuating physical imperfections, while showing a marked preference for spontaneous attitudes: embraces and caresses are in striking contrast with the trends of the preceding period. The Pharaoh's face is depicted with feminine grace; just like that of his wife, their son Tutankhamun and the princesses; it extends forward at the extremity of a very slender neck, with a stretched-out chin and receding forehead in line with the nose. The **relief showing Akhenaten's profile★** and the **head of a princess's statue★★**, in red quartzite with a deformed skull, can be considered extreme examples in this respect. The full-length statuettes of the Pharaoh show a figure with hermaphrodite characteristics, a protruding belly covered with a low-cut loincloth and sagging breasts. There is also a small statue in soft limestone, carved in a workshop no doubt to serve as a model, representing Nefertiti as a real human being, a mature woman with a thin neck, sagging mouth and bosom, dressed in a tight-fitting tunic. The reliefs which show the royal family in the privacy of their daily life, for instance the royal couple holding their children on their knees, express the concept of fertility linked to the worship of the sun god Aten and to his beneficial influence. The polychrome relief of the *stroll in a garden* probably represents Tutankhamun with his wife, leaning on a crutch under his armpit, for he was disabled.

The beautiful set of very expressive **heads of men and women★★**, is also of particular interest among the collection of Amarnian works.

Other objects include part of a painted paving from Queen Teje's palace in El Hawata, depicting ducks flying off through a clump of papyri and, next to it, a funeral relief (*Berliner Trauerrelief*, 1350 BC) on which the gestures expressed by the characters of the lower part still show the influence of Amarnian art, just before the return to Classicism during the Rameses period; also worth noting is the small statue of a scribe writing in a sitting position with one knee raised.

The passageway situated along the right side of the stables leads to a lofty room housing the **columns of King Sahu-Re's temple**.

In the centre of the back room stands an unfinished statue of Akhenaten; the room also contains a **stela representing Bak and his wife Tahere★** (Bak was commissioned by Amenophis IV to supervise the sculptors' work on the temple of Aten) and above all **sketches of animals★** on carved and painted blocks of limestone (*ostraka*). They include a lion licking himself, a sparrow and a delicately drawn horse's head. The drawings depict birds sitting on their eggs as well as lions and baboons.

First floor

★ **"Berlin Green Head"** (5C BC) – It is a remarkable psychological study, expressing carefully stylised realism and thus heralding Graeco-Roman art.

★ **Psammetisch Family** (*c* 600 BC) – This is a set of three wooden statues with smiling expressions. The traditional walking attitude, with raised shoulder and clenched fists, which goes back to the Old Kingdom, was later adopted by the Greeks for the *Kouros* owing to the great number of Greek merchants in Egypt at the time.

★ **Statuette of Amun Meres-Amun's priestess** (850 BC) – During the late period queens and princesses were called divine priestesses and wives of Amun. Some of them dedicated their life to the god and were endowed with great power and wealth.

The Egyptian Museum's prize exhibits

Head of Queen Nefertiti

Strolling in the garden

Akhenaten and Nefertiti with their children

Small cubiform statues of Horus (775 BC) – These funeral statues representing close servants of the Pharaoh were placed in the courtyard of the temples.

★**Funeral chapel dedicated to Amenhotep** – This elegant chapel dating from the Rameses period (1250 BC) is decorated with paintings: easily recognisable are Horus (with a falcon's head), Thot (the god of time and writing, patron of scribes with an ibis's head) in front of Osiris (represented with arms crossed, sceptre and fly fan), and Anubis (the god of the dead, with a jackal's head).

Amenhotep and his wife Hathor (c 1280 BC) – The influence of the Amarnian period is discernable in the shape of the bodies, in the way the folds of the clothing are arranged, in the wigs and in the hymn to the Sun carved on the pedestal.

Container in the shape of the god Bes (c 1360 BC) – The container is in the shape of this beneficent ugly-featured divinity.

★**Glazed pottery** – Three fish with a single head and three lotus flowers are drawn on a small cup. The hippopotamus and the hedgehog (1800 BC) are funeral offerings. The colour of the hippopotamus and the plants drawn on it symbolise the Nile and Noun, the ocean from which all form of life sprang. The mouth of the hippopotamus is wide open in order to chase away evil spirits.

Statue of a goddess with a pig's head – This strange terracotta effigy dates from 3 500 BC.

OTHER SIGHTS

Heimatmuseum Charlottenburg ⊙ – *Schloßstraße 69.*
This small museum, situated at the back of the Egyptian Museum, next to the collection of reproductions, retraces the history of the district.
Behind a model of the Central Block of the castle, made with matchsticks, several prints can be seen illustrating the extension of the castle and the Porcelain Room. In the middle of the room there is a bell (1646) from the old village of Lützow and a model of Luisenkirche with its pointed steeple.

Naturwissenschaftliche Sammlungen/Siftung Stadtmuseum Berlin – *Schloßstraße 69a (next to the Heimatmuseum Charlottenburg).*
The museum hosts special exhibitions covering a whole range of different collection interests, such as insects, apiary, bears, geology of the Berlin area.

Abgußsammlung antiker Plastik ⊙ – *Schloßstraße 69b: next to the Naturwissenschaftliche Sammlungen.*
Re-formed after the war, this collection of reproductions perpetuates a three-hundred-year-old tradition (it was founded in 1695). It was formerly displayed in the New Museum. The range covered comprises idols from the Cyclades as well as Byzantine art, but there is a larger choice of reproductions of master pieces of Greek, Hellenistic and Roman sculpture, kept in various great museums throughout the world. There is a very useful informative panel relating to each sculpture.

Schloßstraße – *110 bus Seelingstraße.* The central reservation laid out as a promenade in 1840 offers a beautiful **view**★ of the green copper dome surmounting the castle. At the end of the 17C, Schloßstraße was known as the "wide street" *(Breite Straße)*, lined with one-storeyed private houses covered with a mansard and occupied by court employees (see the model of the first town hall, built along Schloßstraße, in the *Heimatmuseum*). From 1830 onwards, these houses were replaced by villas and buildings designed for letting. Small gardens were laid out in front of the buildings; **No 67** for instance, built in 1873, is quite typical of the "foundation years" *(Gründerjahre)*. **No 56** and **Nos 45-47** were built by Inken and Heinrich Baller for the **1987 IBA** exhibition in a style that is easily recognisable *(see DAHLEM, Freie Universität, Institute of Philosophy)*.

Schustehruspark – The park used to belong to the Oppenheim villa (1881-82) which can be seen in the southwest corner, partly hidden behind the trees. The large building nearby, in multi-coloured bricks, is a school, formerly *Schlesien-Oberschule*, built a little later. Opposite, on the corner of Nithackstraße, there is a strange-looking modern building with green copper balconies, a work by Baller.

Luisenkirche ⊙ – U 7 *Richard-Wagner-Platz.* In accordance with Frederick I's wishes, this is both a Lutheran and Reformed church; it was built between 1712 and 1716 and entirely remodelled in 1826 by Friedrich Schinkel who added a tower in the *Biedermeier* style. It was at that time that the church was named after Queen Louise. The building has regained its original yellow colour.

Old Charlottenburg – Schustehrusstraße runs through its centre. At **No 13** stands the oldest dwelling in Charlottenburg (1712), the charming former coppersmith's house, painted apple green. The doorway is oval-arched, while the dormer windows are bell-shaped.

The Egyptian Museum's prize exibits

Doorway of the temple of Kalabsha

Psammetich family

Portrait of Queen Tije, the mother of Akhenaten

earthenware hedgehog and hippopotamus

Richard-Wagner-Platz – This former market square (Marktplatz) and the nearby church square (today Gierkeplatz), where Luisenkirche now stands, used to be the two centres of the middle-class town designed by Eosander von Göthe and dependent on the castle.

Rathaus (R) – Ⓤ *7 Richard-Wagner-Platz.* The façade of the building is stocky, but the 88m-high campanile is interesting. It symbolises the spirit of independence of a wealthy municipality which only merged with Berlin in 1920, after showing much reluctance. At the time, the inhabitants did not want to pay taxes for the poorer districts of the town. The town hall was built between 1899 and 1905, for the bicentenary of the foundation of the town, by the architects H. Reinhardt and G. Süssenguth. Its *Jugendstil* decoration on the doorway, in the main hall and on the main staircase is particularly remarkable.

Städtisches Volksbad – *Cross Otto-Suhr-Allee and follow Krumme Straße until you reach Nos 9-10.* The façade of this municipal swimming-pool, the oldest in Berlin (1898), is in Gothic style decorated with attractive *Jugendstil* motifs on enamelled ceramics: Santiago de Compostela shells, water-lily leaves, menacing fish heads and reeds on the column shafts. A saddleback roof and a blue metallic frame cover the pool area.

Villa Kogge und Kraftwerk Charlottenburg – *Follow Warburgzeile, the first street past the town hall as you walk eastwards along Otto-Suhr-Allee.*

Kogge Villa (1864), an elegant Neoclassical villa, overlooks the small square, on the corner of Warburgzeile and Alt-Lietzow. Visitors who walk straight on to the end of Lüdtgeweg will discover an amazing **industrial site★** on the banks of the Spree. Siemenssteg, a graceful metallic footbridge, leads to a neo-Gothic red and white brick castle, which in actual fact is the older part of Charlottenburg power station, driven by heat engines and dating from 1889-90; it was inspired by the architecture of the Brandenburg March.

Gustav-Adolf-Kirche – *Herschelstraße 14-15.*
This concrete and steel church was built by **Otto Bartning** (1932-34) in the shape of a fan. It is one of the most original and interesting churches in Berlin.

IN THE VICINITY

See **FUNKTURM★**, **REINICKENDORF**, **ERNST-REUTER-PLATZ.**

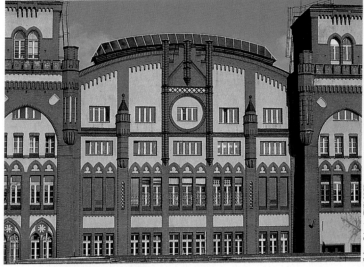

Charlottenbourg power station

DAHLEM★★

Dahlem

See map of the Berlin Conurbation, 🔟, **BV**

This former lord's estate, which was taken over by the state in 1841, used to provide food supplies for the Berlin population. It is now a residential suburb, set in green surroundings and dotted with villas built in a kind of English cottage style, adapted to the Brandenburg landscape by **Hermann Muthesius** (1861-1927, *see the INTRODUCTION, Architecture and city planning*).

It is also a "scientific" suburb. At the beginning of the century, the university acquired 50 hectares in the area, on which several research institutes were established. During the twenties, Berlin had the highest proportion of top-flight scientists in the world. The physicists Max Planck, Albert Einstein, Max von Laue, the chemists Emil Fischer and Fritz Haber worked here with the support of **Emperor William's Society** (Kaiser Wilhelm Gesellschaft), intended to encourage science. After he was awarded the Nobel Prize in 1918, Max Planck declared: "Science is all that the Germans have got left after defeat". Dahlem has a vast university whose buildings, in spite of being relatively low, look rather unsightly among the villas; however, this district is mostly interesting for its museums.

MAIN SIGHTS

Ⓤ *1 Dahlem-Dorf* – This underground station was built (1912-13) according to William II's wishes, in the "picturesque" style of a timber-framed farmhouse.

★**Domäne Dahlem Landgut und Museum** ⊙ – **Ⓤ** *1 Dahlem-Dorf*.
From the underground station, the mansion with its gables and orange-coloured roughcast, which dates from 1650 and is one of the oldest houses in Berlin, is clearly visible. The visitor comes quite unexpectedly upon a piece of Berlin agricultural history, in the form of an ensemble enjoying protected status and comprising a medieval village centre, former manor buildings and the final surviving 15ha free Feldmark community field. The Dahlem estate is currently part of the Stiftung Stadtmuseum Berlin foundation, and is simultaneously a working estate and a museum. The exhibitions are mainly concerned with the history of agriculture and agricultural technology, village development and the supply of food to Berlin. A toy room featuring historical toys is a particular attraction for younger visitors.

A broad range of typical farm animals are either stabled or graze on the estate, including cows, pigs, sheep and chickens, together with geese, horses, ponies and even bees. On the land, on which a seven year rotation system is employed, typical local fodder and market produce are grown. The farm shop sells tasty fresh produce from the market garden.

Rural crafts feature in the everyday life of the museum. Indigo printing, pottery and art metalworking in the historical court forge are all run as independent businesses, while voluntary helpers give demonstrations of spinning, weaving, rural painting and beekeeping.

St-Annen-Kirche – **Ⓤ** *1 Dahlem-Dorf. This small 14C church is closed outside religious services. It was once used as a telegraph relay between Berlin and Koblenz Fortress, which was one of the outposts of the Prussian army.*

Resistance from the clergy under the Third Reich

As soon as the first measures were taken to ensure the predominance of the "Aryan race", the vicar of Dahlem parish church, **Martin Niemöller**, founded a clerical league opposed to these measures, the *Pfarrenotbund*, which was to form the basis of the future "confessing church" (*Bekennende Kirche*). Niemöller was immediately arrested and deported, but the Dahlem parish remained a centre of protest. Other clergymen such as Heinrich Grüber and Werner Sylten helped the persecuted Jews, but ended up in the camps themselves. These ministers were exceptions, for most of the church hierarchy condoned the actions of the Nazi regime. Catholic resistance (10% of the population) was stimulated when youth associations were outlawed and their members tranferred to the ranks of the Hitler Youths. Newspapers, radio programmes and church establishments were forbidden or closed down. The vicar of St Hedwige protested, helped the Jews and denounced crimes against the mentally ill. He died as he was being taken to Dachau.

★★★MUSEUM DAHLEM ⊘ (M³⁷)

Since the art gallery which was housed here until 1998 has now moved to the Kulturforum (the sculpture collection has also now moved out and will be displayed again in the Bode-Museum in 2004), all the vacant exhibition space can now be used to house the collections of the Ethnologisches Museum, the Museum für Ostasiatische Kunst and the Museum für Indische Kunst. This restructuring work means that a few collections are not accessible.

★★★ETHNOLOGISCHES MUSEUM

Ⓤ *1 Dahlem-Dorf; follow Iltistraße immediately to the right as you come out of the station. Entrance in Lansstraße.*

The collections of the kings of Prussia included numerous objects from cultures other that of Europe. They were brought together in 1829 and formed the first "collection of ethnography", but the museum was only founded in 1873; it was located in the centre of Berlin, near the Martin-Gropius Bau (*see KREUZBERG, west side*). It was overcrowded. **Wilhelm von Bode** suggested the creation of a museum complex comprising four buildings, to accommodate all the continents except Europe. The Asian building alone was completed (1908) by the architect Bruno Paul; after the Second World War it was used as storage space by the Museum of Ethnography until the 1950s and subsequently housed the Painting Gallery; It forms the main façade of the Dahlem museums along Arnimallee.

The collections of the Museum of Ethnography rank among the finest in Europe (almost 400 000 exhibits). Particularly in the case of Oceania, they were collected as the result of a series of German colonial expeditions and brought to Europe. Numerous scientific expeditions increased the collections: along the Pacific coast of North America and Alaska; to the heart of Indian country in Brazil; to Mexico and Guatemala; to the centre of Africa; to New-Guinea; to the Bismarck archipelago; to Hawaii; to the Marquesas Islands; and four separate expeditions to Chinese Turkistan (Turfan). Losses due to the war were heavy. The present display is remarkable. The effort made to classify the exhibits has made it possible to clearly distinguish the different cultures. Some of the collections (in particular the musical ethnological collection) have now been given plenty of exhibition space, following the removal of the Painting Gallery to the Kulturforum, making it possible to include the exhibitions entitled "Meisterwerke afrikanischer Kunst" and "Indianer Nordamerikas"..

★★★**Abteilung Alt-Amerika** – Interest never flags in the Pre-Colombian America department. The exhibits are very beautiful and testify remarkably well to the complexity and degree of development reached by this civilisation. The most attractive items are the small clay figures. In spite of lack of space, the South American section has a **Gold Room★★★ (Goldkammer)** containing gold objects and jewellery sets.

★★**Abteilung Südsee** – Having joined the ranks of colonial powers at a late stage, Germany conquered the Caroline Islands, thus acquiring vast territories in the Pacific.

The department of pre-Colombian American art

A selection of interesting and varied items illustrate the different cultures found in the Pacific and Indonesia. The reconstruction of the Belau men's clubhouse, which follows the traditions of the Palaos Islands, and the section displaying **catamarans** *(overall view from the first floor)*, are spectacular. Masks are exhibited in glass cabinets. One, which contains a feather cloak from Hawaï, lights up as you come close.

★**Abteilung Südasien** – Theatrical props from Southeast Asia, India and Sri-Lanka include masks, marionettes, shadow-show puppets and a set of Indonesian *kris* as well as religious statuettes and textiles.

★★**Abteilung Nord- und Westafrika** – This department is still short of space; its most interesting exhibits are pieces of Berber jewellery, **terracotta women's heads from Ife**, famous **bronzes from Benin**, and art from the Cameroon savannah, a former German protectorate.

★**Museum für Ostasiatische Kunst** – The fine paintings on paper and the Japanese prints were not damaged, during the war unlike the rest of the collection which had to be rebuilt. The Chinese imperial throne, made of rosewood inlaid with mother-of-pearl against a background of lacquer and gold, dates from the second half of the 17C. The bronze ritual objects, Chinese ceramics and Japanese lacquer are equally interesting.

★★**Museum für Indische Kunst** – The rich collection of **religious statuettes★★★** is remarkably well-displayed. Bronze figures are followed by **murals from Turfan★★**. This section also includes exhibits from Indochina.

OTHER SIGHTS

★**Museum Europäischer Kulturen (M²⁶)** ⊘ – *Im Winkel 6-8,* Ⓤ *1 Dahlem-Dorf.*
No less a personage than Virchow was behind the establishment of the former "Museum für deutsche Volkstrachten und Erzeugnisse des Hausgewerbes" in 1889. A second folklore museum was established in the western part of the city following the Second World War. The two museums have now been reunited in the Dahlem Museum building.

The museum collects items of popular culture dating from the 16C to the present day. Since the 1990s it has acquired increasing numbers of items originating from neighbouring European countries. The rooms were made accessible once again in the summer of 1999 after renovation work. *The tour commences on the upper floor.*

1st floor: The theme of the permanent exhibition, entitled "Cultural contacts in Europe" is Fascination with Image. It shows the adoption of image, beginning with the splendour of individual religious works of art and ranging through printed images as models for paintings on room walls, furniture and household items, right up to mass-produced items and the current flood of images.

Painted wardrobe from Upper Austria, 1843

MuK/MUSEUM FÜR VOLKSKUNDE · PREUSSISCHER KULTURBESITZ.

Ground floor: Image is initially depicted here in relation to the three world religions of Judaism, Christianity and Islam. Its social role within the 19C and 20C is then highlighted, and finally the visitor is shown the image of foreign cultures to compare against his own image.

★**Botanisches Museum** ⊘ **(M²⁷)** – Ⓤ *1 Dahlem-Dorf,* then *Botanischer Garten.*
The royal herbarium goes back to the 19C. The museum is well laid-out and very informative, but knowledge of German is necessary. Photographs, dioramas and above all models show plants, flowers and bacteria enlarged. It is possible to learn everything about wood, its structure and industry, cereals, vegetable textile fibres and agriculture in ancient Egypt.

★★ Botanischer Garten ⊘ (**B'**) – **U** *1 Dahlem-Dorf, then* **BUS** *Botanischer Garten or* **S** *1*.
The first gardens were laid out on the site of Lustgarten *(see SCHLOSSPLATZ)*;
then, at the end of the 17C, the Great Elector transferred them to the site of the
present Kleistpark in Schöneberg village. They were relaid according to scientific
principles at the beginning of the 19C and moved again to Dahlem in 1897.
These extraordinary gardens, which offer a fascinatingly varied profusion of trees,
plants and bushes from all five continents (18 000 species), are the botanical counterpart of the zoological gardens. They are criss-crossed by a great many small paths
winding their way round hillocks, through woods and dales; a Chinese pavilion is partly
concealed in the "Asian" section. The stroll continues through an arboretum. The **hot-
houses★★★** (1906-7), which offer a good overall view of the gardens *(Café-cum-
restaurant on the terrace, shop-cum-bookseller in the ground floor passageway)*, seem
to be straight out of the imagination of an eccentric millionaire. It seems like another
world, a maze of glass domes, small and large, containing magnificent plants: gigantic
water-lilies, luxuriant tropical vegetation, carnivorous plants, orchids, cacti, etc.

Freie Universität – At the beginning of the 20C, plans were made to tranfer several
university departments into the country. Emperor William's Society (Kaiser-Wilhelm-
Gesellschaft), dedicated to encouraging science, was the only one to settle in Dahlem
where a number of research institutes were based. The physicists Max Planck, Albert
Einstein, Max von Laue and the chemists Emil Fischer and Fritz Haver worked there.
The Independent University was founded by the Americans during the blockade; it
was the starting point of student protest in the sixties. Its buildings, such as the
Institute of Philosophy *(Habelschwerdter Allee 30,* **U** *1 Thielplatz* with its unusual
wrought-iron balconies (1981-83), or the **Henry-Ford Building** *(Garystraße 35/39,* **U**
1 Thielplatz) are scattered throughout the grounds. There are 60 000 students.

★ Albrecht-Thaer-Weg – *(see map of Berlin Town Centre,* **6** *FZ)* – **U**
1 Podbielskiallee, then walk along Schorlemerallee towards the northeast.
This lane goes through an estate which is part of the faculty of Agronomy
(Landwirtschaftlich-Gärtnerische Fakultät) of Humboldt University. It is a perfect
example of what makes Dahlem so attractive: space and nature. The brick houses surrounded by fields offer a charming and unusual picture. A little further on, at
Schorlemerallee 13-23, visitors who like twenties architecture will appreciate the houses
(1925) built by the Luckhardt brothers and Alfons Anker.

Waldfriedhof Dahlem – **U** *1 Oskar-Helene-Heim, then* **BUS** *Am Waldfriedhof.*
This secluded spot is the last resting place of the poet Gottfried Benn, the sculptor
Renée Sintenis *(see OLYMPIASTADION, Georg-Kolbe-Museum)* and the painter Karl
Schmidt-Rottluff.

IN THE VICINITY

See **GRUNEWALD★★, ZEHLENDORF★**.

Another world awaits visitors inside the greenhouses of the botanical gardens

ERNST-REUTER-PLATZ

Charlottenburg

See map of Berlin Town Centre, **7**, **EFGUV**

This large roundabout designed to ease the flow of traffic was named after a mayor of Berlin.

TWO MAJOR FIGURES

Christian Beuth, the man behind the Prussian "economic miracle" – In 1818, at the age of 27, he was already in charge of the government department of commerce and industry. Three years later, he became president of the influential Association for Industrial Promotion which acted as a link between the government and private enterprise. The same year, he founded the Technical School which, after merging in 1879 with the Academy of Architecture *(Bauakademie)*, founded in 1799, became the **Charlottenburg Technical College** with the purpose of encouraging the study of mechanical and electrical engineering, on which the industrial power of Berlin was based. The College became famous for producing engineers with new ideas. The son of a powerful Viennese manufacturer, **Wittgenstein**, who later became a philosopher, began his studies at the College in 1906. In 1822, Beuth organised the first industrial exhibition in Berlin. Seven of the 182 German industrialists who attended were from Berlin. In 1844, Beuth was again the initiator of an industrial exhibition attended by all the member states of the *Zollverein*, the Customs Union of German States. He called on foreign specialists, in particular the Cockerill Brothers from Verviers (Belgium) who set up a wool-mill containing 15 out of the total 26 steam engines operating in Berlin in 1830. Fifteen years later, the capital boasted five large mills and 3 000 steam engines. Beuth's policies were thus crowned with success.

A courageous mayor – Captured by the Russians during World War I, **Ernst Reuter** (1889-1953) adopted the Communist ideology and became one of Lenin's assistants. After his return to Germany, he became head of the Communist Party (KPD). The year 1921 marked a turning point in his career as he left to join the Social-Democrat Party (SPD). Ernst Reuter was very active on the municipal front. He became a member of the Berlin municipal council in 1926 with much protest from his old comrades who did not forgive him his "betrayal". Reuter was put in charge of transport, unified the system and founded the **BVG**, Berlin's public transport network. This conscientious administrator laid down a programme for social (housing construction scheme) as well as technical (modern amenities; "give the older districts more space to breathe") improvements. He concentrated his efforts on the underground. During the twenties, the length of the network increased by 40km. After a long period of exile in Turkey (1935-45), he went back to Berlin, where he resumed his former activity as head of transport, but he was elected mayor of West Berlin in June 1947, during the cold war. On **9 September 1948**, 300 000 people gathered in front of the Reichstag to protest against the division of Berlin. Ernst Reuter addressed the world: "Peoples of the world! Look upon this city and admit that you have no right to abandon either the city or the people, that you simply cannot abandon them!".

MAIN SIGHTS

Hardenbergstraße – The street is lined with the neo-Baroque buildings of the College of Fine Arts *(Hochschule der Künste, No 33)* and the federal administrative courts *(No 31)* which look like castles. There is a small garden in the centre of **Steinplatz** and a cinema showing art house films nearby. If you wish to travel anywhere in Germany by car, and share travel costs *(Mitfahrer)*, you can look at the notice-board in the *Mensa*, the university restaurant *(in the entrance hall on the right)*, where offers are classified geographically. On the corner of Knesebeckstraße stands the **Renaissance Theatre** (1927, **T'**), which has an elegant interior decoration.

★Savignyplatz – **S** *3, 5, 7, 9, 75 Savignyplatz.*
The lively atmosphere in this district is easily explained by the proximity of the College of Fine Arts and the Technical University, which have attracted several large bookshops *(Bogen, Kiepert: see ZOOLOGISCHER GARTEN and above all the chapter ON THE TOWN)*.

Technische Universität – **U** *2 Ernst-Reuter-Platz.* This huge complex extends on both sides of 17-June Avenue. Founded in 1879 *(see below)*, the school became a university after World War II. The vast neo-Renaissance buildings, which were mostly destroyed during the war, have been replaced by modern ones. There are nearly 40 000 students.

Charlottenburger Tor (**A**) – There are bronze statues of Sophie-Charlotte and her husband Frederick I on either side of the monumental gate built between 1904 and 1909. The **flea-market** stretches from Charlottenburger-Brücke to the S-Bahn bridge.

KPM (Königliche Porzellan-Manufaktur)

This royal manufacture ⊙ is situated behind the Ernst-Reuter-Haus building. It succeeded the porcelain factory founded in Potsdam by Frederick-William in 1678, using the Delft works as a model, after various attempts to found a viable manufacture had failed.

Berlin porcelain vase

Wilhelm Kaspar Wegely a native of Switzerland, who was the manager of a wool-mill, founded the first porcelain manufacture in Berlin in 1751, with the full support of Frederick II, a great collector of porcelain ware. A second factory was founded in 1761 by Johann Ernst Gotzkowsky, and various artists, landscape and flower painters, modellers, and miniaturists, continued to arrive from Meißen, the main centre for the manufacture of Dresden china. The two factories merged in 1763. In order to launch the manufacture, the king compelled any Jews, who wished to acquire a house or get married, to buy some of the famous porcelain; this was how the philosopher Mendelssohn became the proud owner of twenty lifesize monkeys! The production was reputed for being particularly refined and the Berlin artists became famous all over Europe for their floral patterns *(see Schloß CHARLOTTENBURG, Belvedere)*.

Strolling northwards, along tiny streets...

The **river view**★ is splendid at the confluence of the Spree River, the Landwehrkanal and the Verbindungskanal, with barges and cruising-boats gliding along. The banks have been specially laid out for strolling. It is difficult to believe that you are in the heart of the city, with so much water around. As you proceed along the promenade, you will notice the Siemens factory *(Zwietuschwerk Siemens, 1925-26, Salzufer 6-7)* and its crenellated gable.

Helmholtzstraße – Former electric bulb factory owned by Siemens & Halske.

Gotzkowsky Bridge – Modern buildings are mushrooming along the banks of the Spree. *The promenade leads to MOABIT.*

Bismarckstraße – Ⓤ 2 Ernst-Reuter-Platz and Deutsche Oper. It is an imposing modern artery, along the same axis as Unter den Linden Avenue featuring a famous theatre, the Schillertheater (1950-51), and an equally famous opera house, the Deutsche Oper Berlin, formerly the Charlottenburg Opera House, where famous conductors performed between the two world wars. The metallic sculpture in front of its blind concrete façade, has been nicknamed "the meat skewer" *(Schaschlik)*.

IN THE VICINITY

See **Schloß und Museumsquartier CHARLOTTENBURG**★★★, **KURFÜRSTEN-DAMM**★★, **MOABIT**★, **TIERGARTEN**★★.

FISCHERINSEL ★

Mitte

See map of Berlin Mitte p. 248-249, PQZ

Fishermen's Island, part of the **Spree Island** in the historical centre of Berlin, was constructed in the **Alt-Cölln** district, and together with the Nikolaiviertel, represented the cradle of the capital. The formerly densely built up district, over which the Petri church tower used to loom, made way in the 1970s for a modern high-rise housing development. Old houses are now rare.

The Spree Island, with the Museum Island in its northern part, and the Palace of the Republic and the Schloßplatz with the royal stud in its central area, is formed by the Spree and the Kupfergraben which flows in a westerly direction to the Historical Port. That section of the Kupfergraben between the Märkisches Ufer and the Spittelmarkt is also known as Friedrichsgracht, because the Spree was made into a canal with the aid of Dutch engineers under the rule of the Great Elector.

The 1848 Revolution (Vormärz) – On **18 and 19 March 1848**, barricades were erected near Brüderstraße. The heaviest fighting took place in the vicinity of the **Cölln Town Hall**. Members of the middle class, mingling with craftsmen and workers, brandished the **black, red and gold** flag over the barricades. The troops were forced to withdraw.

Frederick-William IV, who had to take his hat off in front of the civilian victims (303 in all) inside the castle coutyard, left for Potsdam and from then on he only rarely came back to Berlin, the "disloyal". The citizens acquired various privileges such as the right to smoke in the street; workers formed their own associations. The congress of German workers, which took place at the end of the summer, saw the foundation of the **Workers' Brotherhood**, the first national union in Germany. As the economic situation went on deteriorating, social unrest continued. The Viennese revolution was quelled. The king was determined to strike a decisive blow: "We must lance the Berlin abscess." General **Wrangel** set up siege conditions: former liberties were suspended; the city was powerless. On 6 December, the king granted a constitution, which provided for the election of local councils, but the voting system based on the poll tax favoured certain eminent persons and left aside the great majority of citizens.

ALONG THE SPREE RIVER

★**Märkisches Museum Stiftung Stadtmuseum Berlin** ⊘ – Ⓤ *2 Märkisches Museum*. The picturesque, six part complex of buildings grouped around two inner courtyards *(see Introduction, Architecture)* was constructed between 1899 and 1908 based on plans by the city architect Ludwig Hoffman, in the style of the Gothic and Renaissance architecture of the Mark Brandenburg (Katharinenkirche in Brandenburg, Bischofsburg in Wittstock). Founded in 1874 as a provincial museum for the Brandenburg Mark on the initiative of **Rudolf Virchow** *(see WEDDING)* and city architect Ernst Friedel, the Märkische Museum is now the principal building of the Stiftung Stadtmuseum Berlin which was founded in 1995.
The museum documents the historical and cultural development of Berlin from the initial traces of colonisation during prehistoric and early historic times, through the establishment of the city at the turn of the 12C and 13C right up to the present day. The copy of the larger than life sandstone figure of the Brandenburger Roland dating from 1474, a legal symbol of city freedoms and privileges, stands in front of the museum's entrance.

Until the completion of extensive restoration work, the museum is showing special exhibitions on various aspects of Berlin history on three floors.

Köllnischer Park – The enclosure of the three brown bears, *Schnute, Maxi* and *Tilo*, is what is left of a bastion, for the park was laid out over the 17C fortifications. It is decorated with remnants of stone carvings: Hercules fighting a lion, several putti and a lovely terracotta fountain dating from the end of the 19C. The building *(AOK Berlin)* on the south side of the park, in front of the bears' lair, was erected in 1931 by Albert Gottheiner.

Märkisches Ufer – The March embankment formed part of the Neukölln am Wasser suburb. There is a view of the tower blocks on Fishermen's Island. A group of six private residences, situated between the two bridges, Inselbrücke and Roßstraßenbrücke, gives a fair idea of what the banks of the Spree looked like before the war. The Neoclassical **Ermelerhaus** (**D**) (formerly Breitestraße 11) has a lovely façade. The earthy Raabe-Diele, named after the tobacconist Raabe, is established in the adjacent cellar.

Wallstraße – Ⓤ *2 Spittelmarkt*.

Hermann-Schlimme-Haus is situated at No 61-65, on the left. Opposite stands Cölln College (Cöllnisches Gymnasium); one of its students was Alfred Wegener who laid down the theory of continental drift in 1912. The building situated at No 76-79, dating from 1912 and decorated with terracotta motifs, was used as its headquarters by the central committee of the Communist Party (KPD), headed by Wilhelm Pieck, between July 1945 and April 1946.
The **Museum für Kindheit und Jugend** (school museum) (**M23**), which covers educational and school history from the 16C to the 1950s, is housed in the school building at no 32.

Spittelmarkt – Ⓤ *2 Spittelmarkt*.
It is difficult to imagine that the present square was one of the main shopping centres of pre-war Berlin. Spindler's Fountain (Spindlerbrunnen), dating from 1882, which, owing to the colour of its granite, has been nicknamed the "chocolate fountain", is still here. *Spittel* is short for "Hospital". **St Gertrude's Hospital** *(Gertraudenhospital)*, dating from the 13C, was erected in front of the western gate of Cölln's medieval fortifications. Following the extension of the walls by Gregor Memhardt, it found its place on the site of the present Spittelmarkt. When these defensive works became superfluous, several bridges were built across the moat to link the area to the neighbouring Friedrichstadt district. **Karl von Gontard** decorated the bridge leading to **Leipziger Straße** with two rows of columns. The south row (**Spittelkolonnade, E**) was re-erected near its original site in 1980.

Gertraudenbrücke – A bronze **statue** (1896), representing the patron of hospitals and travellers, stands in the middle of the bridge; St Gertrude's Hospital stood nearby. There is a fine neo-Gothic corner house at No 10-12 Gertraudenstraße. The star-shaped building on the opposite side of the street (corner of Breite Straße/Gertraudenstraße on Fishermen's Island) used to be a self-service restaurant in the days of the German Democratic Republic. Note the overall view of the tower blocks inhabited by 5 000 people, which dominate the southern part of the Spree Island; this kind of town planning continues beyond Gertraudenstraße along Leipziger Straße.

Jungfernbrücke – A shopkeeper called Blanchet, a Huguenot who had emigrated, had two daughters, both skillful lace-makers;

they used to sell their lace on Friedrichswerder bridge, a lovely Dutch-style structure which became known as "Jungfernbrücke". However, the present bridge dates from 1798; it was nevertheless the oldest bridge in Berlin. The arches are in red sandstone; the central part lifted to allow ships through. On this site stood the mills of Werder municipality (Werdersche Mühlen) and the public wash-houses (Waschbänke).

Petriplatz – Erected in 1237, St Peter's Church (Petrikirche) was rebuilt in neo-Gothic style in the mid-19C; at the time, its tower was the highest in Berlin. Its substantial ruins did not survive the GDR's town planning schemes. **No 17 Scharrenstraße**, on the corner of the tiny Gertraudenstraße, is a fine neo-Baroque house.

Brüderstraße – This street used to link Cölln fish market and the dominican monastery. It got its name (*Brüderstraße*: "Brothers' Street") when, early in 1813, the *Landsturm* volunteers were brought together to fight French occupation. Barricades were put up nearby on **18 and 19 March 1848**. **Nicolaihaus**, at No 13, an annexe of the City of Berlin Museum Foundation **F**, was originally a medieval house which had been enlarged several times. It was remodelled in 1787 by Carl-Friedrich Zelter and became the home of publisher and bookseller **Christoph Friedrich Nicolai**. At the end of the courtyard *(right-hand door)*, there is a beautiful **Neoclassical staircase** probably designed by Schinkel, decorated with restored paintings. **Galgenhaus**, at **No 10** (the "Gibbet House"), is more attractive from the ouside owing to its refined frieze with foliage motifs and its bell-shaped dormer windows *(Fledermausgaupe)*.

Mühlendamm – *See NIKOLAIVIERTEL.*

Breite Straße – The Breite Straße connects Schloßplatz with the fishermen's Island, and was Cölln's "Kudamm" after the Second World War. Two interesting buildings remain: **Ribbeck House (Ribbeckhaus)**, at No 35 (**G**), decorated with pinnacled gables, is the only specimen of late Renaissance architecture left in Berlin. It was built by Hans Georg von Ribbeck, a member of the Elector's Council (Kurfürstlicher Kammerrat) and was joined to the old stables next door (**Alter Marstall**, at No 36-37) in 1660. The latter are examples of early Baroque style. The doorway of the **Stadtbibliothek** (**B'**) (No 32-34) is stamped with the letter *A* in different styles and alphabets.

IN THE VICINITY

See **SCHLOSSPLATZ, NIKOLAIVIERTEL★.**

FRIEDRICHSHAIN
Friedrichshain
See map of Berlin Town Centre, **5**, **MTUV**

The road to Frankfurt-on-Oder, called Frankfurter Linden (Linden: lime trees) used to go through the suburb of Stralau and lead to Friedrichsfelde Castle. Very little remains of the Friedrichshain *Mietskasernen*, which have been replaced by the imposing **Karl-Marx-Allee** and the Council flats built by the GDR.

A tradition of violence – Street fighting occurred frequently in this district, for instance in 1919 against Noske's troops, and above all on 29 December 1928. That night, two members of a secret society called Norden, headed by Adolf Leib, alias Muskel-Adolf, stormed into a restaurant and asked the members of another secret society for their help, arguing that one of their members had been stabbed by a carpenter working on the construction of the Breslauer Straße underground station (nowadays Hauptbahnhof). The murderer was identified but he gained the support of his fellow workers; the secret society members, numbering 200 men armed with knives, guns and clubs, arrived on the spot. Fighting went on for 20 minutes. It revealed the extent of the underground work accomplished by the "**Ringvereine**". Founded at the end of the 19C, these were initially networks designed to help released prisoners; they were soon brought together under the leadership of an association founded in 1898, *Ring-Berlin*. These associations became gangs of racketeers, taking over places of entertainment, furnishing alibis, offering bribes to lawyers and putting pressure on witnesses. The funeral services of their members were organised in grand style. Their names are deceptive: Geselligkeit ("Sociability"), Immertreu ("Always faithful"); in 1933, the police recorded 85 such associations. They were tolerated because they ruled over the underworld (Unterwelt) and saved the police time spent on surveillance and enquiries. After the Breslauer Straße fighting, Immertreu and Norden were outlawed. A court action was initiated in Moabit against Muskel-Adolf and seven "Immertreu-Brüder". It turned out to be a victory for the Ringvereine: the defence was efficient and the witnesses did not remember a thing or were confounded; Muskel-Adolf was condemned to 10 months' imprisonment; the two associations could resume their activities. **Fritz Lang** drew upon the character of Muskel-Adolf for his film **M.** in which the actor **Gustav Gründens** is the chief of one of these Ringvereine and takes the law into his own hands to punish a child murderer. The Ringvereine were abolished by the Nazis in 1934. Considered as professional criminals, their members were sent to concentration camps.

The "beast of Silesia Station"

It would take too long to give a full account of criminal activities in Friedrichshain. The district surrounding Silesia Station (Schlesischer Bahnhof), now gone, was, at the beginning of the 20C, one of the shadiest areas in town along with Scheunenviertel. It was in the hands of a gang of young thieves. A number of murderers and other criminals lived along Langstraße. "Captain Köpenick" *(see under that name)* was arrested there, but the most notorious inhabitant was **Karl Großmann**. Up to 1918, twenty-three mutilated bodies were found on park benches, in waste-bins or in the canals in the vicinity of the station. In the end, a 57-year-old pedlar was arrested (Kurz- und Schreibwarenhausierer); although he did not admit to all the crimes, he was undoubtedly a sadistic killer. He was accused of three murders.

The June 1953 uprising – East Berlin was the site of the first uprising to take place in the Communist block. In 1952-53, the situation deteriorated in the GDR. Agriculture was collectivised and production facilities were organised on Socialist principles as part of a five-year plan to boost heavy industry; as a result there was a food shortage and workers saw their working conditions worsen. A massive exodus took place, via West Berlin. The 10% increase in the level of productivity, announced on 28 May 1953, acted as a detonator. On 16 June, 70 builders from "block 40" on the Stalin Allee construction site, who were considered reliable, abandoned their work and marched on Alexanderplatz, holding banners with such slogans as: "No to the productivity increase", soon replaced by political slogans: "Down with Ulbricht"; those who happened to be around started making for the seats of government. A call went out to all workers on **17 June**: protests were heard all over the GDR; there were as many as 400 000 strikers. The demonstrators set fire to the headquarters of the SED newspaper, asking for free elections; prisoners were freed. The Berlin region was the centre of the first uprising inside the Communist block. As the German government seemed powerless, the Russians intervened; a state of emergency and a curfew were imposed; the Red Army tanks were greeted with stones on Potsdamer Platz; the police, who accounted for most of the 21 victims, acted with extreme brutality. The Western powers did not make a move as the spheres of influence had been carefully defined. The 17 June was to be the FRG's National Day until 1990 and an avenue prolonging Unter den Linden was named after the event. *(see TIERGARTEN).*

MAIN SIGHTS

Volkspark Friedrichshain – *No 100* 🚌 *or No 2, 3, 4* 🚊 *Am Friedrichshain.*
This park was originally designed to commemorate the centenary of Frederick II's accession to the throne (1840). However, as soon as it was laid out it became the burial site of the victims of the March 1848 revolution. It is a vast stretch of woodland, with paths winding up the main hill which, like another smaller hill nearby, is flanked by a anti-aircraft defence tower *(flakbunker, see WEDDING, Volkspark Humboldthain)*, but trees and building works hide the view. The neo-Baroque **Fairy Tale Fountain (Märchenbrunnen)** displays an ornamental waterfall. The leisure park (Freizeitpark) offers numerous activities: bowling, sharp-shooting, artificial climbing, miniature golf, table tennis, volleyball, tennis, croquet, "boccia" (Italian bowling) and chess.

Platz der Vereinten Nationen – *No 5, 6, 8, 15* 🚊 *Platz der Vereinten Nationen.*
Formerly called Leninplatz, it illustrates "real Socialism"; the square is outsized with isolated concrete buildings, poorly constructed and already dilapidated. Lenin is gone.

★Strausberger Platz – Ⓤ *5 Strausberger Platz.* The buildings in the fifties-style are impressive; they were designed from the plans of an intersection drawn by Bruno Möhring in 1920. Strausbergerplatz is all the more interesting because of its oval shape resulting in a slight deviation of Karl-Marx-Allee.

★Karl-Marx-Allee – Ⓤ *5 Rathaus Friedrichshain.* One of the GDR's most prestigious avenues, formerly called **Stalin-Allee** (1949-1961), Karl-Marx-Allee is a huge artery which is being completely renovated. It is not until you go through the row of buildings which run along it that you discover that it is a kind of stage-setting: behind are a few smaller blocks of flats, but the main impression is one of emptiness. The best viewpoint is from the Ⓤ *5 Rathaus Friedrichshain Station, next to* the **Frankfurter Gate** (Frankfurter Tor). Two of the buildings are surmounted by domed towers reminiscent of Gendarmenmarkt twin domes; the view extends to the television tower.

Next to the Frankfurter Tor, take the 🚌 *(Kandiner Straße stop). Head either south, alighting at "Oberbaumbrücke", or west to "Hauptbahnhof". Both these stops are near Mühlenstraße.*

★Mauer-Galerie – *Mühlenstraße,* Ⓢ *Hauptbahnhof or* Ⓤ *1, 15 Schlesisches Tor (cross Oberbaumbrücke).* On the West Berlin side, the Wall resembled an open-air art gallery. Entire stretches of wall covered with the most outstanding graffiti have been relocated along Mühlenstraße where they form an amazing sight.

IN THE VICINITY

See **ALEXANDERPLATZ★, KREUZBERG (East part)★★**.

The twin domes of the Frankfurt gate on either side of Karl-Marx-Allee

FRIEDRICHSTRASSE★

Mitte, Kreuzberg
See map of Berlin Mitte p. 248-249, **OYZ**

Friedrichstraße forms part of the new Berlin redevelopment program as the main shopping streeet of the **Mitte** district in the historic centre. Lined with plain but elegant buildings, stocky and compact in typical Berlin style, it looks rather severe. The district is gradually livening up as the end of the rebuilding work draws near and, following in an old tradition, it already has several entertainment establishments, where it is pleasant to take refuge in winter when cold winds blow down the straight adjacent streets.

Urban expansion – When Berlin became a garrison town in 1657 and there was a massive influx of soldiers and French Huguenots, it had to expand. The second princely city was thus founded on land belonging to the Great Elector and named **Dorotheenstadt** after his wife. Friedrichstraße belonged to this district situated north of Unter den Linden. The southern section was, with **Leipziger Straße**, one of the main arteries of **Friedrichstadt**, which developed during the reign of Frederick I, first king of Prussia, after whom it was named. In the 18C, Friedrichstadt was the most spacious and the most populated district of Berlin as well as the capital's cultural centre *(see GENDARMENMARKT)*. Friedrichstraße was lined with lovely two-storeyed houses inhabited by well-to-do families, poets and scientists.

Friedrichstraße in 1878

The heart of Berlin in the late 19C – From 1870 onwards, all the buildings were demolished. While Unter den Linden remained an elegant avenue, Friedrichstraße welcomed hotels, restaurants such as that where **Bernhard Kempinski** regaled Berlin society (his family emigrated to London and opened a restaurant there, but came back to West Berlin in 1945), cafés (the Kranzler, the Bauer, the Kerkau, the café-cum-billiard room run by a former champion), theatres such as the Admiralspalast, the Metropol and the Apollo-Theater where Paul Lincke directed *Frau Luna* in 1899, the variety show theatre *Wintergarten*, cabarets such as Max Reinhardt's famous *Noise and Smoke*, and shops. Cinema producers settled there as well. The southern section of the street was more elegant than the northern section lined with bistros and similar establishments. Workers, who hardly left the northern and eastern districts of Berlin, went on Sundays to the **Kaisergalerie**, an arcade now replaced by the Maritim-Grandhotel, where the wax museum Panoptikum *(see KURFÜRSTENDAMM)* attracted crowds. Between the two world wars, Friedrichstraße was overtaken by Kurfürstendamm but, owing to the proximity of the press district (along Kochstraße), it remained very lively, with its wealth of small theatres and major Broadway music-halls. Factory workers gave way to office workers, including a growing number of women. The advent of Nazism put an end to this endless variety. There was fierce fighting along Friedrichstraße in 1945.

FRIEDRICHSTRASSE

"Tränenpalast" – The "palace of tears" was the nickname given to Friedrichstraße Station, the transit area for visitors from the West, which is currently used for cultural events. The U-Bahn line 6, which used to travel between the West Berlin districts of Wedding and Kreuzburg through walled East Berlin "ghost stations" under constant surveillance, now stops here, as does the north-south S-Bahn. Although Friedrichstraße station, together with the border post, was located in the heart of East Berlin, it was possible to change here on the West Berlin suburban system. The north has continued to offer entertainment with theatres such as the Metropol-Theater (formerly the Admiralspalast), the Die Distel (The Thistle) satirical cabaret, and the Friedrichstadtpalast music hall *(see CHARITÉ)*. Further south, there was a concentration of large hotels, as in Unter den Linden. Some of the buildings covered over with concrete slabs decorated with mouldings date from that period.

ALONG FRIEDRICHSTRASSE

The walk starts from the ⓢ + Ⓤ *Friedrichstraße Station and follows the street of the same name to the* Ⓤ *6 Kochstraße Station.*

Internationales Handelszentrum Berlin – This large, black-and-white, metal-and-glass building which you see as you come out of the station is in striking contrast with the historic surroundings.

Dorotheenstraße 37 – Neo-Baroque façade of the former Splendid Hotel, taken over by the Berliner Volksbank. Brawny telamones support the doorway.

Friedrichstraße/Unter den Linden Crossroads – *No 100* 🚌 *Unter den Linden/ Friedrichstraße.*
The imposing Kranzler and Bauer coffee houses were situated at this busy intersection; the latter is still there. Switzerland House stands on the northwest corner and Linden Corso Business Centre on the southeast corner. From the crossroads there is a splendid view of the tall buildings lining Friedrichstraße.

Friedrichstraße – Ⓤ *5 Französische Straße.*

Friedrichstraße★ reveals its new look south of Unter den Linden. Note in particular:
– Three beautiful **façades** in **Jugendstil** style on the corner of Friedrichstraße and Behrenstraße: **No 165, 166** (neo-Gothic, in red sandstone, 1899) and **167**. Behrenstraße, named after Johann Heinrich Behr, who designed the surrounding streets, was the banking street. Here, for instance, stood the headquarters of Bleichröder's bank, "Berlin's Rothschild" *(see the INTRODUCTION, The Burden of History)*.
The glass **Galeries Lafayette building★** (Friedrichstraße 207 or **"Quartier 207"**), which stands at the intersection of Französische Straße (the only street corner in the district not to be at a right angle), was designed by **Jean Nouvel** and his associate Cattani. The flowing lines of the interior convey an equally strange impression. The Berlin Galeries Lafayette *(see ON THE TOWN, Shopping)*, which is relatively small compared with the huge Parisian store, is built around two large cones. From the ground floor, it is possible

The Galeries Lafayette by Jean Nouvel

to admire the iridescent shimmering light effects on the inverted cone, which provides a glimpse of the shoppers in the delicatessen department. One is tempted to go over the balustrade and slide down the shiny surface; looking up gives an impression of being aboard an airship. The impression is even more striking from the third floor (men's fashion); the conflict between the vertical lines of the cones and the horizontal lines of the counters makes it easy to lose one's sense of direction.

– **"Quartier 206" (H)** was designed by Pei (the architect who designed the Louvre pyramid in Paris), Cobb & Freed, in New York. It is not just a commercial building; provision was made for a great many flats as well. It looks striking at night, when the protruding parts of the building are underlined by luminous bars. The hall contains remarkable marble inlays.

– **Quartier 205 "Friedrichstadtpassagen"**, based on a square shape, is discreetly elegant.

– **Taubenstraße 3** *(on the corner of Glinkastraße,* **U** *2, 6 Stadtmitte)*, is the only 18C house remaining in the former Friedrichstadt. Friedrich D. E. Schleiermacher (1768-1834), a philosopher, theologian and one of the founding members of Berlin University, lived there once.

– **Adler Coffee House** *(***U** *6 Kochstraße)*, formerly the "White Eagle Pharmacy" *(Apotheke zum Weissem Adler*, 1696), is on the corner of Zimmerstraße and Friedrichstraße.

For the following sights, see the map of Berlin Town Centre, **B**, **JKV**.

Leipzigerstraße – **U** *6 Stadtmitte.*
The vast buildings extending horizontally (housing 6 000 people), date from the seventies and are being renovated.

Museum für Kommunikation Berlin (M¹) (KV) ⊘ – *No 142* **S** **U** *Stadtmitte/ Leipzigerstraße.*
The Communications Museum now stands in a truly magnificent setting, in the historical buiding which was home to the old Reich Postal Museum. This sumptuous Wilhelmian palace, takes visitors on a journey through the past, the present and the future of communications.

Museum of Checkpoint Charlie – **U** *6 Kochstraße.*
Five building sites forming part of the "Checkpoint Charlie Business Center" surround the former guardhouse. Office buildings, blocks of flats, and shopping centres built by German and American architects, including Philip Johnson who designed the future "Quartier 106", are going up all around.

Haus am Checkpoint Charlie (M²) (KV) ⊘ – **U** *6 Kochstraße.*
A collection of miscellaneous items selected purely for ideological reasons, illustrating the main stages of East/West confrontation and, along more general lines, of confrontation in general (explanations in German, English and Russian). Audiovisual documents; account of the various, often fantastic, means of "escaping to the West": aboard a tractor, inside the boot of a car, in the space reserved for the battery or the radiator or inside a suitcase, with the help of ladders, by means of a seat suspended from a cable, by jumping from a window *(see WEDDING, Bernauer Straße)*. Most attempts at escaping ended in tragedy; on 17 June 1962, the young Peter Fechter lay dying for an hour after having been shot down by the Vopos. The official number of people killed trying to escape is 80, but there may have been several hundreds. The last victim was Chris Gueffroy who was shot on 6 February 1989. 60 000 people were condemned for having attempted to "escape from the Republic" or simply for having made "preparations".

Mehringplatz und Friedenssäule – *See KREUZBERG (West part).*

IN THE VICINITY

See **CHARITÉ★, GENDARMENMARKT★★, KREUZBERG (West part)★★, POTSDAMER PLATZ, UNTER DEN LINDEN★★.**

FUNKTURM ★

The **Radio Tower** or "Langer Lulatsch", which can be roughly translated as "tall chap" is one of the emblems of Berlin. It forms, together with the congress centre, an interesting townscape, particularly at night when they can be seen towering over the express carriageway *(overall view from the entrance to Halensee, see KURFÜRSTENDAMM)*.

The Radio Tower

Berlin, exhibition town – In the early twenties, Berlin was the most modern town in Germany. It had more businesses (290 000) than Bade and Wurtemberg put together. 2 000 large firms were dominated by the giants of electrical engineering and machinery. The municipal council then had the idea of organising trade fairs devoted to specific fields of activity as opposed to the general fair in Leipzig, for instance. This initiative marked the beginning of the **Radio exhibition** (Funkausstellung), which is now programmed every other year, and is one of the largest trade fairs in the world in the field of electronics and audiovisual equipment. When it was organised for the third time in 1924, it was decided to build a 138m-tower which could be used as a transmitter and a beacon for aircrafts.

MAIN SIGHTS

Theodor-Heuss-Platz – **U** *2 Theodor-Heuss-Platz.*
From the beginning of Kaiserdamm, a huge vista opens up, stretching as far as the Victory Column and even beyond, to the "Red Town Hall" and the Television Tower on Alexanderpaltz. In the centre of the square stands the Blue Obelisk. The banker Heinrich Mendelssohn sensed that an investment in a building project situated on top of the hill, the highest point in Charlottenburg, and following the east-west axis,

---

Am Rupenhorn
(see map of Berlin conurbation, **10**, **AU**)

Those who are particularly fond of architecture might like to take a 149 bus to Ragniter Allee, where they will be able to see one of Erich Mendelsohn's houses, which is not much to look at but happens to be the first cubic building with a terrace erected in Berlin (1923-24). Leave the bus at the Stößenseebrücke stop in order to have a look at **Am Rupenhorn** Street, curved and lined with villas: on the corner of Heerstraße stands a villa built of reinforced concrete by the Luckhardt brothers, in true New Objectivity style; No 6 Am Rupenhorn is a terraced house where Erich Mendelsohn lived and worked from 1930 to 1933 *(difficult to see)*. The weight of **Stößenseebrücke**, a metallic engineering work constructed on sandy soil at the beginning of the 20C, rests almost entirely on the unique central pillar.

could have enormous value; he therefore had **Germany House** (Deutschlandhaus), which housed the first television studio in 1936, and **America House** (Amerikahaus) built on the south side. The metal scaffolding attached to the latter was used to support a giant sign, underlining the new role played by advertising in the facelifted metropolis. A little further south, there is an interesting house designed by Erich Mendelsohn, on the southwest corner of Karolingerplatz *(No 5-5a)*.

★**Haus des Rundfunks** – *Make yourself known to the caretaker at the entrance.*
Built by **Hans Poelzig**, the Broadcasting House, which was the first in Germany (1929-30) is clad with glazed bricks and has a beautiful Art Deco **hall**★ decorated with a statue by G. Kolbe: *Long Night (Große Nacht).*

The hall of the Broadcasting House

Ph. Gajic/MICHELIN

Messegelände – Ⓢ *45 Witzleben.*
The central part overlooking Hammarskjöldplatz, the *Herrenhalle* (1940), with its pillars and two low wings, is the work of Richard Ermisch. It is reminiscent of the New Objectivity style and the monumental architectural style of the Third Reich.

Funkturm Ⓥ – *Entrance opposite the Broadcasting House, on the left of "Herrenhalle". Go through the first building into the garden.*
The Radio Tower (1924-26) ceased to be a radio transmitter in 1962, a role taken over by the 230m-high Scholzplatz mast, near Am Rupenhorn Street. It is now only used by the police and the fire-brigade. Designed by Heinrich Straumer, this metallic structure is surprisingly light (400 tons, compared with 7 000 tons for the Eiffel Tower). It also takes up a very small area (20m x 20m). Situated at the foot of the Radio Tower, the small **German Radio Museum** (Deutsches Rundfunkmuseum) displays many radio sets illustrating the history of radio and television transmission since 1924. German radio transmission first began in Berlin in 1923 in the *Vox* House in Potsdam Street. Sets were mass-produced during the Third Reich in order to bring the price down; radio then became the most efficient means of propaganda, in the form of "Goebbel's mouth". The first-ever television transmission was made from Berlin in 1931.
A smooth climb in the lift to the top of the Radio Tower leads to an exceptional **panorama**★★★ of the Berlin conurbation. Note in particular:
– To the **north**, the red buildings of Siemensstadt.
– To the **south**, Grunewald Forest, split into two by the straight **Avus** motorway. The best way to get an idea of the size of this forest is to remember that the transmitting tower on top of Schäferberg, in Wannsee, marks its southern limits. To the southwest, are Teufelsberg Observatory and the Havel; beyond *(open-air viewing platform)*, the view extends as far as Peacock Island *(Pfaueninsel)*.
– To the **west**, the Olympic Stadium and Le Corbusier's building *(see OLYMPIA-STADION)*.
– To the **east**, the compact mass of the ICC, the dome of Charlottenburg Castle surrounded by its Park, Tiergarten, the Memorial Church, the historic centre of Berlin. Climbing to the top of the Radio Tower offers the best view of the different buildings of the **Exhibition Complex**: the Deutschlandhalle dating from 1935, the ice-skating rink (Eissporthalle) and the various halls, 26 in all, surrounding the oval summer garden (Sommergarten). The strange shape of the **Broadcasting House** isolates the three main recording studios from street noise.

Internationales Congreß Centrum Berlin – This is the Berlin congress centre, the result of a substantial investment which promoted the city to 6th place among all the congress cities in the world. The sculpture standing in front of the main entrance representing *Alexander in front of Ecbatane*, is the work of the French artist Jean Ipoustéguy (1980).

★**Lietzensee** – The district surrounding this lake, split into two by Kantstraße, is probably the most middle-class district of Berlin, considering that it is still in the town proper and not in a residential suburb. The streets, lined with substantial buildings such as **Leonhardtstraße** and the area surrounding Amtsgerichtsplatz, are peaceful. In summer, you can take a pleasant stroll through the district to the southern end of the lake and sit down by a tiered **waterfall** (*access through Dernburgstraße*). Nearby, on the way back to Charlottenburg S-Bahn Station, look at the amazing **IBA 87 Building** at No 17 Rönnestraße.

IN THE VICINITY

See **OLYMPIASTADION★**

GENDARMENMARKT★★

Mitte

See map of Berlin Mitte p. 248-249, **OZ**

With its domes and theatre, **Gendarmenmarkt** is a very handsome square indeed. The edifices bordering it were severely damaged by bombing in 1944. They were rebuilt between 1977 and 1983, with funds from the GDR. Unfortunately, the appearance of the most attractive monumental square in Berlin is partly spoilt by the buildings lining Leipziger Straße to the south.

HISTORICAL NOTES

The Huguenots, French contribution to Berlin life - At the end of the 17C, Berlin set itself apart from the rest of protestant Germany: the prince was a Calvinist whereas the state of Brandenburg had adopted the Lutheran faith; he therefore encouraged

Schauspielhaus and French cathedral

A Huguenot dynasty: the Ancillons

These refugees from Metz in eastern France formed a close-knit, very active group. The Ancillon family founded the Reformed Church in their native Lorraine. David Ancillon supervised the establishment of the Huguenot community in Berlin; his sons Joseph and Charles held high office in the judiciary. Charles was the Great Elector's historian; he was also the headmaster of the French Lycée and took part in the foundation of the Scientific Society, regularly exchanging letters with Leibniz. Louis Ancillon was a vicar and a member of the academy; he read Frederick II's obituary; in the 19C, Jean-Pierre Ancillon was the tutor of the king of Prussia's son and his minister of foreign affairs.

people of his own religion to become influential citizens. An edict establishing religious tolerance was proclaimed in 1664; as a result, some 100 French protestants settled in Brandenburg as early as 1672.

When the Edict of Nantes was revoked in 1685, the **Edict of Potsdam** was proclaimed in order to attract French Calvinists to Brandenburg. There were numerous advantages: exemption from paying taxes for a period of four years, free timber, no guild fee, no obligation to billet soldiers. A vast advertising campaign took place in France and in Frankfurt-am-Main which, in the space of 20 years, received 100 000 Huguenots on their way to other German towns. There were 15 000 in Brandenburg alone and 6 000 in Berlin, who represented a quarter of the total population, and were responsible for the development of the new town of **Friedrichstadt**. The French minority enjoyed special privileges until the 19C. It had its own ecclesiastical and judicial institutions.

The impact of these French immigrants was not only demographic; French influence had lasting results in various ways: about 50 new crafts were introduced into the country, manufactures were created and the textile industry developed, various fruit and vegetables were acclimatised, new dances (the *cotillion*, *gavotte*, *minuet*) became fashionable, and the first inns were opened.

French culture encouraged the blossoming of the Enlightenment in Prussia. One of the best ways to achieve this was through teaching: the young princes, the future Frederick III and the "King-Sergeant", all had French tutors. The **French Lycée**, founded

Ph. Gajic/MICHELIN

in 1689, welcomed the Calvinist élite; today it is the turn of the best German students. A French philosopher, **Etienne Chauvin** founded Berlin's first scientific journal (1696), to which Leibniz contributed. According to a local saying of the time, "he who does not speak French cannot succeed". The **Humboldt brothers** and the novelist **Theodor Fontane** were born of mixed marriages. During the occupation of Prussia by Napoleon, the French Protestants tended to become Prussians: for instance, the name *Blanc* was changed to *Weiß*.

Uninterrupted architectural development – Frederick-William I, who had the reputation of being thrifty, was no great patron of the arts. However, he followed with interest the development of the new town of **Friedrichstadt**, stimulated by the Huguenot contribution. Many churches and private mansions were built. The "King-Sergeant" ordered that a guards regiment should be stationed in it, hence the French name given to the vast oblong square of the new town: *Gens-d'Armes Markt*.

Inaugurated in 1705, the **French Church** was the first public building erected in the new district. It was modelled on the demolished church in Charenton, near Paris. The construction of the **New Church** (Neue Kirche or Deutscher Dom), intended for German Calvinists, was almost simultaneous. During the 18C, several edifices were built between Unter den Linden and Gendarmenmarkt to meet the needs of the French community: church, college, seminary, law courts and theatre.

The layout of the square was completed at the end of Frederick II's reign: between 1780 and 1785, **Karl von Gontard** erected, near the churches, two twin buildings surmounted by melon-shaped domes, as well as a "Comédie Française" which became the German National Theatre after the king's death.

MAIN SIGHTS

Nearest Ⓢ: Ⓢ *Friedrichstraße.*

★★Schauspielhaus (T¹⁵) – Ⓤ *2,* Ⓤ *6 Stadtmitte or* Ⓤ *6 Französische Straße.* Founded in 1786, the **German National Theatre** became one of the main German theatres under the management of the actor Iffland (*see INTRODUCTION, Literature*). Following the fire which destroyed Langhans's building (1817), **Schinkel** rebuilt the **Schauspielhaus** (1820). Budget restrictions compelled the architect to design a plain, functional edifice (another project, this time for the Hamburg opera house, did away with the portico), without any vaulting; its Antique-style decoration consisted mainly of a profusion of pilasters. **E.T.A. Hoffmann** wrote these comments about the interior (nothing remains except the concert hall): "As soon as you enter the new theatre, you feel like spending half a day, and even longer, enjoying the sight... The best artists are working on it and you may say that the smallest detail is a master-piece". Strangely enough, the staircase was reserved for the middle-classes whilst the nobility had its own entrance under the staircase, where carriages could be stored. **Schiller's monument** stands in the centre of the square.

★Französischer Dom (N) ⊙ – In exchange for land given up to carry out Frederick II's projects, the French community was granted the use of the dome which today houses the Huguenot Museum, a library and the community's office.

Dome★ *(entrance on south side)* – It gives the strange impression of going inside the chimney shaft of a factory. The interesting **view★★** extends over the centre of Berlin, a mixture of modern buildings, Neo-Gothic church towers, domes, red-tiled roofs, green open spaces and a forest of cranes. There is also a good view to the west, of the Philharmonie, the Memorial Church, Tiergarten and Teufelsberg beyond; to the north, is the tower of Charité Hospital; to the east, Museum Island and the cathedral, Alexanderplatz and the twin spires of St Nicholas Church.

Hugenottenmuseum – Fine display illustrating the history of the Reformation, in particular of Calvinism, Protestants in France, the revocation of the Edict of Nantes and the way French Huguenots were welcomed in Brandenburg. The documents are plentiful: books, prints, copies of original documents (*ask for the English translation of the explanatory notes at the entrance*).

The **church** *(turn right as you come out of the tower; entrance on the west side)* was remodelled in 1905-1906 and a transverse nave added. It is still used by the French Protestant community. Up to the period preceding World War II, the vicar used to preach in French every other Sunday. The most interesting item is the **organ**, a replica of the original 18C instrument. It is particularly suited to the performance of French classical works (*a free concert is given on every first Thursday of the month, at 7.30 pm*); there are also some original gilt carvings.

★Deutscher Dom (N¹) – The cathedral is being restored to accommodate the exhibition *Fragen an die deutsche Geschichte* ⊙ ("let us consult German history"), which used to be on display in the Reichstag.

Mohrenkolonnaden (**P**) – *Mohrenstraße 37b and 40-41*. These arcades, resting on Tuscan-style twin columns, used to decorate a bridge which spanned the former moat separating Friedrichstadt and Friedrichswerder. Although they are now incorporated in the structure of other buildings, they are the only ones to have remained in their original place. The others, which stood on Königsbrücke (*see ALEXANDERPLATZ and SCHÖNEBERG, Kleistpark*) and Spittelmarkt (*see FISCHERINSEL*) have been moved. The Mühlendamm arcade was demolished in 1892.

IN THE VICINITY

See **FRIEDRICHSTRASSE★**, **KREUZBERG (west part)★★**, **SCHLOSSPLATZ**, **UNTER DEN LINDEN★★**.

GRUNEWALD★★

Wilmersdorf, Zehlendorf
See map of Berlin Conurbation, **10**, **ABUV**

The hunting lodge built by the Elector **Joachim II** in a place called "Zum Grünen Wald" *(see below)* gave its name to Berlin's largest forest and to the district situated on its northeastern border, which is reputed to be the most residential district of the city. Comfortable villas surround the small lakes and line the shaded avenues. The **Avus** motorway, inaugurated in 1921 and running parallel to the S-Bahn line, crosses the forest from end to end. Several lakes suitable for bathing enhance the attractiveness of this area which is ideal for strolling among pines and various deciduous trees.

"AVUS"

The first German motorway was also the first motor-racing track. Originally reserved for private use, it was created in 1909 by the "Automobil-Verkehrs-und-Übungsstraße GmbH" (the initials form the word "AVUS") for the purpose of testing vehicles. The motorway was inaugurated in 1921. Records were set almost from the start, in particular by German manufacturers. During the course of the first race, Fritz von Opel achieved an average of 128.24km an hour and the 261km-an-hour record established before the war was only beaten in 1958. The German Grand Prix was set up in 1926. Ten years later, the track was used for the Olympic Games marathon race.

MAIN SIGHTS

As the forest is very extensive, it is possible to take a walk in two different directions, starting from the Grunewald residential district.

★**Villenviertel Grunewald** – (See map of Berlin Town Centre, **6**, **EY**). **Ⓢ** *3, 7 Grunewald*.
This district became a built-up area in 1889, with the support of Bismarck. There are interesting villas in Kronberger Straße, in Seebergsteig, where a neo-Gothic manor-house (at No 23) stands on the corner of Hubertusbader Straße, in Brahmsstraße (No 4-10, *The Four Seasons Hotel*) and above all in the quiet **Douglasstraße**, in which the South African embassy stands opposite Flechtheim House (No 12), a specimen of New Objectivity; Ribbentrop, who was the head of the diplomatic service of the Third Reich, lived there just before World War II. **Konschewski House** (1922-23), situated at the end of **Gottfried-von-Cramm-Weg** (No 35-37), is an impressive villa (the architect used to build theatres). Its façade denotes the influence of the Rococo style. Hagenstraße before it crosses Wildpfad is also lined with beautiful villas.

TOWARDS THE HAVEL:

Teufelssee and Teufelsberg – **Ⓢ** *3, 7 Grunewald*.
The "Devil's Mountain" *(Teufelsberg)*, a skiing area much appreciated in winter, is also a favourite with locals on New Year's Eve. It is the highest (120 m, 25 million cubic metres) of the nine hills known as Mont Klamott erected in Berlin after the war from rubble left in the wake of the Allied bombings. The top is occupied by a radar station. The small **"Devil's Lake" (Teufelssee)** is, together with Halensee, the meeting-place of nature lovers. *Walk through the pine forest until you reach the Havel.*

Pleasure boats and yachts sail up and down the Havel. All the small sandy patches along the banks are taken over by bathers. A path, following the shoreline, leads to the **Schildhorn** peninsula. The monument erected there in 1845 by order of Frederick-William IV illustrates the legend of the Slav prince **Jaczo of Köpenick**.

The conversion of a fugitive prince

Jaczo of Köpenick was **Albert the Bear**'s *(Albrecht der Bär)* most formidable adversary. He seized Brandenburg by treachery but the city was recaptured in 1157. The gods, called upon by Jaczo during the battle, abandoned him; nor did they help him as he was fleeing after the defeat. As the Christians were catching up on him, he heard their cries. He arrived at the edge of the Havel river and thought: "Instead of helping me, the gods have led me into an impasse!". The prince's faith in Triglav, Belbog and Czernibog weakened. He thought of Christ holding out a helping hand *(versöhnende Liebe)* and he begged him to save him in return for his conversion. As the cries of his pursuers sounded ever closer, Jaczo dived with his horse into the Havel; nobody dared follow him. He spurred his horse on but the animal found it difficult to swim against the current; so he grasped the branch of a pine tree while his faithful horse was swept away. He kneeled down in front of the pine tree and gave thanks to Christ. He hung up his shield *(Schild)* and his horn *(Horn)* on one of the branches, for whatever actions he had done in the name of his old gods, he did not want to perpetrate in the name of the loving Christ. Frederich-William IV had a monument erected in 1844 on the very spot where Jaczo was believed to have landed: it is a sandstone column representing a tree trunk with a shield on it surmounted by a cross.

★**Grunewaldturm** ⊘ – Built in honour of the Emperor William (it is also called Kaiser-Wilhelm-Turm), this neo-Gothic red brick tower is used as a belvedere. From the top, the **panorama**★★★ of the Havel, from Spandau to Potsdam, is splendid. It is difficult to realise that Grunewald Forest, with Teufelsberg rising over its vast expanse, is an integral part of Greater Berlin. The town can be seen in the distance, dominated by the Alexanderplatz Tower and the Radio Tower. On the left of Teufelsberg, the block of flats designed by Le Corbusier is clearly visible and, between the two, can be seen what looks like a medieval tower but is in fact Akazienallee water tower *(see OLYMPIASTADION)*. The view to the south, however, is the most romantic: it embraces the Havel, scattered with islands and meandering between wooded banks as far as Potsdam, with the dome of St Nicholas's Church looking like a pinpoint in the distance.

Linwerder – This small wooded **island** is situated opposite Lieper Bay beach (Lieperbuch) It is possible to reach Wannsee beach by following the Havel and then by road.

Schwanenwerder – *Access via Wannseebadweg.*
This island, which used to be uninhabited, was bought in 1882 by Wilhelm Wessel, a manufacturer who had a bridge built. Bankers, manufacturers, and criminals stayed on the island: Bakounine in 1841, Goebbels after 1933 (it was then nicknamed "bigwigs island"), and the press magnate Axel Springer.

★★**Strandbad Wannsee** – *See WANNSEE.*

THE LAKES

Follow the series of lakes: Grunewaldsee (east bank), Krumme Lanke and Schlachtensee.

★**Jagdschloß Grunewald** (**M²⁸**) ⊘ – *Enter the courtyard.*
This hunting lodge stands in a delightful spot, on the edge of Grunewald lake. Only the tower and its spiral staircase are original. The small museum contains

Ernst Ludwig Kircher:
Berlin street scene (1913)

many **works**★★ by **Lucas Cranach the Elder,** displayed in rooms full of rustic charm: nine scenes from the altarpiece depicting the Passion, originally in Berlin Cathedral, portraits of several Electors *(Joachim Nestor, Joachim II)*, the diptych of Adam and Eve and the delightful *Nymph by the Spring,* which are beautiful examples of nude painting. Also noteworhty is the series of portraits of Roman emperors, and among them Caesar by Rubens. The long servants' building facing the pavilion houses a collection of arms and objects connected with hunting.

★**Brücke-Museum** (**M³⁶**) ⏲ *(see map of Berlin Town Centre,* **G**, **EZ**) – *Bussardsteig 9.* This remote museum was built in 1967 in the heart of a pine and beech forest; it has a very functional style. The exhibition area is small in order to make room for wood carvings. The collection bequeathed by **Karl Schmidt-Rottluff** (who died in West Berlin in 1976), in addition to the thousand or so works donated by Erich Heckel make up the greater part of the stock which is exhibited during temporary exhibitions *(the selection below is given as an indication only)*. The museum also owns a fine collection of cards, painted with watercolours or coloured with pencils, which the Die Brücke artists sent to their family and friends, in particular the woman who inspired Karl Schmidt-Rottluff, **Rosa Schapire**. She collected his works and published the first catalogue of his prints in Berlin in 1924.

The following are particularly noteworthy: *Christ Mocked (*1909) and *Holiday-makers* (1911) by Emil Nolde; pre-1914 works by Rottluff *(Woman Dreaming, 1912)*; *Fishermen's Boat (*1913) by Max Pechstein and above all *Berlin Street Scene (*1913) by Kirchner; *Tübingen (*1920) and *Two Young Girls Bathing (*1921), by Erich Heckel.

★★**The lakes** – Hardly anyone bathes in the **small Grunewald lake (Grunewaldsee)**. **Krumme Lanke,** on the other hand, offers properly equipped if crowded beaches and some lovely views of its wooded banks. The most pleasant lake, however, is

Schlachtensee★ – There is a fully equipped beach near **S** *1 Schlachtensee,* but it is advisable to find a suitable spot between the trees. Only the rumbling of traffic on the S-Bahn belies the impression of being in the heart of the countryside. Bathing here is very pleasant.

Pick up the S-Bahn at Nikolassee Station in order to return to the centre of Berlin or go further out to Wannsee Station.

★★**Strandbad Wannsee** – *See WANNSEE.*

IN THE VICINITY

See DAHLEM★★★, WANNSEE★★, ZEHLENDORF★.

HAVEL★★

Spandau, Wilmersdorf, Zehlendorf
See map of Berlin Conurbation, **10**, **AUV**

It is impossible to speak of the Havel without mentioning **Theodor Fontane** (1819-1898), whose *Hikes across the Brandenburg March* describe the landscapes in a charming fashion and relate the life of the people as well as the events and the history of the region. "The Havel is a special river; considering the shape its course takes, it could be called the Neckar of northern Germany. It describes a semi-circle, flowing from the north and eventually going back north; whoever remembers his childhood swing, a simple rope strung between two apple trees, will have in mind the curved line by which the course of the Havel is represented on maps. Its blue water and numerous bays (the Havel is in fact an uninterrupted series of lakes) make it unique. The land which surrounds it, our *Havelland,* is the cultural birthplace of our homeland. The oldest culture began here; the most recent as well. The building of Prussia began in Potsdam, in the light of Sanssouci. The Havel is therefore one of Germany's cultural rivers".

WEST BANK: from Spandau to Sacrow

★**Spandau** – *See under that name.* **U** *7 Rathaus Spandau. Take* **BUS** *next to the Spandau town hall.*

Weinmeisterhorn – At the end of Zur Haveldüne Street, a belvedere on top of a dune offers a beautiful **view**★ of the Havel which includes the Teufelsberg Observatory and, rising above Grunewald forest, the tower of the same name; in the foreground, the small Schildhorn promontory; buildings and chimney-stacks are never very far though! As you come down the southern slope to take a walk along the river, you will notice, on the right-hand side, a house designed by Hans Scharoun *(Höhenweg 19)*. The **stroll**★ is pleasant.

Go up to a lovely round pavilion capped by a dome, then turn left into Rothenbückerweg which leads into Gatower Straße via Bardeyweg.

Gatow – The main road goes through Gatow. The small church is set inside its close next to the churchyard.

Kladow – There is also a small parish church here as well as a lovely house in the square *(Alt-Kladow 21). Follow Alt-Kladow Street. As you reach the church, turn southwest into Sacrower Kirchweg.* At No 4, behind a brick building, there is an interesting garden with contemporary sculptures *(private property).*

Continue along Alt-Kladow.

From the river bank, lined with restaurants and large villas, can be seen the bathing facilities on Wannsee Beach across the water. The walk is even more pleasant, for Düppel Forest offers wilder scenery than the Havel.

The boat returning to Wannsee comes alongside pier No 3 (Brücke 3). To go to Sacrow, go back up Alt-Kladow Street until you reach the church, then follow Kladower Damm for about 100m and take the bus to Fährstraße.

Sacrow – *(See map of Potsdam and surrounding area, p. 276-277, FT)*
The park and castle form part of Potsdam's royal castles and gardens. The name has Slav roots and means "behind the bush"; it is mentioned for the first time in the *Landbuch* of Emperor Charles IV. In 1773, the site was occupied by a manor-house surrounded by a park in which there was an alleyway lined with chestnut trees. Plans to improve the appearance of the park were drawn up by P.J. Lenné in 1842; he suggested opening new vistas towards Glienicke, Potsdam, and the Babelsberg Flatowturm.

Frederick-William IV commissioned Ludwig Persius to build **St Saviour's Church** (Heilandskirche); work lasted from 1841 to 1844. It is best seen from the opposite bank bordering Klein-Glienicke Park. Seen from this side of the Havel, it certainly deserves its nickname of "the ship". The king and his followers went there almost every Sunday to hear mass. "The lords generally arrived by boat along the blue Havel, just like the inhabitants of Potsdam who almost always went to church in gondolas or rowing boats".

It is possible either to go to **S** *Potsdam-Stadt Station on the bus or, return to Alt-Kladow in the opposite direction and take a boat to Wannsee.*

EAST BANK

From Schildhorn promontory to Klein-Glienicke Park.

Schildhorn, Grunewaldturm, Lindwerder, Schwanenwerder – *See GRUNEWALD.*

★★**Strandbad Wannsee** – *See under that name.*

★★**Pfaueninsel** – *See WANNSEE.*

★★**Klein Glienicke** – *See WANNSEE.*

IN THE VICINITY

See **GRUNEWALD**★★, **POTSDAM**★★★, **SPANDAU**★, **WANNSEE**★.

Calling at Wannsee

KÖPENICK – Großer Müggelsee★★

Köpenick

See map of Berlin Conurbation, **11**, **DV**

Today, Köpenick is a lovely town which has retained its own character, quite different from that of Berlin. Großer Müggelsee and the vast stretches of woodland surrounding it, which were once the "green lungs" of East Berlin, are still a very popular walking area.

HISTORICAL NOTES

The name Köpenick means "settlement on a mound". It was one of the two most important Slav settlements in the Berlin area, the other being Spandau. Extending from the islands to the confluence of the Spree and the Dahme, the site could be easily defended. Castle Island *(Schloßinsel)* had been inhabited since the Neolithic period. A fortress was built on it around AD 825. It remained a centre of Wendish culture until the 12C as well as the seat of political power of the Spreewanes.
In the 13C, the city developed round **Alt-Köpenick** Street, which links the castle to the suburb bordering the Dahme and then spread towards the Old Market (Alter Markt) during the 14C.
Köpenick remembers the "bloody week" of June 1933, shortly after the Nazis came to power, when 500 Communists and Social-Democrats were arrested and tortured and 91 were murdered.

MAIN SIGHTS

★**Oberschöneweide** – In order to make it more easily accessible to visitors, Oberschöneweide is listed under *TREPTOW*.

Ⓢ *3 Köpenick. Walk along Bahnhofstraße, a shopping street which still has its pre-war façades.*

Realgymnasium Köpenick – *No 60, 61, 62, 68* Tram *Bahnhofstraße/Linden-straße.*
This imposing neo-Gothic building standing on the corner of Lindenstraße looks picturesque with its dormer windows, pinnacles and tracery *(see also PANKOW College)*. The staircase is in the tower.

> **How to avoid unnecessary delays:**
> *Visitors, who are staying in the western part of town and intend to travel on the S-Bahn from Charlottenburg Station for instance, are advised not to wait for the direct train to Erkner and instead to get on one of the more frequent trains bound for Ostkreuz (but beware to avoid the* Ⓢ *6 and* Ⓢ *9 which go around the station!). From there, trains to Erkner and Köpenick are more frequent.*

Old town – *No 62* Tram *Freiheit.*
The old town is dominated by the **town hall**, one of the most handsome in the Berlin conurbation, dating from 1904 and clad with glazed multi-coloured bricks.
Continue south along Alt-Köpenick Street.

★★**Kunstgewerbemuseum** (M²⁹) Ⓞ – *No 26, 60, 62, 67, 68* Tram *Schloßplatz Köpenick.*
This museum, the first museum of decorative arts in Germany, has the advantage over its counterpart in the Kulturforum of being housed in a plain yet elegant Baroque castle situated on the banks of the Dahme.
Go into the courtyard.

The **Reformed Church** of the castle (1683-85, *on the left*), built by J.A. Nehring, was the first religious edifice built in Brandenburg according to a symmetrical plan. Go to the end of the gardens in order to admire the Dahme River forming two separate streams.
The excellent quality of the exhibits displayed in the museum is enhanced by the profusely decorated stuccoed ceilings (1684-1690).
The museum is likely to remain closed for restoration work until May 2002. The collections were previously as follows:

Ground floor – Rich collection of gold plate from Augsburg and Nuremberg: Baroque and rococo **epergnes** (the *Man Stooping Under a Heavy Load* is supposed to be an allegorical representation of trade; *Hercules Carrying the World*); the panel of a cabinet consists of a relief depicting *The Temptation of Faith* (Die Versuchung des Glaubens) and 26 bronze and gilt copper plates illustrating some of the virtues. The furniture exhibited includes some handsome chests in Florentine Renaissance style and a **panelled room from Haldenstein Castle★**, near Chur in the Grisons (Graubünden) area (1548). The inlaid panels represent architectonic pictures; the twin-towered stove from Pomerania is extremely rare.

The "Captain of Köpenick"

Born in Tilsit in 1849, **Wilhelm Friedrich Voigt**, a shoemaker's apprentice, left his native province at an early age to go to Berlin. He survived by committing various petty thefts and, as a result, spent half his life in prison. He came out of jail at the age of 56 and immediately bought a coat out of which he painstakingly made a full guards officer's uniform. On 16 October 1906, he took command of two sections at Plötzensee rifle-range, then went by train to Köpenick where, in "his Majesty's name", he arrested the mayor in the town hall and got hold of the tills containing roughly 4 000 RM. He was arrested soon afterwards in his room in Langstraße and condemned to four years' imprisonment. Meanwhile he had become a popular figure. Twenty-four hours only after the event, pamphlets and caricatures circulated everywhere; the international press commented on the incident. Public satire derided people's submissive attitude *(Untertanengeist)* and Prussian respect for uniforms. A Heidelberg business even offered to "borrow" the prisoner for the sum of 150 000 RM, for three months, in order to show him in public. Pardoned by the Kaiser in 1908, he was cheered by the crowd when he was released from prison, went on show at the Berliner Panoptikum *(see FRIEDRICHSTRASSE)*, sold autographed postcards of himself in his captain's uniform (which is now exhibited in the Police Museum, *see TEMPELHOF*) and went on tour in New York. Once he had made his fortune (he is said to have collected 40 000 RM), he retired to Luxemburg where he died in 1922. The playwright **Gerhart Hauptmann** used Voigt's life story to denounce people's natural tendancy towards obedience and their sense of order, while **Carl Zuckmayer** made it the subject of a tragicomedy *(Der Hauptmann von Köpenick)*.

First floor – At the top of the staircase, are some red and gold shelves displaying porcelain ware from Oranienburg Castle (end of the 17C). On the right are several wooden **cabinets** decorated with lacquer and inlaid with hard stones, an ebony wardrobe (Kunstschrank) from Augsburg (*c* 1600) with embossed silver decorations; also an impressive **cupboard** originally owned by the guild of saffron merchants from Basle (Baseler Safranzunft), dating from 1663, with twisted columns surmounted by a row of goblets. The reputation of 18C French cabinet making owes a lot to master craftsmen from Germany. The beautiful collection of German furniture of the period clearly demonstrates this. The **"Neuwieder Kabinett"**★ (Pultschreibschrank) is one of the best examples of what they were capable of: it hides a piano and a flute! The inlaid work, which imitates the art of engraving, is surmounted by a bronze clock with a chime. The Renaissance furniture is darker and more austere; worth looking at though, is the huge 16C Murano glass tray displayed in a glass case. Along one of the corridors, can be seen some **KPM porcelain ware**★, including an amphora decorated with a landscape showing Potsdam and its Russian church seen from Pfingstberg. The flower paintings are amazing. The various pieces from Frederick II's dinner-services, coloured purple, or bistre (representing mythological scenes), or a "faded blue", are remarkably delicate and refined. The top part of the clock standing at the end of the corridor is the work of Charles Cressent (1685-1768).

The **Coats of Arms Room**★ (Wappensaal), which is the finest in the castle, is decorated with the coats of arms of Prussian towns. A small adjacent room contains the reconstruction of the **great silver sideboard**★★ (Großes Silberbuffet) which used to be exhibited in the Knights' Room (Rittersaal) inside Berlin Castle; it shows to what extent the Hohenzollern princes liked to be surrounded by pomp and splendour. Also worth noting is the huge **goblet**★ (post 1719; Münzfaß, als Bierzapfgefäß) inlaid with 688 coins and 46 medals. Fitted with a tap, it held beer for the Tabakscollegium meetings which the "King Sergeant" was only too fond of *(see POTSDAM)*.

During the closure period a few outstanding items, including the Great Silver Chest can be seen in the Kunstgewerbemuseum at the Kulturforum.

Go across *Längebrücke (fine view of the church towers of the old town)*, then follow Oberspreestraße until you reach No 173-181, to see the interesting **Dorotheen-Lyzeum** (1928-29) by Max Taut.

Return to the S-Bahn (take No 68 tramcar Kölnischer Platz or No 26, 60, 62, 67, 68 Tram Schloßplatz Köpenick) and get off at Ⓢ *3 Friedrichshagen Station.*

AROUND MÜGGELSEE

Friedrichshagen – Friedrichshagen is a holiday resort. The high street **Bölschestraße**, is a pleasant shopping street lined with 19C buildings. About 100 weavers from Saxony and Bohemia were enticed by Frederick II to settle there. Müggelseedamm provides no proper view of the lake.

★★Großer Müggelsee – Its oval shape and the gently undulating contours of Müggelberg confer a peaceful atmosphere on the shores of Großer Müggelsee. *There is a well-equipped beach (Strandbad Müggelsee) which can be reached by taking the No 61 [Tram] from* Ⓢ *Friedrichshagen Station.*

Walk along Müggleleseedamm. The Seehof-Hotel (No 288-292) offers a good **view★★** of this expanse of water, which is one of the most beautiful in Berlin. Beyond the hotel, the street is lined with the neo-Gothic pavilions of the **Friedrichshagen hydraulic power station** *(not open to the public)*. The museum is on the right, by the lake.

★Museum Wasserwerk Friedrichshagen Ⓥ – In 1680, the Great Elector ordered that a "street master" should clean up the streets using two carts. In 1700, another decree published by Frederick III stipulated that rubbish should be put back inside houses if it was not swept away; the army was even employed in performing this task in 1735. However, there was no improvement and the unhygienic conditions in the streets remained appalling. In many courtyards in *Mietskasernen*, lavatories and fountains were quite close together, which made it easy for epidemics to spread. The chemist **Justus von Liebig** (1803-1873) proved that the presence of nitric acid *(Salpetersäure)* in the water of a fountain accelerated the decomposition of organic residue. Gutters, about 30 to 80 cm deep, were filled with dirty water letting off foul smells into which refuse from private homes and factories was discharged. In 1850, 250 butchers threw their offal directly into the street. These appalling hygienic conditions were noticed by visiting foreigners, even though industrialisation and technical progress (mechanical engineering, pipe-laying) helped the creation of fountains, pumping systems and hydraulic steam power stations (the first, built in front of the Stralau Gate by the Englishman **Henry Gill**, filtered the water of the Spree). However, between 1851 and 1867, nearly 19 000 people died of cholera and typhus (in 1831, an outbreak of cholera had caused Frederick-William III and his panic-stricken court to flee). Epidemics remained endemic to the area until 1873, when **James Hobrecht** drew the first plans of a drainage system with the help of **R. Virchow** *(see WEDDING)*. Berlin was divided into twelve areas equipped with pumps. The clay or masonry drains carried waste water to sewage-fields *(Rieselfelder)* situated in outer areas, but the system was adopted with difficulty and only became operational in 1876.

The building houses an interesting exhibition *(drawings, photographs, informative panels)* about the Berlin water towers, the history of hydraulic power stations, drainage systems and purification by chemical means. The **steam engine room★** *(Maschinensaal)*, overlooking the lake, is a mixture of neo-Gothic decoration and metal footbridges. One of the engines *(Verbundkolbendampfmaschinen)* is still in working order; it is one hundred years old and ceased to be used in 1979. The wheels weigh five tons (they were made in the Schwarzkopf and Borsig factories).

Take the No 60 [Tram] and get off at Josef-Nawrocki-Straße. Go south to Müggelpark.

★Am Müggelsee – A cool path *(Spreetunnel)* leads to a walk along Müggelsee, among pine trees. There is a cycle track alongside it. *Unless you have a car, if you want to go to Müggelturm, you will have to walk or take the bus, from* Ⓢ *3 Köpenick Station, getting off at Chausseestraße (and you will still have to climb!).*

Müggelturm Ⓥ – The original wooden tower was destroyed by fire in 1958. The restaurant has a terrace which provides a pleasant rest after climbing. From the top of the tower is a vast **panorama★★** of lakes and green open spaces.

Take the staircase and go straight down to the south.

★★Langersee – The Am langen See walk, along the north bank, on the way back to Köpenick, is peaceful and idyllic.

The **Grünauer Wassersportmuseum/Stiftung Stadtmuseum Berlin** stands opposite, on the Grünau side. The building was the garden house of an Art Nouveau villa built around the turn of the century. The exhibitions are concerned with the Berlin "Vikings", the history of water sports in Berlin (1876-1945) and the visit by the Olympic regatta in 1936.

At the end of the promenade, you will notice Wendenschloßstraße, the main street in an area consisting essentially of villas. Take the No 62 [Tram] Wendenschloß to go back to Ⓢ *3 Köpenick Station.*

IN THE VICINITY

See **TREPTOW.**

KREUZBERG★★

Kreuzberg

See map of Berlin Town Centre, **8**, **9**, JKLMXY

Surrounded on three sides by the Wall, this focal point of the alternative movement during the eighties was, before the "turning point", the favourite haunt of the dissident minority: apart from the large closely-knit Turkish community living there, highly conducive to cohabitation and integration problems, squatters, punks, "Green" supporters. Alternative groups and gays were responsible for the unique convivial atmosphere of Kreuzberg. Since reunification of the two parts of the city, the district has become one of the central areas of Berlin and there is every reason to fear the cupidity of investors. What is going to become of Kreuzberg? Apparently, little has changed until now: people still go to the Turkish market along Landwehrkanal; they still listen to music in Mariannenplatz; they take a stroll in Görlitzerpark or stop at a pavement café in Bergmannstraße. There are, in fact, two very different Kreuzbergs: the western part, with a more yuppy atmosphere and the lovely restored *Mietskasernen* façades; and the eastern part, inhabited by many Turks and consequently almost Mediterranean in character.

Berlin Alternative town – West Berlin acted as a kind of laboratory: following in the tradition of the student uprisings of the sixties, members of the Alternative movement were environmentalists and pacifists, setting themselves apart from the parliamentary world and opposed to middle-class values. Women had an important role to play which coincided with a larger number of them going to university, the creation of newspapers and magazines catering to their needs (*Emma* started a debate on abortion), the opening of homes for beaten women, coffee houses, clubs, and professional training centres. In order to live and work in a different way, the Alternatives organised themselves rapidly, founding places like the **Mehringhof** *(See ON THE TOWN)*, became autonomous and took care of the unhealthy districts situated near the Wall, in particular **Kreuzberg**. In 1985, they represented 10% of the total votes expressed at the municipal elections. In Kreuzberg, their list overtook the SPD.

★★KREUZBERG (West part)

The walk can be divided into two parts, starting from the Transport and Technical Museum.

Towards the northeast

★★**Deutsches Technik museum Berlin** ⊘ – **U** 2, 15 *Gleisdreieck or* **U** 1, 15 *Möckernbrücke.*

It is housed in the former administrative buildings of the Refrigerated Warehouse Company. The museum comprises various sections: computer science, television, radio, the railways, the textile industry, inland navigation; there are a number of models; particularly noteworthy is the **collection of railway engines, trucks and carriages★★**, displayed on the rails of the former goods station of Anhalt Station with spectacular results. The museum now includes the collections of the old maritime museum (*on the first floor*: many models of ships and engineering works such as bridges and dockyards). There is a rich vegetation growing over the disused tracks encouraging the development of a strange fauna. This protected natural area includes watermills and windmills.

The **Spectrum★** *(150m east along Tempelhofer Ufer)* is an annex of the museum. A series of manual experiments set out to describe the physical properties of optics, electricity, light and sound waves, radioactivity, light and sound.

Follow Schönberger Straße.

By **Landwehrkanal**, the scenery is a contrasting mixture of willows, metal footbridges and bridges. The **Hebel-Theater** *(Stresemannstraße 29, 1907-8* **T²***)* brought fame to the architect who designed it and thereafter specialised in theatre building. He also built the Volksbühne *(see ORIANIENBURGER STRASSE).*

Reste des Anhalter Bahnofs (**B**) – **S** 1, 2, 25, 26 *Anhalter Bahnhof.*

A wall and part of a portico, where the entrance porch used to be, is all that remain of **Anhalt Station**, once the largest railway station in Berlin. Its ruins were not completely pulled down in 1969 as were those of the other Berlin stations because the demolition company went bankrupt.

Kochstraße – **U** 6 *Kochstraße.*

The street goes through the district traditionally occupied by newspaper publishers. **No 18** is the home of *Tageszeitung*, a fine building with a glass and metal annex; **Axel Springer**'s empire (the publisher of *Bild-Zeitung*) is housed in a tower ostensibly built close to the Wall. A whole block of houses, based on plans by Aldo Rossi, is gradually filling the gap between Zimmerstraße and Schützenstraße. On the corner of Schützenstraße and Jerusalemerstraße, near the Springer building, stands **Mossehaus** (**C**), a fine edifice at present occupied by ELF. It used to belong to the publishing company of press magnate **Rudolf Mosse** (the publisher of *Berliner*

Deutsche Technikmuseum Berlin

Tageblatt). It was built during the twenties by **Eric Mendelsohn** on the site of a 19C edifice, which was damaged during the 1918 revolution but has not entirely disappeared. Its corner façade looks like the front of a car.

Haus am Checkpoint Charlie – **U** 6 *Kochstraße. See FRIEDRICHSTRASSE.*

Oranienstraße 106-109, corner of Alte Jakobstraße – The National Debt brick edifice (Reichsschuldenverwaltung), decorated with terracotta statues, was built in the Expressionist style during the period of inflation.

Lindenstraße – Enter the neo-Renaissance courtyard of No 20, the Victoria Insurance building (Viktoria Versicherung, 1906-13). The façade, an example of heavy historicism, is 130m long and once concealed 12 courtyards. The one seen here shows how modern pavilion-style buildings around a garden can create a harmonious setting.

Jüdisches Museum ⏱ (*Lindenstraße 9-14,* **M³⁸**) – The American architect Daniel Libeskind designed this spectacular, sparkling new building. It is planned to open the museum, which is accessed via the foyer of the Berlin-Museum, in the autumn of 2001. The labyrinthine design, with its empty rooms leading nowhere, is symbolic of the destruction of Jewish-German culture.

The permanent exhibition will show the history of Jews in Germany from the earliest documented evidence right up to the present time. Great emphasis will be placed on the importance of Jews in the development of Berlin from the 18C to 20C, focusing on the Holocaust, persecution and disenfranchisement of Jews during the Nazi era.

1) The Altes Kammergericht (LindenstraBe 14), where the writer E.T.A. Hoffmann used to work, is an annex of the Jewish Museum. The outside of the buildings has been restored in the original late Baroque style. Above the arms of Prussia, the gable wall is decorated with allegorical statues of Justice and Mercy.

It is interesting to wander through the **residential blocks of flats** from the eighties, adjoining the museum and the Victoria Insurance building: Alt-Jakobstraße, **Ritterstraße** (No 63-64), reminiscent of the estates of the twenties.

Mehringplatz und Friedenssäule – **U** 1, 6, 15 *Hallesches Tor.*
The converging vistas, similar to those of the "Piazza del Popolo" in Rome, of the three avenues which formed the backbone of **Friedrichstadt** *(see FRIEDRICH-STRASSE)* were done away with as a result of the war. Wilhelmstraße, slightly to the east, Friedrichstraße and Lindenstraße all met in **Rondell**, the pre-war Belle-Alliance-Platz (the alliance which was at the origin of the Waterloo coalition). The new Mehringplatz was planned by **Hans Scharoun** who designed a housing complex forming two concentric circles.

Starting from Hallesches Tor U-Bahn Station, next to the American Memorial Library (Amerika-Gedenkbibliothek), the southern part of the district can be visited.

Towards the south

★★ Deutsches Technik-Museum – *See p 177.*

Amerika-Gedenkbibliothek ⊘ – **U** *1, 6, 15 Hallesches Tor.*
Donated by the Americans, this is one of the most popular libraries in Berlin. Nex
to it stands the domed neo-Gothic Church of the Holy Cross (Zum heiligen Kreuz'
Behind the A.G.B., there are five of Berlin's important historical **cemeteries**
(entrance through the oldest, situated in Zossener Straße, K¹), which have lai
since 1735 outside the city walls in front of the Hallesche Tor. They house th
tombs of many famous people, from the arts and science in particular, for exampl
the poets ETA Hoffmann and Adalbert von Chamisso, the composer Feli
Mendelssohn Bartholdy, the painter Antoine Pesne, the architects Geor
Wenzeslaus von Knobelsdorff, Carl Ferdinand Langhans and David Gilly.

Mehringdamm – **U** *6, 7 Mehringdamm.*
Kreuzberg's high street is very busy near the intersection where it crosse
Gneisenaustraße, as it is the rendez-vous of cinema lovers, Alternative groups an
the gay community. The elongated shape of former **barracks** (Kaserne des 1. Garde
Dragoner-Regiments) looks like a neo-Gothic castle. The **Mehringho**
(Gneisenaustraße 2) is a former factory building where Alternative groups mee
On the west side, along Yorckstraße, the neo-Gothic **Church of St Boniface** (D) stand
next to an attractive residential complex called **"Riehmers Hofgarten"★** (at No 84) afte
the man who built it. It gives a fair idea of what the "side streets" would look lik
had Hobrecht's plan not been abandoned in order to preserve the *Mietskaserner*
courtyards. Notice also the *Jugendstil* building standing next to No 81. The court
yard of the "Riehmer Hofgarten" offers a cosy setting; come out i
Großbeerenstraße. The tiny theatre in the **Berliner Kinomuseum** ⊘, situated at No 5"
immediately to the right, shows German Expressionist films.

★Viktoriapark – The **National Monument to the Wars of Liberation** (Kriegsdenkmal)
designed in 1821 by Schinkel to commemorate the allies' victory agains
Napoleon's army chased out of Germany, is enhanced by the romantic **setting★** c
a waterfall, a copy of the Zackenfall in the Giants' Mountains *(Riesengebirge,* i
Saxony). The 22m-high Gothic spire, surmounted by an iron cross, gave its nam
to the district *(Kreuzberg:* the "mountain of the cross"). The statues are by Rauch
Tieck and Wichmann. From the top of the hill, formerly occupied by a vineyard
there is a fine **view★★** of Kreuzberg and, immediately to the south, of the neo
Gothic Schultheiss Breweries. Just beyond the Gothic towers of St Boniface':
Church, can be seen modern buildings which used to belong to West Berlin; a littl
further still, the horizontal lines of the Leipzigerstraße complex formed part of th
East Berlin townscape; the view extends along Großbeerenstraße and beyond t
the identical domes surmounting the churches bordering Gendarmenmarkt, in th
Mitte district, which was once in the Soviet zone; it suddenly seems easy to grasp
the real significance of the absurd splitting of the town into two.

★Chamissoplatz – The network of narrow streets east of Viktoriapark forms th
nicest part of West Kreuzberg, and it is the favourite haunt of an elegant Bohemia
crowd. The **Mietskasernen** neo-Renaissance façades in strict alignment are painted i
pastel colours. In Fidicinstraße, there is a neo-Gothic water tower dating from
1887-1889, which houses a café and a centre dedicated to youth, communicatior
and culture, where there are free concerts in summer. **Bergmannstraße** and Zossene
Straße are essentially shopping streets, the former being particularly popular fo
its cafés and *Imbiss* (snack bars). There is a covered market at the intersection o
the two streets. **Marheinekeplatz** nearby, with its children's playground, is the
meeting place for locals.
South of Bergmannstraße are four **cemeteries★** (K²) dating from 1825 and which are
also remarkable in art historical terms. Here lie, among others, the poet Ludwig Tieck
the painter Adolph von Menzel, the philosopher Friedrich Daniel Schleiermacher, the
historian Theodor Mommsen and the politician Gustav Stresemann. A few rathe
extravagant headstones and tombs, for example that of the Oppenfeld family (1828)
which is shaped like a small Egyptian temple, draw the eye.

IN THE VICINITY

See **FRIEDRICHSTRASSE★**, **KULTURFORUM★★★**, **KREUZBERG (east part)★★**
POTSDAMER PLATZ, TEMPELHOF.

★★KREUZBERG (eastern part)

The eastern part of Kreuzberg, which was once surrounded by the Wall on three
sides, is an atypical district. Its atmosphere is both provincial and "with it", often
convivial. Bazaars, snack bars and small Turkish shops (even a large market) stand
next to ordinary bars, restaurants and cafés. People meet in tiny squares and

public gardens, which are often lined with churches and 19C monuments, to take part in various forms of entertainment (cinema, concerts) in the open or in pavement cafés. This former working-class district still has several good specimens of "**Gewerbehöfe**", a type of building with many backyards, still used as living quarters and working premises. The centre of the district lies just north of the **Kottbuss Gate** (Kottbusser Tor), whereas the most peaceful and authentic part is situated between the **Silesia Gate** (Schlesisches Tor) and **Görlitz Park**.

Start from Kottbusser Tor **U** *Station.*

Towards the northeast

U Kottbusser Tor – **U** *1, 8, 15 Kottbusser Tor.*
The Kreuzberg **local history Museum** ⊘ (Kreuzbergmuseum) in Adalbertstraße, is at No 55, on the left, through the children's playground. It organises temporary exhibitions.

Former "Luisenstadt" district – From **Oranienplatz**, green open spaces being relaid and wasteground alternate, extending the view to **St Michael's Church** (Michaelkirche) in the Mitte district. The Wall stood in front of it; the grey and depressing buildings of the former GDR are easily recognisable. The Neu-Cölln am Wasser (1695) suburb, which was the first extension of Köpenick, had its name changed to "Louise's town" (Luisenstadt) in 1802, in honor of the queen of Prussia. **Peter Josef Lenné** designed it in the 1840s along a canal, today replaced by green spaces. Note the splendid courtyards *(Gewerbehöfe)* of the factory buildings in **Waldemarstraße**, in red and beige bricks at **No 33** and white glazed bricks at **No 38**. Follow the lovely **Naunynstraße**. Here, backyards often include a garden, a little patch of green with a small play area for children.

★Oranienstraße – This is quite a pleasant spot for an evening out. From Oranienplatz to **Heinrichplatz**, the street is lined with bars specialising in rock music *(see ON THE TOWN, the Berlin Scene)*. There are boutiques selling clothes for young people, antiques and strip cartoons next to small Turkish bazaars. Fine *Gewerbehöfe* at **No 25**, in contrasting white and green brickwork, and at **No 183**. *(Oranienhof).*

Mariannenplatz – This vast rectangular green space is lined on one side with the former **Bethanien Hospital** (**E**), today a cultural centre (**Künstlerhaus Bethanien** ⊘) which houses a conservatory and a Turkish library. In summer, films are shown on huge screens at the back of the complex *(go round the south side of it)*. **St Thomas' Church**, which stands on the north side of the square, was built by one of Schinkel's students and is today one of the most elegant churches in Berlin. The drum, which would normally support the dome, is particularly remarkable.

Eisenbahnstraße market (**F**) (Eisenbahn-Markthalle), situated along Pücklerstraße, is one of the three remaining covered markets in Berlin *(see WEST KREUZBERG and MOABIT)*. There are pleasant cafés surrounding **Lausitzerplatz**, at the end of Eisenbahnstraße. Also worth noting is the fine *Jugendstil* façade at No 20 Zeughofstraße.

Görlitzer Park – **U** *1, 15 Görlitzer Bahnhof.*
It replaced the old railway tracks of Görlitz Station. Landwehrkanal, flowing past the end of the park *(one can stroll along the banks of the canal)*, marked the border with East Berlin and the district of Treptow. Adjoining streets still have their 19C buildings. Cafés, restaurants, *Imbiss* (snack bars) and small Turkish shops create a lively atmosphere, particularly along **Wrangelstraße**. To the northwest, beyond the intersection with Skalitzer Straße, there is a former barracks, a long and stately red-brick building, which looks like the counterpart of Mehringdamm barracks and has been turned into a school.

Go to Schlesisches Tor **U** *1, 12, 15 Station.*

★Oberbaumbrücke – **U** *1, 15 Schlesisches Tor.*
Schlesisches Tor Station is neo-Gothic. Built in a similar style and recently restored, **Oberbaumbrücke** is, in a way, Berlin's "Tower Bridge". It used to mark the border between East and West. In the 13C, a toll-barrier, known as the **Oberbaum**, stood upstream from Mühlendamm *(see NIKOLAIVIERTEL)*; it consisted of a row of tree trunks *(Baum in German)*, held in place against the flow by oak piles. There was a similar barrier downstream, known as the *Unterbaum*. *Cross the bridge to see the "East Side Gallery" in Mühlenstraße, described under FRIEDRICHSHAIN.*

Take the **U** *1, 15 underground from Warschauer Straße or Schlesisches Tor to Kottbusser Tor and walk along Kottbusser Straße.*

Towards the southwest

★★Landwehrkanal embankment – **U** *1, 8, 12, 15, Kottbusser Tor.*
On both sides of Kottbusser Bridge *(Kottbusser Brücke)*, the Landwehrkanal embankments *(Ufer)* offer one of the most attractive and liveliest townscapes in Berlin:

— **Paul-Lincke-Ufer:** cafés at the beginning of the embankment, fine *Jugendsti* façades. Remarkable *Gewerbehof* at **No 40:** four courtyards in succession! Look als at No 42/43.

— **Maybachufer:** the Friday afternoon **Turkish market★★** is extremely picturesque. offers all the smells and flavours of the Mediterranean: watermelons, vegetables olives, seeds, fish, spices and fabrics. Notice the interesting grooved façade b Bruno Taut at No 2-3 Kottbusser Damm.

— **Planufer:** lovely row of façades in both *Jugendstil* and historicist style, with nec Gothic gables.

— **Fraenkelufer:** Landwehrkanal is lined with willow trees; a lawn makes the bank eve more attractive. The **orthodox synagogue** (Orthodoxe Synagoge am Kottbusser Ufer was profaned by the Nazis and destroyed during the war; today only the white meetin hall *(Gemeindezentrum)* remains. Along this embankment, there are also several inte esting buildings erected for the **IBA 87** *(see INTRODUCTION, Architecture and cit planning)*: the corner building at No 26 as well as **No 38 and No 44★**. You have to g under the span to reach the garden overlooked by other buildings, which are eve more striking with their balconies and pointed dormer windows.

Wassertorplatz and the Ritterstraße district – Ⓤ 1, 8, 12, 15 Kottbusser Tor Elisabethhof, 1897-98. Before World War I, **Ritterstraße** was a centre of the Berli export trade and, in certain fields (precision mechanical engineering, light industry) it even ranked first in the whole of Germany. **Pelikan-Haus** is at No 9/10.

IN THE VICINITY

See **FISCHERINSEL★, FRIEDRICHSTRASSE★, KREUZBERG (west part)★★ NEUKÖLLN, TREPTOW.**

The U-Bahn crossing the Oberbaumbrücke

As early as *1938*, **Albert Speer** had buildings pulled down along entire streets in the well-to-do district surrounding St Mathew's Church, as part of the major projects designed to shape the future "Germania".

The Kulturforum, which used to be bordered on its northern side by the Berlin Wall, remained somewhat on the fringe. It received its name at the end of the 1950s, when Hans Scharoun was planning the Philharmonie and the Staatsbibliothek. It was to be the cultural centre of the former West Berlin and was conceived as a counterpart to the Museuminsel in East Berlin.

The Kulturforum is currently located at the heart of the reunified city, next to the vast building site at Potsdamer Platz *(see under that name)*, precisely where the point of fracture between East and West is to be eliminated by the new plans for the city. The Kulturforum is thus being developed into a new focus of attraction for Berlin.

Nearest U-Bahn and S-Bahn: ⓢ 1, 2, 25, 26 and Ⓤ 2 Potsdamer Platz.

★★★ GEMÄLDEGALERIE (**M⁶**) – *Matthäikirchplatz 6*

Part of the main collection comes from the art collection of Berlin Castle, formed during the reign of the Great Elector (1640-1688), the paintings collected by **Frederick II**, who founded the Painting Gallery in Sans-Souci (1755-1762) and bought works by 18C French artists (after his death, his collections were shown to a restricted number of visitors) and important foreign collections acquired at the beginning of the 19C (Giustiniani in 1815, Solly in 1821). The gallery, which was opened to the public in 1830, was first housed inside the Old Museum built by Schinkel. At the end of the 19C, **Wilhelm von Bode** (*see MUSEUMSINSEL, Bodemuseum*) took advantage of the interest of the Berlin middleclass in art during a period of economic prosperity to encourage the practice of patronage. A systematic approach was used to continue adding to the collections up until World War I. The Second World War brought ruin and disaster: more than 400 paintings were destroyed, including works by Rubens and Caravaggio, inside the anti-aircraft defence bunker in Friedrichshain, reputed to be indestructible. Following the division of the town and the museum collections, the paintings were hurriedly moved to an annex of the Museum of Ethnography in Dahlem where they remained until 1996.

When the Gemäldegalerie moved to the Kulturforum in the summer of 1998 and the collections were combined, it signalled the end of 50 years of division and temporary arrangements. Despite losses during the war, the collection is now once again one of the most important in the world, including as it does selected examples from every stylistic period and school.

The modest building was designed by the architects Heinz Hilmer and Christoph Sattler in such a way that virtually all the rooms are flooded with daylight from above. 53 rooms housing over 1 100 paintings, are grouped in a horseshoe shape around a central foyer. A further 300 substantial works are hung in the Studiengalerie on the ground floor.

The works are hung in chronological order and by schools:

Rooms I-III and cabinets 1-4: **German painting, 13C – 16C** (Late Gothic/ Renaissance)

Rooms IV-VI and cabinets 5-7: **Dutch painting, 15C – 16C** (Late Gothic/ Renaissance)

Rooms VII-XI and cabinets 8-10: **Flemish and Dutch painting, 17C** (Baroque)

Cabinets 20-22: **English, French and German painting, 18C** (Rococo/Classicism)

Rooms XII-XIV and cabinets 23-26, 28: **Italian painting, 17C – 18C** (Baroque/ Rococo); French painting, 17C; **Spanish painting, 16C – 17C** (Mannerism/ Baroque)

Rooms XV-XVII and cabinets 29-32: **Italian painting, end of 15C – 16C** (High Renaissance/Mannerism)

Cabinet 34: **Miniature painting, 16C - 18C**

Room XVIII and cabinets 35-41: **Italian painting, 13C – end of 15C** (Gothic/Early renaissance)

ITALY

Middle Ages

Giotto (1266/67-1337) – The **Death of Mary** is very moving. Attitudes and expressions are extremely varied: Saint-John is wringing his hands in despair above the Virgin Mary's face; another apostle is kneeling down; a third is embracing the body stretched out on a cloth held by two angels. Invisible, Christ is holding Mary's sou in the shape of a child, behind the sarcophagus. This panel formed part of an altar piece kept inside All Saints' Church (Ognissanti) in Florence.

Pietro Lorenzetti (c 1280 - c 1348) – Born in Faenza, of noble parentage, Sain Humility was the founder of an order which built a convent near Florence. The conven originally owned the two paintings depicting scenes from the saint's legend: **Sain Humility Curing a Sick Nun** (note the physician on the left hand side, who looks baffle as he examines the bowl of blood), and **Saint Humility's Ice Miracle** (a piece of ice, foun in a fountain in August, is taken to the saint, who is seriously ill).

Ugolino da Siena (known from 1317 to 1327) – Saint Peter, Saint Paul and Sain John the Baptist formed part of the huge altarpiece (four storeys high!) decorating the main altar of the Santa Croce Church in Florence.

Lorenzo Veneziano (works dating from 1357 to 1372) – This artist freed Venetiai painting from the Byzantine tradition. One of the five predella panels which sur vived the war, **Christ Saving Saint Peter who has Fallen into the Sea**, symbolising divin help, is based on a mosaïc by Giotto, the *Navicella*, which used to decorate th narthex of Saint-Peter's Basilica in Rome.

Lorenzo Monaco (c 1365 - shortly after 1423) – Note the powerful expression depicted on the three predella panels: **The Martyrdom of Saint Catherine of Alexandria The Last Supper**, remarkable for the freshness of its colours, and **The Nativity**, inter esting for its naturalism and its simplicity, particularly regarding the familiar figur of Joseph asleep.

Quattrocento (15C)

Fra Angelico (c 1400 - 1455) – In **The Last Judgement**, Christ in Majesty appears framed within a mandorla, separating the blessed, forming a very graceful group led by angels, from the damned, gathered according to the torture inflicted upon them as described in *Hell*, the first part of Dante's *Divine Comedy*. Sins are named in Latin: pride (*Superbia*) is shown over Satan's three heads.

Masaccio (1401-1428?) – Note the way in which this artist represented the human body; he radically transformed Florentine painting by observing the rules of perspective. Each painting has a strange detail: in **The Adoration of the Magi**, the two men dressed like burgesses are probably the man who commissioned the work and one of his relatives; they are carefully portrayed observing the scene with calm one might almost say with indifference. In **St Peter's Crucifixion**, two henchmen are busy nailing the saint's hands to the cross, in front of a door and two stone pyra mids suggesting the entrance to Nero's arena where St Peter was crucified; in **S John the Baptist's Beheading**, note the realistic details: the soldier holding onto the saint's hair and pressing his neck against the lance thus making sure of hitting straight; the receptacle ready to receive the head and the headsman seen from behind as he prepares to carry out the execution. In **The Death of St Julian's Parents** Julian is raising his sword to kill his parents because he thinks he is seeing his wife and her lover. The **Miracle of St Nicholas of Bari** is the work of a student, based on a drawing by Masaccio: the saint is throwing three gold balls into the bedroom of three young maidens who are too poor to get married.

Domenico Veneziano (1400/10-1461) – It is not surprising that the tondo (circular painting) depicting **The Adoration of the Magi** should have been owned by the Medici, for the main subject of the painting is not so much the Virgin Mary sitting down while one of the Magi is kissing the feet of the Child Jesus than the sumptuous group of kings' followers (actually members of the illustrious Medici family) showing the extravagant and colourful fashion of the Italian 15C. The presence of mottos and numerous animals: a peacock, two camels in a stable, cranes attacked by falcons, and a hunting dog, is reminiscent of Pisanello and models from northern Italy.

Fra Filippo Lippi (1406-1469) – **The Virgin Adoring the Child** used to decorate the main altar of the chapel in the Medici palace in Florence. The purity of the Virgin's face marks a contrast with the landscape of forest and rocks with felled trees and stumps in the background (Luke 3: 9 and Matthew, 3:10: "a tree which does not bear good fruit must be cut down and burnt"). The handle of the axe is stamped with the artist's signature.

Antonio del Pollaiuolo (1431?-1498) – Portraits showing the subject's profile were in fashion in Florence during the 15C. **Portrait of a Young Woman**, wearing richly embroidered garments and with her bust and shoulders turned slightly towards the spectator, is one of the finest of these through the sheer purity of the lines of its drawing and the nobility of the subject's expression.

Giovanni Bellini (1430/31-1516) – The two remarkable children's faces close to Christ's in **The Dead Body of Christ held by two Angels**, make a very fine composition based on a model originally created in France c 1400, known as the *Pietà of Angels*. **The Resurrection** had a strong influence on artists up to the time of Titian. Christ dis pensing his blessing and holding the banner of the Cross is bathed in the delicate colours of dawn against a landscape suggesting the Alpine foreland.

Andrea Mantegna (1431-1506) – An artist and his wife are represented in a painting for the first time, on either side of **The Formal Presentation of Christ in the Temple**. The influence of Donatello's madonnas can be felt in **Mary with Christ Asleep**, a work full of religious fervour in which the Child is being held tenderly against his mother's cheek.

Piero del Pollaiuolo (1441-1496) – The sumptuous interior which forms the background of **The Annunciation** is fascinating because the artist has observed the rules of perspective. Florence and the surrounding countryside can be seen through the twin windows.

Sandro Botticelli (1445-1510) – The Berlin gallery owns some magnificent paintings by this artist, such as **The Virgin with Child Surrounded by an Angels' Choir** (or "Raczynski-Tondo"). *Venus*, which is a workshop copy of the famous painting held in the Uffizi Gallery in Florence, is nevertheless interesting for its flowing movement inspired by an antique statue, the "Medici Venus", also kept in the Uffizi Gallery; another copy of this work was known at the time of Botticelli. Two **portraits** are particularly noteworthy: a likeness of Laurent the Magnificent's young brother, **Julian**, murdered at the age of 25 in Florence Cathedral, and the sharp-looking portrait of a young woman, probably an idealised character, which is also a workshop painting.

Cima da Conegliano (1459/60-1517/18) – The **Enthroned Virgin with Child, Surrounded by Four Saints** used to be kept in the same church, situated on one of the islands of the Venetian lagoon, as Bellini's **Resurrection**. Classical example of Venetian-style composition in a splendid architectural setting. The room which is surmounted by a cupola is decorated with the copy of a mosaïc to be found in St Mark's Basilica in Venice.

Piero di Cosimo (1461/62-1521) – His paintings, which are among the most poetic of his time, and his love of depicting animals (here doves and a rabbit) are pervaded by a sense of humour. In **Venus, Mars and Love**, the god of war is deeply asleep (a remarkable study of sleep), whilst some cupids are playing with his armour against a charming landscape. Botticelli treated the same subject (National Gallery, London) in a stiffer and more aristocratic manner.

Vittore Carpaccio (1465/67-1525/26) – The reflected image of Venetian life characteristic of Carpaccio's great narrative cycles is not to be found in **The Preparation of Christ's Burial**. The painting depicts a macabre scene: two men are opening the tomb and St Joseph of Arimathea is about to wash the body; Christ's body is stretched out on a low table (which used to be a venerated relic in Byzantium); the ground is littered with fragments of skeletons and bodies. The old man leaning back is Hiob, one of Christ's ancestors, revered as a saint in Venice.

Cinquecento (16C)

Giorgione (1477-1510) – There are few of his works left, as he died young; however, like Giovanni Bellini, he played an important role in the development of Venetian painting during the Renaissance and deeply influenced the following generation: Lorenzo Lotto, Palma the Elder and above all his pupil, the young Titian. **Portrait of a Young Man**, characterised by the subject's aloof expression, is the only male portrait painted by Giorgione. The local taste for colour and gracefully rounded forms as well as the diffused light create a harmonious ensemble. The hand resting on the parapet is a detail borrowed from Flemish art.

Il Franciabigio (1482-1525) – His **Portrait of a Young Man**, who was a friend of his, was influenced by Andrea del Sarto in whose studio Il Franciabigio worked.

Raphael (1483-1520) – There is a remarkably serene dignity in the **Terranuova Madonna**, one of the first madonnas painted by Raphael, who freed himself from the conventions of the Umbrian school through his use of *sfumato* (shading off) in landscape painting, as well as the use of freer outlines and softer expressions. Warm, light colours and the spontaneous attitude of the Madonna and Child are characteristic of his **Colonna Madonna**, dating from his Florentine period.

Giovan Gerolamo Savoldo (1480/85-1548) – The **Venetian Woman**, wiping her tears with a piece of her mantilla, her face half lit by the moon, is very mysterious. It is probably meant to be Mary Magdalene on her way to Christ's tomb (the arcades in the background).

Sebastiano del Piombo (1485-1547) – The dark architectural setting and the twilight atmosphere accentuate the impression of mystery pervading the **Portrait of a Young Roman Girl**, which may have been an engagement portrait. It is one of the first Roman works by Sebastiano del Piombo, and its huge size is undoubtedly due to Raphael's influence.

Titian (1488/90?-1576) – His friend Aretino greatly admired the **Portrait of Clarissa Strozzi Aged Two**, one of the first child portraits in European painting. The little girl was born in Venice, where her parents had been exiled; a small scent ball hangs from a thin chain. There are six different versions of **Venus and the Organist**, whic could be a likeness of Philip II of Spain. Attracted by physical beauty, the youn musician seems to forget the beauty of the music and the painting thus seems a invitation to love.

Correggio (1489-1534) – Originally intended for the Duke of Mantua's summe residence, the painting of **Leda and the Swan** was part of a cycle depicting the amorou adventures of Jupiter under various disguises. Before reaching Berlin, it belonge to the king of Spain and to the emperor Rodolphus II in Prague; taken by the Swede in 1648, it became the possession of several Roman princes, then of the Reger Philippe of Orleans, whose son ripped the canvas during a fit of mysticism (Leda' head has been entirely repainted); the work was finally bought by one of Frederic II's agents for the Sans-Souci gallery. According to legend, Zeus took the appear ance of a swan in order to seduce Leda, the king of Sparta's wife. Their unio resulted in the birth, in two separate eggs, of the twin brothers Castor and Pollu and of the twin sisters Helena (the future Helena of Troy) and Clytemnestra.

Agnolo Bronzino (1503-1572) – The background of the **Portrait of Ugolino Martel** is both artistic and intellectual. The young man came from a noble Florentin family. Destined to become a humanist as well as the bishop of Grandèves, i southern France, he is depicted aged 18-20, inside the courtyard of the famil palace, opening a book by the contemporary writer Pietro Bembo (1470-1547) and holding Homer's ninth poem in his right hand. The wax model of David's statu (at the back) by Donatello, is now kept in Washington.

Nicolo dell'Abate (1509-1571) – The **Portrait of a Knight of the Order of St James** i very fine. The order of St James was founded in Spain during the Middle Ages Experts are not absolutely certain that this portrait is in fact the work of Nicol dell'Abate, a Mannerist painter who took part in the decoration of Fontaineblea Castle from 1552 until his death.

Giovanni Battista Moroni (c 1525-1578) – **Portrait of the Duke of Albuquerque** is th work of one of the greatest 16C Italian portrait painters. The motto of the duke who was to become the governor of Milan, is written in Spanish on the base: "Her I am fearless, and death does not frighten me".

Seicento (17C)

Painter from Tuscany (c 1630) – The bees decorating the flag, which are th arms of Pope Urban VIII Barberini, whose troops were defeated by Genera Alessandro del Borroles, make it possible to identify this **Portrait of a Man**. The stron yet jovial face, seen from below, is stamped with a certain dignity.

Ludovico Carraci (1555-1619) – The game is the main subject of **Two Chess Players** a painting which can be compared to that of Paris Bordone, on the same theme The player on the left is totally engrossed in the game while his opponent i watching. The table, covered with an oriental mat, and the richly coloured tapestr hanging on the wall add a touch of warmth to this double portrait whose tense realistic atmosphere anticipates the innovations of the School of Bologna.

Caravaggio (1571-1610) – According to Virgil: "Omnia vincit amor" (Love over comes every obstacle). **Triumphant Love** appears in the shape of an ordinary child looking ambiguously erotic with a mocking smile on his face, surrounded by the attributes of Science (a square and a compass), the Arts (musical instruments laurels of literary fame), Fame and of Power (armour, crown and sceptre, *on th right*). A friend of Marquess Giustiniani, who owned the painting and was the painter's patron, maintained that this picture was the most famous of the collec tion and was kept concealed behind a curtain so that it would not overshadow the other paintings hanging next to it.

Lucas Giordano (1634-1705) – His **Saint Michael Overcoming Satan** is a Baroque work The attitude which was inspired by the famous **St Michael** in the Louvre and the pale colours convey the idea of triumph. Satan's arched body adds to the impres sion of dynamism. The theme, which was popular at the time of the Counter-Reformation and the war against the Turks, was one of the favourite themes of Giordano, better known for his realistic characters representing philoso phers in beggars' clothes.

Settecento (18C)

Giovanni Paolo Panini (1691-1765) – The magnificent horse-drawn carriages depicted in the Departure of the Duke of Choiseul from Saint Peter's Square in Rome (1754) show the splendid lifestyle of Louis XV's ambassador to the Vatican.

Giovanni Antonio Canaletto (1697-1768) – The view of the **Campo di Rialto**, the business centre in Venice, is interesting for its starkness and monumental archi tectural setting. On the left is the goldsmiths' street; the shop signs are visible under the portico. The **Vigilia di San Pietro** and the **Vigilia di San Marta** depict popular

Giotto –
The death of Mary

Antonio del Pollaiuolo –
Profile of a young lady

Titian –
*Portrait of Clarissa Strozzi
Aged Two*

festivities which take place at the eastern and western extremities of Venice, on the eve of St Peter's and St Martha's feast-days; they are the only nocturnal scenes painted by Canaletto.

Pietro Longhi (1702-1785) – **The Music Lesson** depicts an amorous scene, emphasized by the licentious painting hanging on the wall. As she turns round, a young woman playing the spinet is greeted by an elderly knight; the music teacher is standing behind the spinet; the Franciscan friar appears to be very interested.

Francesco Guardi (1712-1793) – **The Ascent of Count Zambeccari's Balloon**, the Venice's first balloon flight took place a year after the Montgolfier brothers' feat. The nacelle was in fact a gondola and the balloon stayed up for 2 1/2 hours before landing in marshland. Guardi's painting depicts it hovering over the Giudecca canal, as seen from the portico of the custom-house.

GERMANY

Middle Ages

Westphalian Painter (post-1250) – This **altarpiece** most probably comes from Soest. The pleats of the garments worn by the Virgin Mary and St John are stylized in a geometric way which confers a strange stiffness to the whole scene. God, holding Christ on the cross, is sitting on the richly decorated "throne of divine grace" (*Gnadenstuhl*). The luminous colours and the golden background are reminiscent of enamel work.

Hans Multscher (1400-1467) – The side panels of the Wurzach altarpiece, a polyptych which has lost its central part, depict episodes in the life of Mary and in Christ's Passion; the characters, including the Holy Family, are represented with striking realism.

Renaissance

Master of the Passion from Darmstadt (active during the 15C) – A native of Hesse or the Rhine valley, he was one of the most important 15C German painters. The two panels of the altarpiece depicting **The Enthroned Virgin with Child** and **The Holy Trinity**, showing Christ on God's knees, used to frame a Crucifixion. Formerly placed on the reverse side, the Romanesque palace in ruins (this style was already considered "old" at the time), which appears in the **Adoration by the Magi**, contrasts with the church being built (painted in a "modern" Gothic style and in red as a symbol of life) in **The Veneration of the Holy Cross**. Kneeling in front of the bishop, surrounded by his deacons, are the emperor Constantine and his mother Helena, who looked for Christ's cross on Calvary.

Albrecht Dürer (1471-1528) – This master of Renaissance painting tried to define a universal type through his portraits, which denote the precision of a skilled engraver. The Berlin gallery owns a good selection of them: portraits of **Hieronymus Holzschuher** and **Jakob Muffels**, both fifty years old, were noblemen from the free city of Nuremberg, of which the painter was a native. The bright colours in **Portrait of a Venitian Woman** and in **The Madonna with the Goldfinch** reflect the Italian influence; they were painted at the end of 1506, during the artist's second visit to Venice.

Lucas Cranach the Elder (1472-1533) – Old women are coming down a barren hill in litters, carts, wheelbarrows and even on men's backs in order to bathe in the pool of **The Fountain of Youth**. The metamorphosis occurs near the fountain's column, which shows Venus and Cupid. Charming young women are playing in the water and are being welcomed by a young squire. They change under tents, putting on elegant clothes and jewelry, and then they enjoy the pleasures of life, music, dancing, and love in a green and fertile setting. The detailed study of the nudes (see also the *Venus* panels), and the care with which the costumes are painted are characteristic of the art of Cranach the Elder who was also a remarkably gifted animal painter.

Albrecht Altdorfer (1480-1538) – In **Resting during the Flight into Egypt**, Joseph brings fruit to Mary who is next to a very attractive peasant's house. Jesus is on her knees leaning over the pool below the Fountain of Life mentioned in the *Song of Songs* and the *Psalms*. The small panel beneath the fountain explains that the painter, a native of Regensburg in Bavaria, has dedicated his work to the Virgin Mary for the salvation of his soul. **The Nativity** is set among ruins where Mary and Joseph, almost hidden, are praying in front of the Child brought to them by cherubs. The luminous atmosphere is unique.

Hans Baldung, alias "Grien" (1484/85-1545) – **The altarpiece of the Magi** comes from Halle's Cathedral; it is one of Baldung's early works. The painter shows the Mannerist's inclination for luminous colours and various kinds of cloth. The scene depicting the Crucifixion is darkened by the presence of black clouds over the cross, with Mary Magdelene kissing its base; a tiny Benedictine abbot can be seen at the bottom, on the right. **The Lamentation of Christ,** portrayed in a mountain setting, depicts the beautifully sorrowful expression of Mary and Jesus; Joseph of Arimathea can be seen in the background holding a jar of ointment.

Bartholomaüs Bruyn the Elder (1493-1555) – The **Portrait of Johann von Reidt** is one of the first full-face paintings in Germany. The mayor of Cologne is portrayed, at the age of 54 in his official dress.

Hans Holbein the Younger (1497/98-1543) – His **Portrait of the Merchant Georg Gisze** shows a young member of a family of merchants from Danzig, sitting at the desk of his London Office. The wealth of details is interesting: oriental carpet on the table, writing material, papers, books and various small objects. There is a vase of red and white carnations which are the symbol of love and fidelity, a reminder that the painting was commissioned for the young merchant's betrothal.

18C

Antoine Pesne (1683-1757) – The **Portrait of the Crown Prince, the future Frederick II,** depicted at the time of his accession to the throne, shows an angelic face and a peaceful expression which was not in keeping with the prince's quick-tempered, irascible character.

FLANDERS

15C and 16C

Jan Van Eyck (1390-1441) – The detail of the turban is fascinating in this **Portrait of Giovanni Arnolfini,** a merchant from Lucca who spent most of his life in Bruges and was depicted with his wife in a famous painting now in London. The **Portrait of Baudoin de Lannoy** shows the unattractive face and resolute expression of the Master of the Duke's House (the stick is the emblem of his rank). Philip the Good, Duke of Burgundy, presented him with the chain of the Order of the Golden Fleece, on 10 January 1430, the very day the order was founded. He met Van Eyck in Lille, where de Lannoy was governor.

Roger van der Weyden (1399/1400-1464) – His altarpieces: the **St John altarpiece,** the **Miraflores altarpiece** and the **Bladelin altarpiece** denote a smooth gentle style. The **Portrait of Charles the Bold** shows the son of the Duke of Burgundy, when he was still only Count of Charolais, wearing the chain of the Order of the Golden Fleece.

Petrus Christus (1410-1472/73) – The young woman who served as the model for this **Portrait of a Young Woman** has not been identified; she is shown in an interior setting, a rare occurence at that time. Her headdress and clothes might be French.

Hans Memling (1435-1494) – The panel representing the **Virgin Mary and Child** is the central part of an altarpiece with an architectural decoration (the bases of two columns can be seen in the two lower corners) which creates an impression of harmonious unity. The counterpart of the **Portrait of an Old Man** is in the Louvre: it is the portrait of an old woman with an interestingly human expression, just like her husband's.

Hugo van der Goes (1440/45-1482) – The gallery owns two magnificent paintings by this artist. **The Adoration of the Shepherds** is an off-centre composition including numerous characters, in which movement is important: the shepherds are arriving in a great hurry; two prophets are drawing a curtain in order to reveal the scene. In **The Adoration of the Magi,** the oldest king has laid down his fur-timmed crown and is kneeling before the beautiful figures of the Virgin and Child; the second king could be a self-portrait of the artist. The irises on the left-hand side, beneath the village street crowded with the kings' followers, are a symbol of Christ's future Passion.

Jan Gossaert (1470/80-1532) – In **Christ on the Mount of Olives,** the moonlit landscape over which hovers an angel holding a chalice intensifies the unreal atmosphere of the scene and the feeling of anguish and solitude. On the right, soldiers can be seen approaching in the dark.

Peter Brueghel the Elder (1525/30-1569) – People, animals and objects illustrate about a hundred Dutch proverbs focused on two main themes: madness and insanity (the earth upside-down in front of the house, on the left), and deceit and hypocrisy (the woman, in the centre of the painting, who is covering her husband with a blue coat).

17C

Peter Paul Rubens (1577-1640) – **Perseus Freeing Andromeda** gave the artist the opportunity to paint some lovely nudes. Several Cupids are helping Perseus free the young woman, mounting the hero's winged horse, Pegasus, and holding the reins, adding a fresh, humorous note. The nephew of the artist, Philip, is represented as a two-year-old boy in **The Child with a Bird.** It would appear that Rubens initially gave the figure an angel's face.

Albrecht Dürer –
Portrait of Hieronymus Holzschuher

Frans Hals –
Young Singer with a Flute

Lucas Cranach
the Elder –
*The Fountain
of Youth*

Caravaggio –
Triumphant Love

Jacob Jordaens (1593-1678) – The theme of **The Return of the Holy Family from Egypt** was taken up by many artists in the 17C. The round figures are full of life. The young Jordaens was apparently influenced by a painting by Rubens or an artist working with him.

Anton van Dyck (1599-1641) – Van Dyck excelled in portraying members of the Genoese and English aristocracy. Although they are somewhat austere, his **Portraits of an Aristocratic Couple from Genoa** give a valuable account of his distinguished style. The senator, a suspicious gentleman dressed in dark clothing, is set against an architectural background; the setting is a little warmer (partly because of the carpet) in the case of his wife, but the attitude is just as rigid. The **Portrait of Countess Geronima Spinola** has its lighter counterpart in the Louvre.

THE NETHERLANDS

17C

Frans Hals (1582/83-1666) – The young men painted by Hals reflect the influence of Italian painters, in particular Caravaggio. The feather on the hat contributes to the spontaneous expression of happiness in the **Young Singer with a Flute**. The painting belongs to a group devoted to the five senses, one of the favourite themes of 17C Dutch painting; here, it symbolises hearing. Another painting, **Malle Balle**, showing a drunken woman with an owl on her shoulder ("To be as drunk as an owl" was a common saying at that time), represents taste.

Pieter de Hooch (1629-*c* 1684) – The background to **The Mother** is a dimly-lit middle-class interior. The light increases along the corridor so that the little girl is standing in front of the door, bathed in golden light. It is one of the artist's best works; note the skillful shading of the different reds, from the cot blanket to the woman's gown and corset and the draping of the bed.

Rembrandt van Rijn (1606-1669) – The Berlin collection is one of the richest in the world: **The Mennonite Priest and his Wife** (he is explaining a passage of the Bible to her); **Portrait of Hendrickje Stoffels**, Rembrandt's companion; **Susanna and the Old Men**. The **Man with the Gold Helmet** is a studio painting, nevertheless fascinating for the rendering of the embossed motifs on the helmet, for the melancholic expression on the man's face, almost inscrutable in the semi-darkness, and for the controlled strength which it implies. This could be a representation of the god of war.

From Rembrandt's studio –
Man with the Gold Helmet

J.P. Anders/GEMÄLDEGALERIE - PREUSSISCHER KULTURBESITZ

Gerard Ter Borch (1617-1681) – The title **Paternal Teaching** dates from the 18C and has nothing to do with the scene depicted in which an officer is showing a gold coin to a young woman seen from behind. Goethe greatly admired her silhouette. **The Knife-Grinder's Family** is one of the rare outdoor subjects ever painted by Ter Borch. There are many details which add a human touch to this backyard scene, depicted with subtle shades of grey: the wall, the wooden roof, the objects scattered on the ground, the mother delousing her child.

Isack van Ostade (1621-1649) – Adraien's young brother depicted a **Farm Interior**, where humans and animals live together.

Jacob Isaacksz van Ruisdael (1628/29-1682) – A feeling of intense poetry pervades the **Oaktree near a Lake**, a rather sad landscape of river banks. The contrast between the trunk of the dead tree and the splendid foliage in the background stresses the concept of the renewal of nature.

Jan Vermeer van Delft (1632-1675) – The **Young Woman with a Pearl Necklace** is a fine study showing how light, even devoid of any warmth, brings out the bright colour of the coat lined with ermine. The fact that the young woman is looking at herself in a mirror underscores the concept of vanity. **The Glass of Wine**, in which another young woman empties her glass while a man hides the jug, is an incitation to drink with moderation.

FRANCE

15C

Jean Fouquet (1420-1480) – The panel featuring **Etienne Chevalier with St Stephen** comes from the tomb of Charles VII's general inspector of the royal treasury, who became Chief Treasurer during the reign of Louis XI and amassed a great fortune; his tomb used to be in Melun Cathedral. The other panel, representing Charles VII's mistress Agnès Sorel as the Madonna, is in Antwerp. The person making the gift is accompanied by his patron saint. The book and the stone symbolise the martyrdom of St Stephen, who was stoned to death. The perspective rendered by the architectural background, decorated with inlaid marble between the pilasters, is one of the first examples of Renaissance ornamentation in French art. The colours have a rather transparent quality.

Simon Marmion (? in Amiens-1489) – The two panels depicting **The Life of St Bertin,** which formed part of the St Omer altarpiece, a gilt-silver altarpiece which disappeared during the Revolution (St Bertin's Abbey was later destroyed), are extremely detailed. In the background, is the cloister decorated with the Dance of Death. Note the serious expression on the monks' faces.

17C and 18C

Nicolas de Largillière (1656-1746) – **The Sculptor Nicolas Coustou in his Studio** is pictured before a study of *Spring,* a statue which decorated the façade of the Hôtel de Noailles mansion in Paris; the building no longer exists.

Nicolas Poussin (1594-1665) – **Landscape with Matthew and the Angel** is one of the artist's early works. In the classical Roman countryside setting, the geometric aspect is emphasized by architectural elements. The angel represents the Evangelist's inspiration.

Antoine Watteau (1684-1721) – **The Dance of the Maiden** is a charming picture. The young girl, elegantly dressed, is getting ready to dance – and to make her social debut – in front of a group of children dressed in shepherds' clothes. The basket full of roses, the arrow and the cartouche, decorated with a heart next to a pillar, express the joys and sorrows of love.

19C

Marie Eléonore Godefroid (1778-1849) – **The Sons of Marshal Ney** admirably conveys the free, affectionate and graceful attitude of the three brothers. The eldest is having fun wearing his father's ceremonial sabre, which Napoleon gave as a wedding present to one of his generals and closest friends. The gun lying on the ground is a reminder of the marshal's modest background. The colours are light; the children's clothes, the silk veil, and the tablecloth are all imbued with the cold elegance of the Empire style. Marie Eléonore Godefroid specialised in children's portraits and this painting was exhibited at the Salon in 1810.

SPAIN

17C

Diego Velasquez (1599-1660) – Velasquez used a limited number of colours to paint the **Portrait of a Lady**. She is dressed in austere clothes, with a faint smile on her face. She could possibly be the Countess of Monterey, the wife of the Spanish ambassador in Rome, who was the painter's patron when he visited the Italian capital.

GREAT BRITAIN

18C

Thomas Gainsborough (1727-1788) – **The Marsham Children** is one of the artist's late works (1787), which seems to lead straight to Impressionism. The free and easy attitudes (young Charles, who later became the second Count of Romney, is picking hazelnuts for his sisters), the charming faces, and the skilful brushwork used for the foliage are quite dazzling.

FURTHER CULTURAL ESTABLISHMENTS

★★ **Philharmonie** (**T**³) – *Matthäikirchstraße 1*
The entrance to the main auditorium (**Philharmonie**, 1960-1963: *see the INTRO-DUCTION, ABC of architecture*), **Hans Scharoun**'s masterpiece, is on the west side and that of the Chamber Music Hall (**"Kammermusiksaal"**), built two decades later (1984-87) by his disciple Edgar Wisniewski after a drawing by the master, is on the south side. These two halls are famous throughout the world for being the

home base of the **Berlin Philharmonic Orchestra** (Berliner Philharmoniker), conducted by Herbert von Karajan from 1955 to 1989. This was the reason for the nickname given to the orchestra was Zirkus Karajani in direct reference to the pre-war Sarasani Circus. When Karajan died in 1989, he was replaced by the Italian conductor, Claudio Abbado. The small **Musical Instruments Museum**★ (Musikinstrumenten-Museum **M⁴** ⊘) nearby is housed in a well-lit, pleasant modern building (1983). The instruments are exhibited round a covered atrium: wind instruments from St Wenzel's Church in Naumburg, "serpent", harpsichords with decorated shutters and panels, organs (including a 17C portable organ from northwest Germany and the strange keyboard of the *Mighty*, an American Art Deco organ).

★★**Kunstgewerbemuseum** (**M⁵**) ⊘ – *Matthaïkirchplatz 8*. The Kunstgewerbemuseum is the oldest museum within the Kulturforum, and was planned by the architect Rolf Gutbrod and opened in 1985. However, the inside is spacious and the exhibits clearly presented, making for a very enjoyable visit. The museum houses a magnificent collection of gold plate. There is another museum of decorative arts in Köpenick *(see under that name)*.

Among the numerous masterpieces exhibited in the musuem, the following items are particularly noteworthy *(from the basement to the 1st floor)*:

– **The Guelph Treasure**★★★ *(Welfenschatz)* – The Guelph, from whom the Hanoverian dynasty is descended, were the most revered royal family in Germany. Their Romanesque treasure comprises some exceptional pieces: the **portable St Elbertus altar** (Cologne 1150), the **Guelph Cross, Duke Otto von Milden's missal**, the **reliquary-head of St Blaise** and the **reliquary in the form of a domed church** (Cologne 1175-80).

– **St George's reliquary**★ from Elbing (1480).

– **The spice box**★ *(Kassette für Spezereien)*, inlaid with hard stones, of Florentine origin (1690-95).

– **The extraordinary Lüneburg Treasure**★★★, including huge vermeil goblets, which once belonged to the municipal council of this small north German city, and objects from the **curios collection** *(Berliner Kunstkammer)*. As in the case of the Green Vault Collections in Dresden, the originality of the figurines made in the workshops of Augsburg, Prague or Nuremberg is fascinating: straight-handled coffee-pot in the shape of a war elephant, drinking horn with Jonah, Diana with a stag or on a goblet, chalice in the shape of a vine stem.

– **Textile** collection.

– **Berlin design** workshop: the "new strictness of the eighties". Eccentric Italian furniture dating from the sixties, pop art objects.

Reliquary, Cologne 1175

Hirmer/KUNSTEWERBEMUSEUM - PREUSSISCHER KULTURBESITZ

The Rathgen research laboratory

Every museum needs accurate information about the material, age and authenticity of its art and cultural historical exhibits. The Rathgen research laboratory undertakes these duties for the national museums in Berlin. It uses the latest technological procedures, for example thermoluminescence analysis, scanning electron microscopy and pyrolysis gas chromatography. It is quite possible to encounter forgeries, and over the past 20 years, 2 000 items have proven to be such.

The laboratory has made major contributions towards conservation research. Not only is it involved in the analysis of causes of damage, but in particular in the development of preventive methods and techniques, with a view to ensuring that visitors to the museums will be able to enjoy the old treasures for some considerable time.

– Drawing-room furniture by Carlo Bugatti (Milan, c1885), denoting the influence of both Japanese and Arabian art. **Costumes** shown in rotation.

– Rococo wooden frame of the "picture of Grace" from the Sonntagberg pilgrimage church (Lower Austria). This frame was used to make an identical silver frame which, together with the picture of Grace surrounded by a glory, formed the centre part of the main altar of the church.

– Chinese cabinet from a palace in Turin (1765) and **mirror cabinet** from Wiesenheid Castle; Chinese scent bottle (black glaze) with French bronze decorations from the first half of the 18C.

– The rich porcelain collection includes candelabra decorated with elephants from Meißen (1735-40) and the "mythological legends" dinner-service (Berlin, 1783).

★Kupferstichkabinett-Sammlung der Zeichnungen und Druckgraphik (M⁶) ⊘ –
This collection also dates back to the Great Elector, who acquired 2 500 drawings and watercolours in 1652. However the collection was gradually built up from 1831, when it opened as a museum.

The collection currently contains around 80 000 drawings, watercolours, gouaches and pastels from the 14C to the 20C, together with 520 000 fine art prints from the late Middle Ages to the present day. The collection of medieval German and Dutch drawings, 80 from Rembrandt alone, is unrivalled the world over. Visitors may ask to view individual works in the study room, without having to wait long. Several special exhibitions are held every year.

Kunstbibliothek – *Matthäikirchplatz.*
It is difficult to imagine a more comprehensive art library, whose individual departments include an aesthetic library, the Lipperheidesche costume library, a collection of ornamental embroidery and a collection of freehand drawings and commercial art, poster and advertising art, photography and the art of books. The library includes a reading and study room. Special exhibitions are held.

St-Matthäus-Kirche ⊘ – It was built in 1844-46 by Friedrich-August Stüler, the architect responsible for the New Museum *(see MUSEUMSINSEL).*

★★NEUE NATIONALGALERIE (M⁷) ⊘ – *Potsdamer Straße 50.*

The building was planned between 1965 and 1968 by the German architect living in America, **Mies von der Rohe**, who was the director of the Bauhaus during the 1930s. The "aerial" part, consisting of a terrace supported by glass walls, is devoted to temporary exhibitions. The museum, which is housed in the upper hall and in the base and lit by means of a sculpture garden, includes some extremely beautiful exhibition areas for 20C art. This is the place to go to for those who like early Expressionism, represented by *Die Brücke* (The Bridge, *see GRUNEWALD*), New Objectivity *(Neue Sachlichkeit)* and the main exponents of modern art. **Hamburg Station – Museum für Gegenwart Berlin** (Hamburger Bahnhof, *see MOABIT*) houses contemporary art.
The following are particularly noteworthy:

Max Ernst, *Capricorne* (1948-64). Near the entrance.

Edvard Munch, *The Frieze of Life for the Max-Rheinhardt Theatre (Lebensfries für das Max-Rheinhardt-Theater in Berlin,* 1906-7); Count Kessler's *Portrait* (Harry Graf Kessler, 1906).

Georg Kolbe, *Dancer, (Tänzerin,* 1911-12).

Ernst Ludwig Kirchner, *Bridge over the Rhine in Cologne (Rheinbrücke in Kölln,* 1914), *Potsdamer Platz* (1914).

Emil Nolde, *Whitsun (Pfingsten,* 1909).

Ernst Barlach, *The Forsaken (Die Verlassenen,* 1913).

Lionel Feiniger, *Teltow II* (1918).

Rudolf Belling, *Triple Chord (Dreiklang,* 1919); *Sculpture 23 (Skulptur 23,* 1923).

Georg Kolbe: Dancer (1911-12)

Calder's stabile

Oskar Kokoschka, *Portrait of Adolf Loos (Der wiener Baumeister Adolf Loos,* 1909).

Otto Dix, *Portrait of the Art Dealer Alfred Flechtheim (Der Kunsthändler Alfred Flechtheim,* 1926); *The Skat Players (Die Skatspieler,* 1920), recently acquired by the museum; *Flanders (Flandern,* 1934-35).

Georg Grosz, *The „Pillaro" of Society (Die Stützen der Gesellschaft,* 1926).

Käthe Kollwirz, *Mother and Her Children (Mutter mit Kindern,* 1932-37).

Max Beckmann, *Birth (Geburt,* 1937); *Death (Tod,* 1938).

The gallery's collections also include paintings by Picasso, Salvador Dali, Robert Delaunay, Fernand Léger, Paul Klee, Laszlo Moholy-Nagy as well as many works dating from the sixties and seventies. A well-stocked bookshop contains an excellent collection of art books and cultural guides.

The capital of psychoanalysis

Doctors played an important role in Berlin life during the twenties: Alfred Döblin, Gottfried Benn, Friedrich Wolf, Richard Hülsenbeck, Magnus Hirschfeld *(see TIERGARTEN).* But the social climate was favourable above all to the development of psychoanalysis. In 1906, Max Reinhardt had staged in Berlin Frank Wedekind's play, banned for 16 years: *The Awakening of Spring (Frühlingserwachen),* which depicts the feelings of two youths and a young girl. The play aroused the interest of the Viennese Society of Psychology meeting in the home of Freud, who had published *Three Essays on the Theory of Sexuality* the previous year. Freud had set his hopes on Budapest, but settled for Berlin. **Karl Abraham,** a psychoanalyst trained by Jung, was the first to set up his practice. The Berlin Institute of Psychoanalysis was founded on 14 February 1920 at No 29 Potsdamer Straße. It was at the same time a research centre, a training centre and a treatment centre which dealt with a great number of service men and civilians suffering from neurosis brought on by the war. The Berlin team which also included Max Elington and Ernst Simmel, was the first to require that future analysts should themselves undergo analysis. The 7th international conference of psychoanalysis took place from 25 to 27 September 1922, in Freud's presence; he delivered a memorable lecture: *A Few Remarks about the Unconscious Mind.* Psychoanalysis was part of the constant cultural activity which took possession of the town between the wars: *Pointing at Shadows (Schatten)* by Arthur Robison anticipated the Pabst film, *The Mysteries of the Soul (Geheimnisse einer Seele),* produced in 1926 by the UFA with the scientific collaboration of Freud, Sachs and Abraham. The latter died on Christmas Day 1925. Students at the "Policlinique", Erich Fromm, Herbert Marcuse, Wilhelm Reich and Manes Sperber became famous while in exile in America and greatly influenced intellectual life in the young Federal Republic of Germany.

★**Staatsbibliothek Preußischer Kulturbesitz** (**M⁸**) ⊘ – *Potsdamer Straße 33.*
It is worth going inside this library, designed by Hans Scharoun between 1967 and
1978, to admire the fitting of the interior. The reading room is a vast curved hall,
very luminous, with reading "terraces" where study desks alternate with filing cabinets. Students are busy working on microcomputers. The store-room occupies the
top part which is covered over, as in the case of the Philharmonie, with aluminium
sheeting and has no opening on the outside. An extension is planned as part of
the works which will eventually link the Kulturforum to Potsdamer Platz.

Potsdamer Straße – The road leading to Potsdam was the first to be paved in
Prussia (1792). It is now a wide shopping street; the Wintergarten variety theatre
(see ON THE TOWN) is also located here.

ALONG LANDWEHRKANAL

Landwehrkanal – *Walk westwards along the bank without crossing Potsdamer
Bridge (Potsdamer Brücke)*
Visitors will walk past the former Navy headquarters and general Army headquarters (1911-14: Reichpietschufer 72-76) taken over by the Ministry of Defence
and Department of Employment (which still has its head office in Bonn), and past
the circular buildings of the Berlin Scientific Centre (Wissenschaftszentrum Berlin).

Shellhaus – *Reichpietschufer 60/62.* The wave-like projections of this building
(1930-31) convey an impression of shape and movement. The architect Emil
Fahrenkamp had to pay the town planning authorities *324 visits in order to explain
his plans.*
Turn right into Stauffenbergstraße.

The German Resistance

Up until 1938, many people risked their freedom to distribute tracts and
underground newspapers, and give help to escaped prisoners. The Church put
up less resistance than isolated individuals and small groups, particularly on
the Left: KPD cells, the young Social-Democrat **Willy Brandt** was, for a few
months, at the head of an organisation which was dismantled in 1939. Most
members of the resistance were arrested and beheaded in Brandenburg prison
(where a thousand more died during the war) or in Plötzensee prison.
The German population remained lethargic. Pre-war successes in foreign politics strengthened the regime; Berlin was at the centre of the repressive system.
Opposition groups developed in the army, the administration and among the
aristocracy. The Red Ochestra, founded by an officer, Harro Schulze-Boysen
and a high-ranking civil servant, Arvid Harnack, sent secret information to
Moscow; the Kreisau Circle of Count Yorck von Wartenburg, influenced by
Christian and Socialist ideas, was at the origin of the attempt on Hitler's life
made by Count Claus von Stauffenberg on 20 July 1944. The repression was
fierce: 7 000 people arrested, 2 000 executed.

Gedenkstätte Deutscher Widerstand (**M⁹**) – *Stauffenbergstraße 11-13.*
The former Navy headquarters taken over by the Ministry of Defence which, from
1935 onwards served as headquarters for the senior commandos of the
Wehrmacht, the general Staff and the Navy, had, since 1938, counted a number
of high-ranking officers who were opposed to Hitler and his warlike plans. Colonel
Klaus Schenk, Count of Stauffenberg, had his office here as did General Friedrich Olbricht
and Albert Ritter Merz von Quirnheim, who prepared the unsuccessful attempt on
the life of Hitler. They were executed in the courtyard the next day, 21 July 1944.
The street was renamed *Stauffenberg* in their honour in 1954. A very comprehensive exhibition *(2nd floor, 1st door on the left in the courtyard)* illustrates the
end of the Weimar Republic, the rise of national Socialism and Hitler's accession
to power, as well as all the different forms of resistance, political, religious, cultural and scientific, conducted from exile during the war. The numerous
explanatory panels are in German, but there is a summary of events in English. It
has become a true research centre *(newspaper cuttings, biographies, trial reports,
films shown in three of the rooms).*
*Return to the Landwehrkanal and continue westwards. Take the first right turn
into Hildebrandtstraße. The* **former diplomatic district,** situated a little further north,
conveys a strange impression: the site has been laid waste and left in that state
so that nature has taken over once more. There are still a few embassies such as
the Italian embassy – now a general consulate – and the Japanese embassy housing
a cultural centre, built in a Neoclassical style which fits in perfectly with Speer's
plans for this district close to the north-south axis.

Stiftung Preußischer Kulturbesitz

The Prussian state was dissolved in 1947 by the Allied Control Council and its collections were stored in the West: should they be divided among the different Länder, which were the legal successors of the Prussian state? The foundation under public law, registered in Berlin, was created by law in 1957. It inherited the name and collections of Prussia and included the following institutes in Berlin: Staatsbibliothek, Staatliche Museen zu Berlin, Staatliches Institut für Musikforschung with the Musikinstrumenten-Museum, Geheimes Staatsarchiv and Ibero-Amerikanisches Institut.

The foundation built the Dahlem extension as well as the Mies von der Rohe New National Gallery, it refurbished the Egyptian Museum opposite the Schloß Charlottenburg, engaged in consistent buying and research and began to combine the separate collections and institutes after German reunification. The neo-Classical villa **Von-der-Heydt** (**H**), which was built between 1860 and 1862 *(Von-der-Heydt-Straße 16)* houses the head office of this most important German complex of cultural institutions.

★**Bauhaus-Archiv (Museum für Gestaltung)** – *Klingelhöferstraße 14*. It is more of a research centre (1979, according to plans by Walter Gropius) than a museum. It depicts the characteristics and main exponents of the movement created in Weimar in 1924, which was later based in Berlin and Dessau. Temporary exhibitions and library.

Two examples of IBA 1987 homes:

The diplomatic district extends towards Tiergarten *(see under that name)*. Worth seeing are the amazing **"Ökohaus"**, at No 11-12 Corneliusstraße, designed by architects and their clients who intended to live in it (its conception is environmentalist: garden-terraces, environment-friendly building materials, economical use of water, including rainwater, and electricity, water recovery for heating purposes) and the rows of IBA 87 villas *(see INTRODUCTION, Achitecture and city planning)* in **Rauchstraße**, surrounding a garden.

Visitors who like this kind of project, might enjoy a ride on the bus along **Lützowstraße**, east of Lützowplatz and up to Magdeburger Platz.

IN THE VICINITY

See **KREUZBERG (west part)**★★, **POTSDAMER PLATZ**, **SCHÖNEBERG**★, **TIERGARTEN**★★.

KURFÜRSTENDAMM★★

Charlottenburg, Wilmersdorf
See map of Berlin Town Centre, **6**, **7**, **EFGHVX**

Kurfürstendamm, which means literally "prince-electors' road", is Berlin's Champs-Elysées; it was laid out by Margrave Joachim II (1535-1571) to link Cölln Castle *(see SCHLOSSPLATZ)* and the Grunewald hunting lodge *(see under that name)*. It was only urbanised in 1886, under the impulsion of Bismarck, who wanted Berlin to be as splendid a city as Baron Haussmann's Paris. In point of fact, soon after the **Memorial Church** (Gedächtniskirche) was built, Kurfürstendamm found itself at the centre of the new residential districts, which were developing fast in the western part of the city, and, just before World War I, it became the new focus of social and cultural activities as well as nightlife, outshining Unter den Linden and Friedrichstraße. Subtantial buildings with front gardens were built along the avenue. Some of them are still there. They contained large flats with a living area of 200 to 300 square metres, equipped with all the comforts (you need only take a room in the vicinity of Ku'damm to realise how large the rooms were in these apartments.). Between the wars, the district was a bustling intellectual and artistic centre with its cafés, theatres, refined tea-rooms and above all its vast cinemas such as the Palast am Zoo or the Gloria-Palast. Goebbels protested repeatedly against this animation from 1926 onwards. After the war, Kurfürstendamm lay in ruins but it was soon rebuilt and became the mirror of West Berlin. Even though it may not be the most authentic part of Berlin, Kufürstendamm is nevertheless a fascinating place, especially at night, and a cosmopolitan avenue, lined with cinemas, cafés and elegant shops, particularly attractive to visitors.

In addition to **S** + **U** **Zoologischer Garten** *Station*, many bus stop in or near Kurfürstendamm **U** *Kurfürstendamm*, **U** *Uhlandstraße, Rathenauplatz, No 100* 🚌 *Breitscheidplatz, No 100* 🚌 *stops at Europa-Center.*

Memorial Church seen through the sculpture entitled *"Berlin"*

STROLLING ALONG "KU'DAMM"

Tauentzienstraße – 🅄 *1, 2, 12, 15 Wittenbergplatz.*
This street offers the best **view★** of the Memorial Church, through the sculpture named Berlin, consisting of two large aluminium links, created by Brigitte and Martin Matschinsky-Denninghoff, which commemorates the 750th anniversary of the town. The main attraction here is the **KaDeWe ★** *(see also ON THE TOWN, Shopping)*. This elegant department store was built in 1906 in a plain style which was unusual at the time.

Europa-Center – *Tauentzienstraße 9:* 🅄 *9, 15 Kurfürstendamm*
In front stands the **"Weltkugelbrunnen"** ("Fountain of the Earthly Globe"; or *Wasser-klops,* "the dumpling"). The Europa-Center is a shopping arcade on several floors *(numerous gadgets for tourists)*. The fountain standing in the middle of the atrium, the *Clock of Passing Time,* is a kind of vertical still, nicknamed "the fruit juice machine" because of the fluorescent liquid circulating inside.

Breitscheidplatz – 🅄 *9, 15 Kurfürstendamm.*
The parvis situated between the Memorial Church and the Europa-Center is a well-known meeting-place. There is always something going on here: street musicians and other buskers, who attract strollers and tourists, as well as roller-skating enthusiasts. At the end of August, festivities are in full swing along Kurfürstendamm and Tauentzienstraße, particularly in this spot. Costume jewellery and hat stalls alternate with food stalls serving hot sausages or Vietnamese and Turkish food. There is also a lovely Christmas market.

★ Kaiser-Wilhelm-Gedächtnis-kirche – 🅄 *9, 15 Kurfürstendamm*
The neo-Romanesque church built between 1890 and 1895 by **Franz Schwechten**, the architect who designed Anhalt Station, and dedicated to the Emperor William I and "Sedan day" (Sedantag), has almost entirely disappeared except for its truncated tower, familiarly referred to by Berliners as "the rotten tooth" or "the hollow tooth" *(Hohler Zahn)*. The new church and tower (the "lipstick and powder case"/*Lippenstift und Puderdose,* as they have been nicknamed with the same popular humour) combine with the ruins to form an original ensemble, which is one of the emblems of Berlin. The blue stained glass windows, made in Chartres, are very effective, either from the interior, decorated with a large gilt Christ on the Cross, or from the outside, at night, when the sanctuary is lit from the inside. In the narthex of the old church, there are mosaics illustrating the family tree of the House of Hohenzollern *(up to the Kronprinz, son of William II, and his wife, on the far right)* and a model of the district and the church before it was bombed in 1943.

★★★ Zoologischer Garten – Ⓢ + 🅄 *Zoologischer Garten – See under that name.*

★★ Kurfürstendamm ⊘ – 🅄 *9,* 🅄 *15, Kurfürstendamm.* This avenue is less straight than the Champs-Elysées, its Parisian counterpart. It is still lined with some fine *Jugendstil* buildings, such as No 234, near Gedächtniskirche, as well as a few others on the corner of several streets which are often more elegant than Ku'damm. For instance, the massive edifice at **No 59**, built in 1905-97 on the edge of Oliaerplatz and surmounted by swollen domes, deserves the name of "monumental safe" given by Christopher Isherwood to similar constructions. This one originally comprised 8 and 11 room flats extending over 410 and 575 square metres respectively. The predilection of Kaiser William's Germany for groups of buildings dominated by prestigious corner edifices, still prevails today as the protruding glass building known as **Ku'70** shows.

Particularly noteworthy are two cafés and a shopping arcade situated between the **KPM** Shop at No 26A and another elegant boutique:

– **The Kranzler Café**: Formerly situated at the intersection of Unter den Linden and Friedrichstraße, it was rebuilt during the fifties on the corner of Joachimstaler Straße. Behind the cafe stands a building based on a Helmut Jahn design. The Cafe Kranzler was restructured at the time, leaving the building front, a listed monument, intact.

– **Ku'damm Karree**: This shopping arcade (at night, the outside is covered with neon lights) houses the **Berliner Panoptikum** *(3rd floor)*, waxworks with a long-standing tradition *(see FRIEDRICHSTRASSE)*. Admission is expensive and the wax figures are poor quality. The most popular attraction is the "medical surgery" (Medizinisches Kabinett, 1890) with its display of casts representing genital abnormalities, difficult childbirths, various diseases (skin diseases: leprosy, syphilis...); next come the torture chamber and busts of famous people.

– **The Möhring Café**: 🆄 *15 Uhlandstraße*, is situated at No 213, opposite the House of France. It is the other famous name along Ku'damm, in true Viennese tradition. *(see ON THE TOWN, The Berlin Scene).*

"Litfaßsäule"

These columns, similar to the "colonnes Morris" in Paris, were invented in 1855 for publicity purposes by the publisher Ernst Litfaß who named them after himself.

★**Fasanenstraße** – 🆄 *15 Uhlandstraße.*
This lovely street, lined with numerous luxury boutiques, gives an idea of what Kurfürstendamm looked like originally; it is lined with villas and private houses, built before the residential blocks of flats designed for letting. The **Literaturhaus**, at No 23, is an attractive house preceded by a garden where tea is served (as well as on the raised verandah which is used as a winter garden). The bookshop is in the basement, level with the foundations of the house. The entrance is on the right for visitors wishing to look at the temporary exhibitions based on literary themes. The **Käthe-Kollwitz Museum** (**M¹⁰**) is situated at No 24. The work of this artist is one long cry of suffering and protest against the misery of the lower classes. The fine-looking **Griesbach Villa** stands at No 25.

Lehniner Platz Ⓥ – 🆄 *7 Adenauerplatz.*

Schaubühne★, which in pre-war days (1927-28) was the Universum Cinema, was designed by **Erich Mendelsohn** together with the Woga block of flats lining Cicerostraße. The interior fittings were completely renewed and it is now one of the most famous theatres in Berlin *(see ON THE TOWN)*. Beyond Lehniner Platz, Ku'damm quietens down and becomes a mere shopping street for the locals .

Rathenauplatz – Ⓢ *9 Halensee.*
The **Halensee** is very close *(walk 100m north along the left-hand side of Halenseestraße)*. In 1904, the *Terrassen am Halensee* used to attract a lot of people as there was dancing and music. They were replaced a little later by a **Lunapark** offering numerous attractions. The official

Kathy Kollwitz: *Complaint*

KÄTHE - KOLLWITZ MUSEUM, Berlin

Käthe Kollwitz: the committed artist

After completing her studies in Munich and the German capital, Käthe Kollwitz only rarely left Berlin. Her husband, the physician Karl Kollwitz, had his practice, which was also used as a family planning office, in the street named after him in Prenzlauer Berg. Having witnessed misery, she gave a full account of its despair throughout her work, which made one of the most important contributions to 20th-century German Realism: *The Trampled On, Death Takes its Due, Mother in Dead Child's Bed; Portraits*. She was a member of the Berlin Secession and was appointed professor at the Fine Arts Academy in 1919. She lived in Berlin until 1943. Her sculptures were almost entirely destroyed during the war. Evacuated to Moritzburg, near Dresden, she died there on 22 April 1945.

name, chosen in 1910, was inspired by Paul Lincke's operetta, *Frau Luna*. The lake is famous because the majority of people who loll along its shores do so in their birthday suits. The other favourite haunt of nudists is Teufelssee *(see GRUNEWALD)*. As Berliners have a simple, direct relationship with nature, nudists are likely to be found in many places, especially near large lakes and in certain parks.

IN THE VICINITY

See **ERNST-REUTER-PLATZ, SCHÖNEBERG★, TIERGARTEN★★, WILMERSDORF.**

LICHTENBERG
Lichtenberg
See map of Berlin Conurbation, **11**, **DU**

The village of **Lichtenberg**, founded in 1230 (the small parish church is still standing in Möllendorfstraße, isolated among modern buildings), retained its rural aspect at the heart of a vast industrial working-class district until the end of the 19C. It was the first to be subjected to a British bombing raid on 25 August 1940, in retaliation against a surprise attack on London. Many more followed and, today, with its large buildings, it is one of the "greyest" districts of Berlin. **Friedrichsfelde Castle** and the **zoo** offer a pleasant contrast. Oscar Gregorovius (1845-1913) played an important role in financing, designing and building the "colony for people of small means" (Kolonie für kleine Leute) in Karlhorst. The successful novelist **Hedwig Courths-Mahler** (1867-1950) was one of the inhabitants of this district before the villas were taken over by various STASI and KGB offices after 1945.
The municipal **Zentralfriedhof Friedrichsfelde** *(Gudrunstraße)* which was opened in 1881 achieved fame during GDR times thanks to the annual mass procession to the "Socialists' Memorial", with the graves of Karl Liebknecht and Rosa Luxemburg, Wilhelm Pieck, Otto Grotewohl, Walter Ulbricht and other leading SED politicians.

MAIN SIGHTS

Rathaus (R) – *No 17 and 23* Tram *Rathaus Lichtenberg.*
The fact that the edifice is situated at the intersection of two streets makes it easier to appreciate its neo-Gothic style with numerous pinnacles and turrets. The small village church still stands a little further north, in Möllendorfstraße.

Fennpfuhlpark – *No 8 and 27* Tram *Paul-Junius-Straße or No 17, 21 and 23* Tram *Herzbergstraße/Weißenseer Weg.*
This green open space , rendered more attractive by the presence of a lake and surrounded by prefabricated buildings, offers a true picture of Lichtenberg.

Schloß Friedrichsfelde ◷ – **U** *5 Tierpark.*
The castle was built at the end of the 17C and was extended to its current size in 1719. Valuable 18C linen tapestries from a number of castles and manor houses in the Mark Brandenburg are hung in the garden room and banqueting hall and also in some of the other rooms.
Works of visual and applied arts dating from the 18C and early 19C are exhibited in the simply decorated rooms (paintings, porcelain, glass, wall hangings, furniture etc). The **concert room★** contains one of the most beautiful early Classical interior decorations in Berlin.

The Treskow family

The Carlshorst Works (Vorwerk Carlshorst) were founded by **Carl Sigismond von Treskow** in the middle of the Friedrichfeld countryside (Friedrichsfelder Feldmark). The Treskow family lived in Friedrichsfelde Castle from 1816 onwards and the municipality prospered under their management. The last owner of the castle, Sigismond von Treskow, who was born in 1864, was evicted in 1945. He died soon afterwards.

★Tierpark Berlin ◷ – It follows on Friedrichsfelde Park. After a number of seemingly common animals the visitor suddenly comes across some magnificent groups of tigers (and a tigon, the offspring of a tiger and a lioness!), white rhinos, elephants, giraffes, fruit bats in a huge hot house and two manatees moving slowly round their large aquarium.

Museum Berlin-Karlshorst (M³⁰) ◷ – *Zwiegeler Straße 4.*
The unconditional surrender of Nazi Germany on 8 May 1945 was signed in one of the rooms of this house, which has been kept as it was at the time. Before this event took place, the building was a casino reserved for the students of the

Wehrmacht engineering corps (Festungspionerschule). It was taken over as their headquarters by the shock troops of the Russian 5th army on 23 April 1945. After 1945, it was occupied by various military authorities from the Soviet bloc. With the help of numerous photographs, uniforms, maps and arms, the museum illustrates the tragic years of the war between Germany and the USSR, and the massacres perpetrated by the "shock troops" *(Einsatztruppen)*. 630 000 prisoners of war and 2.8 million civilians were sent to do hard labour in Germany.

Racing at Karlshorst

The first horse-racing Grand Prix of the Prussian army took place on 24 June 1862 near the Carlshorst Works *(see above)*. It brought a certain prestige to the neighbourhood. In 1893, the steeplechase course was transferred from the Westend *(see OLYMPIASTADION)* to Karlshorst which had its heyday between 1894 and 1914. The first race broadcast live on radio took place on 6 April 1926. After 1945, the Karlshorst racecourse specialised in trotting, and became the most famous racecourse in the GDR.

IN THE VICINITY

See **FRIEDRICHSHAIN, MARZAHN.**

MARZAHN
Marzahn
See map of Berlin Conurbation, **11**, **DU**

It is difficult to be objective about Marzahn. This kind of town planning is hardly the exclusive prerogative of the GDR, even if the shortage of funds make it even more depressing. The suburbs of other western cities have just as many tower blocks which have suddenly appeared in the middle of the countryside. The city of Marzahn, followed by **Hellersdorf** in the east end of Berlin, has the same population as the towns of Ulm and Bamberg put together (about 150 000 inhabitants). This "Trabantenstadt" was built from 1976 onwards and covers 5km. The "Plattenbau" (concrete slab) edifices, the neglected green open spaces, the absence of a focal point such as a square have created a dull grey environment in which all traces of individualism (even inside the flats) have been more or less wiped out. There are few churches and when there are any, they are ridiculouly small; disabled and old people were not allowed in this dormitory town where workers, whose life was regulated like clockwork *(Pendler)*, found all they needed on the spot: swimming-pools, hospital *(Poliklinik)*, nurseries, schools (with their characteristic corrugated roofs) shopping centres, cinemas. The street names have been changed; the plaques mentioning the construction date have disappeared but the PDS (former Communist party) is still in favour; rent increases have led to protests and the smallest plot (green space, parking spaces) arouses questions of ownership.

Visitors and those who have not got the use of a car are advised to discover this new district of Berlin through the *Kulturbüro Berlin*; the guided tour *(Stadtverführung)* programme is available in many museums and cultural institutions. The guided walk (which takes place once a month) lasts for three hours. It is a good way to avoid getting lost in this vast city.

WALKING THROUGH MARZAHN

Start from Marzahn **S** *7 Station. No 6, 7, 17* **Tram** *Marzahner Promenade.*

The **Marzahner Promenade** begins on a square with a modern fountain; shops *(Einkaufspromenade)* and the main amenities *(swimming-pool, municipal library)* are located close together.

Walk across the wide Landsberger Allee and towards the steeple of the small church of Alt-Marzahn.

Alt-Marzahn – Situated only a stone's throw from the recently renovated buildings, the pretty village of Alt-Marzahn, founded a second time by Frederick II after it was destroyed during the Thirty Years War, offers a striking contrast. The stepped gabled

---

High-level spy

Günter Guillaume worked for 18 years with Willy Brandt as his private secretary from the time Brandt became chancellor and, during that time, he passed a lot of information over to the East since he was a captain in the East-German secret service. He was unmasked with the help of a defector but only after having caused the downfall of the Chancellor. He was exchanged for some political prisoners in East Germany.

---

steeple of the church (built at the end of the 19C) dominates the almond-shaped main square of this typical *Angerdorf (see the INTRODUCTION, Architecture and city planning)*. The windmill is the reconstruction of one of the many windmills once scattered throughout the surrounding countryside. **Günter Guillaume**, the spy working for the GDR, who was responsible for the downfall of Willy Brandt, is buried in the cemetery *(Marzahner Friedhof)*. Some of the one-storeyed buildings house museums.

Dorfmuseum Marzahn – Handwerksmuseum and Friseurmuseum collections ⊙ *– Alt-Marzahn 31.*

Friseurmuseum – Barbers' tools as well as those belonging to the wig-maker and the dentist (or rather the tooth-puller) are exhibited. Barbers, who were also physicians and surgeons, were considered as craftsmen who treated wounds, skin diseases, fractures etc. It took 2 to 4 years' study and 4 to 7 years' service under a master *(Gesellenjahre)* to become a barber. The practice of medecine passed out of the hands of barbers in 1843. There were numerous public baths during the Middle Ages, but their number decreased from 1 500 onwards. These professions are at the origin of men's hairdressers *(Herrenfriseur)* who appeared in the middle of the 19C. Note the glass cases full of scent bottles, combs and various hair ornaments. The Art Nouveau decoration★ (1901) of François Haby's establishment comprises exclusively originals, created by Henry van de Velde.

The trendiest hairdresser in Berlin

There were no independent ladies' hairdressing salons in Berlin until the end of the 19C; hairdressing was performed in the customers' homes. **François Haby** moved from Königsberg to Berlin in 1880 and soon became the most famous hairdresser in the capital, having members of the court among his clientele. High society, who set the fashion in Imperial Berlin, met in his salon. He devised advertising slogans for the creams he created: for instance his shaving cream *Wach auf* ("Wake up"), or his lady's shampoo *Ich kann so nett sein* ("I can be so kind"). He used his ointment *Es ist erreicht* ("That's it!") to stiffen *(die Schnurrbartwichse mit zugehöriger Bartbinde)* the moustache of the Kaiser who could not do without his hairdresser even when he was travelling. The salon was decorated according to drawings by the Belgian architect **Harry van der Velde**, a master of Art Nouveau style. There were twelve seats for men and seven for women. Partly destroyed during World War II, the establishment continued to function until 1964 when the building was demolished.

Handwerksmuseum – *Apply to the Friseurmuseum, then go into the building on the right in the courtyard and up to the first floor.*
The guild life of old Berlin is brought to life in a vast loft. Visitors can inspect the frequently crude practices of the journeymen and masters from original trade signs, banners and guild shops. In addition to the cooper's, weaver's, locksmith's and fisherman's workshops, a particular feature of the exhibition is the excellently recreated **guild room**, in which tin goblets, tobacco holders and rare guild standards are kept.

Erholungspark Marzahn (C¹) – *As you come out of Alt-Marzahn, take the bus, and get off at Eisenacher Straße/Gartenschau.*
The green patch stretching along the Wuhle *(Wuhletal)* is bound to the north by Marzahn Park. From the top of Kienberg Hill (101m) there is a panoramic **view★** of Marzahn and Hellersdorf. A strange landscape unfolds before the eyes: a vast expanse of concrete criss-crossed with bars, forming a kind of maze. When the weather is so bad that the tower in Alexanderplatz cannot be seen, the whole of Berlin seems to disappear out of sight.

Allee der Kosmauten – This avenue, which goes round the Springfuhl area, was the first part of Marzahn to be urbanised (1978). It is lined with edifices, sometimes built around a garden *(Wohnhöfe)*; owing to the *Plattenbau* (concrete slab) method of construction used here, there are pointing problems at corners.

Springfuhl – Ⓢ *7, 75, Springfuhl.*
The first council flats were built around the town hall (1984), the post-office and other public buildings; they were clad with ceramics and were regarded at the time as being very beautiful. The hospital *(Poliklinik)* was also considered a fine building because it was made of glass instead of concrete.

Biesdorf – Ⓢ *5 Biesdorf; walk south through Stadtpark.*
Biesdorf-Nord is the residential middle-class part of Marzahn. The Siemens family owned a castle, built by Martin Gropius on the edge of the old village. **Werner von Siemens** conducted his first successful wireless transmission experiments from the top of the tower and he used the park for his electric train trials. There are plans to build a complex of 5,200 homes in south Biesdorf *(Ⓤ 5 Elsterwerdaer Platz).*

IN THE VICINITY
See **LICHTENBERG, WEISSENSEE.**

MOABIT★

Tiergarten
See map of Berlin Town Centre, **3**, GHTU

The name Moabit is derived from "the land of Moab", a barren area in the north-western part of Berlin, which was developed from 1716 onwards by French Huguenots engaged in silkworm-breeding. The silk trade expanded during the reign of Frederick I who subsidised it.

Towards 1850, Moabit became the second most important industrial centre in the capital; it was mainly concerned with mechanical engineering and metal industries: the Borsig factory (see CHARITÉ), established there in 1852, employed 1 100 workers.

Moabit is not included in the usual tourist itineraries, yet it is one of the most inter-esting districts to visit for its wealth of industrial architecture. It is also one of the most popular areas together with Wedding and Neukölln.

MAIN SIGHTS

U *9 Turmstraße. Take the Alt-Moabit-Straße exit. Immediately to the west, inside the park, stands the brick-built Heilandskirche. Walk eastwards.*

Alt-Moabit 90-103 – There is an amazing patchwork of architectural styles along this avenue but also along the banks of the Spree where a promenade has been laid out; the *Focus Teleport Berlin* houses several companies; inside the brick build-ings of the **former Bolle dairy** there is a very nice café-cum-restaurant *(on the ground floor, on the east side)*; next door stands the **Haus am Wasser**, an impressive U-shaped building of pink granite and glass (there is a good view of it from the S-Bahn going towards Friedrichstraße). The opposite bank is lined with willows and private houses dating from the 19C.

St-Johannis-Kirche – The plain nave designed by Schinkel, which is broadly similar to those in Wedding *(see under that name)*, is hardly recognisable with the addi-tions (the steeple) made by the architect's disciple Stüler and the extensions dating from the end of the 19C.
Follow Kirchstraße to Moabit Bridge (Moabiter Brücke or **"Bärenbrücke"**, "Bears' Bridge") from which there is an interesting view.

Neues Kriminalgericht (**J**) – *Turmstraße 91*
Turmstraße is dominated by the imposing façade of the **new court of justice**, best seen from the corner of Rathenower Straße. It seemed only right that the temple of justice should be a source of wonder to ordinary people. The **entrance hall** and the **stairway★**, reminiscent of the vast staircases in Baroque castles, are magnificent. At the back of the court of justice, on the south side, there is a 19C panoptic prison, surrounded by a barbed wire fence.

Ph. Gajic/MICHELIN

The main staircase of the law courts in Moabit is a good example of architecture during the Wilhelmian period.

As you retrace your steps and walk westwards along Turmstraße you will become conscious of a **village-like atmosphere**. Note at **No 21** the fine brick buildings of Moabit Hospital and, going north along Stromstraße, the former Schultheiss Breweries. The town hall overlooking Otto-Platz was built by the Nazis. Behind it lies Bremerstraße, which marks the beginning of the popular, almost village-like section of Moabit. The **covered market** is one of only three similar structures remaining in Berlin *(for the others, see KREUZBERG east and west parts)*; it is a fine brick building with terracotta decorations and rounded windows reminiscent of Roman baths. At No 31 Waldenserstraße, there is a pre-1914 bachelors' home and, at No 27, L. Hoffmann's non-denominational school.

The Reformation Church, one of the numerous neo-Gothic brick churches in Berlin, stands on the corner of Beusselstraße and Wiclefstraße. Beyond lies Rostocker Straße which leads visitors through **Beusselkiez**. The council flats at **Nos 7-8 Sickingenstraße**, built before 1900, look surprisingly modern, with their Belle Époque style, in particular the balconies.

The September 1910 strikes

At the time Moabit had a population of 160 000, which was 100 000 more than at present. Kohlen & Co. belonged to the magnate **Hugo Stinnes**. Workers were asking for a rise in salary for heavy work (what they called *Knochenarbeit*, or "bone work"). A strike was called. Strike breakers accompanied by vehicles loaded with coal tried to make their way along Beusselstraße. Trouble spread rapidly and there was street fighting throughout the whole district. The police acted with extreme brutality against the 20 000 to 30 000 strikers. Foreign reporters were attacked as well, which prompted the British and American embassies to issue a formal prostest. 104 policemen were wounded and many demonstrators were killed or wounded. Pay rises were finally granted on 1 April 1911.

★**The Industrial zone** – The neo-Gothic brick building of A.E.G.'s electric bulb factory stands on the corner of Sickingenstraße and **Berlichingenstraße**, the **series of** industrial buildings lining Berlichingenstraße is interesting. On the corner of Huttenstraße stands **A.E.G.'s turbine factory (A.E.G. Turbinenfabrik)**★★ designed by **Peter Behrens** *(see ABC of Architecture in the INTRODUCTION)*. It was extended by 100m in 1939. The buildings owned by the **Löwe company**, including the milling-machine factory, occupy Nos 42-45 Wiebestraße. Reuchlinstraße is another industrial street, note in particular the fine brick building on the corner of Kaiserin-Augusta-Allee. A completely new townscape is developing along Kaiserin-Augusta-Allee and on the banks of the Spree. Across the river, can be seen the glass rotunda of the Doppe Institute (Doppelinstitut), which belongs to the Technical University.

The vast red brick edifice standing on the corner of Levetzowstraße (No 1-2) and Vikingerufer (No 7) includes a church and houses the Berlin Film Library (Landesbildstelle Berlin).

OTHER SIGHTS

★**Westhafen** – **U** *9 Westhafen, then walk down Westhafenstraße.*
There is a better overall view of Berlin's west harbour, built between 1914 and 1927, from Seestraße Bridge (by car, *see WEDDING*). Situated at the intersection of three canals, it is the most important commercial and industrial harbour in Berlin. It had its counterpart in East Berlin. The **harbour-master**'s tower dominates Dock II but the most interesting building is the large **warehouse** on the south pier.

★★**Hamburger Bahnof Museum für Gegenwart Berlin** ⊙ – **S** *3, 5, 7, 9, 75 Lehrter Stadtbahnhof.*
Hamburg Station is the only one of Berlin's first generation of railway stations (1845-47) to have survived (the other two, Potsdam and Frankfurt stations, have disappeared). The two arched entrances were designed to let the engines inside the courtyard where special rotating rails enabled them to turn around and face the way out. Hamburg station was replaced by Lehrte station and closed to passenger traffic as early as *1884*. The Transport and Railway Museum was housed there until World War II and the great metal hall was built purposely.

After the lavish refurbishment by Josef P Kleihues, it became possible in 1996 to house Dr Erich Marx's collection in an extremely attractive museum.

The huge hall with its three naves and metal pillars, which provides a beautiful and generously proportioned setting, is truly impressive. Admire the glass igloo by Mario Merz (*La goccia d'acqua*, 1987), a work by Richard Long (*Berlin Circle*

1996) consisting of a circle made from pieces of slate, a nail picture by Günther Uecker (*Westtor - vernagelt*, 1996), some profound works by Anselm Kiefer, for example the *Volkszählung*, 1991, made of steel, lead, peas and photographs, *Mohn und Gedächtnis*, 1989, *Lilith am roten Meer*, 1990.

The **West Wing** is reserved almost exclusively for works by **Joseph Beuys**, who has been such an important figure within German 20C art. The ground floor houses environments such as *Straßenbahnhaltestelle*, 1976, *Hirschdenkmal*, 1958-1982, *Unschlitt/Tallow*, a monumental sculpture made of tallow, which was created for an exhibition in Munster, *Richtkräfte*, 1975 and the *Ende des 20. Jh.s*, 1982/83, made of 21 basalt stones. On the upper floor the visitor will find a group of 456 drawings, *The secret block for a secret person in Ireland*, produced between 1945 and 1976, and *Scala Napoletana*, 1985, a ladder balanced between two iron balls.

The **East Gallery** houses works by Robert Rauschenberg (*Pink Door*, 1954, *First Time Painting*, 1961), Roy Lichtenstein (*Imperfect Painting*, 1986) and Cy Twombly (*Empire of Flora*, 1961, *School of Fontainebleau*, 1960) in a generously proportioned environment flooded with natural light. The collection of pictures by **Andy Warhol** is extremely extensive. *Do it yourself (Seascape)* 1962, ironically shows the mechanical copying of a motif. Repetition is also the subject of *Twenty Jackies*, 1986, *Double Elvis*, 1963 and *Mona Lisa Four Times*, 1978. *Ambulance Disaster*, 1963, deals with death, a motif frequently addressed by Andy Warhol.

IN THE VICINITY

See **CHARITÉ★, ERNST-REUTER-PLATZ, TIERGARTEN★★, WEDDING★**.

Situated in Berlin's city centre, **Museums Island** was one of the richest museum complexes in the world before World War II. At the beginning of the 19C, the northern part of Spree Island reclaimed marshland through which a canal once flowed linking the Spree and the Kupfergraben; this was used as storage space by the Customs Authorities (*Packhof*, built by Schinkel). The Altes Museum was erected by Karl Friedrich Schinkel at the beginning of the 19C on top of the filled-in trench, along the central axis of the castle portal. While he was still only the Crown Prince, **Frederick-William IV** thought of turning it into "a sanctuary of Art and Science" and he set about realising his plan at the beginning of his reign in March 1841. Prestigious edifices reflecting Germany's new greatness were erected throughout the 19C. After 1871, political and economic expansion were matched by massive buying of works of art, spurred on by two exceptional general administrators, **Richard Schöne** (1879-1905) and **Wilhelm von Bode** (1905-1920). Hitler's coming to power threatened the future of the collections, in particular the collection of contemporary German painters whose works were mostly destroyed or sold under the pretext of fighting against "degenerate art".

Access via the S-Bahn

The S-Bahn passes right across the Museums Island (unfortunately it does not stop on the island itself). Consequently it is necessary to walk a short distance from the following stops Ⓢ + Ⓤ *Friedrichstraße and* Ⓢ *3, 5, 7, 9, 75 Hackescher Markt.*

The war was responsible for serious damage to the museums and quite a few of the treasures; the rest were taken away then shared out between the two Berlins. After four decades of slow restoration work intended to carry out the most urgent repairs and to make the museums accessible once again, Museums Island has become one of the largest projects in the new capital. The antiquities collection is to be brought here.

THE MUSEUMS

Lustgarten and Berliner Dom★ – *See SCHLOSSPLATZ.*

★★**Altes Museum** (**M**¹⁸) ⊘ – *No 100* 🚌.
The idea of a public museum was conceived around the end of the 18C and the beginning of the 19C, in an attempt to improve the general education system. **Wilhelm von Humboldt** founded the first Prussian museum. Frederick-William III's decree of 1810 specified the complementary aspect of the collection which "should thus be in close contact with already existing artistic and scientific institutions..." Standing opposite the castle, near the Arsenal and the cathedral, the **Old Museum** was yet another symbol of royal power; it originally housed 1 200 paintings and the main part of the collection of antiquities. Its design in the style of a Greek temple unquestionably makes it one of the finest museums in Europe and the most magnificent edifice built by **Schinkel** in Berlin, crowning of the architect's career. It was completed in 1830. The portico with its 18 Ionic columns and a façade length of 87m is a picture of majestic harmony and perfect proportions. The architectural peak is the **rotunda**, for which Schinkel was inspired by the Pantheon in Rome. It is decorated with statues of gods and goddesses and enhanced by subtle polychromy. The ascent of the double staircase, from the first relatively dark flight to the brightly lit top where the **Warwick Vase** is displayed and which offers a fine vista through the portico towards *Lustgarten* (and in the past towards the castle), is particularly imposing. The visitor is lifted from

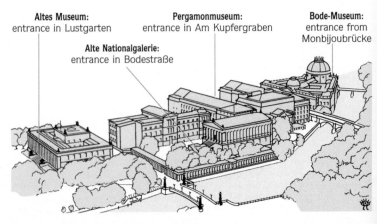

Altes Museum: entrance in Lustgarten

Pergamonmuseum: entrance in Am Kupfergraben

Bode-Museum: entrance from Monbijoubrücke

Alte Nationalgalerie: entrance in Bodestraße

the earthly world to the ideal world of beauty and art. The walls used to be completely covered with murals on mythological themes, which played an important role in the initial programme of educating people through beauty. The plan of the museum is logical and harmonious and the rooms housing the painting collection are arranged round the central rotunda where sculptures are displayed. Part of the **collection of antiquities**, specifically the smaller items, is housed on the ground floor (the monumental architecture is exhibited in the Pergamonmuseum). The tour through Greek art and cultural history begins with the marble idols of the Cyclades (Millennium BC), and passes through the Archaean period (7C to 5C BC) and the Hellenist period right up to the Etruscan and Roman civilisations. A few different topics are dealt with in different sections, for example *The Heroes, The Greek City, Sport amongst the Greeks, Temples and Shrines.*

The **antique jewellery** in two treasure vaults is absolutely fascinating, and includes the **gold treasures** of Vettersfelde (500 BC) and Tarent (3C BC) and the **Hildesheimer silver treasure**★★★ which dates from Roman times. The so-called **Praying Boy**★★, which was created on Rhodes around 300 BC, is an outstanding and famous bronze statue. It is still not known whether the figure depicted is Apollo, Ganymede or simply a praying boy.

Numerous vases, amphoras and raters bear witness to the important ceramic art of the Greeks. Examples include the **amphora of the so-called Berlin painter**, produced in around 490 BC. works are ascribed to this artist, one of the most important vase painters during the transition from Archaic to Classical art, although he never signed them.

Visitors will find it hard to tear themselves away from the other fascinating works of art, which include a marble bust of the Gaul **Julius Caesar**★★ (1C BC), the **Centaur's family fighting beasts of prey**★, a mosaic based on a Greek original and dating from the first half of the 2C, which was found in Hadrians Villa in Tivoli, and **Nile mosaic**★, a Late Hellenic work from Palestrina.

A number of major works from the Alte Nationalgalerie are on temporary display on the 1ˢᵗ floor.

Neues Museum (M¹⁹) – *No 1 and 13* Tram *Am Kupfergraben.*
Built between 1843 and 1855 in an elegant Classical style by Schinkel disciple, **Friedrich August Stüler**, the building was almost entirely destroyed during the Second World war. Before the war, it used to house the Egyptian collections; *Nefertiti* was exhibited there in 1926 and it contained a courtyard imitating that of an Egyptian temple. A large proportion of the interior decoration has been preserved. However the way in which it should be rebuilt has become a subject of controversy. A competition was won by the plan submitted by the architect David Chipperfield, who envisages a link with the adjacent Pergamonmuseum. It remains to be seen whether and how this will be realised. The work is due to be completed in the year 2010.

★★ALTE NATIONALGALERIE

(M²⁰) ⏱ – Ⓢ *3, 5, 7, 9, 75 Hackescher Markt*

Encouraged by the support obtained from the 1848 Frankfurt Parliament, a group of "patriotic artists" demanded the creation of a national museum devoted to contemporary German art. The gallery was finally constructed between 1866 and 1876 based on plans by Stüler. This Corinthian temple, raised on a pompous pedestal, houses works from the 19C and the first half of the 20C, spread over three floors. Jewish traders and bankers helped the museum to acquire the collection of French Impressionists. The gallery's losses under the Nazi regime were enormous. *The Alte Nationalgalerie will probably remain closed until 2001. The statue of Princesses Louise and Fredericke of Prussia, sculpted by Johann Gottfried Schadow, and Adolph Menzel's famous Flute Concert, will then be back on display for visitors to admire. The renovated gallery will then provide a worthy*

Johann Gottfried Schadow: *Princess Louise and Princess Fredericke of Prussia* (1797)

The struggle of a modern art supporter

The director of the National Gallery was a civil servant of the Reich who was not under the control of the royal Prussian museums. **Hugo von Tschudi**'s (1851-1911) taste for French Impressionist paintings did not get the approval of the Emperor and his followers who did not appreciate them. However, the works were taken into the gallery and exhibited on the top floor. And what a collection it was! Hugo von Tschudi had excellent taste and he was advised by **Max Liebermann** (1847-1935), who had connections in Paris. Tschudi acquired Manet's *Winter Garden*, the first work of the artist sold to a European museum; he went on to buy works by Cézanne, Renoir, Van Gogh and Sisley. Members of the Jewish upper middle class enabled him to buy paintings without having to be subjected to the control of official commissions. The director offered to resign in 1909, following a violent scene. Transferred to Munich (where he bought another important Manet: *Lunch in the Studio*, held by the new paintings gallery of that town), he gave his support in 1911 to the small group of the *Blue Cavalier*, which had just been founded by Marc and Kandinsky, and died the same year.

---

setting for the major works of the classicists, the German Romantics (Anselm von Feuerbach), the French Impressionists (Edouard Manet's "Le Jardin d'hiver") and German artists they inspired. During this period the major works from the collection are being exhibited on the upper floor of the Altes Museum.

★★★PERGAMONMUSEUM ⊘

Time: allow 3 hours. No 1 and 13 🚋 *Am Kupfergraben.*

The museum's edifice was constructed between 1909 and 1930 based on plans by Ludwig Hoffman and Alfred Messel. Originally the project included an avenue linking it to Humboldt University, thus underlining the didactic purpose of the museum. The visit is extremely interesting and a free audio-guided tour in several languages (*including English*) with comments about the main exhibits is available at the entrance. The collections were assembled rather late and rapidly, soon after the birth of the German Empire, at the time of the important archaeological excavations interrupted in 1914: the aim was to build collections which would rival those of the British Museum and the Louvre. They are famous all over the world because they give a lifesize picture of Antiquity. The beauty of the highly elaborate reliefs of Pergamum was in harmony with the neo-Baroque trend of the period.

TOUR *Allow 3 hours.*

★★★**Pergamonaltar** – "From the death of Attalus III, the Romans not only admired but loved foreign splendours" (Plinus the Elder). **Pergamum**, (whose name means "the citadel"), was a royal capital at the centre of a rich region and a well-governed state as well as one of the most extraordinary successes of Hellenistic town

Detail from the Pergamum altar: *Athena, crowned by a victory, separates the giant Alkuone from his mother Gaia.*

Ischtar gate

Pergamum altar, general view

Gateway to Milet market

A brilliant dynasty

The history of the Attalid kings starts with a betrayal. The successors of Alexander the Great (the **Diadochi**) fought for his empire. One of them was the king of Thrace, Lysimachus; he entrusted the treasury to Philetaerus (282-263 BC) in Pergamum, who used the money to impose his own authority. In 263 BC, he adopted one of his nephews, Eumenus I and founded the **Attalid** dynasty. Eumenus I and Attalus I *(whose portrait can be seen in another room)* were victorious over the Seleucids (a Greek dynasty, founded by one of Alexander's generals and established in Syria and Asia Minor) and the Gauls (Galatians). Having extended his territories, Attalus I took the title of "king". A powerful state was thus established in Anatolia: an ally of Rome, it became a buffer zone between the Macedonian kingdom and the Seleucid empire. **Eumenus II** (197-159 BC) had to rely on his own strength and sometimes go against Rome's wishes in order to fight his Bithynian and Galatian neighbours whom he defeated in 168 and 165 BC. The altar is a memorial to these victories. The son of Eumenus II, **Attalus III**, bequeathed the kingdom of Pergamum to Rome, who turned it into the Roman province of Asia.

planning. The Attalid kings, who were greedy for glory, built an acropolis with the intention of creating a new Athens, a centre of Greek civilisation in Asia Minor. Constructed on a 300m-high hill, at the foot of which lies the modern town of Bergama, the ancient city displayed its porticoes on different levels laid out as terraces following the contours of the terrain. The altar dedicated to Zeus and Athena was situated near the library containing 200 000 scrolls, which rivalled Alexandria's famous library (the word parchment, *Pergament* in German, is derived from Pergamum). It ranks among the most significant works of Hellenistic art.

The frieze decorating the base is *120m long and 2.30m high; it depicts a recurrent theme in Greek art: the* **battle** of the Olympian gods against the previous generation of Giants, sons of Gaia (Earth), which represents the fight of order against chaos but also that of the Pergamenes against the enemies of the kingdom; it is therefore a work intended to promote the glory of the king. The style is dramatic: there is spirit and romantic beauty in the suffering expressed by the tormented faces and bodies of the Giants, mercilessly destroyed. The group in which Athena, armed with a shield, clutches Alcyoneus' hair to tear him away from his mother Gaia, whose contact ensures his immortality, can be compared to the *Laocoon*, now in the Vatican Museum.

The sacrificial area was situated at the top of the stairs, behind the portico surmounted by tritons, griffins, teams of horses and statues of divinities. The walls were decorated with a smaller frieze depicting the story of **Telephus**, the son of Heracles (Hercules) and mythical founder of Pergamum. The kings claimed to be his descendants.

The altar was destroyed during the Byzantine period and pieces from it were used to reinforce the town's fortifications against Arab assaults. The marble reliefs were found there at the time when **Carl Humann** led the German excavations (1878-1886). It took years to put them together again *(the history of the excavations and the reconstruction of the altar is recounted in a corridor situated under the altar, at the end of the room).*

★★**Gateway to Milet market** – Built in AD 120, it formed the centre of the Roman city together with the town hall and a nymphs' sanctuary *(the model of Milet city centre, which can be found on the terrace, helps to locate these various monuments).* It was included in the Byzantine fortifications and destroyed by an earthquake in 1100.

The acroteria surmounting the pediments of temples such as the Trajaneum and the temple of Dionysus in Pergamum clearly show the refinement of the architectural style.

★★★ **Hellenistic architecture** – *Entrance through the glass entrance foyer. Turn left into room 8 from the room housing the Pergamon altar.*
– **Façade of the santuary of Athene Nikephoros**★ in Pergamon (1st half of 2C). The inscription on the gable reads: "King Eumenus, to Athena who alone brings victory".
– **Huge column from the temple of Artemis** from Magnesia-on-Malandros/Menderes; **Temple of Zeus Sosipolis** on the market square; columns from the temple of Athene Polias in Priene.

★★★**Greco-Roman Antiquities** *(rooms 9-18):*
– **Lion resting**, from Milet. 1st half of the 6C BC *(room 9)*
– **Goddess on her Throne**★★, from Tarentum, 480-460 BC *(room 11)*
– **Funeral relief in honour of Thraseas and Evandria**★, from Athens, 350-340 BC *(room 11,*

– **Bust of Doryphoros**★ (the spear-bearer). Roman copy of a Greek original by Polyc-itus, c 440 BC *(room 14)*

– Statue of **Athene**, from Pergamon, c 150 BC *(room 14)*

– **Wounded Amazon**, from an original by Polycitus in the sanctuary of Artemis, 400-430 BC *(room 14)*

– Relief of **Medea and Pelias's Daughters preparing a fatal bath for their father**★. Roman copy after the altar of the 12 gods in Athens, end of the 5C BC *(room 14)*

– **Portrait of a king of Pergamum**★, probably Attalus I, Pergamon, c 200 BC *(room 16)*

– **Young Girl playing with Knuckle-bones**, Roman copy of a Hellenistic original from the 2C BC *(room 16)*

– **Triglyph and Metop** from the north west corner of the Temple of Athene in Troy, depicting 1st third of the 3C BC *(room16)*

– **Antique coins** and **collection of Greek, Hellenistic, Celt and Roman medals**★ *(room 17)*

– **Bacchus wearing a crown**, Roman bronze statue, 2C *(room 18)*

– **Sarcophagus depicting Medea's legend**★★. Roman work from the middle of the 2C *(room 18)*

★★**Gate of Ishtar and reconstruction of the Processional Way in ancient Babylon**
– The wall surrounding Babylon included five gates, each named after a divinity. The reconstructed doorway displayed in the museum is lower than the original which preceded a loftier one. A **sacred way** passed through the town. The New Year procession went through the north gate or Gate of Ishtar, mistress of the sky, goddess of love and patron of the army. The works undertaken by **Nebuchadnezzar II** (605-562 BC) entailed the reconstruction of this part at the beginning of the 6C BC, using sumptuous materials. The brickwork was glazed over and decorated with low reliefs. Rows of dragons, the emblem of the god Marduk, patron of the city, alternate on the doorway with rows of bulls, the animal of the god of storms, Adad. The lions on the processional way were Ishtar's sacred animals. This recon-struction leads to the Near Eastern Antiquities.

★**Vorderasiatisches Museum** – *From the Gate of Ishtar, on the ground floor. This section contains many reproductions.*

– **Stela**★ depicting King Assarhaddon of Assyria with his two sons.

– **Base of a column supported by two sphinx**★; remains of a palace in the citadel of Samal/Zincirli (Northern Syria); reconstruction of the monumental entrance and surrounding wall (10C-8C BC). The lions bring some kind of magical protection as do all the representations of mythological characters, humans or animals. The city and state of Samal was conquered by the Assyrians in the 7C BC.

– **Monumental statue of Hadad, the god of time**, with traces of alphabetic writing; relief depicting lion hunting *(Reliefplatten mit Darstellung einer Löwenjagd, 750 BC)*; monumental statue of a bird, part of the entrance to a palace-temple in Tell Halaf, 9C BC.

– **Brick façade of the Temple of the Goddess Innin in Uruk**★: cone-shaped mosaics.

– **Assyrian crypt** *(reproduction)*.

– **Model of Marduk Temple** in Babylon; **cylinder seals**; glass cabinet containing **tablets**: diplomatic letters, contracts in cuneiform writing, Babylonian writing; terracotta and glass receptacles.

– **"Immortal"** of Darius I in Susa.

– **Assyrian reliefs from the palace of Ashurnasirpal II**★★ (883-859 BC) in Kalhu/Nimrud: winged genii, lion hunting scene, noblemen. Reproductions of winged bulls with human heads, the originals being kept in the British Museum.

– **Reliefs from the palace of Sennacherib**★ (704-681 BC) in Nineveh: soldiers of the royal guard, officers, musicians.

– **Ritual basin**★ (period of King Sennacherib of Assyria), from Ashur; each side is decorated with a water divinity and priests wearing fish-shaped costumes.

★★**Museum für islamische Kunst** – *1st floor; (Access via the Vorderasiatisches Museum)*.

– **Reliefs from Ctesiphon**★, capital of the Sassanian Empire of Persia until 637, and from Samarra, seat of the Abbasid caliphs.

– **Collection of carpets**★ (Asia Minor, Egypt, Iran and the Caucasus); also the oldest Spanish carpet (14C), made by the interlocking stitch method.

– **Façade of Mschatta**★★, the caliphs' castle.

– **Illuminations, carved wood panels**★ (Seljukian lectern – or "rabla" - from the 13C; sar-cophagus from Iran, dating from 1423.

– **Mihrab**★ (niche used to show the direction of Mecca for the prayer) **from the Maidan Mosque** in Kasan, Iran, dating from 1226. Damascene **basin** from Syria dating from the end of the 13C.

Bode-Museum

– **Pottery from Iznik** and **panels from Ispahan** depicting two young servants.
– **Room from a house in Aleppo★★** ("Aleppo-Zimmer", Syria, 1603), reception room of a
Christian merchant's house.

★★BODE-MUSEUM ⏱ *Time: 2 hours*

The royal architect **Fritz von Ihne** (1848-1917) made the best of a poor site at the
tip end of Museum Island (an important amount of preparatory digging was necessary) and managed to fit an impressive number of exhibition rooms of varying
sizes, in a relatively small area. The interesting interior design of this museum,
which used to be called the *Kaiser-Friedrich-Museum* (1897-1904), is what makes
it particularly attractive. The large stuccoed cupola and the double flight of stairs
with its wrought-iron banisters form an imposing setting for the replica of
Frederick-William III's equestrian statue by Andreas Schlüter (the original stands in the
main courtyard of Charlottenburg Castle, *see under that name*), and other statues
by the same artist, which used to be in Berlin Castle. Before World War II, the
museum housed the finest treasures of the Renaissance, including paintings, sculptures and furniture. The Bode-Museum will be closed for five years from the middle
of 1999 to allow for its complete renovation and refurbishment and to utilise the
outstanding potential of the building with its three exhibition levels and four inner
courtyards. When it reopens in 2004, the Bode-Museum will house the entire reunified **sculpture collection** in the **Museum für spätantike und byzantinische Kunst** and the
Münzkabinett, which will depict the history of coins and money.

It is planned to present the history of European sculpture from Greco-Roman times
to the birth of Early Classicism, via careful selection from the extremely broad collection which is available. The result should be extremely exciting!

Frühchristlich-byzantinische Sammlung – *Closed. Due to reopen in 2004.*

Skulpturen-Sammlung – *Closed. Due to reopen in 2004.*

The "pope" of the Berlin museums

Wilhelm Bode (1845-1929), "von" since 1914, was an art historian and a
lawyer. He began his work for the museums in 1872; he was appointed
director of the sculpture collection in 1883 and director of the painting
gallery in 1890. He was the *condottiere* of international museology, a scientist, an expert, a man of diplomacy, "the pope of museums"; he felt as
much at ease when he was at court as in the company of bankers or
members of the aristocracy. Being himself a patron of the arts, he managed
to encourage donations and obtain subsidies. He was the general manager
of the Berlin museums from 1904 to 1920. From the beginning of the 20C,
he found his match among wealthy American art collectors.

★★**Ägyptisches Museum und Papyrussammlung** – *Closed. It will be possible to view part of the collection in the Pergamonmuseum. At the time of publication, it was not known which of the following works will be exhibited there.*

Old Kingdom:

– **Collection of reliefs★**, including one from the Meten offering chamber *(Opferkammer des Meten)*, Saqqara, 2 600 BC: a senior civil servant can be seen bare-chested and wearing a wig. Note, on one of the reliefs *(symbolische Darstellung der ägyptischen Überlegenheit über das Ausland)*, the god Seth with his strange greyhound head, beneath a row of chained strangers. See also the *Representations of Various Gods* (with traces of polychromy); the *Return from Syria of the Egyptian Merchant Fleet; Hunting Scenes with Royal Figures* and *Scenes of Country Life during the Four Seasons.*

– **The Manofer simulated door** *(Scheintür)*, through which the soul of the deceased was said to pass from the tomb to the place where the offerings were deposited.

– **The Merib offering chamber,** Giza, 2 450 BC (renewed paintings, reproduction).

Middle Kingdom:

– **Statue of King Amenemhet III standing up** in an attitude of prayer (1 800 BC).

– **The collection of papyrus** in Latin, Aramaic, demotic, hieroglyphs, hieratic characters, Arabic, Coptic and Greek shows the evolution of the different languages in Egypt *(explanatory panels in German).*

– *Ram,* Amun's sacred animal, 1380 BC; many statues of the goddess Sekhmet in a standing or sitting position; **cubic statue of Senenmut** (governor of Hatshepsut's palace and tutor of the princess whose head can be seen) and Queen Hatshepsut's *sphinx* (1 480 BC).

– **Wooden models:** small figurines of animals, illustrating life on the Nile and the peasants' daily work.

New Kingdom:

– **Group representing Pathmai** (Ptah's officer then priest) **and his family★** (1250 BC).

– **Funeral mural★** representing Queen Ahmes-Nefertari and her son Amenophis I, revered by the craftsmen and artists of Thebes necropolis as having a protective influence (1 200 BC). The costumes are splendid; the black colour of the queen's skin suggests a ritual statuette.

Ptolemaic and Roman Egypt:

– **Portraits and masks of mummies★★**: remarkable facial expression of **Aline,** called Tenos, who died aged 35 in AD 25 in the Fayoum oasis colonised by the Greeks, and of a bearded man, who died aged 30 in 200 AD. Clothing and jewellery are in Alexandrian fashion. A shroud represents a deceased man accompanied by Anubis and Osiris (AD 180). The masks (their gold colour is a sign of the deceased's divine state) are in true Egyptian tradition.

J. Liepe/AGYPTISCHES MUSEUM - PREUSSISCHER KULTURBESITZ.

Portrait of *Aline*

Münzkabinett – *Closed for refurbishment.*

IN THE VICINITY

See **ORANIENBURGER STRASSE★, SCHLOSSPLATZ, UNTER DEN LINDEN★★**.

NEUKÖLLN

Neukölln

See map of Berlin Town Centre, **9**, **LMYZ**

The former municipality of **Rixdorf** merged with Britz, Rudow and Buckow villages and took the name of **Neukölln** in 1912. It soon became a dormitory town, with an exponential growth (90 000 inhabitants in 1900, 200 000 nine years later); the inhabitants who for the greatest part were blue-collar workers and office staff, were packed inside living quarters often consisting of no more than one room. In 1919, the Spartakist Group took over the town hall and proclaimed the "Neukölln Republic". The district remained outside the feverish activity which characterised Berlin between the wars. Owing to inadequate transport, it carried on living at a provincial pace, its nightlife only consisting of a municipal theatre, a few cinemas and cafés, popular dances and beer festivals. Today it is still one of Berlin's popular districts, with the highest population count. Like Kreuzberg, it has a large Turkish community, but it manages to keep out of the news. No striking examples of fringe behaviour, no Alternative groups either. Life in Neukölln is no different from the rest of Berlin. The district is polluted, traffic is dense between Karl-Marx-Straße and Sonnenallee. The area adjacent to the Wall which has retained its no-man's-land on the border with Treptow, is depressing. On the corner of Wildenbruchstraße and Heidelbergerstraße, can be seen imbricated buildings from the former Western and Eastern parts of Berlin (brown façades).

A WALK THROUGH THE DISTRICT

Hermannplatz – **U** 7, 8 Hermannplatz.
There are many shops near this busy intersection. It used to be dominated by the towers of the Karstadt department store, directly accessible from the underground station. Inaugurated in 1929, the building was thought to be the best illustration of modern day America.

Volkspark Hasenheide – It is in this park (the name literally means "warren") that **F.L. Jahn** trained his young disciples in the practice of gymnastics (monument in the northwest corner). In 1814, some patriots organised festivities at Hasenheide, a traditional public meeting ground. A gymnastics show took place in front of 10 000 people and Jahn's disciples decided to meet every year in the same place in order to celebrate those memorable days. The Socialists had the same idea, which prompted their mortal enemy, Bismarck, to say that "one did not engage in politics in Hasenheide". On Sundays, whole families would take a stroll in the park, which provided carousels and swings for the children; some people would drink large tankers of pale beer in the Biergarten. Today, the park is a vast expanse of lawn, slightly scorched in summer.

Friedrich Ludwig Jahn (1778-1852), the initiator of gymnastics

F.L. Jahn's initiative to combine physical exercise, moral instruction and patriotism met with immediate success among grammar school and university students. The sports ground, equipped with various apparatus, was very plain. The "gymnasts" were taught to develop a strong German identity, free of any foreign influence. The **German League**, founded by Jahn in 1810, included around 100 members recruited among the "gymnasts"; from 1812 onwards, it strived to put an end to the Franco-Prussian alliance. In 1813, Jahn was a member of the most famous of the special force regiments (that of General **Lützow** from Berlin, which was later decimated). But this kind of patriotism was looked upon with suspicion by the government; the Berlin section of the students' corporation was dissolved; the Hasenheide grounds were closed in 1819. Suspected of having carried out subversive actions, Jahn was imprisoned until 1824, in spite of the fact that his friend E.T.A. Hoffmann had proved his innocence. He remained under police surveillance until 1841.

Karl-Marx-Straße – **U** 7 Rathaus Neukölln.
This is Neukölln's main thoroughfare, a very polluted shopping street. Along Karl-Marx-Straße and nearby streets, stand the **town hall (Rathaus)** (**R**), the **Museum of Local History** (**Emil-Fischer-Heimatmuseum**, in the adjacent Ganghoferstraße 3-5, in the courtyard on the left), and the **opera house** (**T⁵**) (**Neuköllner Oper**, between Nos 129 and 135) housed in a beautiful building set back from the street, which provides access (Kino Passageway) to Richardstraße. The **Puppet Museum** (Puppentheatermuseum, at No 135) (**M¹¹**) ⊘ contains characters from German folklore and legends.

Böhmisches Rixdorf – Ⓤ *7 Karl-Marx-Straße.*
Serving as a kind of backstage to the noisy Karl-Marx-Straße, the old village of
Rixdorf is no more than a group of village houses and barns situated between
Richardstraße and Kirchgasse. A sizable community of Protestant weavers arrived
from Bohemia in 1737. A statue of Frederick I decorates the attractive Richardplatz; north of the square stands the old **Bethlehem Church (Bethlehemskirche)**. *Return
to Karl-Marx-Straße.*

Körnerpark – This lovely park was laid out (1912-16) over a gravel pit *(Kies-
grube).* The difference in level of 5 to 7m (16 to 22ft) with adjacent streets,
explains the presence of terraces and stairs which are reminiscent of Italian Baroque
gardens. There is an orangery alongside the park; unfortunately, the fountains do
not work.
For the following sights, see the map of the Berlin conurbation, **⑪, CDV.**

BLUB (Berliner Luft und Badeparadies) – Ⓤ *7 Grenzallee (then walk south and cross
Teltowkanal).* This is Berlin's "water world", with several huge slides and fitness
centres.

★**Britz** – Ⓤ *7 Blaschkoallee.*
This village, situated on the outskirts of Berlin, includes several groups of fine buildings dating from the twenties (1925-27). Along Fritz-Reuter-Allee and in the
famous **"Hufeisensiedlung"★★ (D¹ CV)** there is a complex of more than a thousand
council homes designed by Bruno Taut, which are almost luxurious: small gardens,
reasonably low high-rise buildings, a variety of colours and shapes, in accordance
with the criteria of "light, air and sun" advocated at the time. Further west, stands
the small **Britz Castle (Schloß Britz)** behind a rose garden. Further still, along Fulhamer
Allee, there is a charming little village **church (Dorfkirche)**, near a pond.

★**Britzer Garten** – Laid out for the 1985 Flower Show, this vast park *(which can
be visited aboard a small train)* offers pleasant walks; you can stroll along, put out
chairs on the lawns, or even sit down at the top of a hill and admire the view of
Berlin's southern districts. There is no risk of getting lost as there are signs showing
the way out and the way to attractions such as the butterfly house. The decoration of the follies, like that of the orangery, which is a kind of spike-covered shell,
is rather ugly. A lake with a sinuous shoreline lies at the centre of the park and,
to the east of the bridge *(Hauptbrücke)*, there is a kind of tiny harbour for the
use of model ship owners.

Buckow – Charming village church *(Dorfkirche)* dating from the 13C.

Gropiusstadt – Ⓤ *7 Lipschitzallee.* These grey towers of various shapes scattered
in the greenery, were originally designed by Walter Gropius. Built between 1962
and 1973, the estate is similar to *Märkisches Viertel (see REINICKENDORF)*; it is
inhabited by 50 000 people.

Rudow – At the end of the Ⓤ *7 line (Berlin's longest line: 31.8km covered in
56min),* there is a small village church.

IN THE VICINITY

See **KREUZBERG (East Part)★★, TEMPELHOF, TREPTOW.**

NIKOLAIVIERTEL★

Mitte
See map of Berlin Mitte p 248-249 **PQYZ**

Considered to be the cradle of the city of Berlin, **St Nicholas district** was reconstructed
round the church of the same name, with its characteristic twin spires, for the 750th
anniversary of the foundation of the town, which was celebrated in 1987. Berlin is
supposed to have been mentioned for the first time in an official document in **1237**,
but this date was arbitrarily chosen by Goebbels, who wished to celebrate the city's
anniversary in 1937. The restoration of St Nicholas district marked a change of attitude on the part of the GDR authorities in regard to their national heritage. Whereas
precious relics from the past had been razed to the ground up to then, this attempt
at restoring Old Berlin showed that their policies in future would tend to be more
respectful of the collective conscience. In spite of this, houses were built of concrete
slabs; however, near the vast open spaces of Alexanderplatz, there is an attractive
network of narrow streets with definite human qualities and the fact that there are
small but interesting museums nearby makes it all the more pleasant to stop for a
coffee in the small square surrounding the church.

A WALK THROUGH ST NICHOLAS DISTRICT

St Nicholas district is easily accessible from the Ⓢ + Ⓤ *Alexanderplatz Station.*

★**Nikolaikirche Museum Nikolaikirche(Q)** ⓥ – Ⓤ *2 Klosterstraße* – The oldest preserved edifice in Berlin was built around 1230. Of the three-naved late Romanesque basilica, only the stone base of the tower remains together with the west portal. The Gothic chancel dates from 1380, the naves of the "hall-church" *(see the INTRODUCTION, ABC of Architecture)* from the 15C. The church was restored between 1876 and 1878 (the twin towers were erected at that time) after its destruction during the war. A museum was opened here in 1987 (a branch of the Märkisches Museum, *see FISCHERINSEL*). Artistically outstanding Baroque creations include the entrance portal to the vault of the goldsmith Daniel Männlich, erected by Andreas Schlüter in 1701, and the **Chapel of the Chancellor of the Exchequer Krautsch★** designed by Schlüter's student Johann Georg Glume (for the Prussian Chancellor of the Exchequer Johann Andreas von Kraut). Also noteworthy are models of the first church and the twin cities of Berlin and Cölln in 1220-30 and in 1450, the funeral chapel of Carl Constantin von Schnitter and his wife *(Grabkapelle des Königlichen Obristen Carl Constantin von Schnitter)* as well as table linen from the Cistercian convent of Zehdenick *(Hungertuch, Leinen aus dem Zisterzienserinnenkloster Heiligkreuz in Zehdenick)* dating from the beginning of the 14C (*c*1300).

Nikolaiviertel – *Zum Nußbaum* was the oldest inn in Berlin until it was destroyed in 1943. Situated in Cölln, Fischerstraße 21, and dating from 1571, it was a favourite haunt of Heinrich Zille and Otto Nagel. It was restored in 1986-87. The **Knoblauchhaus museum building** ⓥ **Stiftung Stadtmuseum Berlin★** (Knoblauchhaus, *Poststraße 23*, **M²¹**) was built during the 18C and was redesigned in the Classical style in the early 19C. Exhibits depict the history of the Knoblauch family from the 18C to the early 20C. Eduard Knoblauch, the architect of the New Synagogue *(see*

Balconies on the façade of the Ephraim Palace

ORANIENBURGER STRASSE) is also honoured. On the first floor there are six rooms decorated in the Biedermeier style. A historic public house (Historische Wein-stuben) occupies the ground floor. Zur Gerichtslaube House, with its light green Renaissance gable, stands on the site of Berlin's old town hall in Poststraße, near Marx-Engels Forum. **Ephraim Palace★** Stiftung Stadtmuseum Berlin (**S**) *(on the corner of Poststraße and Mühlendamm)*, adorned with elegant gilt rococo balconies, was built for the court jeweller and royal mint-master **Nathan Veitel Ephraim**, one of the rare Jews to have held an important office during the reign of Frederick the Great. It is in fact a reconstruction since the original building was demolished in 1936 for the widening of Mühlendamm. Berlin works of art ranging from the time of Frederick the Great to 1945 are on display, together with city views depicted on Berlin porcelain by KPM dating from 1800 to 1900.

The Schwerin'sche Palais stands opposite Ephraim palace, next to the new Mint built by the Nazis.

Mühlendamm – In the 13C, a toll-dyke formed by four watermills stood on this site which marked the entrance to the town. It is the oldest crossing point between Berlin and Cölln. Outside traders were compelled to sell their goods in both towns or pay a heavy toll. Mühlendamm owes its name to the **Mühlenhof (Amt Mühlenhof)**, an office responsible for the running of the watermills and the prince's possessions in the vicinity of Berlin, as well as for providing the court with adequate food sup-plies and wood. It was therefore necessary to maintain large stocks (400 people and 200 horses had to be fed), slaughter cattle, brew, weave, and have large quan-tities of leather brought in. The Mühlendamm Manager was the representative of the official authority and it was in his house that justice was administered to the peasants.

Molkenmarkt – The "Whey Market" is the oldest square in Berlin; it was formed by the intersection of two roads near a crossing point on the Spree. The view extends over a heterogeneous group of buildings of different styles: St Nicholas' Church, the lantern of the cathedral *(see SCHLOSSPLATZ)*, the "Red Town Hall", the Television Tower *(see ALEXANDERPLATZ for the last two sights)* and the "**town house**" or "**Stadthaus**" with its 109m-high tower.

Parochialkirche ⊘ – Ⓤ *2 Klosterstraße*. This Baroque church, built with three apses according to a centred plan, is being restored. On the corner of Parochial-straße and Klosterstraße stands **Podewils Palace** (**V**) which houses a café. Note the *Jugendstil* façade of No 64 Klosterstraße.

Franziskaner Klosterkirche (**W**) – Ⓤ *2 Klosterstraße*. The 13C-14C three-naved basilica founded in 1249 was almost entirely destroyed during Allied bombing raids and only the walls are still standing. They form an original setting for open-air sculpture exhibitions. The ruins were reinforced in 1951. The church was adjacent to the "**grey cloisters**" *(see below)*. Two capitals from Berlin Castle have been placed in the park where the convent stood.

The "Grey Cloisters"

Grey was the colour of the robe of the Franciscan monks with whom the Ascanian Margraves had close contacts. When a piece of land situated near the Berlin walls was granted to them, they erected "grey" cloisters and a brick church. Members of the aristocracy and the upper middle-class were buried in the adjacent cemetery. In spite of the Reformation and the secularization of the Catholic clergy's possessions, the Franciscans remained until the last member of their community had died (1571); the humanist **Thurneisser** then occupied the monastic buildings, which have now disappeared, and set up the first printing press in Berlin. In 1574, the "Grey Cloisters" grammar-school was founded in the former monastery. It was highly appreciated by the Berlin middle-class and counted many future celebrities among its students. In the 18C, it became the focal point of Russo-German relations and, during the Wars of Liberation (1813-1815), Professor **Friedrich Ludwig Jahn**, who was the ini-tiator of gymastics *(see NEUKÖLLN)*, taught there. The establishment had in its ranks the young Schinkel, Schadow, Schleiermacher and Bismarck.

Next to the ruins of the Franciscan church stands a pompous **municipal court of justice** (**J**) in Baroque and *Jugendstil* style which, like the courts in Moabit and Wedding *(see under these names)*, houses a magnificent **staircase★**. The **wall** which once sur-rounded Berlin and Cölln *(Littenstraße, southwards)* is surmounted by a small row of houses seen to greater advantage from Waisenstraße, in particular the tradi-tional public house *Zur Letzten Instanz*.

IN THE VICINITY

See **ALEXANDERPLATZ★, FISCHERINSEL★**.

OLYMPIASTADION★

It is on this site, which still has striking examples of Nazi architecture, that the 15-day mascarade of the **1936 Olympic Games** was staged. Goebbels had asked the Berliners to be "more charming than the Parisians, more jovial than the Viennese, more voluble than the Romans, more cosmopolitan than the Londoners, more practical than the New Yorkers". The town was cleaned up, restored and decorated. Antisemitic propaganda became very discreet. Berlin wished to be a city "like any other" under a "respectable" regime. In the end, it was a "clean" town under strict surveillance from the police, relieved of potential opponents and the dissident minority alike *(see MARZAHN)*. An impressive programme of propaganda ensured that the games were a success and allowed the producer **Leni Riefenstahl** to shoot *The Stadium Gods*, "a hymn to beauty and strength", which showed sport in a new light. The victory of the black runner **Jesse Owens** displeased Hitler; Germany gained the highest number of medals, which strengthened the superiority complex of the whole German youth kept under strict control. However this attempt at seducing the outside world was only partially successful. It is true that some French newspapers acclaimed Hitler's pacifist attitude, but a New York Times reporter wrote: "The greatest propaganda stunt ever". In spite of this, from the point of view of Hitler, who had just reoccupied Rhineland, the 1936 Games amounted to a skilful operation aimed at building up the Nazi "myth", demonstrating his popularity among the masses and securing a certain respectability on the international scene.

Olympiastadion

MAIN SIGHTS

Friedhof Heerstraße – The graves of this peaceful wooded cemetery are laid out on terraces around an expanse of water. The entrance is in Trakehner Allee, near the cemetery office building.

★**Olympiastadion** – **U** *2, 12 Olympia Stadion (Ost).*
The top of the bell tower affords the best view of the reinforced concrete stadium (Hitler would have preferred stone, a nobler material) which could accommodate 120 000 spectators. Although its proportions are harmonious, it was deemed "too small" by the Führer. Albert Speer later built a Stadium for 400 000 spectators in Nuremberg. Monumental statues by Arno Breker and Joseph Thorak illustrate Nazi visions in the shape of brutal naked giants.
The sports ground *(accessible by an extension road and S-Bahn line)* was built between 1934 and 1936 on an area of 130 hectares. The stadium is reached via a wide pathway which ends in front of two towers. The architect, **Werner March**, has skilfully made use of the contours of the terrain to bury the stadium which seems low from the outside (17m, 12 of which are below ground). Behind the stadium was the May field (Maifeld) on which 500 000 people could crowd to hear the Führer. The Olympic stadium will be closed until 2004 for renovation work.

Glockenturm (E¹) ⊘ – The May field is a huge expanse of lawn dominated by the **bell tower**, which has a 10-tonne bell bearing the inscription: "I appeal to the youth of the world". There is a vast **panorama★★** of the town *(ascend by lift)*: to the north, Spandau and the stacks of Ernst-Reuter power station, and *Waldbühne* below; to the east, the Olympic Stadium, the red brick Siemens factory complex *(see SIEMENSSTADT)* on the left along with the black tower of the Charlottenburg town hall; to the south, Teufelsberg overlooking Grunewald Forest and, in the distance, the dome of St Nicholas' Church in Potsdam.

Waldbühne (T²⁰) – This was part of the Olympic sports ground and was modelled on antique theatres. Since the war, it has become one of the most prestigious cultural venues in Berlin.

Sportmuseum Berlin ⊘ – Bus *218 Waldbühne*. In the "Deutsches Sportforum" on the Olympic site, the museum exhibits memorabilia concerned with the history of gymnastics, sport and games in Berlin-Brandenburg and their influence on national and international sport development.

★**Le-Corbusier Haus (F¹)** – *Reichssportfeldallee 16.*
It is necessary to go through the building into the garden in order to see the façade from the other side. The different arrangement of the balconies adds variety.

Georg-Kolbe Museum (M³¹) ⊘ – *Follow Heilsberger Allee then Sensburger Allee.* The museum houses a beautiful collection of works by **Georg Kolbe** and other sculptors from the first half of the 20C such as **Renée Sintenis** (1888-1965). Lifesize sculptures in the garden.

Westend – Ⓤ *2, 12 Neu-Westend*. Quiet residential district with small villas (much less attractive than Friedenau). The Akazienallee **water-tower**, consisting in fact of two water-towers joined together, one dating from 1878 and the other from the beginning of the 20C (1908-1909), is a fine brick building which looks like a castle keep. The top of the tower has been equipped for radio transmission.

IN THE VICINITY

See **FUNKTURM★, SPANDAU★**.

ORANIENBURGER STRASSE★★

Mitte

See map of Berlin, Mitte p. 248-249 **OPQXY**

Between Oranienburgerstraße and "Hackescher Markt" beats the heart of Old Berlin. Dilapidated façades, walls riddled with bullet holes, buildings covered with graffiti or taken over by squatters, old deserted streets, Jewish cultural institutions dominated by the gilt dome of the new synagogue, numerous cafés and restaurants, restored courtyards and backyards: evidence of the past is present everywhere, and visitors can expect to find the liveliest nightlife in the eastern part of town.

From the suburb of Spandau (Spandauer Vorstadt) to the "Barn District" – During the second half of the 17C, Berlin slowly recovered from having been ruined by the Thirty Years War. In 1679, street lighting by torches and then by lanterns was imposed by decree. In order to limit the risks of fire, the order banned thatched roofs and relegated barns outside the city walls. They gave their name to a shady suburb, **"Scheunenviertel"** or "Barn District" which, owing to urban development, became one of the most central districts in the capital, a stone's throw from the cathedral and Museums Island. During World War I, it was a place of refuge for many poverty-stricken Jews, who either arrived as immigrant workers or were trying to escape pogroms in eastern Europe. Unlike wealthier Jews, who often despised them, or White Russians who took up residence in the west after the Revolution, many "Jews from the east" *(Ostjuden)*, dressed in black, found in *Scheunenviertel* the end of the line which was to lead them to America. They represented a quarter of the 172 000 Jews living in Berlin. They evolved a particular lifestyle, hanging on to their customs and their languages. Small shops, gambling houses, shady deals, and prostitutes formed the usual street scenery at the back of Alexanderplatz.

A memorial district for the dead – When the Nazis came to power, they immediately clamped down. The Gestapo asked the Jewish community to organise itself and provide information. During the war, the Jews were assembled in an old people's home before being deported. The synagogue, which was profaned during the "Night of the Broken Glass" in November 1938 and then bombed in 1943, remained in ruins until 1990. The year 1943 witnessed a very strange event: 5 000 Jews were among the last about to be deported since they had been protected by their German wives. The latter raised protests and organised demonstrations. It would have been easy for the Gestapo to disperse them. Instead they were given their husbands back and these formed the majority of the survivors.

The Night of the Broken Glass

On 9 Nobember 1938, a huge pogrom was organised on a national scale following the assassination in Paris of a secretary of the German embassy by a desperate young Polish Jew. Shops were looted, synagogues burned down, 91 people murdered. Those who were arrested were interned in Sachsenhausen camp, opened two years earlier near Oranienburg. The Jews were made to sweep the pavements littered with broken glass.

ALONG THE OLD STREETS

Oranienburgerstraße – Ⓢ *1, 2, 25, 26 and No 1 and 13* 🚋 *Oranienburgerstraße.* The street is lined with café-cum-restaurants. It has even become a recognised tourist attraction. It is sometimes more interesting to walk along the narrow back streets.

"Tacheles" *Oranienburger Straße 54-56.*
A new building will no doubt replace this favourite haunt of members of the Alternative group, situated in the ruins of a former shopping arcade *(see ON THE TOWN, The Berlin Scene)*. From the end of the street, opposite Tacheles, there is a strange view, at night, at the gilt dome of the new synagogue and the Television Tower enhanced by green lighting. At **No 69,** you can see a beautiful hall and staircase dating from the "foundation years" *(Gründerzeit).*

Old post office in Oranienburger Straße

★**Ehemaliges Postfuhramt** – *Oranienburger Straße 35-36 (on the corner of Tucholskystraße).*
This splendid building (1875-81) is in glazed brick, with terracotta decorations. The stables lining the courtyard could accommodate 200 horses on two levels. There was already a "post" *(Postillonhaus)* on this site at the beginning of the 18C. The Royal Mail was founded in 1827; its 36 postmen wore the arms of the king as well as a horn, still used as the emblem of their profession.

Neue Synagogue ⊙ – *Oranienburger Straße 30:* Ⓢ *1, 2, 25 Oranienburger Straße.* The façade *(the light-coloured stones mark the refurbished parts)* and the cupola are the only restored parts of what was once the largest and the finest synagogue in Berlin, built by **Eduard Knoblauch** *(see NIKOLAIVIERTEL, Knoblauchhaus)* between 1859 an 1866. The sanctuary, which was one of the most beautiful edifices erected in Berlin during the 19C, was destroyed. In its place there is an open space; the plan is visible on the ground and the apse has been outlined. A glass lining protects the inner wall. The ground floor houses an exhibition on the history of the

New synagogue

synagogue, its architecture and restoration (pieces from the former building, religious objects); on the first floor there is a rich exhibition (unfortunately the numerous explanatory panels have not been translated) on Berlin's Jewish community through the centuries, the essential economic and cultural role it played and antisemitism.

Große Hamburger Straße – *Follow Oranienburger Straße towards Hackescher Markt, then turn left.* The **old Jewish cemetery (Alter jüdischer Friedhof) (X)** is the oldest Jewish cemetery in Berlin which is still recognisable as a burial place. It was used from 1672 to 1827 and destroyed in 1943 on the orders of the Gestapo. A tombstone made in 1990, to which there have been three predecessors, was erected as a memorial to the philosopher **Moses Mendelssohn** (1729-1786). Nearby, along Sophienstraße (**stela**), stood the Berlin's Jewish community's oldest almshouse *(Altenheim)*: in 1942, it was turned into a meeting place by the Gestapo. 55 000 Berlin Jews of all ages were exterminated in the Theresienstadt and Auschwitz concentration camps. The primary and secondary schools of the Jewish community have been restored. Mendelssohn founded the first Jewish school in Berlin. The tower of **Sophienkirche** ⊘ (1712-1734 (**Y**), set back from the street, has an elegant Baroque steeple. The interior, also in Baroque style (but renewed in 1892), is quite plain: lovely cartouche surrounded by a glory on the ceiling. The historian **Leopold von Ranke** is buried here.

Walk along Große Hamburger Straße until you reach St-Hedwigs-Hospital, then turn right into Sophienstraße.

The Jews, cultural life and discriminaton

By the 18C, the specific persecutions to which the Jews had been subjected during the Middle Ages and the Renaissance had stopped, but Frederick-William I and Frederick II's general regulations imposed tight restrictions. The Jewish community represented 2% of the population but its members were professionally confined to the fields of finance and manufacture. Heavy taxes were levied on their activities and they were under constant threat of expulsion. Frederick II forced them to buy often mediocre porcelain from his newly founded manufacture in order to get it going. For instance, **Moses Mendelssohn** was obliged to buy 20 lifesize porcelain monkeys before being allowed to get married. However, Jewish financiers and manufacturers found their rightful place in the changing economic context of Berlin during the Enlightenment period: **Ephraim** was responsible for the royal mint *(see NIKOLAIVIERTEL, Ephraim Palace)*; **Itzig** was the official supplier of the king's army and, if his naturalisation must be considered as exceptional, it nevertheless testifies to the struggle led by enlightened Christians and Mendelssohn. Impoverished aristocrats turned to wealthy Jewish women: Sara and Marianne Meyer respectively married a baron and a prince. The salons of these rich, beautiful and intelligent ladies were very fashionable. As a result, the first reactions were voiced against the "huge influence" of the Jews.

★**Sophienstraße** – *No 2, 3, 4, 5, 15, 53* [Tram] [U] *Weinmeisterstraße.*
This lovely restored street is lined with 18C and 19C houses with painted façades. There is an attractive view of the east end of Sophienkirche and its garden. Note, at Nos 18-18A, the double neo-Gothic or Renaissance gateway of the **Berlin Craftsmen Association (Berliner Handwerker-Verein)** and, in particular, the frieze.

★**Hackesche Höfe** – *Sophienstraße 6, corner of Rosenthalerstraße.*
This group of eight picturesque and splendidly restored courtyards clad with ceramic tiles houses cafés, shops, galleries, restaurants, a theatre, a cinema, a nightclub, antique shops, an art and architecture bookshop and even a Museum of Eroticism *(see ON THE TOWN, The Berlin Scene)*.

Monbijoupark – Ⓢ *3, 5, 7, 9, 75 Hackescher Markt; No 1, 13* [Tram] *Monbijouplatz.* Nothing remains of the castle built by Eosander von Göthe *(see Schloß CHARLOTTENBURG)* and lived in by Sophie-Dorothy, the wife of the King-Sergeant. Destroyed during the war, it was razed to the ground by the GDR. The park is just a plain green open space offering a view of the dome of the New Synagogue.

Hackescher Markt – Ⓢ *3, 5, 7, 9, 75 Hackescher Markt, No 1, 13* [Tram] *Monbijouplatz.* The heart of the "Barn District" is an ordinary square and a tramway junction. The whole area is the subject of a huge restoration campaign. There is an old chemist's shop on the corner of Rosenthalerstraße and Neue Schönhauserallee *(note the lovely staircase at No 8)*. The school standing on the corner of Rosenthalerstraße and Weinmeisterstraße is a Nazi building (note the frieze depicting young boys and girls with their "instructors"). **Mulackstraße** and **Linienstraße**, once notorious for their gambling houses and prostitutes, are both interesting. Black crosses shaded by trees mark the site of the **Garrison Church cemetery** (Friedhof der Garnisonskirche – **K⁴**), dating from 1722, where many military leaders are buried.

Volkspark am Weinberg – *See map of Berlin Town Centre,* 🔲, **KLT** – [U] *8 Rosenthaler Platz; No 6, 8 and 50* [Tram] *Brunnenstraße/Invalidenstraße.* This pleasant sloping park (in the past, there was a vineyard – *Weinberg* in German – on Barnim hillside) is situated at the heart of a busy shopping district. The suburb which developed in front of Rosenthal Gate was named *Neu-Voigtland* because the builders and carpenters who settled in it were natives of Saxony. The district had its own scaffold which was dismantled in 1842, after the last public execution. In 1843, Bettina von Arnim talked to the king about this poor community. **St Elizabeth's Church**, which is being restored, is one of those small suburban churches designed by Schinkel, who tried many various plans *(see the Church of Nazareth and St Paul's Church in WEDDING)*. St Elizabeth's is a perfectly harmonious building. **Sion Church** (Nos 13, 50 and 53 [Tram]) was the meeting-place for those for whom the Protestant church was the last bastion of free speech in the GDR; it stands at the centre of a peaceful attractive district with blocks of rented apartments similar to those in the nearby Prenzlauer Berg district *(see under that name)*.

Rosa-Luxemburg-Platz – Ⓤ *2 Rosa-Luxemburg-Platz.* It is in this crowded district that the Social-Democrats, who wanted to rouse the interest of the general public in popular theatre, decided to found the Popular Theatre Association (Volksbühne) which eventually had 70,000 members. Between the wars, the **Volksbühne★** attracted several famous directors. Its curved façade, designed by Oskar Kauffmann *(see POTSDAMER PLATZ, Hebbeltheater)* is plain and imposing. Nearby are the Karl-Liebknecht-Haus and the Babylon cinema which shows many classics from abroad.

The theater *Volksbühne*

IN THE VICINITY

See **ALEXANDERPLATZ★, CHARITÉ★, FRIEDRICHSTRASSE★, MUSEUMSINSEL★★★, PRENZLAUER BERG★★.**

PANKOW★

Pankow

See map of Berlin Conurbation, **⑪**, **CT**

German occupation of the district of Pankow goes back further than in many other parts of the Berlin area. The valley *(Panketal)* of the **Panke** River is a natural water way leading to the Oder and the Baltic, which the Margraves controlled from 1214 onwards; it has given its name to the village founded around 1220, at the same time as Buchholz, "Nedern Schonhuszen" (Niederschönhausen), Blankenburg, Buch and Karow. The village, which is mentioned for the first time in 1311, was bought by Berlin in 1370 together with Niederschönhausen; like all the Barnim villages, it was plundered by the **Quitzows** in 1410 *(see TEGEL).* In order to escape from the numerous conflicts which preoccupied his mind, the Elector Prince **Johann Cicero** (who ruled from 1486 to 1499) had a retreat (Vogelherd) built in Pankow, at the heart of a forest of oak trees where he could indulge his passion for hunting. Last century, the Berlin middleclass had summer residences built there. The district, which includes a great number of villas (No 16 Kreuzstraße is a fine example), badly needs restoring. Relatively spared by the war, Pankow became the first capital of the GDR; many writers and leaders of that country lived there.

MAIN SIGHTS

Gesundheitshaus – *Grunowstraße 8-11:* Ⓢ *8, 10 Pankow.*
The house, which is very close to the S-Bahn Station, was built (1926-28) in a late Expressionist style, at the centre of a working-class district developing on either side of Florastraße.

★**Heimatmuseum Pankow** ⊙ – *See map of Berlin Town Centre* **④***,* **(LR)** – *Heynstraße 8. Entrance in the hall on the right; 1st floor; ring the bell.*
The museum is housed in the former home (1890) of a rattan manufacturer, Fritz Heyn. This substantial Baroque and rococo residence was damaged in 1943. The

façade has been stripped of its decorations and coated with ordinary roughcast, but the **interior**, occupied by Heyn's two daughters until 1972, is still intact. It is a perfect example of *Gründerzeit* style, pompous and newly rich, favoured by middle-class people who wanted to live like lords and ladies of the manor. Ceilings richly decorated with mouldings, huge stoves, old clocks ticking, painted walls (medallions with the daughters' portraits are even painted below the cornice of the drawing-room) create an old-world atmosphere which is not without charm. There is a cigar-holder *(Zigarrenständer)*-cum-watch which plays a tune every hour. The corner room is a typical example of *Berliner Zimmer*, with the rest of the apartment overlooking the courtyard. It often served as a dining-room, since the kitchen *(go to the end of the corridor)* was next door. One room of a working-class home has also been reconstructed. The museum recalls the history of celebrities connected with the district and interesting buildings: the mathematician **Paul Nipkow** (1860-1940) who invented the basic principles of television (at the time, his invention unfortunately went unnoticed); Rheinhold Bunger, the inventor of the vacuum flask; the Garbaty cigarette factory. Small informative temporary exhibitions are regularly held in the museum.

Gymnasium Berlin-Pankow – *Görschstraße 43-44*. This building in German neo-Renaissance style (1909-10) with characteristic gables decorated with volutes is, together with the town hall, an imposing landmark in the centre of Pankow.

Rathaus Pankow (R) – *Nos 52, 53* [Tram] *Rathaus Pankow*. Its style denotes a mixture of influences. A little further south, at No 32 Neue Schönholzerstraße, there is an interesting neo-Romanesque house and an old brewery.

Alte Pfarrkirche – Founded 1230 by Cistercian monks. Stüler built a neo-Gothic church with two towers onto it. It was then completed with a narthex and a portal in around 1900.

Bürgerpark – *No 52, 53* [Tram] *Bürgerpark*.
Theodor Hermann Karl Julius, Baron Killisch von Horn, was one of the thirteen children of a counsellor of the Bromberg Chancellor's Office. He acquired his title from the Republic of San Marino. Having become a rich industrialist and founded the *Stock Exchange Publication (Börsenzeitung)*, he set out in 1868 to improve the layout of the park, decorating it with rare plants (which he subsequently removed to his own residence), pagodas, pavilions and a "mice castle" *(Mäuseburg)* for guinea pigs and white mice. He was buried in the family vault situated next to the lovely neo-Renaissance gate which marks the entrance to the park. Today, only the **music pavilion** remains; it is a meeting-place for strollers. The Panke River flows through the park which offers pleasant walks and includes *(on the west side)* an aviary with peacocks, pheasants and goats.

Wohnanlage Grabbeallee – *Northeast exit from the park*.
A private road, Paul-Francke-Straße, goes through this estate (1908-9) which is a kind of garden city with corbelled façades, gables and bay windows opening onto superimposed loggias.
Turn east into **Majakowskiring**, a pathway in the shape of a horseshoe which goes through another estate where several politicians (Wilhelm Pieck, the first president, and Otto Grotewohl, the first prime minister of the GDR), artists and writers lived.

An unfortunate wife

Frederick II was only attracted by the male sex. His wife, **Elisabeth-Christine of Brunswick-Bevern** (her portrait by Antoine Pesne hangs in Charlottenburg Castle, *see under that name)*, born in 1715, was chosen by the King-Sergeant, after other matrimonial plans with the British royal family had fallen through. The marriage was celebrated in June 1733 in Wolfenbüttel. At first, the couple lived apart; they only lived together after 1736, in Rheinsberg. Upon his accession to the throne (1740), Frederick II gave the Schönhausen estate to his wife and work began immediately. Thereafter, Elisabeth-Christine lived in **Schönhausen** (and in Berlin Castle in winter), while Frederick II lived in Potsdam. She was no longer invited to family gatherings, but foreign princes, diplomats and artists were expected to pay their respects (Aufwartung). Until her death in 1797, the queen devoted her time to her estate. She founded a colony (Kolonie Schönholz) whose members were natives of Bohemia; their duties consisted in looking after the royal gardens and, in exchange, they were granted a piece of land and a house: this scheme was called the "Queen's Plantation" (Königin-Plantage); she also founded a school for the children. Her castle was devastated during the Seven Years War. The garden was turned into an English-style park by Lenné in 1828-31.

Schloß Niederschönhausen (**G¹**) – *Access via Majakowskiring and Ossietzkystraße. Not open to the public.*
It was in this unassuming Dutch-style 18C residence, built of brick and white stone, that Frederick II's wife was confined. It was also the official residence of Wilhelm Pieck.

★**Maria-Magdalenen-Kirche** (**H¹**) – *Platanenstraße 20-21. No 53 tramcar Platanenstraße or via Waldstraße, then Treskowstraße.*
Some of the villas in this area have been restored. The catholic Church of Mary Magdalene (1929-30) is one of the most irresistible Expressionist sanctuaries in town *(see also WILMERSDORF, Kreuzkirche).* Note the terracotta reliefs above the doorway.

★**Höllanderhaus** (**P¹**) – *On the corner of Platanenstraße and Dietzgenstraße.* Charming house with carved wood gables.

Buch – Tower blocks, green shirts and shaved heads; Buch is not very inviting. It is on the edge of town and is due to become a technological centre specialising in biomedical science.

300m south of the S-Bahn Station; go through the park diagonally towards the southeast.

The small **castle church** *(Schloßkirche)* is charming, in spite ot having lost its bell tower.

IN THE VICINITY

See **PRENZLAUER BERG**★★, **REINICK-ENDORF.**

Ph. Gajic/MICHELIN

Höllanderhaus

POTSDAMER PLATZ-Wilhelmstraße

Kreuzberg, Mitte, Tiergarten
See map of Berlin Town Centre, **B**, **JKVX**

Between the two world wars, **Potsdam Square** became a myth, the symbol of the modern capital and Europe's busiest crossroads. The first traffic lights were installed here in 1926.

A crossroads at the entrance to the city – It was originally just a crossroads situated in front of the gate of the same name *(Platz vor dem Potsdamer Tore)*, with roads leading to Schöneberg, Potsdam or Charlottenburg. Unlike the adjacent "octagon", it was not included in the town planning projects of Baroque Berlin. Then, at the end of the 18C and the beginning of the 19C, a number of inn-keepers settled there. The urbanisation process was concentrated around **Potsdam Station** (1838), which was the terminus of the first Prussian railway line (the Berlin-Potsdam line), and the famous Anhalt Station *(see KREUZBERG, west part).* Wealthy members of the middle class erected country houses and people talked about the "millionaires' district", *Millionärsviertel.* Hotels, restaurants, cafés such as the Bellevue or the Josty flourished. Finally, in 1926, Erich Mendelsohn erected his **Columbushaus**, one of the most modern office buildings in Europe.

> **A treacherous escape route**
>
> In time, it became impossible to get over the Wall. There were innumerable obstacles: a white 3.5 to 4.2m-high wall topped by a concrete pipeline which prevented any sort of hold either by hand or grapnel, then a large strip of wasteland, a deep moat filled with water, guards (there were as many as 14 000 of them), dogs, an automatic firing system and... another wall.

Berlin, a metropolis of the fu

After World War II – The ruined square found itself at the junction of the Western sector and the Soviet zone. Its buildings were razed to the ground and, after the construction of the Wall, a vast no-man's-land separated the two Berlins.

The new look Potsdamer Platz – Now that the Wall has crumbled, Potsdamer Platz is once more gradually becoming a strategic intersection and large companies have bought plots of land on which to build their headquarters. Each firm in turn organised a competition. Acting on behalf of Daimler-Benz, **Renzo Piano** solved the problem caused by the necessity of joining the new district to the Kulturforum and its isolated monuments; **Helmut Jahn** designed the Sony European headquarters. **Giorgio Grassi** is responsible for the ABB buildings extending to the Landwehrkanal. The vast site, dominated by a forest of cranes, has become a tourist attraction.

MAIN SIGHTS

Potsdamer Platz – Ⓢ *1, 2, 25, 26,* Ⓤ *2 Potsdamer Platz.*
The buildings on the square, many with avant-garde inspiration, shot up in record time, including Sony's European headquarters, designed by the architect, Helmut Jahn. The complex is also home to the Berlin Filmmuseum, a media library and two cinemas. The DaimlerChrysler and debis buildings were designed by Renzo Piano and Hans Kolhoff. A theatre designed for musicals and an Imax cinema, with a powerful dome, are also Renzo Piano works. The Cinemaxx cinema palace boasts no less than 19 cinemas. The Potsdamer Platz Arkaden shopping centre takes in some 50,000 visitors each deay. In the midst of these futuristic surroundings, the Weinhaus Huth, the only historical edifice (1911) left standing after the war, provides a touch of nostalgia. Giorgio Grassi's ABB buildings stretch all the way down to the Landwehrkanal. The Potsdamer Platz is als home to two luxury hotels and Germany's biggest casino.

Leipziger Platz – In 1814, the **"Oktogon"** of the Friedrichstadt new town was renamed after the town in which Napoleon suffered defeat, which prompted him to withdraw from Germany. Once a well-known shopping area, it needs to be entirely rebuilt. It used to be lined on the east side by the Wertheim department store.
The Upper House (Herrenhaus) of the Prussian Diet moved into No 3 Leipziger Straße in 1850. Bismarck fought hard to obtain the subsidies he needed to carry out his military plans and this largely governed his foreign policy. No 4 was occupied from 1761 to 1871 by the royal porcelain factory *(KPM, see ERNST-REUTER-PLATZ)*, where the Reichstag provisionally met until it moved in 1894.
Opposite the Martin-Gropius-Bau, there are 1987 IBA building blocks along Stresemannstraße, Bernburger Straße (Nos 22-23/26) and Dessauer Straße (No 9-10). The Bundesrat was transferred to 3-4, Leipziger Platz in August 2000.

★★ Martin-Gropius-Bau ⊘ – The appeal of this neo-Renaissance brick building (1877-1881), inspired by Schinkel's Academy of Architecture *(see SCHLOSS-PLATZ, Friedrichwerdersche Kirche)*, is enhanced by its refined decoration of ceramics, mosaics and stone friezes which makes it look like an Italian palace. It was the work of **Martin Gropius**, the uncle of Walter Gropius who designed the Bauhaus. It was once the Museum of Decorative Arts and was surrounded by other museums which have now disappeared: the Ethnological Museum, and the Fine Arts Library. Note the glass roof of the beautiful columned inner hall. The

sdam Square and the Octagon in Leipzig Square

building is the counterpart of the Grand Palais in Paris, a place where important temporary exhibitions are held, such as *Prussia, an evaluation attempt* in 1981, when restoration work had just been completed, and *Berlin-Moscow* in 1995. The Berlin Wall went through the centre of the street. Opposite, the former **Prussian parliament (Preußischer Landtag/Abgeordnetenhaus von Berlin**, 1892-1904, at Nos 3-5 Niederkirchnerstraße) (**P**) is now the Council Chamber of Berlin County; it also houses the annexes of ministries, which have remained in Bonn.

"Topography of Terror" Exhibition (**S**) ⊘ – "Prince Albert's land", which lined Prinz-Albrecht-Straße (today Niederkirchner Straße) where the palace of the same name was situated, formed part of the Wilhelmstraße district where government edifices were once concentrated. Only the foundations of these various buildings remain. There is now a stretch of wasteland *(climb on top of the mound to have an overall view)* next to Martin-Gropius-Bau, where the official buildings of the Third Reich's authorities once stood. The secret police *(Geheime Staatspolizei* or **Gestapo**) took over the former School of Decorative Arts which included a prison in the south wing; the SS general headquarters *(Reichsführung SS*, headed by Himmler) occupied the Prinz-Albrecht Hotel next door; the SS security services *(Sicherheitsdienst der SS* or *SD)* were housed in **Prinz-Albrecht's Palais** which became in 1939 the governing body of the Gestapo, the criminal police and the SD under the name of the "Reich Central Security Service" *(Reichssicherheitshauptamt)*, presided by **Heydrich**. These parallel authorities *(Gestapo* next to the police, SS next to the army) were the cause of numerous conflicts of competence and, often kindled a spirit of "competition" in the exertion of oppression. The building situated on the southwest side houses an exhibition *(English translation, DM 1.-)* on the history of the district, the official services involved in repression, their members, the Jews between 1933 and 1938, the German Resistance and the "final solution" concerning the Jews and Gypsies. Construction work on a new building, designed by the Swiss architect, Peter Zumthor, has been dogged with delays. Part of the Wall runs along the street to the north.

Wilhelmstraße – In the new Friedrichstadt, three avenues converged towards Belle-Alliance-Platz *(see KREUZBERG, west part)*. One of them was named Wilhelmstraße at the end of the 17C in honour of the Crown Prince Frederick-William *(Wilhelm* in German), the future King-Sergeant. During the 18C, Wilhelmstraße was sought after by the aristocracy who had French-style mansions built on both sides of the street. From 1871 to 1939, the eyes of the world were focused on Wilhelmstraße as they are today on the White House or the Kremlin for, along this street, which has lost its original appearance and is today lined with ordinary homes, stood the Chancellor's Office, the Ministry of Foreign Affairs and the Presidential Residence. Hitler's new Chancellery was built in record time in an adjacent street (only the underground bunker remains), with luxury materials, immediately before the war. The huge building standing on the corner of Leipzigerstraße was the **Air Ministry (Reichsluftfahrtministerium)**, where Goering had his office; designed by Ernst Sagebiel and erected in 1935-36, it was the main example of Nazi architecture until the new chancellery was built. During the war, the resistance group called **"the Red Orchestra"** ("Rote Kapelle"), led by Harro Schulze-Boysen, worked on the premises. However all its members were executed in 1942. After the war it became the Ministries House (Haus der Ministerien) of the GDR, and was occupied from 1990 to 1994 by the Treuhandanstalt (the organisation responsible for privatisation of the GDR's companies); there are plans for the building to house the

The assassination of Walter Rathenau (1867-1922)

Born in Berlin, Walter Rathenau was a brilliant man, from the point of view of his bearing as much as of his attitude of mind. He was equally interested in economics and in philosophy, and dreamt of a society which would evolve beyond the division between capitalism and socialism. At the beginning of the 20C, he was the author of the catch-phrase: "Athens-on-Spree is dead, Chicago-on-Spree is now growing". He founded the Raw Materials Department of the War Ministry and succeeded his father on the board of AEG. Having engaged in politics, he took part in the preparation of the Peace Conference in Versailles, which put him in close contact with the victorious powers and led him to study the problem of compensation. He became Reconstruction Minister, then Foreign Affairs Minister. Shortly after having signed the **Rapallo Treaty** with the newly founded Soviet Union, which marked the first international recognition of the new state, Walter Rathenau was assassinated in his car on 24 June 1922, by two anti-Semitic former officers belonging to the extreme right-wing organisation Consul. This crime was the logical continuation of the violent repression which followed the 1918 revolution and the warning of much more to come. 200 000 people were present at the funeral as panic started the uncontrollable rise of inflation. His old friend **Stefan Zweig**, who met him a few days before his death, described him in his autobiography *Yesterday's World (Die Welt von Gestern)*.

treasury. To the south, Wilhelmstraße offers a few interesting buildings by Aldo Rossi on the corner of Kochstraße; to the north, a plaque marks the house lived in by **Konrad Adenauer** (1876-1967), who was Mayor of Cologne and President of the Prussian State Council from 1931 to 1933 and became Chancellor of the FRG.

IN THE VICINITY

See **FRIEDRICHSTRASSE★, KREUZBERG (West Part)★★, REICHSTAG★, KULTURFORUM★★★, UNTER DEN LINDEN★★**.

Postdamer Platz in 1930
(in the bottom left hand corner: Europe's first traffic lights)

PRENZLAUER BERG★★

Miraculously spared during the last war, **Prenzlauer Berg** has retained its old blocks of rented apartments, the *Mietskasernen* with their symmetrical façades, around the two main arteries, Prenzlauer Allee and Schönhauser Allee. The district, reputed to be the most tolerant in Berlin, offers both a convivial atmosphere and a lively nightlife.

Prenzlauer Berg: before and after restoration work

The rise of Social Democracy – The Socialist influence became apparent as soon as the Empire was founded. It made an impact on the working-class districts of Wedding, Friedrichshain and Prenzlauer Berg and replaced the liberal movement which until then dominated political life in Berlin with the support of a powerful press and outstanding personalities such as the surgeon **Rudolf Virchow**, strongly opposed to Bismarck, and the historian Theodor Mommsen. In 1862, **Ferdinand Lassalle** submitted a programme intended to improve the life of the working class. The following year, he was elected president of the general association of German workers. Bismarck then retaliated with two contradictory measures: taking as a pretext an attempt on the Emperor's life, he enforced the **laws against the Socialists** between 1878 and 1880 and, in a typical turn-around, he initiated laws on health insurance (1883), industrial injury (1884) and pension schemes, which put Germany well ahead of European nations in the field of social welfare. However, these laws only slowed down the progress of the Socialist movement: just before World War I, 3/4 of the members of the Reichstag belonged to the SPD, intent on changing German society pacifically; Eduard Bernstein even spoke of an "evolutionary" kind of Socialism. The Socialist ideals expressed in the newspaper *Vorwärts (Ahead)*, caused the conservatives to react sharply and a revolutionary minority headed by Karl Liebknecht and Rosa Luxemburg formed to break away from the main current *(see TIERGARTEN)*.

The "Kreuzberg of the East" – Prenzlauer Berg owes its charm to the poetry pervading its disused backyards, its buildings occupied by a radical Alternative community and its cafés full of activity at all times. The district is now considered to be

Jewish cemetery

the "Kreuzberg of the nineties", and it can indeed quite rightly be compared to what Kreuzberg was like for several decades. An easygoing way of life, a strong community spirit and the mingling of generations are the main characteristics of these two districts.

MAIN SIGHTS

★ **Jüdischer Friedhof** ⊘ – *Schönhauser Allee 23-25* Ⓤ *2 Senefelderplatz.*
Open in 1827; owing to the density of the trees, an intense charm permeates this place. Here lie among others, the composers Giacomo Meyerbeer (1791-1864), the painter Max Liebermann (1847-1935) and the publisher Leopold Ullstein (1826-1899).

★ **Kollwitzplatz** – *Walk along Kollwitzstraße.*
This lively square *(see ON THE TOWN, The Berlin Scene)* has managed to retain its peaceful atmosphere. Children play in the garden; local life, typical of Prenzlauer Berg, quietly goes on. Slightly to the southeast, a disused **water tower**, turned into homes (it already included several homes on four levels), stands in front of the highest hill in the area *(Berg* in German), which does not offer any view. Built in 1877 to a height of 44m, it used to be called *Dicker Herrmann ("Big Hermann")*. Opponents of the Nazi regime were tortured there and murdered in the cellars and in the engine-room. The main synagogue in Berlin stands at No 53 Kybestraße. Restoration work is still going on through most of the district.

Return to Käthe-Kollwitz-Platz. **Husemannstraße** is a lovely street lined with numerous restaurants and cafés.

★**Schultheissbrauerei** – *Schönhauser Allee 36-39;* Ⓤ *2 Eberswalder Straße.*
This huge building (1891) looking like a medieval fortress is a busy cultural centre which draws large crowds at night *(entrance in Knaackstraße; see ON THE TOWN The Berlin Scene).*

The Kiez dialect

The *Kiez* spirit is more alive in Prenzlauer Berg than anywhere else. To become acquainted with it, you have to experience it. In order to make it easier for you and help those who wish to acquire a better knowledge of German, here is a small glossary containing typical words from the Berlin *Kiez* dialect :

Keule instead of *Kumpel* or *Bruder:* "brother", "pal".
Kiez is the equivalent *of Heimisches Wohnviertel:* "district", "village".
Eine Molle for Ein Glas Bier: "a beer".
Schusterjunge for Brötchen: "small brown buns".
Schrippe for weißes Brötchen: "small bun".
Schnieke: "chic".
Etepetete: "delicate", "affected".
Stino(s), stinknormale for vollnormal: "boring", "square".
Schau for schön and toll: "super", "great".
Schlauchen for betteln: "to beg", "to pass the hat round".
Wa? idiom for "isn't it!"
Wat? instead of *was?:* "pardon?"
With the Kiez accent:
Ich: "I" becomes *Icke.*
Auch: "also" becomes *och.*
Gut: "fine", "good" becomes *jut.*

The **Sammlung Industrielle Gestaltung/Stiftung Stadtmuseum Berlin** has found a home on the site of the former brewery, which has been given protected status. It houses items relating to both product culture and everyday culture and to designs for the Soviet Occupation Zone and the GDR.

Danziger Straße – Visitors, who choose to continue eastwards *(for instance to go to Friedrichshain Park)* along Danziger Straße, will need to turn north into Prenzlauer Allee if they wish to see the Zeiss **Planetarium** ⊘ (Zeiss-Großplane-tarium: ⑤ *10 and* ⑤ *85 Prenzlauer Allee*). Further on (⑤ *8, 10 Greifswalder Straße)*, at the back of **Ernst-Thälmann Park**, there is a monument to the head of the Communist party who was arrested by the Nazis in 1933 (he had left his hide-out to spend the night with his girlfriend) and died in Buchenwald. Sur-rounded by tower blocks built by the GDR, the park stretches along the long and monotonous Greifswalderstraße.

Schönhauser Allee – Ⓤ *2 Eberswalder Straße.*
As far back as the Middle Ages, this avenue led from the Spandau Gate to the vil-lages of Pankow and Niederschönhausen and to the castle of the same name (*see* PANKOW). It is a shopping street which brings life to the whole district. The ele-vated S-Bahn line has been nicknamed *Magistratschirm* ("the municipal council's umbrella"). From **Eberswalderstraße** Station (note the lovely façade of **No 55 Schön-hauserallee**), one can wander through several interesting streets. **Prater**, one of the oldest inns in Berlin, is situated in Kastanienallee (Nos 7-9). The buildings have not all been renovated by far, but those which have been restored look fine. **Oderberger Straße** was a dead end before the Wall came down, since it ran along the north-western end of the street; beyond lay the French sector *(see WEDDING)*. A strong feeling of solidarity united the inhabitants of this no-through road and discussions went on in backyard gardens. The layout of the buildings is identical: the owners' homes overlook the street; the workers' overlook the first courtyards; and work-shops (small industries) are confined to the backyards. All this amounts to a network of communicating courtyards running behind the façades.

Walking north:

Groterjan-Brauerei – *Nos 50 and 53* 🚋 *Milastraße; on the corner of Milastraße.* Built in German Renaissance style, the edifice houses shops, cultural institutions and homes-cum-workshops.

Gethsemane-Kirche – Fine group of brick buildings in Buchholzer Straße. On the corner of Stargarder Straße and Greifenhagenerstraße, interesting buildings and **Church of Gethsemane** where Christian demonstrators met when the "turning point" came.
Beautiful *Gründerzeitstil* houses line Kuglerstraße and Erich-Weinert-Straße (⑤ *8, 10 and* Ⓤ *2 Schönhauser Allee)*.

IN THE VICINITY

See **ALEXANDERPLATZ★, FRIEDRICHSHAIN, PANKOW★, WEISSENSEE.**

REICHSTAG★

Tiergarten
See map of Berlin Historic Centre Mitte p. 248-249, **NYZ**

Few monuments are as deeply symbolic as the **Reichstag**, unified Germany's parliament, built in the 19C at the time of the Empire, burnt down by the Nazis in 1933, situ-ated for four decades on the border of East and West, like its neighbour the Brandenburg Gate (which was in the Soviet sector). This monument, whose original role was restored amid general rejoicing on 20 December 1990, after the first general elections in unified Germany will be at the centre of a vast town planning project aimed at removing all traces of the split between the two parts of the city: the **meander of the Spree** or "Spreebogen" which is due to link up the parliamentary institutions. Just before work began, it was wrapped up in a most spectacular way by **Christo**.

Lehrte Central Station
Built on the north bank of the Spree and closely linked to the government offices district, it will be used by long distance trains, suburban trains, the S-Bahn, the U-Bahn (the Ⓤ 5 line will be extended to Pariser Platz and the station) and cope with 200 000 passengers a day. The north/south lines will go underground while the east/west lines will be elevated. The Spree will have to be diverted northwards in order to build the tunnels intended for long-dis-tance lines, the U-Bahn and the express way B96 which will go under Tiergarten and link up with Potsdamer Platz Station. The works will be completed in 2002.

THE UPS AND DOWNS OF HISTORY

The Alsenviertel – From the 16C onwards and for 200 years, the meander of the Spree was used for economic and military purposes. In the middle of the 18C, it became, together with Tiergarten, a favourite destination for family outings. In 1839, Lenné and Schinkel began to remodel this part of town. In 1843, the former parade ground (Exerzierplatz, today **Republic Square**) was redesigned; the middle-class district of Alsenviertel gradually developed and attracted offices, companies and diplomatic delegations (such as the Swiss Consulate which is still there)

The Reichstag fire – At **Goering**'s instigation (he was head of security), the Reichstag burnt down on **27 February 1933**; the fire had started in several places at once as the chief of the fire brigade noticed when he arrived on the spot; he was assassinated a few days later. A Dutch communist, Van der Lubbe, was arrested. The next day, left-wing parties were banned and their members persecuted. The remaining members of parliament took refuge on the opposite side of the square, in Kroll Opera House. The Reichstag was used for showing propaganda films and would have looked insignificant next to the "People's Hall" designed by Albert Speer, a 200m-high dome which could contain 180 000 people.

Systematic demolition began before 1939 to make room for Hitler's megalomaniac schemes which included his own palace, the military Headquarters and the "People's Hall". This was to be the heart of State bureaucracy, at the centre of the new "**Germania**".

The "Spreebogen project" – The district was razed to the ground after the war. The proximity of the Wall prevented urban development until the 1980s. After reunification and the transfer of the capital to Berlin, the decision was taken in 1991 to locate the parliamentary buildings and government offices together in the bend of the Spree. This move had already been proposed during the Weimar era.

An international urban design competition for the "bond of the Spree" was launched in 1993. The project was put forward by the Berlin architects **Axel Schultes** and **Charlotte Franck**.

To the west of the "Innerer Spreebogen", they created the federal chancellery building and a garden, with the Forum in the middle and the buildings containing the members' offices to the east; these buildings are grouped into three complexes on the two banks of the Spree. Stéphane Braunfels designed the Alsen and Luisenblock complex, while the Dorotheenblock was the work of a consortium.

The inscription: "To the German people"
was added at the time of the Weimar Republic

MAIN SIGHTS

★**Reichstag** ⊘ – ⑤ *1, 2, 25, 26 Unter den Linden; No 100* 🚌 *Reichstag.*
The construction of the Reichstag (1884-1894) became urgent as the members of parliament of the newly founded German Empire were short of space inside the former porcelain factory situated in Leipzigerstraße *(see POTSDAMER PLATZ)*; it was financed by war damages paid by the French treasury but became a subject of controversy between the architect **Paul Wallot** and Emperor William II who was afraid lest the edifice, in particular its cupola, should be higher than the castle. A compromise was found in the form of a glass and steel cupola, but this did not prevent the largest building in the Imperial capital from having a ridiculously small serviceable area and being declared too small shortly after its inauguration in 1894. Being a member of parliament during the Wilhelmian period had a somewhat ambiguous meaning since power entirely rested in the hands of the emperor and his chancellor. William II called the Reichstag "the Imperial monkeys' cage". In 1926, the inscription *Dem Deutschen Volke* was added whilst the Weimar Republic was being torn apart by the demons of authoritarianism. With its shrapnel-riddled façade chosen by every photographer at the end of the war as the symbol of Berlin's collapse, the Reichstag could not, during the time when Germany was still divided, serve any real purpose nor accommodate all the parliamentary groups. Odd groups, committees and institutions met there, congresses were held and there was also an exhibition called *A look at German History* which attracted 12 million visitors (it has been moved to the German cathedral, *see GENDAR-MENMARKT*). In 1995, the Reichstag was wrapped up by **Christo** and his wife Jeanne-Claude, according to whom this wrapping up symbolised the "different questions one might ask oneself about its use and the political future of Germany". The operation attracted more than five million visitors.

The refurbishment of the Reichstag was entrusted in 1993 to the British architect **Sir Normal Foster**. One year later he presented his plan, which was based on three basic principles: to facilitate the functioning of the Parliament, to respect the history of the building and to create a new administrative concept. A new glass dome, different from the original, was thus raised to the top of the federal Parliament building in 1999, although the structures of the building designed by Paul Wallot have been preserved. This dome, which includes a **panoramic platform★★** accessible to the public, will quickly become a new urban point of reference, thanks to its splendid nocturnal illumination, the symbol for Germany in the Millennium.

Platz der Republik – The former Royal Square (Königsplatz) was used as a parade ground. Berliners would come and watch the garrison inspection in May. The construction of the Reichstag, various embassies and the general headquarters turned it into a political centre, a role which it will assume once again after the *Spreebogen* project has been completed. The Victory column *(see TIERGARTEN)* used to stand here until 1937. 300 000 Berliners gathered in the square in 1947 to hear **Ernst Reuter**, the mayor of the west part of the town, denounce the city's division *(see ERNST-REUTER-PLATZ)*. Reunification was celebrated here on **3 October 1990**, Germany's new national day.

Sowjetisches Ehrenmal – *Along the 17 June Avenue.* The marble used for this monument came from the ruins of Hitler's new chancellery. The tank was the first to enter Berlin.

IN THE VICINITY

See **TIERGARTEN★★, UNTEN DEN LINDEN★★**.

REINICKENDORF
Reinickendorf
See map of Berlin Conurbation, **⑩**, **BCT**

It has been inhabited for a very long time. Places such as Lübars, Tegel, Waidmannslust, Hermsdorf and Wittenau have been settled since the Bronze Age (1100 BC). A graveyard and traces of a village, dating from the time of the Germanic migrations (5C), have been found in Waidmannslust. The urbanisation of Reinickendorf followed the construction of the Northern railway line (Nordbahn); subsequently, the district became "the Iron North" *(Der eiserne Norden)*, specialising in tools and machinery. The decline of this activity began in 1960. Reinickendorf is a large industrial area situated on the periphery of the town. This urban district and the neighbouring villages annexed in 1920 *(see the INTRODUCTION, The Burden of History)* are well outside the centre of Berlin. It is preferable to visit them by car. There are old almond-shaped village squares with ancient and often charming parish churches in the middle as well as interesting estates and, sometimes, stretches of countryside, but there are no great attractions.

MAIN SIGHTS

Borsigwerke (Q¹) – Berlinerstraße 27; **U** Borsigwerke The U-Bahn exit (take the exit at the head of the train, then on the left, Berliner straße, Gewerbepark) is adjacent to the Gothic style brick entrance porch of the Borsig factory.

August Borsig, the "railway engine king" *(see CHARITÉ),* set up a factory in Tegel with 4 800 workers and 500 employees (the *Babcock* company took over the Reinickendorf buildings). The **tower★** an administrative building of 11 storeys, was Europe's first sky scraper (1922-24); it inspired the Ullstein House tower *(see TEM PELHOF).* The lancet windows and the broken outline of the top are Expressionist details. It is possible to have an overall view of the build

Borsig Factory Tower

ings from the underground exit situated at the beginning of Ernststraße.

Arbeiterkolonie Borsigwalde – *Follow Ernststraße and take the metal footbridge over the railway lines. Turn right into Räuschstraße.*
The homes specifically built for the workers of the Borsig factory were the first block of working-class tenements in Berlin (1899-1900). The influence of historicism can still be seen: graceful timber-framed Renaissance gables, in brick Gothic style, decorate the façades.

Russischer Friedhof – The Russian Orthodox St Constantin and St Helena Chapel with its bulbs and roofs painted blue makes the cemetery, which dates from 1893, one of the most noteworthy in Berlin, an honour which it shares with the Muslim cemetery in Neukölln, Columbiadamm, which was opened in 1866. Among those buried in it are Tsar Nicholas II's war minister who signed the 1914 declaration, and also Nabokov's and Eisenstein's fathers. A commemorative stone recalls the composer Michail Glinka, "the father of Russian music", who died in Berlin in 1857.
Return to the underground via Wittestraße.

Reinickendorf – **U** 8 Paracelsus-Bad.
Small parish church. Slightly further south, on the other side of Lindauer Allee and along Aroser Allee, stands the elegant **"White City" ("Weiße Stadt", 1929-31)** built by Otto Rudolf Salvisberg.

Russians in Berlin during the twenties

It is estimated that up to 300 000 Russians and citizens of the former Austro-Hungarian empire settled in Berlin. Their community included 6 banks, schools and an organisation to help refugees. Charlottenburg was renamed *Charlottengrad.* There were numerous meeting places between Zoo and Charlottenburg stations, such as the music-hall Der Blaue Vogel *(The Blue Bird,* in Goltzstraße), a small shadow-show theatre where Russian artists sang, danced and played sketches and which was famous for the originality of its stage scenery. The Haus der Künste *(Arts House),* founded by Andreï Biely, Alexis Tolstoï and Remizov was based in Leon am Nollendorfplatz Café: political discussions went on in a smoke-filled atmosphere. A second organisation called Schriftstellerklub *(Writers' Club)* was created. But apart from this colony of refugees, Berlin was not a truly cosmopolitan town: in 1925 there were only 1 437 British subjects, 1 030 Americans and 688 French citizens! Foreign nationals only represented 2.39% of the population.

Wittenau – Ⓤ *8 Rathaus Reinickendorf.*
Set among trees, the small church and its shingle-clad bell tower form a charming picture.

Märkisches Viertel – *Wilhelmsruher Damm.*
It is, along with Gropiusstadt *(see NEUKÖLLN),* one of the largest estates built in Berlin during the sixties : note the layout of the various buildings (painted yellow, red and blue) and the numerous amenities (shops, swimming-pools, etc.).

Lübars – Berlin's loveliest village, together with Marienfelde, has retained its natural setting. Small bungalows surround the elongated village square. Some of the buildings house well-known restaurants.

Hermsdorf – Ⓢ *1 Hermsdorf.* The charming square in front of the parish church makes this village look like a real country place. The **local history museum★** (Heimat-museum Reinickendorf) Ⓥ **(M³²)** is one of the best-appointed museums in Berlin. It houses fine reconstructions of different workshops (a carpenter's, a joiner's, a book-binder's, a cobbler's, a saddler's, a blacksmith's), many objects, dioramas such as that depicting the ambush set by the **Quitzow** robber barons to trap the citizens of Berlin *(see TEGEL),* and reconstruction of a reindeer hunter. In the courtyard, at the back of the house, there are several reconstructed cottages from a German village of the 2C and 3C, with thatched roofs sloping down to the ground: there is the cottage where spinning and weaving was performed, the store-house, the home which also included the stable. Upstairs, before you reach the classroom and the dining-room, note the well-lit drawing-room which contains extremely graceful yet unsophisticated *Biedermeier* **furniture**.

★Gartenstadt Frohnau Ⓥ – Ⓢ *1 Frohnau.*
Designed between the two world wars, the Frohnau garden city is a harmonious ensemble. It has two centres: Zeltingerplatz, shaped like an arch, and the square situated in front of the S-Bahn station, surmounted by a tower (1909-10) with a restaurant. At the top of a hill, **The Buddhistischen Haus** Ⓥ (No 54 Edelhofdamm), was a Buddhist community from Sri-Lanka *(in winter, beware of the ice on the steps, which makes them extremely slippery; go round the house from the left).* The monastery comprises the library, a pleasant room with a bay window over-looking the garden and an altar decorated with flowers, and the temple *(leave your shoes at the entrance).*

IN THE VICINITY

See **TEGEL★★**, **WEDDING★**.

SCHLOSSPLATZ

Mitte

See map of Berlin Mitte, p. 248-249 **PYZ**

The vast open space marking the site where the Hohenzollerns' castle used to stand offers good views of the surrounding monuments.

THE MISSING CASTLE

The Prince's initiative – **Cölln Castle**, which was built on the island of the same name, was the very first residence of the House of Hohenzollern in Berlin. It dated back to the 15C: in fact, Margrave **Frederick II**, who called it **"Iron Tooth"**, laid the first stone on 31 July 1443. During the rebellion of 1448, the site was flooded, but this did not stop the building from being pompously inaugurated in 1451.

An administrative complex – The residence became really worthy of a prince during the reign of Elector **Joachim II** (1535-1571) who extended and embellished it, taking as models the castles of Saxony. **Caspar Theiß** had several features added including a square tower, corner towers and gabled roofs (the spiral staircase was a copy of the famous one in Torgau). When the Renaissance came to Berlin, the castle made the city look like a town of residence. After the Thirty Years War, the castle had to be refurbished in order to become an administrative centre aimed at making it easier to reorganise the electorate. It was rebuilt between 1698 and 1707 by **Andreas Schlüter** and became a symbol of centralised absolute monarchy during the Baroque period *(the model is on show on the ground floor of the Knobelsdorff wing, in Charlotten-burg Castle, see under that name).* The architecture of the second courtyard was particularly remarkable. The dome of the chapel was built by Stüler around 1850.

From stateliness to destruction – According to **Jules Laforgue**, a French reader in the service of Empress Augusta, wife of William I, life at the palace "went on with con-stant monotony". After World War I and the first damages caused by the revolution, the castle was turned into a Museum of Decorative Arts (1921), but the public had little time to admire the splendid interiors, which bore witness to the evolution of taste through five centuries. The castle was badly damaged in 1944 and 1945; in 1950 the GDR authorities, in particular **Walter Ulbricht,** decided to have it demolished. It was necessary, as in Potsdam, to wipe out all trace of Prussia's military power. In June 1993, metallic scaffolding covered with a piece of painted canvas made up a dummy façade, designed by a French company, and thus recreated part of the castle for a few weeks in order to promote the idea of its rebuilding and enable people to form their own opinion...

MAIN SIGHTS

Berliner Dom ⊙ – *No 100* 🚌 *Lustgarten.* This imposing edifice was built between 1894 and 1905 on the site of

Access by S-Bahn
Castle Square is situated within equal distance of 🅢 + 🆄 *Friedrichstraße and of* 🅢 + 🆄 *Alexanderplatz Stations.*

an 18C **cathedral** remodelled by Schinkel. William II, and above all his wife Augusta, who was a devout person, wished for a Lutheran church worthy of the Imperial capital; the result was <u>an ostentatious and splendid **interior**</u>★★ (note the organ), which gives a good idea of the <u>predilection of the Prussian court for pomp.</u> This exuberance, in true Wilhelmian style, was matched on the outside: the dome and lanterns were laden with ornaments which made this enormous mass look ridiculous. The plain restoration work has only left the impression of hugeness.

On the south side of the nave *(opposite the organ)*, can be seen the **ceremonial coffins** of King Frederick I, from a sketch by Andreas Schlüter, and his second wife Sophie-Charlotte *(see Schloß CHARLOTTENBURG)*. Under the organ, there are more ceremonial coffins, less obviously Baroque and more elegant, this time of the Great Elector and his second wife Dorothy. Their names can be seen in a small corner of the **Hohenzollern crypt** *(Entrance south of the nave; put the card through and go quickly past the gate; going the other way, press the button and go through the gate. Tickets are on sale in the bookshop on the left-hand side of the narthex).* The vaulted part, supported by massive sandstone columns was damaged by bombs and is being restored. It houses about 100 graves including those of the Great Elector, Frederick I and Sophie-Charlotte, and Frederick-William II (the tomb is covered over with the Hohenzollern colours), the nephew and successor of Frederick the Great (the latter is buried in Potsdam).

Lustgarten – These were once the private gardens of the Great Elector (Kurfürstlicher Lustgarten). Like most Renaissance gardens, they were both a kitchen garden and an ornamental garden. Having acquired numerous exotic species, they became Berlin's first botanical gardens. When Tiergarten was laid out, they lost some

The cathedral seen from the castle bridge

of their appeal and were used as a training ground during the King-Sergeant's reign. The flower-beds, which bridged the gap between the Castle and the Old Museum, were removed in 1935.

Palast der Republik (**Z**) – *No 100* 🚌 *Lustgarten.*
The GDR's People's chamber sat in this building until 1990, and it was a cultural centre "open" to the people, with cafés and space for various leisure activities. Currently negotiations concerning the development of the Schloßplatz are still in progress.

Neuer Marstall (**Z¹**) – *Corner of Schloßplatz and Breite Straße.*
These monumental stables, which used to face the castle across Schloßplatz, were equipped with a mechanical elevator system for horses. They could house 300 horses. There is a good view from **Rathausbrücke.**

Staatsratsgebäude (**Z²**) – *Schloßplatz 1.*
After the castle was blown up with dynamite, the GDR authorities had the balcony, from which the Republic was proclaimed by Karl Liebknecht on 9 November 1918, fixed to the façade of the State Council (1964). It is supported by telamones and is the work of **Balthasar Permoser**, the sculptor who decorated the Zwinger in Dresden.

"Germany fell asleep under the Empire and woke up under the Republic"

This famous sentence by the chief editor of *Tageblatt* sums up the abrupt political change which occurred after the abdication of William II in November 1918. The main headline of the newspaper *Die Rote Fahne*, owned by the extreme left-wing Spartakist party, was: "The red flag is flying over Berlin!"; however, the Social Democrat government did not agree with this and tried to relieve tension by instituting universal suffrage and took precautions to avoid looting and incidents. Demonstrations were cancelled and regaining hold of the castle turned out to be a bloody operation.

Werderscher Markt – This square was occupied right up to Werderstraße by the extension of the Foreign Office. The building, which housed the central committee from 1959 to 1989, was erected between 1934 and 1938, during the Nazi regime, as the headquarters of the Reichsbank. At the "turning point" in 1990, it served as the "House of the East German members of Parliament". The ministry of Foreign Affairs of the ex-GDR which stood opposite (to the north) has been demolished. Schinkel's famous **School of Architecture** (**Bauakademie**, 1831-1836) will be rebuilt in its place. Owing to its strictly functional role, its new technology using iron and brick, in particular all the technical and aesthetic possibilities of these materials, and its terracotta decoration, this building is considered to be one of Schinkel's principal architectural works. The planned reconstruction is based on an absolute consensus between all those responsible, together with two associations involved in the reestablishment of the School of Architecture. Shortly before the church stands the **Bear Fountain.**

★**Friedrichswerdersche Kirche** ⊘ (**M²²**) – The suburb of the same name developed from 1662 onwards *(see the INTRODUCTION, The Burden of History)* and the church standing on the market square was built in 1700. For its reconstruction, Schinkel suggested several styles for the same kind of church: Neoclassical or neo-Gothic. Neo-Gothic, which was thereby used for the first time in Berlin, was finally chosen; in spite of this, the edifice has extremely clear-cut lines. The interior has strange polychrome decoration: the vaulting (brickwork and ribs) and the pillar stones are painted to give the illusion of marble; the gallery and the pulpit are made of wood; the apse is decorated with stained glass. The church houses the **Schinkel Museum (Schinkelmuseum)** which, together with the Schinkel Pavilion *(see Schloß CHARLOTTENBURG)* is the place to visit if you wish to learn about the great Berlin architect Karl Friedrich Schinkel. Explanatory panels in German give details about his main achievements: the **Old Museum**, the **Academy of Architecture,** the elegant School of Artillery (Artillerie- und Ingenieurschule), and, in Unter den Linden, the Packow, the Taxes Building as well as the projects he could not realise such as the State Library and the **Department Store in Unter den Linden** (1827), a splendid idea which fell through because the king was apprehensive about the possible concentration of two hundred shops in one place. All these projects have in common the originality of their design which heralds industrial architecture, their clear-cut lines, the elegance and simplicity of their interior decoration. The lovely **terracotta decorations★** intended for the Academy of Architecture together with one of its **doorways** *(which can be seen a few steps away, behind the church, in Oberwallstraße),* denoting perfect elegance and refinement, as well as the doorway of the church, show that all the details of Schinkel's buildings are there to enhance the ultimate beauty of the work. The church has become a focal point for art lovers, thanks to an exhibition of 19C sculpture (principally from the Classicistic period) and bust likenesses.

IN THE VICINITY

See **FISCHERINSEL★, GENDARMENMARKT★★, MUSEUMSINSEL★★★, UNTER DEN LINDEN★★**.

SCHÖNEBERG★

Schöneberg

See map of Berlin Town Centre, **7**, **8**, **GHJXYZ**

Less typically middle-class than its western neighbours Wilmersdorf and Charlottenburg, Schöneberg is the meeting-place of a certain Bohemian youth which includes students, gays etc.; it is a fairly large district with several lively centres. The northern part, between Wittenbergplatz and Nollendorfplatz, is the favourite haunt of Berlin's large homosexual community (together with West Kreuzberg and Prenzlauer Berg). Further south, a great number of cafés and fashion boutiques are gathered round Winterfeldplatz and along Goltzstraße, while in the southernmost part of the district, Friedenau is a residential area beside a busy shopping street.

Modest beginnings – *"Sconenberghe"*, which was officially mentioned for the first time in 1264, was bought on behalf of Joachim I and administered by the Mühlenhof *(see NIKOLAIVIERTEL, Mühlendamm)*. Twenty gipsies settled in the area around 1750, shortly before the village was destroyed during the Seven Years War. At the beginning of the 19C, Schöneberg was a popular destination for excursion trips; there were many public baths along Potsdamer Chaussee and the Schafgraben, which is now the Landwehrkanal. The development of the railways (in 1838, the first Berlin-Potsdam line went through the municipal grazing grounds) was the main factor which determined the growth of the village.

New western districts – In their effort to get away from the industrial city, the well-to-do settled in front of the Potsdam Gate and beyond the Landwehrkanal which marks the limits of Berlin, thus starting the general tendancy of the middle class to move westwards. During the "foundation years" *(Gründerjahre)*, large landowners and unscrupulous promoters set the trend for wild speculation and were followed in this by peasants who sold their land at a very high price. The "millionaire farmers" from Schöneberg had large mansions built in the new "Bavarian district" and in Friedenau. Artists, writers and scientists followed. A mixture of "rented apartments" and small companies, particularly concentrated in the south, characterises urban development in Schöneberg, where there were many civil servants and soldiers; the district was granted town status in 1898. From 1875 to 1905, the population multiplied by twenty. The period was marked by the struggle with Charlottenburg for the privilege of having the first S-Bahn. Schöneberg and Friedenau were incorporated into Greater Berlin in 1920.

The Sports Stadium: from the Six Cycling Days to the declaration of "total war". A sports venue during the twenties (great enthusiasm was shown for the **Six Cycling Days**, broadcast at length on radio), the **Sports Stadium**, in Potsdamer Straße, was also a venue for political meetings which, at the beginning of the thirties, resounded with the fiery eloquence of popular leaders. Communist speakers sometimes followed Hitler onto the platform; fighting often broke out and the police had to clear the stadium. It was however full of carefully selected sympathisers when, on 18 February 1943, **Goebbels** launched a propaganda operation intended to boost the people's morale. To the question: "Do you want total war?" an overwhelming "yes" was roared back.

After the war, Schöneberg, which was situated in the American sector, played a major role *(see below Rathaus Schöneberg and Kleistpark)*.

A few celebrities from Schöneberg:

Albert Einstein resided at No 8 Nördlinger Straße from 1905 to 1912.

Else Lasker-Schüler (1869-1945), who represented and promoted Expressionist literature, lived in a Schöneberg hotel from 1924 to 1931. Being Jewish like her colleague the poet **Nelly Sachs**, she emigrated to Switzerland in 1933. The famous conductor Wilhelm Furtwängler (1886-1954) was a native of Schöneberg.

Marlene Dietrich was born in "Red Island" *(see below)* and lived in Kaiserallee (now Bundesallee) until 1930. She left for the United States in 1930 and, in 1934, she turned down Goebbels's offer to go back to Germany.

MAIN SIGHTS

Rathaus Schöneberg (**R**) – **U** *4 Rathaus Schöneberg.*
This was the home of West Berlin's Senate until 1990 *(the Senate of the reunified town now sits in the "Red Town Hall", see ALEXANDERPLATZ)* and the administrative centre of the town. It became famous on 26 June 1963 when J.F. Kennedy pronounced the following famous words from the balcony: "All free men, wherever they may live, are citizens of Berlin. And therefore, as a free man, I take pride in saying: "Ich bin ein Berliner".

Rudolph-Wilde-Park – This is a pleasant stretch of woodland, with lawns and ponds, which extends *(Volkspark)* westwards to Wilmersdorf. In the hollow, the underground has been admirably installed under the bridge. A golden deer *(Goldener Hirsch)* stands on top of a column.

Dorfkirche – The cemetery situated next to the church contains the graves of the "millionaire peasants". **Hauptstraße** is a shopping street linking Schöneberg's village church and Kleistpark.

Kennedy in Berlin

Dalmas/SIPA PRESS

"Rote Insel" – **S** *1, 25, 26 Yorckstraße (Großgörschenstraße)* or **U** *7 Yorckstraße.* Wedged between the S-Bahn lines and the disused railway tracks of Anhalt Station, **"Red Island"** got its name from its working-class population which voted for the Communists between the two world wars. In this working-class district there were many *Schlafgänger*, people who could only afford a bed for the night. It has kept its community spirit set apart from the rest of the metropolis, and reminds one of *Beusselkiez* in Moabit *(see under that name)*: similar lifestyle, similar small shops. **St Matthew's cemetery** (St-Matthäus-Kirchhof) is very romantic. The Grimm Brothers are buried here (map of the cemetery with mention of the most important graves at the entrance).

Kleistpark – **U** *7 Kleistpark.*
This small park was the first site of the botanical gardens before they moved to Dahlem. It gives on to Potsdamerstraße through a double 18C colonnade by Langhans, which used to decorate the **Royal Bridge,** near Alexanderplatz. The park serves as the gardens of the imposing neo-Baroque **law courts** which, from 1945 to 1990, housed the Allied Control Council.

Winterfeldplatz – This square, together with **Goltzstraße** and Maaßenstraße, is a hub of activity *(see ON THE TOWN, The Berlin Scene).*

Bayerisches Viertel – **U** *4, 7 Bayerischer Platz.*
Around 1900, the Berlin Real Estate Company (Berlinische Bodengesellschaft), which was the biggest land investor in Schöneberg, entered into negotiations with the banks and cooperated closely with the municipal administrative authorities to

---

A Prussian is always on duty...

Among the exhibits in the **Local History Museum** ⊘ (Schöneberg Museum, *Haus am Kleistpark, Grunewaldstraße 6-7),* there is a collection of Prussian lead soldiers inside a very small glass case. In itself, the collection is of no particular interest except for the fact that Prussian lead soldiers, as the true heirs of Frederick II's army, are always shown fighting. Where then are the military orchestras, the drinkers, the dancers which liven up the daily life of an army when it is not at war? Fortunately, Bavarian and Austrian lead soldiers are more inclined to be *bons vivants*. Their heads had to be cut off and replaced with Prussian heads and all the uniforms repainted.

Claire Waldoff (1884-1957):
"Everyone in Berlin is mad about my legs!»

The music-hall star of *Les tilleuls (Linden)* and *Roland von Berlin* was a native of Silesia. She first settled in Friedenau, then in Schöneberg. During the twenties and until 1933, she lived in the *Bayerisches Viertel*. She was small but had the banter and humour of Berlin's female workers; she also sang like "a Berlin sparrow, in a carefree cheeky manner" (Kurt Tucholsky). Her talent as a singer and a story-teller was comparable to that of her French counterpart, Yvette Guilbert. In spite of her sprightly insolence and her sense of the absurd in comic situations, she never failed to show tenderness. Her songs could be heard in the streets and are still popular today. The composer of light operas **Walter Kollo** (1878-1940), who also lived in the "Bavarian District", supported Claire Waldoff throughout his life. As soon as the Nazis came to power, she found herself in a difficult situation, but she overcame it and died in Bavaria, almost blind, having survived on a measly honorary pension granted to her by the West Berlin Senate.

---

agree on the road layout. It designed the "Bavarian District", as a result of property speculation in Berlin's expanding western areas, and then carried on its activities in Wilmersdorf where it erected even more sumptuous buildings. Large-scale destruction caused by the war has spared very few of the many large houses inhabited by university staff, Jews in particular (among them, Albert Einstein), except in **Viktoria-Luise-Platz** which still has a number of façades dating from 1900-1910. The rest of the district no longer forms a harmonious whole. Several wide crisscrossing streets (such as Innsbrucker Straße) are lined with anonymous buildings.

Nollendorfplatz – Ⓤ *1, 2, 4, 12, 15 Nollendorfplatz.*
Before the war this was the theatre district, including such establishments as the giant **Metropol** (1906; **T°**), in which **Erwin Piscator** staged some of his productions and which has now been turned into a discotheque.

"An der Urania" – This is a very modern square. The arch was a present from France. **Urania** is a cultural centre *(closed in summer)*, where many lectures are given.

Wittenbergplatz – Ⓤ *1, 2, 12, 15 Wittenbergplatz.*
Dominated by **"Kaufhaus des Westens"** or **KaDeWe★** department store, this square marks the border between Schöneberg and Kurfürstendamm *(see under that name)* districts. The underground station (the first to actually be underground) was built by Alfred Grenander, who also built a number of others during the 1910s and 20s.

TWO OTHER SIGHTS :

★**Ceciliengärten** – The street has been turned into a square and a long garden decorated with two fine statues by Georg Kolbe *(see OLYMPIASTADION, Georg Kolbe Museum)* to complete this beautiful estate (1924-26) comprising two-storeyed corbelled buildings with loggias. Some of the entrances are shaped like horseshoes and adorned with terracotta lattice-work. Each apartment was equipped with a kitchen and a bathroom; the average area of a two-room flat was 72 square metres.

"Stop Berlin! Think a little! Thy dancer is Death."

Paul Zech (1881-1946) is the author of *Deutschland, dein Tänzer ist der Tod (Germany, Thy Dancer is Death)*, the first part of which was written in 1933 in Schöneberg and the second in exile. A native of the Rhine region, Paul Zech grew up in the Ruhr valley. Having been influenced by Expressionism, he published his first poem in Herwalth Walden's periodical *Der Sturm* and depicted the condition of the working class in *Das Schwarze Revier (The Black District,* 1913). His abundant production, which included about thirty plays and more than a hundred prose works, made him, in the mid-twenties, a successful author politically committed to the SPD (Social Democrats). In 1926, he adapted Rimbaud's *Le Bateau ivre (The Drunken Ship)* for the theatre; Piscator's production featured stage sets by Grosz. Zech went into exile in Buenos Aires where he survived in miserable conditions. His body was repatriated in 1946 and buried in Friedenau cemetery.

Amazing view over a couple of estates *(for there is another one opposite Ceciliengärten)* in Rubensstraße.

★**Friedenau** – This extremely pleasant residential district with Friedrich-Wilhelm-Platz in its centre *(the layout becomes evident on a map)* has retained some splendid *Jugendstil* façades along some of its quiet shaded streets. **Rheinstraße** is a shopping street which leads to Steglitz. **No 45** houses a small industrial concern *(Gewerbehaus)* called Becker & Kries located in a particularly fine setting: note the two neo-Gothic courtyards where red bricks alternate with white roughcast.

IN THE VICINITY

See **KREUZBERG (West Part)**★★, **KURFÜRSTENDAMM**★★, **STEGLITZ**★, **TIERGARTEN**★★, **WILMERSDORF.**

SIEMENSSTADT-HECKERDAMM★
Spandau, Charlottenburg
See map of Berlin Town Centre, **2**, **3**, **EFGST**

The main interest of this district for visitors lies in the Siemens factory complex. Before the war, Siemens had its headquarters in Berlin (it has now moved to Munich) and, like the Borsig Company *(see REINICKENDORF)*, the group had a model estate built for its employees.

The Siemens empire – In 1847, **Ernst Werner Siemens** ("von" after 1888) founded a telegraph line installation business in collaboration with the engineer **Johann Georg Halske.** He discovered the basic principle of the dynamo-electric machine and, in 1881, he launched the first electric tramway in Lichterfelde *(see STEGLITZ)* and then converted the railway and the underground. This marked the birth of electrical engineering which became, with mechanical engineering and the steel industry, one of the pillars of Berlin's economic activities. The **Siemens & Halske** company subsequently diversified into electric bulbs, the telegraph, and facsimile transmission, occupying 2 000 hectares between Charlottenburg and Spandau, known as «**Siemensstadt**", with its own S-Bahn line. This huge industrial complex was spared during World War II because some American companies had vested interests in it.

MAIN SIGHTS

★**Siemensstadt** – *(See map of Berlin Conurbation, ⑩, BU)*. *In order to avoid having to retrace your steps, start the visit from Paulsternstraße* **U** *7 Station*. It has never stopped expanding since 1897. Modern extensions are mostly one-storeyed buildings.

Reuter Kraftwerk (Reuter Electric Power Station) – This huge edifice with three identical stacks was built by Siemens in the 30s. Badly damaged during the war, then dismantled and finally demolished, it was eventually rebuilt because military authorities considered it was vital to West Berlin's electricity supply. The entire equipment was brought over by plane during the blocus.

Schaltwerk (Commutator Station) – *Nonnendammallee 104*. Europe's first industrial building.

Bereich Antriebs-, Schalt und Installationtechnik – *Opposite, Nonnendammallee 72*. In the distance, towards the south, the **OSRAM factory** (electric bulbs).

Siemens administrative buildings – *Nonnendammallee 101*. In the classical style.

Röhrenwerk – *Rohrdamm 88, on the corner of Rohrdamm and Nonnendammallee;* **U** *7 Rohrdamm*. Good view from Rohrdamm.

★**Wernerwerk** – *(See map of Berlin Town Centre, **2**, ET)*. Follow Wernerwerkdamm and Ohmstraße or take the **U** 7 to Siemensdamm. Vast complex of rectangular dark red brick buildings, overlooked by the **clock tower** (70m) of the factory producing measuring equipment. Good view from the underground station entrance.

★**Großsiedlung Siemensstadt (Siemensstadt Estate)** – *See map of Berlin Conurbation, ⑩, BU S¹* – **U** *7 Siemensdamm*. The Siemens factories had 50 000 employees. There was an undeveloped piece of land south of the Jungfernheide and the firm was about to build a new underground line *(Siemensbahn)*; on **Martin Wagner**'s recommendation, six architects in the *Der Ring* (The Ring) Group, among them **Hans Scharoun**, **Walter Gropius**, Hugo Häring and others from the Bauhaus, were chosen to design a new estate. Rents were so high that there were more tenants among white collar workers and civil servants than among workers from the

Wernerwerk

Ph. Gaïc/MICHELIN

Siemens factories! The inhabitants also included artists and journalists; Hans Scharoun himself lived there for nearly twenty years. Three-storeyed bridge-type buildings, with roughcast façades, were built round St Joseph's Church *(good view from the corner of Goebelstraße and Quellweg as well as from the corner of Schuckertdamm and Quellweg).* The lovely Lenthersteig leading to St Christopher's church *(Christophoruskirche)* is also worth seeing.
The walk continues along **Heckerdamm** (Charlottenburg) up to the Plötzensee Memorial.

★**Volkspark Jungfernheide** – Ⓤ 7 *Halemweg.*
The Jungfernheide was a hunting ground until the beginning of the 19C, when it became a parade-ground and rifle-range. The Charlottenburg municipality bought 208 hectares of the available land in 1908, at a time when it was not yet completely surrounded by the town. It was laid out after World War I, together with another piece of land in the northern part of Charlottenburg. It is a very pleasant park with a central lawn overlooked by a **watertower** (1926); there is an expanse of water, covering an area of 7.5 hectares, where bathers and dinghies can move about freely. Go round the lake and onto the island which is an interesting nature reserve and is linked to the shore in the north and south by two wooden bridges. There were plans to erect several buildings on it, including a library and a lecture room. The planning programme was typical of the 20C, combining culture with leisure. The park architect, **Erwin Barth** (1880-1933), who was in charge of the Charlottenburg gardens and then of all Greater Berlin parks, took part in changing the layout of numerous green open spaces which are still remarkable today for the clever use that was made of them.

North Charlottenburg Estate – Ⓤ 7 *Halemweg.*
Garden-city where one can admire **Hans Scharoun**'s buildings: Halemweg 31-43 as well as the large building on the corner of Toepler Straße and Schneppenhorstweg.

Maria Regina Martyrum ⊘ – Ⓤ 7 *Jakob-Kaiser-Platz.*
Without its campanile and golden cross, this edifice would not look like a church. In the churchyard, there is a bronze set of the *Stations of the Cross (Der Kreuzweg)* along the wall. The lofty church nave is a large concrete and wood rectangle decorated with a frieze at the back of the altar.
To the right of the church, along Heckerdamm, a panel shows the map of a large **"Laubenkolonie"** ("allotments colony"), a network of alleyways and straight narrow paths lined with sheds surrounded with tiny lovingly tended gardens. In summer,

the *Laubenkolonie* are permeated with the fragrance of a multitude of flowers; they form part of the enjoyable activities which Berliners go in for during their leisure time.

Gedenkstätte Plötzensee ⓥ – *If you do not have the use of a car, we would advise you to take a taxi in front of Maria Regina Martyrum Church (the number to call is indicated on a pillar: 345 76 50; it will cost you roughly 20 DM). If you are on foot, follow Heckerdamm, Friedrich-Olbricht-Damm. A small panel indicates Plötzensee along Hüttigpfad.*
Inside the perimeter of this prison, more than 1 500 opponents of the Nazi regime were executed.

IN THE VICINITY

See **SPANDAU★, TEGEL★★**.

SPANDAU★

Spandau

See map of Berlin Conurbation, 10, **AU**

Like its counterpart Köpenick, Spandau one of those towns of Greater Berlin which have retained their specific character testifying to a long history.

REFUGE AND PRISON

Slav origins – The islands, formed at the mouth of the Spree by the numerous arms of the Havel, were used as defensive positions as early as the Stone Age. A ford decided the site of the city where some Slavs settled in the 8C. It was the capital of the **Stodor** district *(Gau)* and it became an important cultural and economic centre, which controlled the waterways and trade route leading to Köpenick south of the Spree and linking Magdeburg with Kiev.

German settlement – The first consequence of the German settlement under Otto I who established a feudal fort *(Turmhügel)* as part of a first line of defence, was to lead to an uprising of the Slavs in **983** and to the destruction of the village. Rebuilt in the 11C, it had 250 inhabitants.
Spandau is first mentioned in a donation recorded in **1197** *(facsimile displayed in the local history Museum, see below)*. At that time the Margrave of the Northern March, **Albert the Bear,** conquered Brandenburg and German colonisation made considerable progress in the Spree valley.

The princes' fortress – The trade route shifted slightly northwards, following what is now Nonnendamm, and went through Berlin which quickly eclipsed Spandau. However, the fortress remained one of the favourite residences of the Ascanian margraves. The **Juliusturm** was erected at the beginning of the 13C; it received the treasure and the archives. During the second half of the 14C, a palatial edifice *(Palas)* was joined onto it; Jewish tombstones were used in its construction. Emperor Charles IV stayed in it and the *Great Land Book (Landbuch)*, which he commissioned, specified that all the Berlin mills, representing an important source of income for the margrave, were to be administered from Spandau.
Prince **Joachim II** of the House of Hohenzollern chose the city as a place of refuge, because it was conveniently linked to Berlin by waterways. A new **fortress** was built between 1560 and 1594. In 1567, he organised a kind of game, the "club war" and asked Berliners to launch an assault agains Spandau, but the latter resisted victoriously. The margrave was so furious that he had the tower of St Nicholas bombarded and the mayor imprisoned.
The withdrawal of the French army in 1813 had catastrophic consequences: 3 000 men took shelter inside the fortress which was besieged for two months by Russo-Prussian troops. The town was severely bombarded.

Hitler's heir – Born and brought up in Egypt, **Rudolf Hess** was one of the first followers of Hitler with whom he took part in the Munich Putsch in 1923. In 1939, the Führer named him his second official heir after Goering. In May 1941, Hess flew secretly to Britain, most probably in an attempt to seek a separate peace treaty. His plane crashed in Scotland. Taken prisoner, he was condemned by the Nuremberg Tribunal to life imprisonment. He remained a prisoner in Spandau military prison (now razed to the ground and replaced by a shopping centre), situated in the British sector, for 42 years; he committed suicide in 1987. Between 1935 and 1945, the fortress served as a secret laboratory for experimenting with various gases.

★ZITADELLE *Allow 1 hour*

U *7 Zitadelle, exit Zitadellenweg; continue west along Am Juliusturm for 200m. The red brick fortress and its gateway can be seen behind the trees, on the right-hand side.*

In 1559, the cities of the Brandenburg March had to pay between 14 000 and 20 000 thalers for the construction of a new fortress; brickyards were set up nearby. Work began under the supervision of an Italian engineer, **Francesco Chiaramelle da Gandina**, once commissioned by the Republic of Venice. The fortress had all the characteristic features of a Renaissance citadel and was the most modern defensive work in the region, which did not prevent it from being siezed by the Swedes during the Thirty Years War. Whilst the Austrians camped in front of Berlin during the Seven Years War (1756-1763), the Queen and the Margravine of Bayreuth, Frederick II's favourite sister, found refuge there together with the royal silverware. A curved pediment bearing coats of arms decorates the gateway.

Stadtgeschichtliches Museum Spandau ⊘ – *Entrance immediately to the right; go up to the first floor. Time: 45mn.*
There is more to read than to see: a collection of Prussian helmets; panels and models illustrating the evolution of fortifications from the medieval *Burg* (the fortress has been reconstructed to look as it did during the second half of the 15C) to the bastions designed by Italian engineers; utensils, ceramics, arms and documents, maps; and a brief survey of the local fauna and flora (the fortress is inhabited by owls, falcons and martens). A hand-operated mill has been reconstructed – around 1200, watermills were unknown east of the Elbe; this hand-operated mill produced a very coarse type of flour which contained chips off the grindstone and could injure the palate and spoil the teeth.

The **Juliusturm** was built in brick over a granite base. It was used as a defensive redoubt and then as a prison until 1876. Its first prisoner was the robber baron **Dietrich von Quitzow** *(see TEGEL)*. Others included Joachim II's widow, detained on the orders of her son; the wife of a war minister dismissed by the King-Sergeant who, for two days each week, was deprived of food, bed and light (she remained a prisoner for one year); one of Frederick II's servants who poisoned his hot chocolate during the Seven Years War (another servant, who had a similar idea, spent 23 years in a dark cell); and even F.L. Jahn, the initiator of gymnastics *(see NEUKÖLLN)*; all endured the same fate. Near the museum exit there is a spiral staircase leading to the top of the tower, which has a beautiful timber frame: good **view★** of the historical centre of Spandau dominated by the tower of St Nicholas's Church and that of the town hall *(the sloping path situated immediately to the right of the museum door leads back to the courtyard).*

The courtyard of the fortress, lined with recent buildings *(one of them houses a collection of cars, ask at the museum ticket office)* is used as a setting for temporary events. Walking west along the moat provides a view of the very interesting **King's bastion**.

Entrance and moat of the citadel

> ### A wandering engineer: Rochus Guerini, Count of Linar (1525-1596)
> Chiaramella's successor was a native of Tuscany, where his father had taken refuge after a quarrel had ended in bloodshed *(Blutfehde)*. Having entered the King of France's service, he took part in the defence of Metz and was entrusted with the mission of erecting a citadel. He lost an eye *(see his portrait)* during the course of a battle. Converted to the Protestant faith, he was compelled to leave France and served various German princes, including the Elector of Saxony, for whom he supervised construction of the Dresden fortifications. After being the victim of several plots, he entered the Elector of Brandenburg's service in 1578; his duties included the supply of munitions, the maintainance of all artillery gear, the arsenals and fortresses, in particular the Spandau fortress. In addition to this, he wrote *Articles about the Construction of Fortresses (Artikel für den Festungsbau,* 1578) and continued to serve the Elector of Saxony, the landgrave of Hesse, the prince of Anhalt and the Count Palatine of the Rhine. He also designed the building separating the two courtyards of Berlin Castle and worked on the Köpenick and Grunewald castles. Not satisfied with the deployment of such tireless energy, he reorganised the salt monopoly and became *Salzdirektor,* a position he held until his death. He was buried beneath his altar inside St Nicolas's Church, in the presence of the Elector John-Sigismund.

★ALTSTADT SPANDAU *Time: 1 hr*

U *7 Altstadt Spandau.*

Walk along the avenue Am Juliusturm; soon after the bridge, follow Behnitz Street which leads to the **locks.** Joachim II ordered them to be built in 1556. Owing to the proximity of the Citadel, they only allow medium-sized ships to pass between the Hohenzollern Canal and the lower Havel.

The old town of Spandau has retained some features which the centre of Berlin has lost such as the rows of old houses on either side of Carl-Schurz-Straße, the town's main shopping street. **Ackerbürgerhaus,** also called "Wendenschloß" *(Kinkelstraße 35, on the corner of Ritterstraße),* which dates from 1681 and was rebuilt in the 60s, Benn Hotel in Ritterstraße and the house next door *(Ritterstraße 1, on the corner of Carl-Schurz-Straße)* are old timber-framed houses. The physicist Ernst Ludwig Heim lived from 1776 to 1783 *(plaque)* in another house in Reformation Square (Reformationsplatz). In the same square stands **St Nicholas's Church** (St-Nikolai-Kirche), **(V¹)** ⊙, in brick Gothic style; the tower, surmounted by a Baroque steeple, was for a long time the highest tower in the March. Joachim II's monument, placed in front of the entrance, is a reminder that it was in this church that he was converted to the Reformation and the whole of his State with him. Next to E.L. Heim's house, an excavation can be seen behind a shop window, revealing a private well dating from Frederick II's reign, once currently used in public inns.

The market square marks the centre of the city; a little further on stands the imposing and severe looking **town hall** (Rathaus Spandau) **(R)**. Spandau was granted its charter in 1230, before Berlin.

★**Zeppelinstraße Estate** – This amazing estate (1926) shows all the various aspects of Expressionist decoration: oriels, corbels and triangular windows, zigzag motifs, all enhanced by polychromy. The **Falkenseer Chaussee** crossroads seems to have come straight out of a film. It is, however, only a façade, as the design of the houses in the estate is traditional.

Go back along Zeppelinstraße and take the bus to Gartenstadt Staaken.

★**Gartenstadt Staaken** – The residential estate designed by Paul Schmitthenner between 1913 and 1917 is his answer to the densely populated *Mietskasernen* of the late 19C. Curved streets, small low houses with a maze of tiny back gardens *(Am Langen Weg),* gabled houses inspired by Hanseatic buildings, either brick-built *(Heidebergplan)* or roughcast and preceded by short flights of stairs *(Zwischen den Giebeln,* which means "between the gables"), enhance the impression of a small idyllic yet closed community. The square in front of the church is simple and charming, but the sound of aircraft and trains spoils these harmonious surroundings.

IN THE VICINITY

See **HAVEL★★, OLYMPIASTADION★**.

STEGLITZ★

Steglitz

See map of Berlin Conurbation, ⑩, **BV**

Some of the streets of this residential district, lined with villas, are among the most pleasant and charming in Berlin. The panoramic restaurant, Bierpinsel, a blue and red mushroom-shaped tower (1972-76), dominating the access to the ring road, is the emblem of the district. Schloßstraße, which is the continuation of Rheinstraße in Friedenau *(see SCHÖNEBERG)*, is a particularly busy shopping street near the town hall.

A VERY ANCIENT PAST

Around 10 000 BC, mammoths, bison and rhinoceros, whose bones were discovered during the excavation of the Teltow canal, used to graze on the plateau of the same name, thus attracting groups of hunters who settled there. Traces of a Bronze Age village (1100-100 BC) were also found. A basin for offerings had been fitted out in the hollow trunk of an oak tree. It contained several hundred clay receptacles filled with honey, cereals and spices. Discoveries from the Iron Age include a Germanic urn field dating from the 2C and 3C AD. Villages were founded around 1225, at the time of the German occupation of the area. In 1920, Lichterfelde, Lankwitz, Südende and Steglitz (which was the largest Prussian village with 93 000 inhabitants) are now a part of Greater Berlin.

MAIN SIGHTS

Wrangelschlößchen – *Schloßstraße 19;* Ⓤ *9 Schloßstraße.* The general, nicknamed "Daddy Wrangel", who restored order in Berlin after the 1848 revolution, used to spend the summer in this small castle, built in 1804 for Karl Friedrich von Beyme *(see WILMERSDORF)*. Designed by **Heinrich Gentz**, it is the only specimen of Neoclassical architecture inspired by Claude-Nicolas Ledoux and Etienne-Louis Boulée *(Revolutionsarchitektur)* remaining in Berlin, since Gentz's famous Mint in Werderscher Markt *(see SCHLOSSPLATZ)* has now disappeared.

Rathaus Steglitz (**R**) – Ⓢ *1,* Ⓤ *9 Rathaus Steglitz.*
Good example of neo-Gothic architecture. Some of the streets at the back of the town hall are lined with beautiful *Jugendstil* houses *(decorated with plant and animal motifs)*. Quite near, in Südstraße *(go under the motorway bridge)*, there is an interesting neo-Gothic post office.

★**Lichterfelde West** – Ⓢ *1 Lichterfelde-West.*
One of the owners of Lichterfelde, a village founded *c*1225 at the time of the German occupation of the area, was Nikolaus von Béguelin. In 1747 he became the revered tutor of the future Frederick-William II. The king ennobled him, then bought the estate and gave it to him.

In front of West Lichterfelde Station

The first railway line from Berlin to Potsdam (1837-38) by-passed the village until **Johann Carstenn** built an estate consisting of individual houses (1865). A small station was then built in the style of an Italian villa. It was also here that, in May 1881, **Werner Siemens** tested the world's first electric tramway.

Outside the station, one is pleasantly surprised to find a charming light opera setting which includes the *West-Bazar* (1897) and houses with timber-framed gables, turrets and finials. Shaded streets lined with villas, such as **Curtiusstraße**, are very attractive. The **Local History Museum** *(Museum Steglitz at No 64a Drakestraße.)* contains (**M³³**) a drawing-room furnished in *Biedermeier* style.

"The Migrating bird from Steglitz" (Steglitz Wandervogel)

The excursions committee was founded in the cellars (which in Germany are often used as restaurants) of the Steglitz town hall, by an A level student, Karl Fischer. This modest association which longed for a rural lifestyle, away from the developing industrial civilisation, organised long-distance hikes. It grew in importance, was recognised around 1903 and became the *Frei-deutsche Jugend* (Free German Youth Movement) in 1913. It was dissolved by the Nazis in 1933 and founded a second time after the war *(Karl-Fischer-Bund)*.

The **parish church** *(Dorfkirche)*, dating from the 14C, was remodelled in 1939; the steeple is made of wood. The nearby neo-classical **castle** *(Hinderburgdamm 20, c1780)* which was the starting point of the Lichterfelde estate, has been renamed "Carstenn-Schlößchen" ("Small Carstenn castle").

Lilienthalpark – The hill commemorates **Otto Lilienthal**'s first free flight; he killed himself on his *2 000th attempt*.

IN THE VICINITY

See **DAHLEM★★★, SCHÖNEBERG★, TEMPELHOF.**

TEGEL★★
Reinickendorf
See map of Berlin Conurbation, **⑩**, **ABT**

Tegel, a pleasant little town to visit, is on the banks of the Havel where it widens into a lake.

HISTORICAL NOTES

Traces of human presence go back a long way, since around 8000 BC tribes from the northern part of the Berlin area settled along the **Tegeler Fließ** (which flows into Tegel harbour), a stream which appeared after the last ice age and was the only means of communication between north and south, through the forest. These men were nomadic reindeer hunters who watched out for reindeer herds travelling through in springtime. In the autumn they erected tents shaped like teepees (14 different camps have been discovered, *see REINICKENDORF, Local History Museum)* near the ford, in the narrowest part of the valley. The first village appeared around 1100 BC; it was later occupied by the Germans. At the beginning of the 14C, the Tegel watermill was one of many such mills along the Tegeler Fließ; together with the village of Tegel, it belonged to the Benedictine monastery in Spandau.

It is no easy task to catch a Quitzow... – Around the year 1400, many of Berlin's citizens owned agricultural land on the outskirts of town. It was the time when the robber baron **Dietrich von Quitzow** and his brother Johann plundered the countryside, robbing merchants and burning villages. For a time, they were the protectors of the towns of the March on behalf of Berlin. On 3 September 1410 they went through the Jungfernheide Forest, which was much larger than the present park *(see SIEMENSSTADT)*; they came out into the open without warning and stole the cattle grazing in front of Berlin's fortifications. The shepherds immediately warned the citizens, who were outraged and rushed in pursuit of the thieves. The latter were hindered in their progress by the animals, who ended up quenching their thirst near the Tegel mill, roughly where the Alter Fritz Inn *(see below)* is now. Some of the robber barons hid behind the mill while the rest tricked the citizens into believing they were retreating. The first group then fell upon the citizens and took sixteen prisoners, including the Council's President, **Niclas Wyns**, who spent a year in one of Quitzow's castles before being released for a ransom. Dietrich von Quitzow was delighted to hold this particular prisoner, whose brother Martin Wyns, mayor of Frankfurt-on-Oder, had rejected him when he had asked for his daughter's hand in marriage.

The Humboldt Brothers' House – **Alexander von Humboldt** (1769-1859) was a geographer and a cosmopolitan traveller who ended up knowing 40 languages. He lived in France for more than 30 years. His brother **Wilhelm** (1767-1835), who was also a linguist, helped to restore Prussia's power. As a high official in the Home Office, and then in the Ministry of Education, he precipitated foundation of the Berlin University *(see UNTER DEN LINDEN)*, which was named after him, and supported freedom of teaching, thus encouraging progress. In 1819, the prevailing reactionary climate forced Wilhelm to resign his official position. He retired to Tegel castle, which he had inherited *(see WEISSENSEE)*, whilst Alexander "could not get over his longing for Paris". He invited **Schinkel**, who had met the Humboldt family during his stay in Rome, to refurbish his manor house. The edifice, which houses the collection of antiquities brought back from the Eternal City by Wilhelm when he was a diplomat there, was one of the first public museums in Prussia.

Wilhelm and Alexander von Humboldt

Experiencing total freedom – During the summer of 1922, three teachers, including W. Blume, who had adopted the new ideals of the youth movement *(see STEGLITZ, box on the Wandervogel)*, settled on **Scharfenberg Island** and founded a boarding-school for 22 Tegel students. It was only one of many such experiments carried out in an attempt to rescue education in Prussia, but it lasted longer than any other and was encouraged by the authorities until 1933. The teaching principles were new: no classrooms, no marks, no reports, no timetable and no punishment, just a permanent commitment towards others. Groups identified by different colours were formed as the students arrived, and all of them learned together. Lessons took place in the open air and were based on a common theme, which was continued for several weeks. An old barn was soon turned into a refectory and a dormitory. There were small workshops next to the garden whose upkeep was a useful exercise in physics and biology and also served to improve eating conditions. This ideal miniature society soon became the prey of the Nazis who imposed an authoritarian, hierarchical system. In 1941, the island was turned into a military drill-ground.

STROLLING THROUGH TEGEL

★Tegeler Hafen – **Ⓤ** *6 Alt-Tegel. Starting from the underground station, walk towards the northwest along Berliner Straße.* The **IBA 87** (1985-87) project is has a playful side to it. Variegated pavilions stand in front of an S-shaped building, while some taller buildings conceal courtyards which look like cloisters surrounding gardens. Water and nature are everywhere (it is possible to stroll along the Tegeler Fließ and join up with the Greenwichpromenade). Note the Humboldt Library which forms part of the project and is reflected in the waters of the Tegeler Fließ. The dimensions are moderate but there is a feeling this architecture is intended more for pleasure than to serve a real urban purpose.

Alt-Tegel – The intersection of Berliner Straße, Gorkistraße and Alt-Tegel is a busy shopping area. **Alt-Tegel** is a pedestrian street, lined with cafés and restaurants as well as a double row of trees. **Greenwichpromenade★** is quite pleasant in spite of being lined with ordinary buildings. It is more enjoyable to follow the edge of the lake which offers a lovely **view★**. The Tegel Harbour **Bridge** (Tegeler Hafen-Brücke) is an elegant piece of engineering in red-painted metal.

★★Tegeler See – Just before you reach **Greenwichpromenade**, you will see a great number of panels mentioning the various boat trips available from Tegel Lake to Nieder-Neuendorfer See, Berlin or Wannsee *(imminent departures are announced, all you have to do is ask for the price)*. The average boat trip on **Tegeler See** lasts *2 hours* *(allow 4-5 hours to Berlin or Wannsee)*. On the way, you can spot the **Borsig villa,** hidden behind trees, and **Tegel beach** (Freibad Tegeler See) equipped with slides. The boat follows an interesting route round the southern part of the lake, among small islands and at the meeting point between the lake and the Havel, in the little community of **Tegelort**, the water's edge is lined with small houses, sailing boats lying alongside their moorings, and café-cum-restaurants. The Upper Havel power station (Kraftwerk Oberhavel) and its high chimney can be seen at **Heiligensee**, towering above the river which is less developed there.

★**Schloß Tegel** (**X**) ⊘ – This manor house dating from the Renaissance *(entrance is through the Renaissance part of the house)* was extended and remodelled by **Schinkel** using local materials. The architect retained the 16C building to which he added a loggia and rectangular corner turrets decorated with pilasters and figures representing the gods of the winds, inspired by the Tower of the Four Winds in Athens. The Neoclassical interior *(guided tour; tickets for sale in the kitchens; go round the castle in a westward direction)* is very light and airy and plain: the austere rooms are painted with pastel colours; most of the statues are reproductions.

Tour – The **library** was **Alexander von Humboldt**'s study. The two female busts belong to a group of three Graces brought back from Greece by an officer in Napoleon's army. The **staircase** is decorated with extremely fine paintings by Schinkel *(note the first floor loggia)*. The **Blue Drawing-Room** used to be decorated with numerous family paintings by some of Schinkel's contemporaries. The **Antiquities Room** housed the first collection of antiquities open to the public prior to the inauguration of the Old Museum *(see MUSEUMSINSEL)*. Alexander von Humboldt supervised the return of the objects stolen in Italy by Napoleon. As a token of his gratitude, the pope gave him the interesting **head of the Rondanini Medusa**. The three small marble **reliefs** found their rightful place again after the fall of the Wall. In the **study**, there is a statue of Carolina von Humboldt in the guise of Psyche (1810) by Thorvaldsen.

"Der Alte Fritz", "Die Alte Waldschenke" – These two ancient inns are housed in lovely timber-framed buildings.

Alt-Heiligensee – The village comprises houses concealed by greenery, streets covered with old paving-stones, and an attractive church surrounded by a churchyard. *If you wish to bathe in the Heiligensee, you should take the bus Strandbad Heiligensee.*

Tegelort – Follow the path along the bank, generously lined with restaurants; ferry to Hakenfelde, Saatwinkel and the islands of Valentinswerder and Marienwerder.

A USEFUL SIGHT

Flughafen Berlin-Tegel – One of the characteristics of Berlin's airports is that they are relatively central. This is true in the case of Tempelhof, but also in the case of Tegel, located on a former rifle-range turned into an airstrip for **Count Zeppelin**'s airships at the beginning of the 20C. In 1931, Professor Oberth tested the first rockets there, with Werner von Braun's help. It was during the Berlin blockade that the site became an airport. Tegel has been West Berlin's main airport since 1976. **Schönefeld**, East Berlin's former airport, has been chosen to replace Tegel in 2006, once it has been extended.

IN THE VICINITY

See **REINICKENDORF, SPANDAU★**.

TEMPELHOF

Tempelhof

See map of Berlin Town Centre, **8**, **9**, **JKYZ**

The various sights offered by this vast district are fairly spread out. The area has played an important role in Berlin's recent history.

FROM THE KNIGHTS TEMPLAR TO THE BLOCKADE

Rural connections – A commandery of Knights Templar gave its name to **Tempelhof**. Peasants settled under the protection of the Knights Templar in **Mariendorf** and **Marienfelde**, both named after the Virgin Mary, patron of the order.
In 1800, the southern part of Berlin was not yet urbanised: a path lined with poplars and inns (including the popular Cave Obscure) leads to the village of Tempelhof.

The astrologist of Margrave Joachim I (1499-1535)

The deplorable state of his finances explains the tyrannical behaviour of the Margrave, who became very unpopular. In 1522, he had a young astrologist brought to his court. The young man predicted that Berlin would be engulfed by floods on 15 July 1524. On the morning of that day, the Elector and his court went up to the top of Tempelhof Hill in order to observe the phenomenon. Nothing happened. On the way back, a coachdriver and four horses were struck by lightning.

The Ullstein Empire – The Ullstein Brothers Group, which included five newspapers, four weekly and ten monthly periodicals, was, together with **Mosse** and **Scherl**, one of the main publishing houses in Berlin. It initiated the concept of modern magazines with the *Berliner illustrierte Zeitung*, a periodical with a large circulation and the only one to enjoy nationwide distribution. Some remarkable journalists were employed by the group but their articles could not compete with those of the heavyweight of the reactionary press, **Hugenberg**, which became Hitler's sponsor. Once the Nazis were in power, the press was silenced (the number of newspapers was halved) and followed instructions from the ministry of propaganda. The Ullstein and Mosse empires, which belonged to Jews, were bought for an absurdly low sum and liquidated. Even the old *Tante Voss*, which was almost a hundred years old, ceased publication.

"The islander keeps on hoping / That his island will once more be joined to the continent." – With these words, the music-hall singer Klaus-Günter Neumann, who had once performed in the Katakombe, summed up Berlin's situation during the **blockade** enforced by the Soviets between 24 June 1948 and 12 May 1949. Agreements signed in 1945-46 had only specified the conditions of access by air to the western sectors of the capital. Three corridors had been granted. The United States devised *Operation Vittles* and from 25 June they established an **airlift** with American and British planes. This saved the city from starvation, but the people were compelled to relive the end of the war, with its curfew, restrictions, errands on foot or on bicycle. Unemployment increased; the mayor, **Ernst Reuter,** made a speech before the Reichstag; however, inside the besieged town, the Allies became friends and the recently created FRG (Federal Republic of Germany) sided with the western powers. The airlift continued until 30 September 1949. During the 462 days it lasted, 944 000 tons of coal, 224 000 tons of food supplies and the parts needed to build a complete power station *(see SIEMENSSTADT)*, were transported to Berlin; 16 000 tons of *Made in blockaded Berlin* goods were exported; it cost the lives of 79 people. Berliners never forgot this gesture nor the taste of dehydrated food and chocolate bars brought in by "sweets bombers" *(Rosinenbomber)*.

TALLANDIER

At the beginning of the cold war, the airlift ensured Berlin's freedom

MAIN SIGHTS

Platz der Luftbrücke – U *6 Platz der Luftbrücke.*
This is probably the most polluted crossroads in Berlin, owing to particularly dense traffic. The **Airlift Monument** (Luftbrückendenkmal) is a memorial to this important episode in the cold war, which increased West Berlin's isolation within Communist territory. It well deserves its nickname: "the fork of hunger" *(Die Hungerharke).* It was on the first anniversary of the airlift that Ernst Reuter gave its present name to the crossroads in front of Tempelhof Airport.

Dudenstraße 10 – U *Platz der Luftbrücke.*
The building housing the Association of Printers (Verbandhaus der Buchdrucker), erected in 1925-26 by Max Taut and Franz Hoffmann, marks the beginning of the New Objectivity (particularly in the courtyard, where concrete is visible).

Flughafen Tempelhof – U *6 Platz der Luftbrücke.*
Opened in 1924 and extended by the Nazis, this airport was intended to be an important feature of Hitler's *Germania.* The megalomaniac hugeness of the circular part testifies to the frame of mind of a man who wanted to build "edifices such as no one has built for 4000 years". One of the runways was supposed to be lined up with the Kreuzberg monument. The airport is now restricted to short distance flights (Prague, Warsaw, Riga, Strasburg, Copenhagen).

Polizeihistorische Sammlung (M[13]) ⊘ – *Enter the Police headquarters (Polizeipräsidium), in the centre of the airport's west wing. The attendant will tell you which way to take: go through the hall on the left; go down the stairs immediately on the right, behind the glass door (on the landing: model of the first traffic lights in europe, on Potsdamer Platz); the museum entrance is then indicated.*
This small police museum offers detailed information about the history of the Berlin police with its ups and most of all its downs, for it is concerned with the dregs of humanity: uniforms, explanatory panels about daily life, instruction, history and social events, decorations, arms etc. The creation of a police force gave the Hohenzollern a new opportunity to curtail the prerogatives of the municipal council. The **Polizeidirektorium** was founded by Frederick III in 1693, at the time when Berlin and Cölln merged with the suburbs of Friedrichswerder, Dorotheenstadt and Friedrichstadt. In 1718, the King-Sergeant appointed the first police inspectors and created a special force instructed to keep a close watch on taverns engaged in prostitution and to fight against fraud. In 1787, new regulations compelled prostitutes to spend a few months in a workhouse and to sweep squares and bridges. Smoking was forbidden owing to the risk of fire. The political police force, which watches foreign residents and diplomats, was set up during the reign of Frederick II and placed under the leadership of Kircheisen. The military police force was founded in 1812, and later a distinction was made between the **Schupo** (*Schutzpolizei:* police) and the **Kripo** (*Kriminalpolizei:* the CID). After the 1848 revolution, the *Kripo* was reorganised by Hinckeldey. The first Black Maria was seen in 1866; it was called "**grüne Minna**" ("green Minna"). The exhibits include the original uniform of "the Captain of Köpenick" (*see under that name*).

An inflexible commissioner

Between 1848 and 1856, Berlin was controlled by the chief constable and then by the commissioner of police and head of Prussian security, **Carl Ludwig von Hinckeldey** (1805-1856), who crushed the Democratic movement during the revolution. This was a test from which the police, reorganised along the lines of its London counterpart, emerged even stronger: 2000 "privileged strollers" wandered through the streets wearing a blue uniform and a black hat and armed with a sabre. Hinckeldey established a repressive system based on censorship, searches and denouncements. The Democratic movement and the reactionaries were both under threat. The aim was to maintain order. Gaming houses favoured by the nobility also came under attack from the police and there was a raid in a very select club. Hinckeldey's rigorous approach made him popular with the liberal middle class. In the same way as it happened in Paris with Baron Haussmann, the State, through Hinckeldey, used dictatorial powers to control growth and deprived municipalities of all means of action. Road repairs and cleaning, fire fighting: Berlin gradually became a thriving metropolis but, for economic reasons, wealthy districts were privileged at the expense of northern and eastern working-class areas. Hinckeldey was killed in a duel with an aristocrat, supposedly for a question of honour: "The middle class, civil servants and all the citizens are inclined to side with Hinckeldey because they hate *Junkers,*" said Karl August Varnhagen von Ense. More than 100000 Berliners followed his funeral procession.

The room concerned with the Nazi period, when parallel police forces (Gestapo, Goering's police and Lichtenberg cadets) increased in number, deals with sombre events. The post-war period, during which the police were used for mine-clearing operations, is illustrated by uniforms, masks, murder weapons (and disturbing photographs of victims) and even a periscope used by the curious.

Siedlung Neutempelhof – Ⓤ *6 Paradestraße.*
The middle-class apartment buildings dating from the beginning of the 20C, which line the shopping street Manfred-von-Richthofen-Straße, correspond to the first type of housing designed for the "Tempelhof Fields" (*Tempelhofer Feld*). Neutemplehof garden-city developed after World War I (1920-28). It offers a striking contrast with Dudenstraße, for it is just like being in the countryside!

★**Ehem Reichspostzentralamt** – *Starting from Tempelhof* Ⓤ *6 Station, follow Ringbahnstraße for 300m going west.*
Imposing Expressionist façade (1925-28) in purple brick *(pay particular attention to the doorways).*

Tempelhofer Damm – Ⓤ *6 Alt-Tempelhof.*
Tempelhofer Damm is a busy shopping avenue on either side of **Alt-Tempelhof**. The Old Park (Alter Park) and Tempelhof village church *(Dorfkirche Tempelhof)* form a charming setting: a church with a timber-framed steeple, set among trees beside a small lake.
For the following sights, see map of Berlin Conurbation, ⒒, **CV**.

Ullstein-Druckhaus (**Z**) – **Tempelhof Harbour** (Hafen Tempelhof) offers an industrial landscape dominated by the buildings of **Ullstein Printing Works★**. This red brick fortress (1925-26) with its clock tower is quite impressive in spite of being only 80m high. It was the largest printing concern in Europe and the highest concrete building on the continent. The back of the building consists of a huge brick wall.

Alt-Mariendorf – Ⓤ *6 Alt-Mariendorf.*
The interesting little **Museum of Local History** ⊘ (Heimatmuseum Tempelhof) (**M³⁴**) stands next to the village church. It illustrates the history of Berlin from the Middle Ages to the 19C, and also deals with the tragic events of the 20C: Tempelhof as a drill-ground and airfield; the sinister Gestapo prison, Columbiahaus; the airlift. A kitchen and dining-room from the *Gründerzeit* period have been reconstructed.

Lichtenrade – Ⓢ *2 Lichtenrade.*
The S-Bahn provides a glimpse of the neo-Renaissance gables of the **Malt-house** (*Steinstraße 40-41*). The **village church** (Dorfkirche), stands in a charming setting, its steeple rising above willow trees on the edge of a pond.

★**Marienfelde** – Well-preserved street village with a serie of houses and farms. The granite **parish church**, standing in the middle of its close-cum-churchyard, is simple yet attractive; it is the oldest church in Berlin. There is an imposing front porch and the tower has a saddleback roof.

IN THE VICINITY

See **KREUZBERG (West Part)★★**, **NEUKÖLLN**, **SCHÖNEBERG★**, **STEGLITZ★**.

TIERGARTEN★★

Once situated on the outskirts of Berlin, the vast green open space of Tiergarten is today one of the lungs of the capital. Strolling about is quite pleasant during the day: there are lawns, woodland, quiet paths, winding lanes, ponds and small lakes. At weekends, Turkish families organise barbecues, and all open air enthusiasts do the same. At night, it is the local counterpart of the Bois de Boulogne in Paris, with large areas reserved for prostitution. Evenings can become heated, even dangerous.

A FASHIONABLE PLACE FOR A STROLL

From hunting-ground to drill-ground – Around 1650 the forest west of Berlin at the end of Unter den Linden avenue *(see under that name)* laid out at the same time was turned into a wild animal preserve, surrounded by a fence and stocked with deer and grouse. It had been an enclosed hunting ground since the reign of Joachim I (1499-1535). This "animal garden", or Tiergarten, was deforested at the time of Frederick-William I and used as a parade-ground; it became "Berlin's Sahara". Every year, large crowds applauded the royal regiment parade.

"The Tents" – Frederick II wished to turn it into a "leisure park for the people". Tiergarten was converted into a landscape-garden by the court gardener **Sello** (Lenné continued his work during the first half of the 19C) and a popular destination for outings. In 1740, two Huguenots were granted a permit to erect some tents in the park with a view to serving refreshments in summer. A fellow-countryman followed in their steps and founded an establishment called *The Tents* which gave its name to the place (the word tent is *das Zelt* in German; an avenue near the *Kongreßhalle* still bears the name *In den Zelten*). Bandstands, merry-go-rounds and swings standing next to popular dance halls contributed to the popularity of Tiergarten which, by that time, was the "Berliners' favourite haunt for a stroll". Aristocrats and members of the middle class strolling side by side were represented in **Chodowiecki**'s etchings. In March 1848, *The Tents* became for ten days the focus of revolutionary unrest as Berliners discovered the thrill of democracy: ideas were exchanged, quarrels flared up, citizens congregated and wrote an appeal to the king, asking him to guarantee basic liberties.

Imperial pomp – **William II** was very fond of sculpture: "In my kingdom, everything is larger than life". He had ugly monuments, often mocked by Berliners, erected all over the capital. For instance, he had Victory Avenue (Siegesallee) laid out across Tiergarten from the column of the same name over a distance of 700m. On either side of the yew-lined avenue, the emperor's favourite sculptor arranged thirty-two monuments made of Carrara marble, a gift from the Kaiser to his capital, which represented the monarch's glorious ancestors, each one accompanied by two statues of the prince's friends. Ordinary people marvelled at what they called the "dolls". Tiergarten's trees were far more useful to Berliners when they were felled at the end of World War II to provide heating for the city's population during two hard winters.

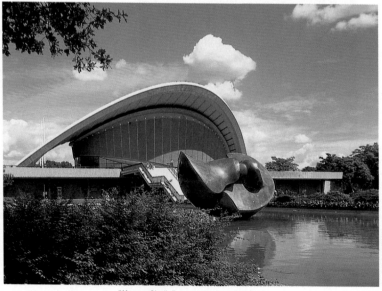

"Kongreßhalle", now a cultural centre

Ph. Gajic/MICHELIN

THE NORTHERN PART OF TIERGARTEN

★**Reichstag, Platz der Republik, Sowjetisches Ehrenmal** – *See REICHSTAG.*

Hansaviertel – Ⓤ *9 Hansaplatz.*
The tower blocks in this model district (5 000 inhabitants), which are all different and scattered among greenery, were designed by famous architects: the Finn Alvar Aalto, the Bresilian Oscar Niemeyer, the Frenchman Le Corbusier and the German Walter Gropius for the 1957 Architectural Exhibition. They were based on the principle that everyone should be able "to live in the city centre with plenty of light, air and sun" *(Im Herzen einer Weltstadt in Licht, Luft und Sonne leben)*, but they are less convincing today. The district has been equipped with modern amenities: two churches (Kaiser-Friedrich-Gedächtniskirche, St-Angar-Kirche), a school, a kindergarten, a small shopping centre, a cinema, a library, a theatre and the Academy of Arts (Akademie der Künste) (**Q**). There are interesting views of the tower blocks lining Bartningallee, on the corner of Hanseatenweg. The **English Garden**★ (Englischer Garten) is lovely: lanes wind round the pond, amidst bamboo and flowers. It goes close to **Bellevue Castle** Park.

Schloß und Park Bellevue – Ⓢ *Bellevue; No 100* Ⓑ *Schloß Bellevue.*
This 18C castle (1785) built for Frederick the Great's younger brother has a harmonious Neoclassical façade. It is the official residence of the Federal Republic's President.

★**Haus der Kulturen der Welt** (**V**) ◷ – *No 100* Ⓑ *Kongreßhalle.*
The former **congress hall** (ehem Kongreßhalle), nicknamed "The pregnant oyster" *(Schwangere Auster)* was a present from the Americans on the occasion of the 1957 International Architecture Exhibition. The roof, which appears to be floating but actually rests on the two outside pillars, collapsed in 1981 and was rebuilt in 1987 for the city's 750th anniversary. The **bronze** sculpture (1956) placed in the middle of the pool is by Henry Moore. The "House of World Cultures" (Haus der Kulturen der Welt), which is the forum of non-European cultures, has been holding numerous events there since 1989. There is a **chime** nearby.

Straße des 17. Juni – *No 100* Ⓑ *Großer Stern.* Great Star Square (Großer Stern), which is the converging point of eight avenues, was created in the 18C, at the time when Tiergarten was being laid out. The sixteen sandstone sculptures, which used to decorate it, were nicknamed "the dolls". The **Victory Column** ◷ (Siegessäule), surmounted by an allegorical figure, known to Berliners as "Golden Else" *(Goldelse)*, was erected on the Royal Square *(Königsplatz)*, opposite the Reichstag, to commemorate Prussian victories of 1864, 1866 and 1871. Measuring 67m in height, it was transferred to the Great Star Square in 1938. It served as an optical relay along the triumphal axis which led from Unter den Linden to Exhibition Park, where the Nazi authorities planned to build a university. The climb is tiring but the **panorama**★★ is exceptional and extends towards East Berlin, Moabit, the Hansa District *(Hansa Viertel)* and Kreuzberg.

THE SOUTHERN PART OF TIERGARTEN

★★★**Zoologischer Garten** – *see under that name.*

Schleuseninsel – Ⓢ *Tiergarten or* Ⓢ + Ⓤ *Zoologischer Garten, then skirt the zoological gardens westwards.*
The large variegated pipes of the experimental station run by the Technical University's Institute of Hydraulic Construction

"Gold Else" on top of the Victory Column

Ph. Gajic/MICHELIN

and Shipbuilding look like a sculpture. Under the bridge, there is a plaque in memory of **Rosa Luxemburg**, who was murdered and thrown into the canal in this particular spot.

The path which skirts the north bank of the Landwehrkanal (Tiergartenufer) is lit with lampposts from various European towns.

Neuer See (Lichtensteinbrücke) – **Karl Liebknecht** was executed here in 1919, at the end of the Spartakus uprising.

The assassination of the Spartakus leaders

In **January 1919**, the members of the Spartakus movement left the USPD and founded the Communist party (KPD). Setting aside parliamentary procedure, they went into action. **Rosa Luxemburg** disagreed with this as she thought the time was not ripe. "The whole of Berlin looks like a bubbling witch's cauldron in which violence and ideas are whirling round" (Count Kessler). The Social-Democrat government set about to crush the movement with the help of volunteers recruited by the military staff, who doubted the troops' reliability for the reason that they were too easily influenced by events in the street. Special regiments were created; **Gustav Noske**, who called himself the "bloodthirsty dog" was given the task of eliminating the centres of insurrection. Revolutionary committees were led by Spartakus member **Karl Liebknecht** and the Communist Wilhelm Pieck, but the Social-Democrats held government buildings. Noske prepared to regain control from the outside. His units of volunteers entered Berlin and recaptured the buildings held by Spartakus members with extreme brutality. On the 15th, Karl Liebknecht and Rosa Luxemburg were assassinated in Tiergarten. The body of the latter was found months later in the waters of the Landwehrkanal. These murders, which were the first of a long list, tended to justify assassination as a political means, since those responsible were protected.

Rousseau- und Luiseninsel – The walk along the bushy shores of the Tiergarten lakes is a pleasant one. There are lovely flower-beds in front of Queen Louise's monument.

★★★Kulturforum – *See under that name.*

IN THE VICINITY

See **KULTURFORUM★★★, KURFÜRSTENDAMM★★, POTSDAMER PLATZ, UNTER DEN LINDEN★★, ZOOLOGISCHER GARTEN★★★.**

TREPTOW
Treptow
See map of Berlin Conurbation, **11**, **CDUV**

Spread over a large area, wooded and still relatively rural (particularly around Königsheide), this district has no major sights to offer. The Wall was not far from here. Buildings are being stripped of the GDR's brownish roughcast and gradually given a face lift.

HISTORICAL NOTES

Treptow was the last stage before Berlin along the Köpenick Road (Köpenicker Landstraße) which went through fertile land rich in silt. Frederick II founded settlements in Schöneweide, Adlershof and Johannisthal. Inns and cafés made the place popular, but there were only 60 inhabitants at the beginning of the 19C. Industrialisation changed all that. Large private houses were erected alongside Treptower Park in the second half of the century, and the façade of the new town hall modelled on them.

MAIN SIGHTS

Treptower Park – Ⓢ *6, 8, 10 Treptower Park.*
Deforestation of Cölln Heath (Cöllnische Heide), which has belonged to Berlin since the 13C, began in 1840, with the exception of two places including Treptower Park, laid out between 1894 and 1896. The industrial exhibition (Gewerbeaustellung) was held in the park and it became an important meeting-point for the Social-Democrats. In 1911, August Bebel and Karl Liebknecht made speeches here about the growing danger of war. The **Soviet Memorial** (Sowjetisches Ehrenmal) (**A¹**) is a reminder of the enormous sacrifices made by the Red Army. It takes up a large

area within Treptow Park. A methodical design gave this open space an imposing dimension thus creating an almost holy atmosphere. Allegorical figures of kneeling soldiers frame the entrance to the esplanade. At the other extremity, there is a hill surmounted by the effigy of a soldier holding a child, with his sword pointing downwards. The mosaic decorating the base is a tribute to the USSR and the Red Army. The texts engraved on the bas-reliefs, in German and Russian, which sum up the main episodes of the war, are by Stalin.

An exit makes it possible to go behind the hill and see the Carp Pond (Karpfenteich). The Archenhold Observatory (Archenhold Sternwarte) is being restored.

Insel der Jugend – A charming bridge framed by a pair of towers gives access to this small island. There is a view of the two huge stacks of the **Klingenberg power station**, built during the mid-twenties in anticipation of electrification of the S-Bahn. It was placed on the banks of the Spree in order to have a constant supply of cooling water as well as a suitable port for the delivery of coal. *Enter Plänterwald Park.*

★**Spreepark** – This leisure park has a Ferris wheel, a roller coaster and a water slide.

Plänterwald – *Follow the path along the Spree.* Barges gliding along the river form a melancholy landscape. On the opposite bank, taken up by various industries, note the Oberschöneweide Broadcasting House (Rundfunkgebäude), one of the broadcasting stations of GDR Radio.

Arboretum (**B**²) – Ⓢ *6, 8, 9, 10, 45, 46 Baumschulenweg.*
The Institute of Biology of Humboldt University is housed in Franz Späth's House where he lived from1874 to 1913. The horticultural farm, founded in 1720 started to spread to the meadows between Alt-Treptow and Johannisthal in 1864. The school of tree cultivation (Späthsche Baumschule) was founded the same year. It gave its name to Baumschulenweg and stimulated its development. This walk will be of interest mainly to botanists.

Niederschöneweide – Ⓢ *6, 8, 9, 10, 45, 46 Schöneweide.*
A settlement known as *Auf der Schönen Weide* ("on the lovely meadows") was founded at the end of the 18C near the site of the present Oberspree Station; twenty people lived there in 1858. Industrialisation modified the aspect of the river banks. *Spreesiedlung* Estate (1930-32; Hainstraße) is dilapidated but the scenery and the walk along the Spree are remarkable. There are views of the imposing industrial landscape on the opposite bank, in Oberschöneweide.

Adlershof – Ⓢ *6, 8, 9, 45, 46 Adlershof.*
Within the urban sector situated northeast of the station, buildings which were neglected at the time of the GDR, are being restored and their façades are once again as smart as they were at the turn of the century.

Wissenschafts- und Wirtschaftstandort Berlin-Adlershof (WISTA) – Ⓢ *6, 8, 9, 45, 46 Adlershof.*
Between Johannisthal and Adlershof, a scientific town will be developed until 2003 over an area of 76 hectares, round a vast park which used to be the training-ground of Stasi regiment. This pole of development will include the research and economic institutes of most large German industries (200 companies and 14 research institutes are already there), as well as studios, workshops, high-tech industries (chemicals, electronics, medical technology), the natural science faculty of the Humboldt University and the BESSY particle accelerator. Thirty thousand researchers will work there and a residential district for 15 000 people has also been planned.

★**Oberschöneweide** – *Starting from* Ⓢ *6, 8, 9, 10, 45, 46 Schöneweide, take No 61 or 67 tramcar to Wilhelminenhofstraße/Edisonstraße et Rathenaustraße.*
An uninterrupted row of industrial buildings stretches along the Spree River, between Rummelsburg and Oberschöneweide, in the district of Köpenick. The Oberschöneweide **industrial complex**★★ is one of the finest in Berlin. It includes a large **AEG building** on the corner of Edisonstraße and Wilhelminenhofstraße, comparable to those in Moabit and Wedding *(see under those names)*. The renovation project known as "Spree Knee" (Spreeknie) concerns Wilhelminenhofstraße as well as the beautiful edifices of the KWO cable company, built in ochre-coloured brick. The **Rathenau villa** surrounded by a park has been preserved at No 76-77.
Standing at the end of the street is the **Peter-Behrens Bau**★ (**C**²), the former headquarters of the largest audiovisual equipment company in the GDR, called Werk für Fernsehelektronik (hence the *WF* sign at the top of the tower). Go into the base of the tower then turn immediately left; ask the caretaker if you want to go upstairs and see the **hall**, a lofty arcaded room covered with a glass roof.

IN THE VICINITY

See **KÖPENICK**★★, **KREUZBERG (East Part)**★★, **NEUKÖLLN**.

UNTER DEN LINDEN★★

This wide avenue, originally lined with four rows of walnut and lime trees and whose name **Unter den Linden** means "under the lime trees", was laid out in the mid-17C (1647) at the beginning of Frederick-William's reign. The new aristocratic district it goes through, **Dorotheenstadt,** which had not yet been built, was named after the Great Elector's second wife. Its growth (it only obtained its urban charter in 1674) was due to the Huguenots *(see GENDARMENMARKT).* During the reign of **Frederick II,** the old houses lining the avenue were replaced by uniform four-storeyed residences (the standard height imposed at that time); moreover, the construction of the "**Forum Fridericianum**" and of many palaces (Prince Henry's Palace, Crown Prince's Palace, Princesses' Palace) is a clear indication that the town centre was moving west. Unter den Linden began to look like a royal avenue, lined with numerous cafés: the National, the Royal, the Imperial, the Café Richard, the favourite haunt of persons of private means. Today, the avenue has no beginning and no end. **Pariser Platz** and its prestigious embassies, which used to surround the Brandenburg Gate, has not yet been rebuilt and, at the other end, the castle to which the avenue formed a stately approach, has disappeared. However, there are still many monuments left, that symbolise the history of the town and of Prussia.

BERLIN'S PRESTIGIOUS AVENUE

The visit starts at the Brandenburg Gate and ends at Castle Bridge (Schloßbrücke).

★★**Brandenburger Tor** – 🚇 *1, 2, 25, 26 Unter den Linden; No 100* 🚌 🚇 *Unter den Linden.*
This symbol of the division of Berlin and of Germany was built between 1789 and 1791 by **Carl Gotthard Langhans,** who took as a model the Propylaeum of the Acropolis in Athens. The gate is surmounted by the **Quadriga** by **Johann-Gottfried Schadow,** led by a Victory who recovered her eagle and her iron cross after 1989 following some controversy, since these warring attributes were designed by Schinkel at the request of King Frederick-William III, when the *Quadriga* came back on 7 August 1814. The king had created the Iron Cross the year before. However the *Quadriga* was originally designed with peaceful intentions. The Victory faced the city as a symbol of the triumph of peace. Hitler had it turned towards the west to express his lust for conquest. It was on the occasion of the 1814 Paris Treaty, which sealed Napoleon's defeat and the end of the German "Wars of Liberation", that Frederick-William I's "**Square**" became the **Pariser Platz.** Situated near the Wilhelmstraße district where government edifices were once concentrated *(see POTSDAMER PLATZ),* the square was lined before the war (and this will no doubt be reinstated in the near future) by the French Embassy housed in a Classical-style mansion (1883), the British Embassy, the American Embassy (mansion where Marshal Blücher lived, at No 2) and the famous Adlon Hotel *(see below).* These edifices formed, with others built in the *Beaux-Arts* style, including the house of the artist Max Liebermann, an elegant gateway to the historical centre.

Adlon Hotel – The most famous palace-hotel in pre-war Berlin. Charlie Chaplin stayed there in 1931.

Botschaft der Russischen Föderation (**A**¹) – *Unter den Linden 63-65.*
The Russian Embassy, in rigid Stalinian style (1950-53), has 334 rooms. It stands on the site of a former palace which had housed the Russian Embassy since 1837.

Schadowhaus (**C**²) – *Schadowstraße 10-11.* This Neoclassical house was the home of the sculptor **Johann-Gottfried Schadow,** who was the artist responsible for the stucco work on the ground floor.

Komische Oper (**T**¹⁶) – *Behrenstraße 55-57.* Erected in 1947 on the ruins of the *Metropoltheater,* it has not kept its original façade, rebuilt in 1967 in true GDR style.

Intersection Unter den Linden / Friedrichstraße – 🚇 + 🚇 *Friedrichstraße or* 🚇 *6 Französische Straße.*
This crossroads situated at the heart of Dorotheenstadt was a very busy intersection between the two world wars. The six-storeyed stone buildings are decorated with colossal pilasters or engaged columns. Elegant boutiques occupy the ground floor. **Switzerland House** is still there. In 1825, the court confectioner who was a native of Austria set up shop at the crossroads. His café rapidly became the rendez vous of Berlin's fashionable circles.

Deutsche Staatsbibliothek (**B**²) ⊘ – *Unter den Linden 8.* Founded in 1661 by the Great Elector, the library was transferred by Frederick II, who had enlarged its collections, to the curved building of the *Forum Fridericianum (see below).* Schinkel's project was never realised. The new Prussian National Library was built between 1903 and 1914 by von Ihne, the architect who designed the Bode Museum, in the same pompous style as the latter.

Gouverneurhaus (G²) – This former governor's residence was a municipal tribunal from 1808 onwards. The façade has been moved to the site of a palace destroyed during the war. The building belongs to the Humboldt University.

Denkmal Friedrichs II (D¹) – A monument was already planned during Frederick II's lifetime. Schinkel made many different drawings of such a monument to be erected either along Unter den Linden or near the castle. **Christian Daniel Rauch**, a student of Schadow, was finally commissioned to do the work in 1836 but the monument was only completed in 1851; it was taken as a model for other monuments (which grew in size and monstrosity such as William I's monument standing in front of the castle's main gate, nicknamed by Berliners "the emperor in the lions' den"). Between 1951 and 1980, Frederick mounted on his war-horse was exiled in Potsdam.

★**Forum Fridericianum (Bebelplatz)** – *No 100* 🚌 *Deutsche Staatsoper*. Frederick II's ambitious town planning project for Berlin included an opera house, a new palace and a fine arts academy.

★**Staatsoper Unter den Linden** (T¹⁷) – This was the only part of the project to see the light of day (1741-1743), at a time when no opera house had yet been built in France, to comply with the specific wishes of the sovereign who, according to Voltaire, secured the services of "the finest singers and the best dancers" out of his own privy-purse. **Knobelsdorff** erected an elegant Corinthian portico, which makes the building look like Apollo's temple, separated for the first time from the royal palace. The inauguration took place before the work was completed, in cold muddy weather and, for this occasion, a performance of *Caesar and Cleopatra* by Carl Graum was given, with **Carl-Philipp-Emmanuel Bach**, Johann-Sebastian's son, playing the harpsichord. The opera house, in which the Italian dancer Barberina *(see Schloß CHARLOTTENBURG, Knobelsdorff Wing)* delighted the king who paid her as much as three ministers, and the school of music formed the core of Berlin's musical tradition. The stalls could be removed and the hall used as a ballroom.

Alte Bibliothek★ (1775-1781) – It occupies the site originally intended for the academy. The building's convex façade corresponds to the King's request to have it modelled on a curved chest of drawers, as it is aptly nicknamed by Berliners today. It is in fact inspired by plans for the Hofburg in Vienna which was built on a grander scale a long time after its Prussian copy. It was reputed to hold 160 000 volumes at the end of the 18C.

Altes Palais – It was built in 1834-37 next to the library. The future king William I resided there.

St.-Hedwigs Kathedrale (F¹) – Berlin's Roman Catholic cathedral (1747-1773) was built for a community whose importance was constantly growing in Prussia. St Hedwige was the patron of Silesia and Frederick II, who had just conquered this

The Brandenburg Gate

> ### "Wherever books are burnt, men will eventually be burnt"
> ### (Heinrich Heine)
>
> A plaque commemorates the dreadful *auto-da-fé* which took place on **11 May 1933**, when students threw into a bonfire thousands of books by "non-German" authors. In reality, the books did not burn very well until firemen poured petrol onto the fire. The students formed a human chain in order to throw whole packs of books into the flames, accompanied by noisy cheering from the crowd, whilst someone read aloud the names of the authors concerned and what they were being blamed for. After Marx and Kautsky, came the names of nineteen writers: Heinrich Mann and Erich Kästner, Sigmund Freud, Werner Hegemann, Theodor Wolff, Erich Maria Remarque, Alfred Kerr, Kurt Tucholsky and Karl von Ossietzky… At midnight, Goebbels arrived and made a speech on the emergence of a new order.

province, thought it a clever move on his part to dedicate an edifice to her. The shape of the building is inspired by that of the Pantheon in Rome, but a legend has it that it looks more like an upside-down cup.

Humboldt-Universität – *Unter den Linden 6. Nos 100* 🚌 *Deutsche Staatsoper*.
The palace of Prince Henry, Frederick II's brother, was planned as part of the Forum Fridericianum, but by 1766 only the main courtyard had been built. The building became an annex of the new university founded in 1810. **Wilhelm von Humboldt** *(see TEGEL)* had conceived the project in 1807. The university was named after Frederick-William. The philosopher Johann-Gottlieb Fichte *(see the INTRO-DUCTION, The Burden of History)* became the university's first dean; lectures were given by about 50 professors: among them, the lawyer Savigny, the philosophers Schleiermacher then Hegel, and the historian Ranke who aroused the enthusiasm of young students such as Schopenhauer. The university developed, particularly after 1815; it ranked first among German universities and enjoyed a great deal of independence. Its teachers spurred German patriotic fervour. Students became part of the Berlin landscape along with their brawls and multi-coloured clothing. Although they date from 1913-20, the present buildings were inspired by the Classical style in fashion at the time of Frederick II. The modern university, whose personnel was entirely renewed after the Wall came down, accommodates 20 000 students.

Neue Wache – *Nos 100* 🚌 *Deutsche Staatsoper*.
It serves as the FRG's official monument in memory of the victims of war and tyranny. Frederick-William II had the building erected between 1816 and 1818, according to

drawings by **Schinkel** who introduced four re-entrant angles to give it the shape of a Roman camp. The Victories of the entablature, made of zinc, are the work of Gottfried Schadow. The building had two storeys (as the side windows show) and it housed the royal guards until 1918. In 1931 it became a "monument in memory of soldiers killed during World War I". Restored in 1960, it was turned into a "memorial to the victims of Fascism and militarism". From 1969 onwards the building housed the mortal remains of an unknown soldier from the battlefields and of an unknown prisoner from a concentration camp. An enlarged reproduction of Käthe Kollwitz's sculpture: *Mother with her Dead Child* stands in the middle of an impressive void.

Maxim-Gorki Theater (T¹⁸) – *Am Festungsgraben 1/2; at the back of the Neue Wache*. As soon as it was founded in 1791 by the virtuoso harpsichord player Carl Fasch, the **Academy of Singing** (Singakademie) showed signs of a promising future. At the time of the founder's death, 147 choristers, who came mainly from middle-class backgrounds, gave recitals at the Academy. His student, Karl Friedrich Zelter, housed the choir in the elegant building designed by Schinkel and offered the public the possibility of rediscovering Bach's works under the baton of **Felix Mendelssohn-Bartholdy**. In 1848, the new National Assembly of Prussia sat in the Academy. Next door is the Palais Am Festungsgraben.

Ph. Gajic/MICHELIN

BERLIN
HISTORIC CENTRE

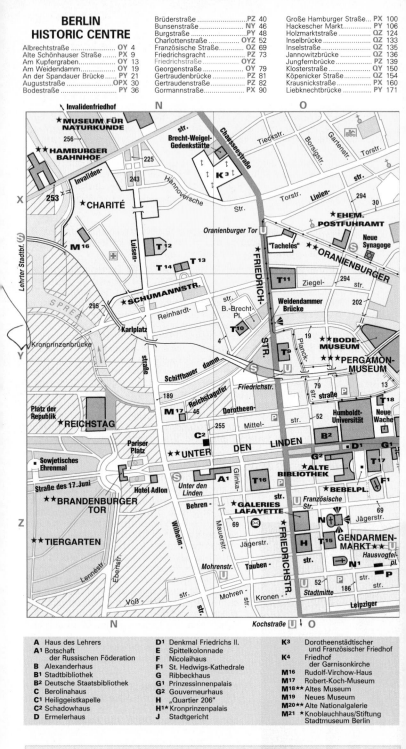

To each social class its own pastimes

During the Wilhelmian period, high society, which included the aristocracy and the upper middle-class, was a small social group numbering fewer than 2 000 people. It had its favourite haunts: the Kaiserhof Palace, the salon of the wife of the knighted Jewish banker Paul von Schwabach, the Bauer café, where aristocrats went after the opera. The pastimes of the working class were simpler: the beach at Wannsee, Hasenheide, the Kaisergalerie in the town centre *(see FRIEDRICHSTRASSE)*, cafés on street corners.

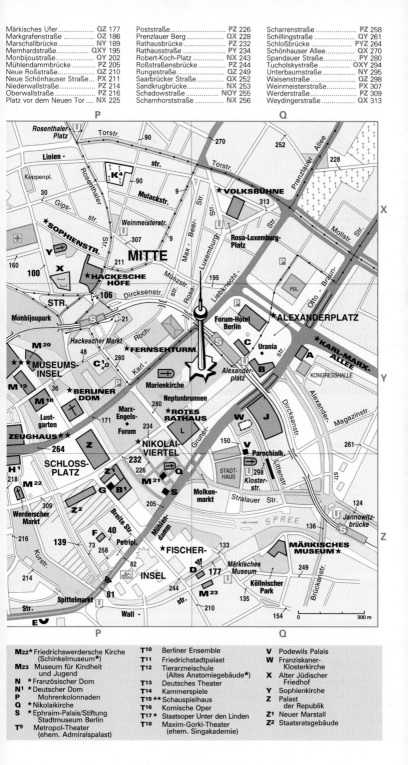

M22★ Friedrichswerdersche Kirche
(Schinkelmuseum★)

M23 Museum für Kindheit
und Jugend

N ★ Französischer Dom

N1 ★ Deutscher Dom
Mohrenkolonnaden

Q ★ Nikolaikirche

S ★ Ephraim-Palais/Stiftung
Stadtmuseum Berlin

T9 Metropol-Theater
(ehem. Admiralspalast)

T10 Berliner Ensemble

T11 Friedrichstadtpalast

T12 Tierarzneischule
(Altes Anatomiegebäude★)

T13 Deutsches Theater

T14 Kammerspiele

T15★★ Schauspielhaus

T16 Komische Oper

T17★ Staatsoper Unter den Linden

T18 Maxim-Gorki-Theater
(ehem. Singakademie)

V Podewils Palais

W Franziskaner-
Klosterkirche

X Alter Jüdischer
Friedhof

Y Sophienkirche

Z Palast
der Republik

Z1 Neuer Marstall

Z2 Staatsratsgebäude

★★ Zeughaus – *Unter den Linden 2. Nos 100* 🚌 *Deutsche Staatsoper or Lustgarten.*
The façades of Berlin's most handsome Baroque monument have been repainted
a pale pink. The construction of the edifice began in 1688 under the supervision
of the Huguenot military engineer Jean de Bodt and the Dutchman J.A. Nering,
with later contributions from Andreas Schlüter. The building was completed in
1730. A knowledge of German is needed to read the very interesting panels in the
German History Museum★★ (Deutsches Historisches Museum) which offers a remarkably
well-illustrated journey through the country's fascinating history. Simple and

Eduard Gaertner, Unter den Linden (1853) / From left to
the opera house and

clear information, which does not attempt to render less abhorrent the nation's sometimes heavy heritage (a frank approach which is repeated in many exhibitions). In the courtyard, there are 22 **grotesques** sculpted by **Andreas Schlüter** and his students, which represent the faces of dying soldiers.

Prinzessinnenpalais (**G¹**) – *Oberwallstraße 1-2.*
This palace was entirely rebuilt to house a café *(Operncafé, see ON THE TOWN, the Berlin Scene).*

★**Kronprinzenpalais** (**H¹**) – *Unter den Linden 3.*
The royal apartments, with their splendid furnishings, and the salons are open to visitors. The concert hall is a particular favourite, with a view overlooking the lake on three sides, as is the Eastern chamber.

★**Schloßbrücke** – This is another of **Schinkel**'s works (1821-24) which replaced the wooden "Dogs' Bridge"; it is set askew and unusually wide. The statues of warriors guided by Victories are a little pompous but the bronze reliefs decorating the parapet, with tritons and dolphins, are typical of Schinkel's elegant style.

★**Friedrichswerdersche Kirche** – *See SCHLOSSPLATZ.*

IN THE VICINITY

See **FRIEDRICHSTRASSE★, GENDARMENMARKT★★, MUSEUMSINSEL★★★, SCHLOSSPLATZ, TIERGARTEN★★**.

J.P. Anders/Nationalgalerie - Preussischer Kulturbesitz

: the university, the castle (now gone),
erick II's memorial monument

WANNSEE★★

Zehlendorf

See map of Berlin Conurbation, **10**, **AV**

This "country" resort situated between one of the arms of the Havel, the Großer Wannsee, and Düppel Forest is a popular destination for pleasant outings. There are numerous villas and a choice of walks for nature lovers which include forest trails and the first of a series of royal castles and parks.

HISTORICAL NOTES

Heinrich von Kleist (1777-1811) and the romantic crisis – Towards the end of Frederick II's reign, Prussian society came to a standstill: the aristocracy monopolized all the interesting positions; the absence of university education prevented social promotion and deprived Berlin's younger generation of a suitable start in life. The young therefore became fascinated with everything that was irrational. The various strata of society, including the court, were contaminated by mysticism; an uncontrollable passion for gambling spread everywhere whilst mesmerizers, healers, visionaries and prophets proliferated. The young middle-class elite, looking for recognition, turned to literature. From October 1810 to March 1811, **Heinrich von Kleist** was the news reporter for the evening newspaper, *Berliner Abendblätter*. This news coverage was the first of its kind in Berlin and it launched the newspaper. Kleist got hold of his information directly from his friend **Justus Gruner** who had reorganised the police. Among other news items, he reported on the wrongdoings of Horst's gang of incendiaries (Horst'schen Mordbrennerbande) who held the March to ransom. He probably did not suspect that he would himself become hit news. In November 1811, the bodies of the playwright and of his friend Henrietta Vogel, who followed him into death, were recovered in the waters of the small Wannsee. The *Berliner Abendblätter* is no longer printed. Tormented and rebellious at the same time, Kleist symbolised a generation which had lost its sense of purpose and had been sacrificed.

The "final solution to the Jewish problem" – One hundred and sixty thousand out of a total of 500 000 German Jews lived in Berlin, mainly in Wilmersdorf, Charlottenburg and the Mitte District. They worked in industry and trade or belonged to the professional classes.

Wannsee beach

1 April 1933 – Jews were gradually excluded from all economic activities. Their shops were boycotted; administrations, businesses, department stores, newspapers and publishers dismissed or were forced to dismiss their Jewish employees; bankers, barristers and doctors were no longer allowed to practise.

1935 – The **Nuremberg laws** deprived the Jews of their civil rights. Mixed marriages were forbidden and the right to go to the cinema, cultural institutions, sports grounds, beaches and fairgrounds was denied. The Jewish Cultural League, closely watched by the Gestapo, was encouraged to emphasise the difference between Jewish and "Aryan" cultures. Humiliations and persecutions inflicted daily were intended to chase the Jews out of Germany against payment of a "tax for fleeing from the Reich" and the surrender of all possessions (in particular the numerous apartments situated in western residential districts). In 1938, there were still 140 000 Jews left in Berlin.

9 November 1938 – The **Night of the Broken Glass** *(see ORANIENBURGER STRASSE)*, a nationwide pogrom on a huge scale, was organised after the assassination of a member of the German embassy in Paris by a desperate young Polish Jew. Shops were plundered, synagogues burnt, and 91 persons murdered. Those who were arrested swelled the prisoners' ranks in **Sachsenhausen** concentration camp, which had been set up two years earlier near Oranienburg. Jews were made to sweep the pavements strewn with broken glass. The rest of the population mostly remained passive.

1941 – The survival of the Jewish community became more and more problematic: it was impossible to leave Germany and all Jews had to wear the star of David; living conditions were almost unbearable. Massive deportations began even before the **Wannsee conference** took place. The first train load left on 18 October from **Grunewald Station**. Alois Brunner's "Jewish police" put up a desperate fight. There were two resistance groups: the Chug Chaluzi network which organised escape routes and the "Jewish cell" (with the young Communists Herbert and Marianne Baum).

RELAXING IN WANNSEE

★★Strandbad Wannsee (D²) – Ⓢ *1, 3, 7 Wannsee.*
The facilities on this large beach along the bank of the Havel, which was inaugurated in 1907, are good examples of the New Objectivity architectural style (1929-30). Sport and health were among the social concerns of the Weimar Republic. Wannsee is the largest inland beach in Europe; fitted with huts, terraces, a covered walk and shops, it is a very popular attraction *(animals and portable radios are forbidden)*; however bathing is better in Schlachtensee. On the opposite bank is the villa in which the Wannsee conference took place in January 1941.

Kleistgrab (E²) – *Walk along Kronprinzweg starting from the S-Bahn station; cross Königstraße and turn slightly left into the small Bismarckstraße.* The extremely plain grave merely consists of a stela carved with the name of the poet.

"Because National-Socialists, with their technique of unscrupulous imposture, were careful not to show how extreme their intentions were, before people had been hardened. They applied their methods with caution; doses were increased progressively, and there was a short pause between each dose. They never gave more than one pill at a time, then they waited for a moment to make sure that the effect had not been too strong, that the conscience of the world could still stand the last dose." (Stefan Zweig, *Yesterday's World*).

Am großen Wannsee – This curved street, shaded by trees, is lined with substantial villas (and numerous rowing clubs):

– Coloniestraße 3, on the corner of Am großen Wannsee: this is the place where the artist **Max Liebermann** worked *(note the inscription on the entablature)*. Opposite, Am Großen Wannsee 39-41.

– Small yellow brick mansion at No 52.

– At **No 58, Wannsee Conference Memorial** (Haus der Wannsee-Konferenz) **(F²)** ⊘ – This imposing villa on the edge of the river was the venue, on 20 January 1941, for the conference at which the decision was taken to apply "the final solution to the Jewish problem", i.e. the extermination of the Jews in occupied Europe, which was the inevitable outcome of the Nazi ideology.

★**Heckeshorn** **(G²)** – Next to No 58 there is a small promontory with a platform offering a pleasant **view**★ of the Großer Wannsee and Wannsee Beach. There is also a convenient restaurant and a snack bar. The Flensburg Lion (Flensburg is a town in the northern German region of Schleswig-Holstein) commemorates a Danish victory during the struggle for the possession of the duchies in 1864 *(see the INTRODUCTION, The Burden of History)*. Victory having been followed by defeat, the lion was taken as a trophy but given back in 1945. The Wannsee Lion is a copy.

The walk along the Havel (Uferpromenade) is popular at weekends. It leads to Peacock Island.

★★**Pfaueninsel** **(AV)** – *See map of Potsdam and surrounding areas* **(GT)** – *Time: 3 hrs. A shuttle ferry service links the island to the shore.*

Peacock Island used to be called Rabbit Island. **Frederick-William II** (1786-1797), nicknamed "Fatties" by Berliners, who was disliked by his uncle Frederick II because of his dissolute lifestyle, became the talk of the town through his numerous marriages. The small **castle**★ **(GT)**, which is a fake ruin, was built as a setting for the love-affair between the king and the beautiful **Wilhelmine Enke,** the daughter of a court trumpet-player. The love-affair, sumptuous presents and the fact that the favourite was made countess of Lichtenau, gave rise to sarcastic comments from the people. However the castle was only completed the year the king died.

★**Castle** ⊘ – The footbridge linking the towers was made in the Royal Ironworks *(see CHARITÉ)*. The small statue of the actress **Rachel,** standing in front of the entrance is a reminder that in July 1852 she recited extracts from the French

Peacock island shelters several birds of that species

Ph. Gajic/MICHELIN

theatrical repertoire in front of Frederick-William IV and his brother-in-law, Tsar Nicholas I. The **interior★** is simple, elegant yet exotic (the tearoom is next to the "Tahitian Cabinet"); it has not changed since 1800. The ground floor was reserved for the royal family, the first floor for the king. It is also possible to see the bedroom of Queen Louise, who liked to stay on Peacock Island.

★★ Park – It contains peacocks as well as cormorants. The landscape garden was used as a menagerie *(see ZOOLOGISCHER GARTEN)*. A palmarium, a kind of large green-house in oriental style, was its most fantastic building.

The estate is studded with follies such as Switzerland House, the charming **Gothic dairy★ (Meierei)**, situated at the northwest extremity of the island *(view of the forest, Grunewald Tower and Teufelsberg)*, a false ruin which offers a contrast between white roughcast and red bricks; the original porch of Queen Louise's Mausoleum *(see Schloß CHARLOTTENBURG)* and the **Knights' House (GT)**, built by Schinkel, who reused the façade of a Danzig Gothic house bought by the king.

In the centre of the park, there is an aviary stocked with golden pheasants, macaws, cockatoos *(one of them enjoys having his neck stroked)* and peacocks.

Take the ferry back to Wannsee and follow Nikolskoer Weg.

The sights described below are located on the map of Potsdam and surrounding areas (**FGTU**).

★ Nikolskoe – The religious fervor of a Prussian princess made her wish to hear bells in this spot, at the highest point of a vale which offers a **vista★** of the Havel. This is how the lovely **St Peter and St Paul's Church** came to be built. **Blockhaus Nikolskoe** Restaurant, built in wood in a similar style to that of the Alexandrovna Estate *(see POTSDAM)*, has a terrace with a splendid **view★★** of Peacock Island and the Havel.

Moorlake – Walk down to the river to see Moorlake creek, a popular bathing place, lined with inns and restaurants.

Sacrow – *See HAVEL.* A few benches and a kind of peninsula brings **Heilandskirche** nearer; this small neo-Romanesque basilica looks as if it were built on water (the same architect erected Friedenskirche on a similar site in the Sanssouci Park). The **view★★** extends from Peacock island to the two square towers of the Belvedere, seen above the wooded top of Pfingstberg *(see POTSDAM)*. The border between East and West ran through the middle of this narrow channel in the Havel.

★★Volkspark Klein-Glienicke (Klein-Glienicke Estate) – The village is mentioned for the first time in 1375 under the name of *Parva Glinik* (in Slavonic language: "sandstone place" or "land of clay") in the *Landbuch* of Emperor Charles IV. A hunting-lodge belonging to the Elector Frederick-William, was turned into a military hospital during the reign of the King-Sergeant and in 1816 became the property of Chancellor Hardenberg. In 1824, it was bought by Prince Charles, the brother of Frederick-William III, who had the park laid out by **P.J. Lenné.**

The architect of the Prussian royal gardens

Peter Josef Lenné (1786-1866) came from a long line of horticulturists from Bonn. With Schinkel, he changed the face of Berlin during the first half of the 19C. However, his masterpiece was the shaping of the Potsdam landscape. In 1833, he made plans to embellish the Potsdam environs. He also embellished the banks of the Havel, creating new pathways, supervising the planting of trees, the laying out of meadows, linking the different parks to the rivers and the surrounding fields. After being a civil servant in Potsdam since 1816, he became general manager of the royal gardens in 1854.

Tour – Is there a more attractive place than Klein-Glienicke? The park, which is alpine and dark in the north, becomes Italian and light in the south, studded with small plain castles and refined buildings. It is one of the best examples of Lenné's work. The walk along the Havel leads to the **Hunters' Gate (Jägertor)**, built in Tudor style (1828), and the **Devil's Bridge (Teufelsbrücke)**. A little further on, the elegant **Maschinenhaus** is an introduction to Italian taste. Leave the estate and approach the river in order to see the façade of the **casino★ (C)**: with its terraces, pergolas and two protruding wings, on either side of the façade, it is one of the most exquisite of Schinkel's creations. There is a romantic **view★** of the Pfingstberg and of the Belvedere towers (here too, the Wall ran in the middle of the water). The **Big Curiosity★** (Große Neugierde) **(D)**, an elegant rotunda built a year after Glienicke Bridge (1835) and supported by 18 cast iron Corinthian columns (note the detailed work on the gilt balustrades), offers a splendid **view★** of Babelsberg Park and Castle. The peaceful atmosphere of the park is slightly disturbed by traffic noise from the road linking Berlin to Potsdam via Glienicke Bridge *(see POTSDAM)*. There are some strange column fragments on the lawn, next to the Big Curiosity.

Glienicke Castle★ is plain, in Biedermeier style, with its green shutters (a graceful fountain with a broken pitcher stands in front). The Lions Fountain enhances the view of the castle from the street. Note the refinement of the neo-Greek

Griffin gateway

decoration, even on the **gatehouse** (Pförtnerhaus) (**K**), adorned with caryatids, which is adjacent to the southeast entrance to the park; the gate is guarded by two gilt griffins. The **Small Curiosity** (Kleine Neugierde, 1825) (**E**) was made to look like a tent; there is a view of Potsdam and the dome of St Nicholas's Church.

Go across Königstraße.

★**Glienicker Brücke** – This is the famous "Spy Bridge", a metallic structure built in 1905-07, which marked the frontier between East and West, and was used when spies from both sides were being exchanged. A wooden bridge had, linked Potsdam Island to the village of Glienicke since 1660.

Jagdschloß Glienicke – This neo-Renaissance building is now a school. From the garden alongside the Havel, there is a **view**★ of Babelsberg Castle, Potsdam, Glienicke Bridge and, immediately opposite, the much talked-about residential blocks built in 1995.

IN THE VICINITY

See **HAVEL**★★, **GRUNEWALD**★★, **POTSDAM**★★★.

WEDDING★

Wedding

See map of Berlin Town Centre, **3**, **4**, **HJKRS**

"Wedding the Red", the bastion of Communism is, like Moabit and Neukölln, one of Berlin's working-class districts and one of the most interesting to visit for those who wish to get a taste of daily urban life. Between 1945 and 1990, Wedding formed part of the sector occupied by the French and, like Kreuzberg, it represented a kind of outpost of the Western zone facing the East. Neglected by visitors, Wedding offers nevertheless a choice of sights and green open spaces. The quality of its homes, which are unpretentious but well designed, is the essence of Wedding's quiet charm.

HISTORICAL NOTES

An important civil servant employed at court founded a dairy (Meierei) in Wedding at the beginning of the 17C. It was purchased by the Elector and became a small agricultural concern (Vorwerk Wedding) administered by the Mühlenhof *(see NIKOLAIVIERTEL, Mühlendamm)*. Farmers from Vogtland (Saxony) settled there during the reign of Frederick II. They often went back home in winter, but they supplied the town with fresh fruit, vegetables, milk and butter. There were many watermills along the Panke, including a paper-mill, owned by a certain Schulze, who was given the title of Court Purveyor. The reforms concerning freedom of trade, initiated by Hardenberg and von Stein, encouraged Wedding's industrial growth. The mills, which were the forerunners of steam engines, provided energy for home as well as industrial flour-milling and sword and knife sharpening. The Panke water-mill (Wassermühle an der Panke) was bought by the state in 1803 and used to supply energy to the Royal Iron-works *(see CHARITÉ)*. In 1825, there were 22 windmills in Wedding; it was the highest concentration of windmills on the outskirts of Berlin; competition was ruinous. In the mid 19C, Wedding's landscape revealed a mixture of windmills, tanneries, tile-works and glue factories. In 1861, Wedding became part of Berlin.

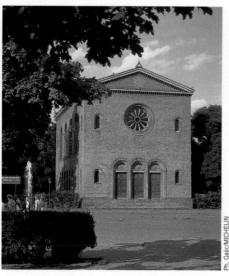

The church of Nazareth

MAIN SIGHTS

The visit is centred round two separate places: the **U** *6, 9 Leopoldplatz Station and the* **U** *8 Pankstraße Station. Several other underground stations can be used to reach the different sights. We have chosen as a starting-point Leopoldplatz Station, which makes it possible to reach other places of interest later.*

From the **U** 6,9 Leopoldplatz Station

Müllerstraße is the main shopping street, particularly between Leopoldplatz and Seestraße. The area is in the direct flight path of planes taking off from Tegel Airport.

Nazarethkirche – **U** *6, 9 Leopoldplatz.*
In spite of being unpretentious, the church is stamped with the elegant simplicity of Schinkel's art *(see also ORANIENBURGERSTRASSE, St Elisabeth's Church)*. The architect was inspired by Umbrian churches.

Rathaus Wedding (R) – *Müllerstraße 146.*
It is a brick building erected in the twenties.

Walking south along Müllerstraße

Anti-Kriegs Museum – *Müllerstraße 158.* Founded in 1923, this anti-war museum was sacked by the SA in 1933 and its founder, Ernst Friedrich, had to escape to Belgium, taking the archives with him. He founded a second museum which was destroyed in 1940 by the Wehrmacht. Drawings by Käthe Kollwitz, photographs showing horrible wounds inflicted on soldiers during World War I, the recollection of Hiroshima's inferno, all contribute to denouncing the horrors of war.

Schering Pharmaceutical Company's Head Office – *Müllerstraße 18;* **U** *6 Reinickendorfer Straße;* A consistant research policy has turned this small company into a multi-national which occupies a group of modern buildings.

Abspannwerk Scharnhorst (W) – *Sellerstraße 16-26;* **U** *6 Reinickendorfer Straße.* This transformer building appears like a huge isolated wall, concealed behind the head office of the Schering Pharmaceutical Company. The **west side★**, in the shape of a zigzag, has adopted one of the favourite motifs of the Expressionists and turned it into the symbol of electricity. The setbacks on the façade concealed the cable networks.

The founder of a pharmaceutical empire

Ernst Christian Friedrich Schering (1824-1889) was born in Prenzlau (Ucker March, northeast of Berlin), a small city which possessed the oldest licensed chemist's shop in Germany (1305), called the "Green Pharmacy" *(Grüne Apotheke).* It was in Berlin, during the revolutionary unrest of 1848, that Schering finished his studies to become a dispensing chemist. In 1851, he bought a pharmacy in Chausseestraße (where many businesses settled at that time, *see CHARITÉ*) and gave it the name of the old chemist's shop in his native town. He set up a chemistry laboratory which was also used for photography. Schering was a forerunner in his field and became known for the quality of his products. He set up a chemicals factory, in Fennstraße, on the site of the present head office, and, in 1868, he was a co-founder of the German Chemistry Company. During the Franco-Prussian war, he was in charge of medical supplies for the army, a task which he fulfilled admirably well. His company subsequently became a public company. However, he hardly had time to reap the fruit of his labour, for his health started to deteriorate in 1882. Schering took care of the well-being of his employees, and set up a foundation, long before the first social laws were implemented.

Walking towards Amrumer Straße

Universitätsklinikum Rudolf Virchow – *Augustenburger Platz 1;* Ⓤ *9 Amrumer Straße*
The hospital was built at the turn of the century in a poor district, as a result of Bismarck's policy of introducing hygiene and social welfare into German society. The **main courtyard★ (Brunnenhof)** is in neo-Baroque style: it is very similar to the Hofburg in Vienna. Modern buildings (75% of the hospital buildings were destroyed during the war) line the main pathway.

Rudolf Virchow (1821-1902)

R. Virchow was a doctor of medecine, a hygienist, an anthropologist, a politician and a Democrat, in short one of the greatest scientists and professors of his time. He finished his studies in Berlin and became the assistant-dean of Charité Hospital *(see under that name)* at the age of 25. Having taken part in the 1848 middle-class revolution, he was compelled to leave Berlin; he came back in 1856, having already acquired international recognition. He then became head of the University's Institute of Pathology. His influence on the policies of the capital (over-populated and under-equipped until the 1870s) in matters of hygiene proved decisive. He designed a system of mains and drains together with the town planner James Hobrecht and spread the basic principles of local hygiene by giving numerous lectures. As a member of the municipal council in Berlin, he took part in the foundation of several large hospitals and had trees planted along the capital's streets and avenues in order to purify the air. **Robert Koch**, who identified the tuberculosis germ *(see CHARITÉ)*, visited hospitals all over the world, but he acknowledged that his colleague's hospital was the best from the point of view of its architecture and hygiene conditions.

Estate at No 10-2 Amrumer Straße – The apartments of this estate, decorated with corbels and loggias, overlook a large garden.

Zuckermuseum (M¹⁴) ⊘ – *Amrumer Straße 32; situated on the 3rd floor of the Sugar Industry Institute.* What is sugar? The answer can be found in this small museum: the visit begins with the chemical composition of sugar, the photosynthesis process and the assimilation of sugar by the body. The history of sugar illustrates the use of natural sources of sugar (maple syrup, honey) and above all a colonial product, sugar cane, which led to an economic system based on plantations and slavery. Faraway Prussia was quite willing to take part in the "triangular trade" between Europe, Africa and America: the ships of the Brandenburgisch-Afrikanische Kompanie carried 30 000 slaves from Africa to the Caribbean, with the support of Großfriedrichsburg Fort situated on the coast of modern Ghana. A model shows the inside of Krayn sugar factory in Silesia, *c*1805. The sudden expansion of sugar beet farming at the beginning of the 19C marks the beginning of beet sugar production on an industrial scale; this activity necessitated an abundant seasonal workforce, which included women and children well into the 20C and was called *Sachsengänger*. Many tools, gold plate (sugar bowls, baskets and sugar-tongs), as well as information on by-products, including alcohol, complete the instructive display about this essential product.

★Westhafen – Continue west along **Seestraße**. From Seestraße Insel Bridge, there is an interesting view (if you're travelling by car) on the **West Harbour** dockyard (**Westhafen**, *see MOABIT*).

Estate at No 14-41 Afrikanische Straße – It was designed (1926) by Mies van Rohe.

★Volkspark Rehberge – Ⓤ *6 Rehberge or* Ⓤ *9 Amrumer Straße.*
There is a beach on the western shore of **Plötzensee** *(see SIEMENSSTADT-Heckerdamm on the memorial)*. A large meadow occupies the centre of this vast green open space. wild-boars, doe, pheasants, cocks and turkeys are kept in pens fenced off by wire-netting.

In the vicinity of the Ⓤ 6 Rehberge Station

There are some interesting streets and settings in the "African" district and the "British" district, situated on either side of Müllerstraße. Togostraße, lined with very plain houses, leads to the **Dauerkolonie Togo** (entrance between No 25o and 25p or between No 106 and 105 Müllerstraße) which surrounds a *Laubenkolonie*. Dubliner Straße and Edinburger Sraße lead to Schillerpark dominated in the south by terraced gardens which look as if they have been fortified.

Return to Leopoldplatz Ⓤ *6 Station. If you are on foot, pay particular attention to the level you want (and go in through the correct entrance, since it can be different depending on where you wish to go). Change at Osloer Straße and take the* Ⓤ *8 line to Pankstraße.*

From the Ⓤ *8* Pankstraße Station

The clear-cut lines of Schinkel's buildings are recognizable in **St Paul's Church** (St-Pauls-Kirche, 1828-1835), decorated with Corinthian pilasters.
Follow Prinzenallee.

Groterjanbrauerei – *Prinzenstraße 78-79*. The façade, on the street side, which is incomplete, shows plain Expressionist features *(doorway)*. The façade overlooking the courtyard is more interesting, with its simple, purely functional outline.
Retrace your steps and follow Badstraße.

Luisenhaus – Note the lovely *Jugendstil* façade of **Luisenbad** *(Badstraße 35-36)*, with Mercury in its centre, and **Luisenhaus** *(Badtraße 38-39)* built of muti-coloured glazed bricks. Last section of the Walter-Nicklitz Promenade along the **Panke** River and lovely façade of a former restaurant with musical entertainment (ceramic tiles inscription: "Café Küche"), turned into a library. Some fine modern buildings erected for the IBA 87, with bold curved lines, contribute to the architectural appeal of the intersection between Schwedenstraße, Koloniestraße and Badstraße with its old brick buildings, which is one of the best-designed crossroads in Berlin.
Walk along Gropiusstraße.

Amtsgericht (J) – The tribunal is one of the finest neo-Gothic buildings in Berlin. The **staircase★** is particularly remarkable with its amazing criss-cross of flamboyant vaulting (liernes and tiercerons), Gothic banisters and pendants, which follow a similar design to that of the tribunal in Moabit *(see under that name)*. Fine view of the building at the bottom of the garden, near Pankstraße.

Heimatmuseum Wedding (M¹⁵) Ⓥ – *Pankstraße 47, 1st door on the left, in the courtyard*. This small museum houses reconstructions of a working-class home with its bedroom, kitchen strewn with children's toys, the communal launderette with the first hydraulic and mechanical washing-machines (which were only installed in the best apartment blocks) and a classroom. The tour continues on the 1st floor with displays on the French occupation, the famous entrepreneur Schering, the AEG and the Luisenbad.

★**Volkspark Humboldthain** – Ⓤ *8*, Ⓢ *1*, Ⓢ *2*, Ⓢ *25*, Ⓢ *26 Gesundbrunnen*. This pleasant, peaceful park is less neglected than Friedrichshain *(see under that name)*. Like the latter, it was laid out on top of a mound of debris, at the foot of which lies a rose garden (on the east side). What remained of the anti-aircraft bunker, built by Speer at the beginning of 1941 was cast in a concrete wall now used for climbing practice. At the top, there is a belvedere which offers an interesting **view★★** over the town, at the point where East meets West.

"Gesundbrunnen": the "health fountain"

The discovery of a ferruginous water spring prompted **Dr. Heinrich Wilhelm Behm,** the official court chemist (königlicher Hofapotheker), to suggest in 1757 the foundation of a spa (Bade- und Trinkkuranstalt), the first of its kind in the vicinity of Berlin, intended for wealthy citizens and members of the court. The establishment, which has large grounds, was situated between the present Osloer, Prinzen, Pank and Thurneysser streets and the Panke River. Behm wanted to turn the path which led to the fountain, the future **Badstraße,** into a prestigious avenue. He invested his entire fortune in it, confident that he had the king's support. In 1808, **Queen Louise** allowed the establishment, which had just been renovated, to be named after her. The area became an elegant resort, extended and embellished once again during the 1820s (model in the Heitmatmuseum in Wedding), and, in summer, a popular destination for middle-class family outings. People enjoyed meals in select restaurants, or drank milk in local dairies. When Wedding was gradually industrialised in the 1850s, the *Luisenbad* and its surroundings naturally became places of entertainment for the workers and lower middle class. After 1860, the *Mietskasernen* town planning programmes included the establishment, and the fountain finished up in the cellars of **Luisenhaus.**

Law courts

Ph. Gajic/MICHELIN

★★Ehem. AEG Gebäude – The **AEG buildings** (taken over by Siemens-Nixdorf) are wonderfully functional. Ackerstraße industrial estate soon covered 20 000 square metres. There was a neo-Gothic entrance (which still exists) in Brunnenstraße and the estate had its own railway line. The factory produced small appliances: electric motors, plugs, switches, glow-lamps or Nernst lamps. It is one of the main ensembles of industrial architecture in Berlin. The buildings lining Voltastraße stretch over a distance of 300m: the **Kleinmotorenfabrik** (1910-13), decorated with engaged columns; the **assembly shop (Montagehalle für Großmaschinen**, 1912), on the corner of Voltastraße and Hussitenstraße, designed by **Peter Behrens** *(see also MOABIT and TREPTOW)*, whose outline denotes a remarkable simplicity. Go round the block along Hussitenstraße and Gustav-Meyer-Straße in order to see the rest of the buildings (Hochspannungfabrik) and the courtyard.

On the corner of Max-Urich-Straße and Ackerstraße, is the entrance to the three courtyards of the **AEG Apparatfabrik★**, built by Franz Schwechten, the architect who designed the Gedächniskirche *(see KURFÜRSTENDAMM)*, and had not quite given up historicist-style ornaments; today it is the Berlin Centre of Business Innovation and Creation (BIG) founded in 1983.

★Hussitenstraße 4-5 – This is a group of amazing buildings in which each illustrates a different style as you walk through a series of three courtyards (originally there were six for 1 000 people): neo-Romanesque, brick neo-Gothic from the March (the finest and best preserved part) and neo-Renaissance.

"The largest factories, with the best equipment and the most advanced scientific approach"

This 1921 evaluation was already true at the end of the 19C. A very interesting room in the **Heimatmuseum Wedding** illustrates the foundations of **AEG**'s success. The photographs give an idea of the working conditions and rationalisation of the production process in the Wedding electric motor factory: huge halls were filled with similar pieces of machinery; men with bowler hats and bow-ties walked along the rows of workers in order to keep an eye on the production rate. Punctuality was not a vain word in the AEG factory. The 20C had arrived, bringing with it division of labour and mass production, which required a large number of unqualified workers and, among them, women who were paid even lower salaries and whose fine fingers were very useful in handling wire and manufacturing glow-lamps. It was a totally different world from that of William II's ostentatious court festivities. This mechanical work force was later used in the trenches during World War I. Between 1914 and 1918, women replaced most of the male workforce, and had to do hard physical work; they reverted to their usual tasks after the war. The workers in the Brunnenstraße and Ackerstraße factories marched in great numbers towards the castle during the November 1918 revolution. A 1920 popular song said:

> "He who has never worked for
> Siemens-Schuckert,
> A.E.G. or Borsig,
> has not tasted life's misery,
> He still has a lot to learn,
> for you are nothing; you become nothing,
> even though your stomach may rumble
> That's how it is at Borsig's, A.E.G.'s,
> Siemens's and Schuckert's."

Bernauer Straße – **U** *8 Bernauer Straße*. Today Bernauer Straße is nothing more than the boundary between the districts of Wedding and Mitte, but the Wall stood here from 1961 to 1989. The former no-man's land is still a wasteland. The **Gedenkstätte Berliner Mauer** has stood since 1998 on the site of the Sophiengemeinde cemetery, at the intersection with Ackerstraße.

IN THE VICINITY

See **MOABIT★**, **REINICKENDORF**, **SIEMENSSTADT★** *(for the Plötzensee Memorial)*.

Escaping to the West

Dramatic incidents took place in this street which belonged to the western sector but whose buildings on the south side were situated in the Soviet sector. When the Wall was erected, people jumped out of windows as builders, ordered to wall them up, barged into the apartments of the upper floors accompanied by guards. A 77-year-old woman remained suspended in mid-air for a quarter of an hour, held securely on one side, with a safety net below. Threats from the crowd caused her pursuers to let go. Many fugitives missed the safety net and were seriously hurt. Along the same street, inside an old bakery, was the exit of the longest tunnel (145 m) dug 12 m underground beneath the east/west border; the entrance was located in some backyard toilets.

WEISSENSEE

Weißensee

See map of Berlin Conurbation, **11**, **CTU**

Berliner Allee is the main thoroughfare and shopping street in Weißensee which owes its name to a small lake *(Der Weiße See:* the white lake). The district began to develop in 1873, when the site of Neu-Weißensee, the area surrounding Meyerbeerstraße, was built on by an important wholesale merchant from Hamburg. The mayor, Carl Woelck, took the initiative of erecting municipal buildings (Munizipalviertel) around the tiny **Kreuzpfuhl** Lake; the new district eventually reached Prenzlauer Allee. Pleasant sites are to be discovered at random, in particular along Pistoriusstraße.

MAIN SIGHTS

★**Jüdischer Friedhof** – *No 2, 3, 4, 13, 23, 24* 🚋 *Albertinenstraße. Entrance in Herbert-Baum-Straße; head gear compulsory.*
Taking a stroll in this 115 000 grave cemetery inaugurated in 1875, which was and which is the largest of its kind in Europe, is a very moving experience. The cemetery, with its many important examples of monumental art ranging from 19C Historicism to the Cubism of Walter Gropius, is the resting place of some outstanding scientists, artists, entrepreneurs and politicians.

Pistoriusstraße – Slightly north of Pistoriusstraße, at No 109 Berliner Allee, stands a small chemist's shop called Flora-Apotheke, which has retained the rural aspect of houses in the more remote suburbs. The Local History Museum **(Stadtgeschichtliches Museum Weißensee)** ⊘ holds temporary exhibitions on a regular basis. The isolated tower of the church of Bethany (Bethanien-Kirche), in brick Gothic style, can be seen at the end of the street.

A provident mother

The Humboldt brothers' mother, **Marie-Elisabeth Colomb**, who owned an estate in Falkenberg and was buried in the parish church, now disappeared, was a descendant of Huguenots from Burgundy. The grandfather was a Parisian wholesale merchant. It is interesting to note that she had the same name as the citizen of Genoa who discovered America, for her son **Alexander**, who was a great traveller and linguist, "discovered" America scientifically. Their mother's intelligence was to a great extent responsible for the destiny and brilliant career shared by the two brothers. When their father died, they were brought up by Christian Kunth, an open-minded tutor, who became a friend of the family and the trustee of the estate. Marie-Elisabeth made it possible for her sons to study at the university of Frankfurt-on-Oder, and did not encourage them towards a military career even though it was the acknowledged ambition of all Prussian aristocrats. The clever administration of her estate (the **Tegel** domain – *see under that name* – was acquired in 1765) ensured a solid financial base for Alexander's travels and Wilhelm's career.

Woelckpromenade – On your right as you walk along Pistoriusstraße, there is a small green open space round Kreuzpfuhl Lake. Opposite, an imposing school dominating the willow trees along the shore makes a lovely picture. Slightly further north, near a pond, some **council flats**★ built of dark bricks in 1908 (*enter the courtyard laid out as a garden*) are the most interesting sight in the area. Their stepped gables make them look like Dutch buildings.
A lovely school stands on the corner of Parkstraße and Amalienstraße.

Trierer Straße Estate – *Nos 2, 18* 🚋 *Falkenberger Straße/Berliner Allee*. The colour scheme of these variegated council flats was designed by **Karl Schmidt-Rottluff** (*see GRUNEWALD, Brückemuseum*).

IN THE VICINITY

See **PANKOW**★, **PRENZLAUER BERG**★★.

WILMERSDORF
Wilmersdorf
See map of Berlin Town Centre, 🄶, 🄷, **EFGXYZ**

Like its neighbour Charlottenburg, Wilmersdorf is a middle-class district; it is no doubt more lively in the evening (*see the chapter, ON THE TOWN, The Berlin Scene*), but has few historical monuments and consists mainly of large houses along shaded streets which make the western part of Berlin look like a garden-city. Artists settled here at the beginning of the century.

HISTORICAL NOTES

Peasant origins – Like Schmargendorf, Wilmersdorf is a village surrounding a small square (*Angerdorf, see the INTRODUCTION, Architecture and City planning*), founded shortly after the successors of Albert the Bear acquired the Teltow and Barnim plateaux in 1231 (first mention of Wilmersdorf in 1293). The green space which splits Wilhelmsaue Street into two (🅄 7 *Blissestraße)* marks the site of the first

---

Thoens the handy-man ("Thoens der Bastler")

The Wilmersdorf chronicle relates the story of **Friedrich Thoens** (who died in 1798), the son of a shepherd and a shepherd himself *(Hirte,* then *Büdner).* From a very early age, he tried his hand at carving wood while his flock was grazing in the fields, in spite of threats and ill-treatment from his father. Once he had freed himself of his father's domination, he began to make all sorts of clocks, sun dials, optic glasses *(Stubenuhren, Repetieruhren, Sonnenuhren),* cart wheels and spinning wheels *(Karrenräd, Spinnräder).* Through reading, he acquired extensive knowledge in the fields of history and geography (as well as *Dogmatik)* and he conceived a whole philosophical system, but he remained a day-labourer *(Tagelöhner)* and was paid accordingly.

---

settlement. However, whereas Schmargendorf, Dahlem, Steglitz and several other villages in the Teltow area, became the property of aristocratic families, Wilmersdorf was governed by the **Mühlenhof** (Amtsdorf), an official body responsible for supplying the court *(see NIKOLAIVIERTEL, Mühlendamm).* Wilmersdorf's peasants were mentioned for the first time in 1591. At the end of the Thirty Years War, there were only five of them left.

A good place for entertainment – At the beginning of the 19C, Wilmersdorf, together with Schöneberg, was the favourite destination of Berliners when they went on an outing; they travelled on foot or in a "Kaleschwagen", drawn by four horses and able to hold six to twelve people, and picnicked in the open. They found tables and chairs in the inns; they looked at farm animals and went horse-riding. At the end of the century, Wilmersdorf was well-known for its entertainment establishments *(see also KURFÜRSTENDAMM, Hallensee):* the *Tanzpalast,* situated on the shores of Wilmersdorfersee (a small lake, no longer in existence on the southern edge of the village), attracted 2 000 visitors a day; young people gathered there on Wednesday evenings, and they also attended public balls in Schmargendorf.

"Wealthy peasants" – The village was caught up in Berlin's expansion. Parcelling out of the land began around 1850; most peasants did not become millionaires *(see SCHÖNEBERG)* but joined the ranks of the urban proletariat, but **Georg Christian Blisse** was lucky enough to become one of the richest. Having no children, he bequeathed three million RM to the municipality in order to have an orphanage built (Blisse Foundation). Six hundred thousand RM were used to erect the building; the rest was absorbed by inflation. The Viktoria-Luise Schule, which was the first teaching establishment of a high standard for girls, was also located in Wilmersdorf.

MAIN SIGHTS

Bundesallee – Ⓤ *1, 9 Spichernstraße.*
Note the architectural style of the **Fine Arts College**, the first monumental building in the western part of Berlin, a former high school (Joachimstalsches Gymnasium). Nearby: **Musical Theater Berlin** (T⁷).

★**Ludwigkirchplatz** – The district surrounding the small church offers many possibilities of having an enjoyable time in reputable establishments: bars, American restaurants or Tex-Mex, *Imbiss* (snack-bars) and cafés *(see ON THE TOWN, the Berlin Scene).* Take a stroll along shaded streets, very pleasant in summer: Pfalsburgerstraße, Emserstraße, Pariserstraße (intersection with Sächsische Straße). The area is lively as far as **Olivaer Platz**.

Kirche am Hohenzollernplatz ⊙ – *Hohenzollerndamm 202-203;* Ⓤ *1 Hohenzollernplatz.* The church is clad with glazed bricks. Note the entrance in Nassauische Straße, a Gothic arch between two cylinders remarkable for its simplicity.

Fehrbelliner Platz – Ⓤ *1,* Ⓤ *7 Fehrbelliner Platz. About this name, see the INTRODUCTION, The Burden of History, under 1675.*
It was a kind of forum under the Nazi regime. The semi-circular buildings of that period are still there on the south side. A flea market is held here on Sundays

Wilmersdorf Museum ⊙ – *Apply to the cafeteria attendant at the Kunstgalerie, Hohenzollerndamm 176.* This museum is interesting for its informative panels about the living conditions of peasants in a village in the Berlin area.
Follow Barstraße, where you will see a picturesque **Mosque** and Pakistani cultural centre, then skirt Wilmersdorf's cemetery on the right.

Russische Kirche – *Hohenzollerndamm 166*
The Russian church was inaugurated after most of the Russian community, exiled as a result of the October Revolution, had already fled Nazism and Berlin. Today, it is still the seat (and, as such, it is a cathedral) of the orthodox bishopric of Central Europe.

Doorway of the Holy Cross Church

M. Chaput/MICHELIN

★**Kreuzkirche** – Holy Cross Church is one of the finest Expressionist churches in Berlin (1927-29; *see also PANKOW, Maria-Magdalenen-Kirche, and WANNSEE, St Michael's Church)*. The pagoda-shaped **doorway** is noteworthy with its cladding of blue glazed enamel tiles. The tower is separate from the polygonal nave.

Schmargendorf – The former *Margrefendorf* (i.e. *Mark Grafendorf*) mentioned in 1275, has a splendid **town hall** (**R**) with alternating red bricks and white roughcast forming a pleasant contrast; it is a good example of a return to brick Gothic style from the March.

IN THE VICINITY

See **DAHLEM★★★, GRUNEWALD★★, KUFÜRSTENDAMM★★, SCHÖNEBERG★**.

An eminent lawyer: Carl Friedrich Beyme (1765-1838).

When Baron von Stein undertook his reform of the State after the Prussian defeats, he dismissed all the members of the government except **Carl Friedrich Beyme** who became chancellor before being given other important positions. Before that, he had been a member of Frederick-William III's secret council (Geheimer Kabinettsrat). After being made a peer in 1816, he lived in Steglitz from 1820 until his death. In his Schmargendorf estate, he was noted for his kindness towards his farmers. For, even though slavery was officially abolished on 9 Octobre 1807, it was not before the 1848 revolution had taken place and in fact not until 1865 that equal rights became general practice.

ZEHLENDORF★

In many ways, Zehlendorf is a much nicer residential district than Grunewald. The war had little impact on it and it is pleasant to stroll along streets lined with *Jugendstil* façades. The town's shopping centre stretches along Teltower Damm, which prolongs Clayallee to the south from Zehlendorf **S** *1 Station*.

NATURE, VILLAS AND... MUSEUM OF MEDIEVAL LIFE

Dorfkirche – **S** *1 Zehlendorf.*
An oak tree, which is over a hundred years old and called the "Oak of Peace" *(Friedenseiche)* because it was planted in 1871, stands in front of the **Local History Museum** (Heimatmuseum Zehlendorf) ⏲, near the small cemetery surrounding the charming hexagonal parish church (1768). Along Teltower Damm, traditional shops occupy the ground floor of handsome buildings with interesting façades such as **No 25** and **No 20** opposite.

★★Onkel-Toms-Hütte – **U** *1 Onkel-Toms-Hütte.*
This is probably the finest housing estate in Berlin, designed between 1926 and 1931 by **Bruno Taut, Hugo Häring** and **Otto Rudolf Salvisberg** and built in an idyllic setting. Salvisberg also designed the S-Bahn station which included a shopping parade, a post office and a cinema. No two rows of buildings are alike and there is a great variety of doors and windows; the houses are all of moderate size (with one storey and an attic). Strolling along the streets of this garden-city, which provided homes for 15 000 people, brings surprise upon surprise for town planning here has been conceived as a game.
It is possible to go back to the centre of Zehlendorf village along **Riemeisterstraße**. This street is lined with splendid villas; note in particular the stately residence standing on the corner of Schützallee (**No 27-29**).

★S 1 Mexikoplatz – *This S-Bahn station, shaped like an egg in an egg-cup (1904-5), is the most original in Berlin. It is one of the best examples of Jugendstil, owing mainly to its corrugated roofs and windows. The towers of the large apartment blocks surrounding the square are reminiscent of those in Nuremberg.*

Museumsdorf Düppel/Stiftung Stadtmuseum Berlin (**M³⁵**) ⏲ – In the Museum of Mediaeval Life which opened in 1975, cottages with thick thatched roofs sloping down to the ground give a good idea of life in a village of the Brandenburg March during the 13C. In springtime, when the trees are in blossom, the scenery is charming. Interiors are very rustic, but all the necessities of daily life as well as various craftsmen's tools are there: grinding stones, looms, ceramics, hearth with metal grate. People work in the pottery workshop or look after the garden. Farm animals: oxen (trips in carts pulled by oxen are available), wild-boar and their young, goats, rams and sheep make up a genuine country setting which children love. Home-made bread and mead (honey wine) are on sale.

IN THE VICINITY
See **DAHLEM★★★, GRUNEWALD★★, WANNSEE★★**.

Museum of medieval life in Düppel

Inmates of the Zoological Gardens

ZOOLOGISCHER GARTEN★★★

Tiergarten

See map of Berlin Town Centre, **7**, **GHV**

Berlin's zoo ⊘ was created at the end of the 18C on **Peacock Island** *(see WANNSEE)*, where a menagerie and hothouses were built. The zoo sheltered 850 animals. It was moved in 1844 to the outskirts of Berlin and was laid out by the landscape gardener **P.J. Lenné** *(see WANNSEE)*. The zoological gardens, which were Germany's first, were influenced by urban development to the point that, at the beginning, the various pavilions were built in the style of the country of origin of the animals they contained; later they became more functional.

Knautschke, the survivor...

The end of the war was a very hard time indeed for the zoo's inmates, for they were used to feed Berliners, just like the Tiergarten trees were used to keep them warm. A writer (Stefan Reisner, in *Stadtfront, Berlin West Berlin*, 1982) remembers that his father once brought back a camel's hump which melted in the frying pan. But Knautschke the Hippo was luckier. He went under water during the last days of the conflict and reappeared once the bombing had stopped, thus becoming a hero.

This zoo is extraordinarily rich in rare animal species, birds in particular: eagle owls, condors, harpy eagles and parrots, can be seen next to seals, varans, snakes, okapis, beavers, pandas, brown and polar bears, and there is also a well-stocked aquarium... more than 15 000 animals in all. The wild animals are magnificent and quite awe-inspiring. The fact that they have young ones with them is a sign that captivity has not affected their well-being. An underground passage running beneath the wild animals' dens, leads to some glass cages where lemurs live in semi-darkness. Allow three hours for a tour of the zoo.

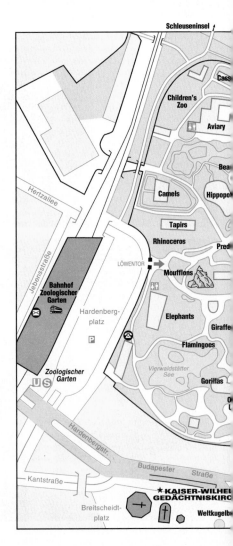

OTHER SIGHTS

Bahnhof Zoologischer Garten – Ⓢ + Ⓤ *Zoologischer Garten.*
Situated next to the zoo, the **station** of the same name appears to be strangely suspended. At night, with its base lit by conical lights (the 1935 design, inaugurated when the station was extended for the Olympic Games, has been retained), it looks more like a ship about to sail than a terminus. A large population of dropouts mingles with passengers constantly coming and going and the station adds an industrial touch to the townscape of ultra-modern neon lights flashing over Kurfürstendamm. This is Berlin's main western station pending the construction of Lehrte Main Station (Lehrter Stadtbahnhof, *see REICHSTAG).*

Kantstraße – The neo-Baroque façade of the *Theater des Westens* (**T⁸**) (1895-96), fixed onto a picturesque timber-framed building, seems to ignore the innovations of the *Jugendstil* trend. The street is lined with some interesting·cafés in the vicinity of Savignyplatz. The **stock exchange,** whose design was inspired by the scaly carapace of a pangolin, is being built in Fasanenstraße. Kantdreieck, a building surmounted by a shark's finn, looks somewhat aggressive. This is the setting seen from the train just before arriving at Zoo Station or just after leaving it.

★**Savignyplatz** – Ⓢ *3, 5, 7, 9 Savignyplatz.*
This square, located at the heart of a peaceful residential district, and the forklike intersection of Grolmann, Knesebeck and Carmerstreets, the favourite haunt of students from the Fine Arts College and the Technical University, are more interesting for visitors who intend to use the information contained in the chapter *ON THE TOWN*.

IN THE VICINITY

See **ERNST-REUTER-PLATZ, KURFÜRSTENDAMM★★, TIERGARTEN★★.**

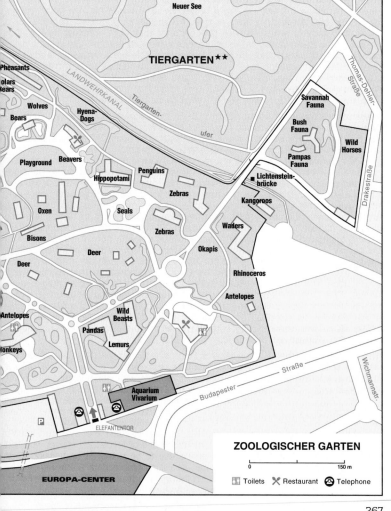

This small fishing village, older than Berlin and of Slav origin, which became a garrison town, an aristocratic city and a royal residence, represents the essence of Prussian refinement. The lake setting; enhanced by a ring of dark forests, is idyllic: "The **Potsdam** area is very beautiful. There are paths in front of every town gate; as one draws away from the town, one often encounters forest streams, wooded hills and vineyards. Some of the surrounding hills offer a choice of fine views of the city, the Havel, which is very wide at that point, the lakes, the villages as well as the parks, forests, castles and royal edifices, essentially built on top of small hills" (Christoph Friedrich Nicolai). All the Prussian monarchs embellished the city in which the French cavalry was stationed during Napoleon's occupation. Shortly before the surrender of Berlin and the end of World War II, British bombs destroyed the town centre, causing major damage which, for ideological reasons, the GDR made sure would be irreparable. However, there is still enough to see to warrant spending a day in Potsdam. There are choices to be made though, the various royal castles are quite far from each other and the town itself has a rich heritage.

TO THE GLORY OF PRUSSIA

"The whole island is to become a paradise..." – It was its beautiful setting which brought notice to the city which a friend of the Great Elector, **Jean-Maurice de Naussau-Siegen**, suggested as a royal residence. The new absolute power vested in the State made it necessary to build a modern castle in a region where the monarch had vast hunting grounds. The prince therefore had his second residence built there in 1657 by a Frenchman of Italian descent, **Philippe de la Chieze.**

The King-Sergeant's simple taste – Frederick-William I preferred Potsdam to Berlin. As Chateaubriand remarked, he turned the town into "golden barracks" and surrounded it with fortifications. Every day, accompanied by his son, he would watch the guards' parade in front of the Town Castle. He liked to see his "tall guys" *(Lange Kerls)* marching along; they were at least 1.83m tall and he called them his "dear blue boys" because of the Prussian blue uniforms they wore. Whether he stayed in Potsdam or in Berlin Castle, he would organise a *Tabakscollegium*, "and evening gathering", and his guests would sit round a large rustic table and converse while smoking, drinking beer and eating cheese. They would help themselves to beer from a huge hanap fitted with a tap, inlaid with 688 Thaler and 46 medals, now exhibited in the Museum of Decorative Arts in Köpenick *(see under that name)*. One month before he died, the king said: "Good bye Berlin; I want to die in Potsdam!".

Frederick II's traumatic youth – Born in Berlin on 24 January 1712, the young prince was soon confronted with strong hostility from his father who wanted to educate him in a Spartan way whereas the boy was more attracted by books and above all, by music and dancing. This hostility grew into real hatred and Frederick decided to flee to Britain. However, he was betrayed at the last minute and locked up in Küstrin fortress where he was compelled to watch the execution of his friend and accomplice, Katte. The King-Sergeant thought of having his son executed too. Instead, he forced him to work as a simple employee in the War and Estates office in Küstrin. Later the young prince was given command of a regiment in Neu-Ruppin, where, among the officers, he met the architect, painter and ornamentist, **Georg Wenzeslaus von Knobelsdorff.** In 1733, the prince married, without great enthusiasm, Princess Elisabeth of Brunswick-Bevern *(see PANKOW)*, started an exchange of letters with Voltaire and, from 1736, he began to get acquainted with Freemasonry. Like a true Hohenzollern, he sacrificed everything to the higher interests of the State and put his trust in the Prussian army. As his father's death drew nearer, Frederick adopted his views regarding administrative and military organisation. **Rheinsberg** Castle, 80km north of Berlin, was fitted out according to his wishes. The Crown Prince spent happy days there, practising philosophy, music, dancing and gambling, collecting paintings by his favourite artist **Antoine Watteau** (1684-1721) and by his disciples Nicolas Lancret (1690-1745) and Jean-Baptiste Pater (1695-1736), and reconstructing, within his small court, a dream world of gallant festivities after Watteau. He became king on 31 May 1740.

The enlightened monarch – The name of Potsdam is forever linked to that of **Frederick II** who, in spite of unhappy childhood memories, turned this "austere Sparta" into a "resplendent Athens", as **Voltaire** put it. The philosopher, with whom Frederick had corresponded since 1738, while he was still only the Crown Prince, stayed in Potsdam from 1750 to 1753. Their relationship was cordial at first, but eventually became stormy. Their misunderstanding got worse in 1752, when Voltaire stood up against the mathematician **Maupertuis**. He was allowed to leave Berlin to go and take the waters in Plombières. Feeling out of reach, Voltaire wrote more pamphlets, but had to suffer the "Frankfurt insult", when he was detained for more than a month by one of Frederick's envoys who had come to ask for the king of Prussia's poems due to be published by Voltaire. Their exchange of letters was resumed much later. As a sign of reconciliation, the king ordered a bust of Voltaire from the Berlin porcelain factory. The philosopher concluded that, in Sans-Souci, Frederick "lived without court, without counsel and without religion".

POTSDAM
and surrounding areas

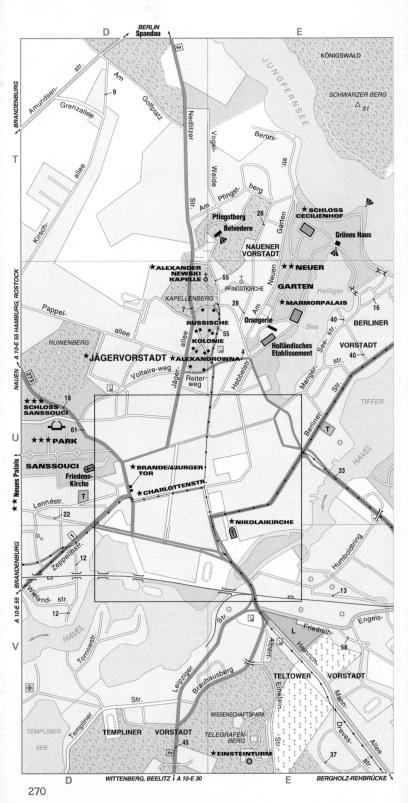

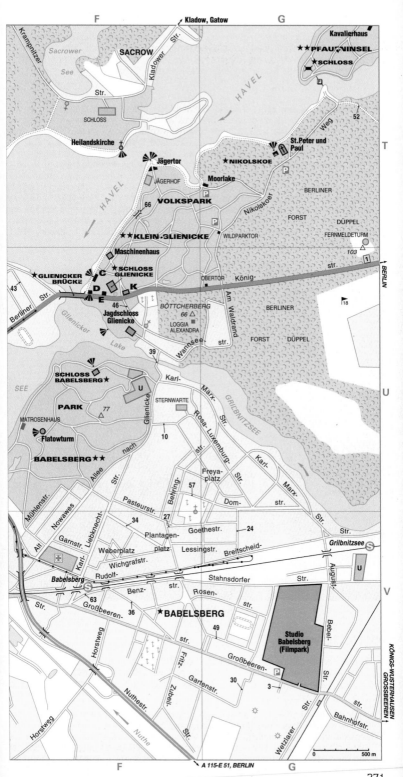

271

> ### "And yet...and yet..."
>
> "The king's suppers are delicious, the conversation centres on reason, wit and science; freedom prevails; he is the soul of all this; no bad temper, no clouds, or at least no storms. My life is free and busy; and yet..and yet..Operas, plays, parades, suppers in Sans-Souci, war exercises, concerts, studies, reading; and yet..and yet...Berlin, a large town, more rationally laid out than Paris, palaces, theatres, kindly queens, charming princesses, beautiful, shapely ladies-in-waiting, Lady Tyrconnell's house always full and often too full; and yet...and yet..., my dear child, the weather is beginning to turn to fair but cold."
> (Voltaire, *Letter to Madame Denis*, 6 November 1750).

A royal patron of the arts – **Frederick-William IV**, the eldest son of Queen Louise, was confronted with the major political problems of the 19C: industrialisation, poverty, national identity and the wish to move towards a constitutional state. The "Romantic on the throne" had conservative ideas and accused Berlin of being "unfaithful" following the 1848 revolution. His attitude was, however, more constructive as far as the arts were concerned. He had collected books since his childhood and appeciated the Frederician rococo style; he asked his father to buy paintings by Caspar David Friedrich and launched the Museum Island project. While he was still only the heir to the throne, he dreamt of continuing the work of **P.J. Lenné** *(see WANNSEE, Volkspark Klein-Glienicke)* and turning Potsdam into an artistic ensemble in which landscape and architecture would blend harmoniously. He completed the layout of the parks which had already been established and created Sakrow Park. He died on 1 January 1861, mentally diminished, as a result of having contracted syphilis.

Sans-Souci Castle and terraces

Ph. Gaïc/MICHELIN

★★THE TOWN

The historical centre did not survive the 1945 bombing nor the GDR's policy of replacing most of the evidence from the past with anonymous modern buildings.
Start from Potsdam-Stadt S-Bahn Station and walk towards the high dome of St Nicholas's Church.

Alter Markt – Immediately after *Lange Brücke*, a column fragment is the only trace of the former **Town Castle** (Stadtschloß), once the residence of the Great Elector, remodelled by Knobelsdorff, in which Voltaire most probably stayed. The *Merkur* Hotel marks the place where the castle stood. St Nicholas's Church, the town hall and the castle gate surrounded the elegant **Old Market Square** or **Alter-Markt**, right in the town centre. An obelisk stands on the site. **St Nicholas's Church★** (Nikolaikirche) was designed by Schinkel and remodelled by his students (the former church burnt down in 1795). Persius built the dome, similar to that of the Pantheon, between 1843 and 1849 together with the four corner turrets. The interior is huge and cold. The **old town hall** (Altes Rathaus, *Am Alten Markt 1-2*) is surmounted by a gilt statue of Atlas. *Follow Breite Straße.*

Marstall – *Schloßstraße 15.*
The stables, decorated with fine trophies, house a **Cinema Museum★** ⊘ (Filmmuseum): reconstruction of stars' dressing-rooms (with wax figures and some memorabilia: Marlene Dietrich, Lilian Harvey, Zarah Leander and Marika Rökk, stars of the Third Reich period, Renate Krößner, an actress from the GDR; gruesome setting used for films about the camps, information about Fritz Lang's *Nibelungen* and Expressionist films: *Doctor Caligari's surgery, Tired Death (Der müde Tod), Golem (Golem, wie er in die Welt Kam), Faust, Doctor Mabuse*; the film-makers who emigrated: Babelsberg between 1933 and 1945 and films from the Third Reich. Many photographs of films and actors as well as extracts can be seen along the way.

Am Neuen Markt – *At the back of the stables, along Schloß-, then Siefertstraße.* This small square gives a good idea of what Potsdam was like in the past. One-storeyed houses have almost all been restored except for the coach-house (Kutschstall; *on the west side at No 9*). There are more interesting buildings in **Yorckstraße,** but the whole street needs to be done up. Fine Baroque ensemble along **W.-Staab-Straße.** The concave outline of **"Acht-Ecken-Haus"** (**A**), with its green and white roughcast, underlines the intersection of Friedrich-Ebert-Straße and Ebräerstraße.

Bassinplatz – Rows of Dutch-style houses. Mozart stayed in **No 10** at the beginning of 1789. Neo-Romanesque Catholic church and 18C French church *(at the end of the square, on the east side)* surmounted with a flattened dome.

★**Holländisches Viertel** – The district was built for the Dutch craftsmen Frederick-William had sent for. Stand on the corner of Benkertstraße and Mittelstraße in order to admire the alignment of the houses.

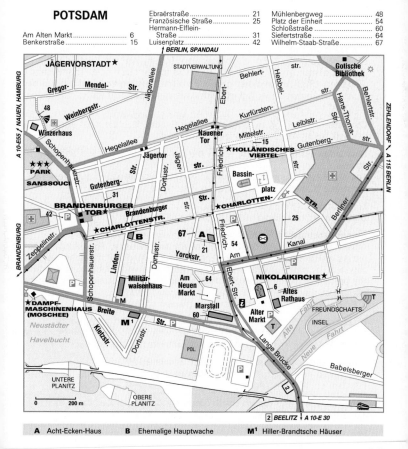

A Acht-Ecken-Haus   B Ehemalige Hauptwache   M¹ Hiller-Brandtsche Häuser

Ph. Gajic/MICHELIN

Houses in the Dutch district

Nauener Tor – This is one of the first neo-Gothic monuments in Europe (1755). Behind it stands the imposing government building (Regierungsge-bäude) topped with a green copper dome.

From there, one can reach the Russian quarter (Russische Kolonie) and Pentecost Hill (Pfingstberg) or carry on walking to the New Garden (Neuer Garten).

★**Jäger-Vorstadt** – This "Hunters' suburb" consists of refined-looking villas. There are quite a few in **Gregor-Mendel-Straße**: the Siemens Villa at Nos 21-22 and, opposite, an odd *Jugendstil* villa; walk to the right of it. From the steps of Mühlenbergweg, there is a good view of Potsdam's centre (St Nicholas, Telegrafenberg). **Weinbergstraße** is lined with lovely villas in antique style, such as the Thieck Villa (now the *Haus der Technik*, 1843-46), on the corner of Schopenhauer Allee. The **Vine-grower's House on Mühlenberg** (No 25 Gregor-Mendel-Straße), situated opposite, is being restored.

To continue the tour of the town, rejoin Brandenburger Straße.

Brandenburgerstraße – This pedestrian precinct is the old town's shopping street; the **Brandenburger Tor★** (Brandenburger Tor), built by Karl von Gontard and his pupil Georg Christian Unger (1743-1799), marks the entrance to it. The **"Hunters' Gate"** (Jägertor, 1733) is the oldest gate in Potsdam. **Gutenbergstraße**, which runs parallel to Brandenburgerstraße, is lined with uniform houses, sometimes dilapidated and occupied by squatters.

★**Charlottenstraße** – With its fine Baroque façades, it is the most attractive street in town. **No 41** was built by Unger *(see above)*.

Ehemalige Hauptwache (**D**) – *On the corner of Lindenstraße and Charlottenstraße.*
The arcade is supported on twin Tuscan columns. Beyond Charlottenstraße, Lindenstraße is lined with some lovely one-storeyed houses.

Lindenstraße – Note the fine Baroque building of the **orphanage** (Militärwaisenhaus, *Dortustraße 36)* situated at the beginning of the street.

★**Dampfmaschinenhaus (Mosque)** ⊘ – *Zeppelinstraße 176.*
Amazing yet successful combination of art and industry. The interior is as surprising as the exterior: the machinery is hidden behind multifoiled arches, under a cupola lit by moucharabies and vaulting decorated with Moorish motifs. Note, in the preceding room, *Young Boy with a Dolphin*, after Schinkel, executed for the pavilion of the Roman Baths lake *(see Sanssouci Park)*.
Grey depressing tower blocks stand at the end of Breite Straße.

Kietzstraße – *Retrace your steps: take the Wall am Kiez to the south.*
It is worth walking along Kietzstraße lined with one-storeyed houses, characteristic of Potsdam, and along Dortusstraße with its fine old façades.

Hiller-Brandtsche Häuser (**M¹**) – *Breite Straße 26-27.*
They house the municipal museum (**Potsdam-Museum**: exhibition on the bombing of Potsdam on 14 April 1945).

Breite Straße – The **Garrison Church** (Garnisonskirche), famous for its chime, stood along this symbolic street.

Marstall – *See above.*

Inside the "Mosque" (Dampfmaschinenhaus)

Ph. Cajic/MICHELIN

A national sanctuary

The presence in the church of the remains of **Frederick-William I**, who had it built, and of his son **Frederick II**, turned the building into a symbol of national greatness. As such, it became the setting of political meetings: during the night of 5 November 1805, Frederick-William III, his wife Louise, who became the soul of the resistance against Napoleon and Tsar Alexander I, took an oath of alliance on the tomb of Frederick II; one year later, the victorious Napoleon spared the church out of respect for the same tomb, next to which he stood in silent homage. After the fire which damaged the Reichstag, the inaugural sitting of the new parliament took place in Potsdam, during a huge ceremony organised by Goebbels, the brand new propaganda minister. On 21 March 1933, the town was hung with imperial flags and, in the presence of the imperial family (William II's seat remained empty), **Hitler** officially became part of Prussian tradition and made a speech about the "marriage of past greatness and of new strength". This is what the French ambassador, **André François-Poncet,** who was there, called the "Potsdam comedy". He described it in these terms: "It is not the union of two generations which is sealed in Potsdam; it is the eviction of one by the other: the young generation raised its hat to the old one, then cocked a snook at it in its back."

★★★SANSSOUCI PARK

A bus leaves from the station and takes passengers to various sights within the Sanssouci Park.

Once inside the park, the visitor is pleasantly surprised by the great variety of small gardens; and, indeed, the attractive **Sanssouci Park** (290 hectares) offers a series of surprises. Various buildings in picturesque settings appearing unexpectedly at the turn of an alleyway, near a pond or at the top of a hill, secret Italian gardens, symmetrical formal gardens, landscape gardens, all add to the exquisite charm of this domain which includes numerous sights.

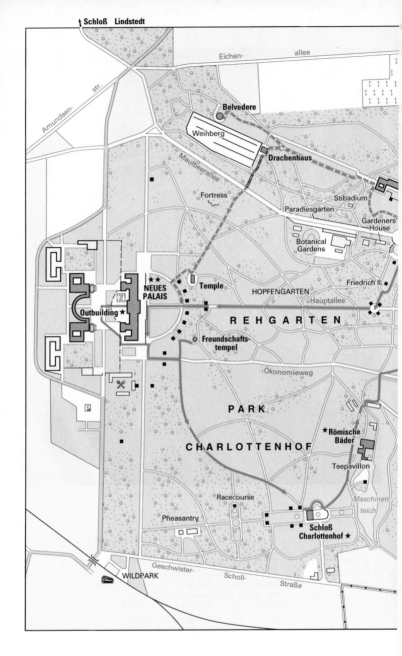

"Am Obelisk" – The hieroglyphs on the **obelisk** are purely decorative; the entrance gates are in keeping with the modest proportions of the castle. The main path is stately and stretches to the New Palace over a distance of 2.5km.

Friedenskirche – *On the right after the entrance to the obelisk; small classical doorway.*

Good view of the apse of the church, modelled on St Clement in Rome, standing on the edge of the pond, its campanile, its colonnade and the small dome of the mausoleum. This basilica, in ancient Christian style, was meant to be the resting-place of Frederick-William IV. The magnificent **mosaic★** (1st half of the 18C) decorating the apse comes from Murano. Note the columns of the baldachin above the altar and the copies of antique candelabras. The mausoleum houses the sarcophagi of Frederick III, who reigned for only three months (March to June 1888) between William I and William II, and of his wife, and, since 1995, of the King-Sergeant. There is a lovely view of the gardens through the cloister.

Running alongside the Italian-style buildings next to Friedenskirche, *Am Grünen Gitter* ("with green railings", elegantly fencing off the alleyway), leads to a site which offers an imposing **view★★** of the terraces in front of Sanssouci Castle.

Continue along the main paths.

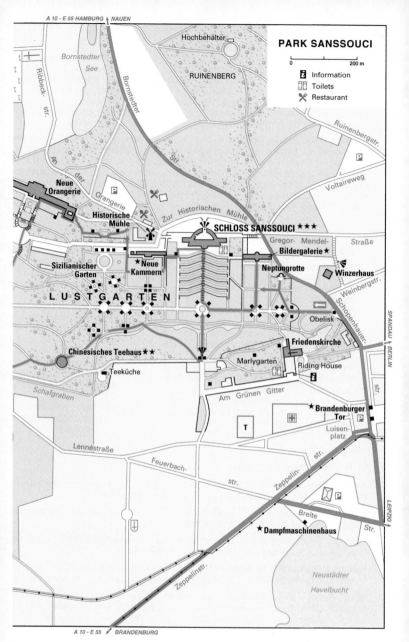

PARK SANSSOUCI

0   200 m

🛈 Information
🚻 Toilets
✗ Restaurant

Neptungrotte – Neptune's Grotto was Knobelsdorff's last work (1751-57). The architect did not see it in its finished state since he died in 1753. The fountain, clad with shells in true Baroque fashion, only worked in the 19C.

Bildergalerie ⊘ – This gallery was built between 1755 and 1764 by J.C. Büring who replaced Knobelsdorff as the official royal architect. It is one of the oldest museums in Germany, since it was purposely created to house a collection of paintings. It contains 124 works by Italian, Flemish and Dutch masters (Caravaggio, Reni, Rubens, Van Dyck), all purchased by Frederick II. There is a lovely view over the Dutch garden below.

★★★ Schloß Sanssouci – Between 1744 and 1747, **Frederick II** undertook preparatory work on the site; he had a hill razed and made excavations in order to build tiers of terraces for hothouses and vineyards which would eventually be dominated by a summer palace. The king did not want a new Versailles, but a modest retreat. He designed it himself and gave the plans to his architect friend **Georg Wenzeslaus von Knobelsdorff;** he specifically asked for the castle to be set back from the edge of the upper terrace which became one of his favourite spots. Sanssouci was really the domain of Bacchus and pleasure. The king led a simple life: he only had five valets and six page-boys at his service; he got up very early, dealt with the affairs of state, had a frugal meal, read and played the flute (an occupation he particularly enjoyed; he composed more than 100 sonatas for the flute), accompanied at the harpsichord by **Carl Philipp Emanuel Bach**, one of Johann Sebastian's sons; he dined in select company. These "philosophical dinners" which the king, as an enlightened monarch, enjoyed very much, brought together in the marble room men of letters who conversed only in French (the cook himself was French...). The period immediately preceding the Seven Years War was the happiest of Frederick the Great's reign. The castle was full of guests: diplomats, philosophers, artists, writers.

Exterior – The park was laid out in the 19C by the famous landscape-architect **Peter Joseph Lenné**. Beautiful sculpture groups by the Adam brothers and Jean-Baptiste Pigalle (note *Mercury Tying Up his Sandal*) surround the pool at the bottom of the terraces. There are open vistas of the Chinese Tea-House, the mill peeping above the trees, the golden top of the Painting Gallery and the New Rooms. The view from the upper terrace is spoilt by the tower blocks built at the time of the GDR. Termini *(see ABC OF ARCHITECTURE)*, representing bacchantes and smiling satyrs, make up the graceful decoration of the façade and support the entablature, enhancing the impression of lightness. Note also the small lattice-work pavilions (Laubenpavillon mit Sonnenemblem), on each side of the castle, with a symbol of the sun. Inside the elegant main courtyard, once the main entrance to the castle, a semi-circular colonnade appears to be suspended above the trees. It offers a view of the **"Ruins Mound" (Ruinenberg)**, which was meant to conceal the reservoirs and pumps supplying water to the various pools in the park.

> **The return of Frederick the Great's remains**
>
> The remains of Frederich II and of his father were exhumed in 1943 to preserve them from damage by bombing. They were taken to the seat of the Hohenzollern family *(in the Swabian Jura)*; they came back to Potsdam in 1991, inside a railway carriage which had belonged to William II. 50 000 people paid their respects to the sarcophagi. Frederick-William I is now buried in a mausoleum within Sanssouci Park while Frederick II rests at last, according to his wishes, next to his dogs, in a vault built during his lifetime on the terrace of his palace (funeral plaque near the exedra on the east side).

Guided Tour ⓧ *(1 hour)*

Antechamber – Elegant, sober decoration in grey and gold (stuccos representing the *Bacchanalia*). The ceiling was painted by Harper in 1746.

Small Gallery – 18C French paintings by J.B. Pater and N. Lancret; on the mantelpiece, busts of Frederick II and his brother Henry.

Library – Small room in the shape of a rotunda. The beautiful cedar-wood panels have gilt bronze decorations. The sun adorns the ceiling.

Frederick the Great's Bedchamber and Study – Neoclassical decoration. Portraits of the royal family as well as Frederick II's table and the armchair in which he died.

Music Room – It is a masterpiece of German rococo style and was Frederick II's favourite room. On the walls there are murals by Pesne on the theme of Ovid's *Metamorphoses*. A painting by Menzel represents Frederick II playing the flute in this very room *(see MUSEUMSINSEL, Alte Nationalgalerie)*.

Audience Hall – Ceiling by Pesne *(Zephyr and Flora)*. Paintings by Coypel and Van Loo *(Medea and Jason)*.

Marble Hall – Splendid pavement in Carrara and Silesia marble. Beneath the cupola, there is a bust of Richelieu by Bernini; also, allegorical stucco figures *(Music, Architecture, Astronomy, Painting)* and gilt chequer-work on the ceiling. Statues of Apollo and Venus by F.G. Adam, a French sculptor sent by Louis XV, who was in charge of Frederick II's decoration workshop from 1742 to 1760.

The beds in the **guest rooms** appear to be small inside their alcoves, but in fact they are between 2m and 2.20m long. "Voltaire's Room" is exquisite: yellow walls with painted birds and flowers made to look as "natural" as possible. There is a replica of the writer's bust by Houdon (1774). It would seem that Voltaire stayed in the Town Castle *(see above)*.

★**Damenflügel** ⓧ – These two wings were built at the beginning of his reign by Frederick-William IV, who made Sanssouci his summer residence without making use of Frederick the Great's apartments, The **Dream Room** (Traumzimmer), which the king had seen in a dream, was decorated according to his description.

★**Neue Kammern** ⓧ – *Guided tour 1 hour*. The Old Orangery (Alte Orangerie), designed by Knobelsdorff, was turned into apartments between 1771 and 1774 by G.C. Unger. With its arched doors open, it offers the best series of rooms in

Adolf von Menzel, *The Flute Concert* (1850-52)

Potsdam. The rococo decoration is neat and very beautiful: the circular dining-room with its sideboard and vases on console tables, **Ovid's Gallery★**, whose gilt wood panels, depicting scenes from the Roman poet's *Metamorphoses*, are extremely erotic, and the Jasper Room decorated with busts from Berlin Castle. The marble comes from Silesia. The Guest Rooms are adorned with *Views* of Potsdam. The wood panels are inlaid with fruit and flower motifs.

Historische Mühle – This mill is the subject of a famous anecdote which illustrates to perfection Frederick II's respect for the State and his enlightened way of ruling. The noise of the mill annoyed the king. He tried to convince the miller to stop his activity or to move elsewhere. Persuasion, compensation, threats: nothing succeeded. Frederick instituted legal proceedings against the miller and lost: " In the law courts, the law must be heard and the king must remain silent".

Sizilianischer Garten – There is a lot of charm in this eclectic ensemble of bowers, balustrades, statues, small palm-trees, flower-beds and various species of trees (palms, agaves, bitter orange trees).

Neue Orangerie ⊘ – Designed by Frederick-William IV and modelled, as far as the central part is concerned, on the Medici Villa in Rome, it looks more attractive from afar, seen as a whole with the garden and the double staircase, than at close quarters, when its hugeness (the façade is 330m long) conveys an impression of coldness. The apartments of Tsar Nicholas I and of his wife, the king of Prussia's sister, are sumptuous, in particular the **Malachite Room** which formed part of the tsarina's apartments. However, the **Raphaël Room★**, in which 47 copies of the most famous works of the Italian master are displayed, is more original and in keeping with the 19C taste for splendidly appointed museums.

The sights described below are less important; however they are marked on the map and joined by a red line to guide the visitor with more time to spend.

Drachenhaus – This small pagoda (there are sixteen gilt dragons on the ridge of the roof) is now a tea-room. It was built in 1770 by Karl von Gontard near the vineyard planted the year before on the southern slopes of the hill (Drachenberg). It was the home of the vine-grower. Chinese buildings were in fashion during the 18C.

Belvedere – It was the last structure erected in Potsdam during the reign of Frederick II; the king was not entirely pleased with it although it is a charming and light edifice, restored after having been neglected for many years. Look at the **antique temple** (Antikentempel) before you reach the New Palace.

★★Neues Palais – Frederick II wanted to show the world that, having come out of the Seven Years War (1757-1763, *see the INTRODUCTION, The Burden of History*) as a victorious power, Prussia had not suffered any ill effects from such a long

Lindstedt Castle (1845-1858)

Although situated outside the Sanssouci domain *(Lindstedter Chaussee; follow a path on the left)*, this small castle, built for Frederick-William IV who intended to settle there in his old age, is not very far from the New Palace. It is a minor sight, but noteworthy for its garden, peristyle and portico. The asymmetrical building stretches its wings as if to offer more varied views of nature.

conflict. This "fanfaron-nade", as the project was called by the sovereign himself, who thus employed thousands of craftsmen, is the largest palace in Potsdam. It was intended for members of the royal family. Built in a rococo style that was no longer in fashion but that Frederick II liked nonetheless (and which he had chosen "fifty years too late" according to Voltaire), it is an extravagant and pompous edifice. It would seem that the desire to attract attention at all costs had become an obsession, a supposition confirmed by the motto inscribed on the eagle of the central pediment: "Non Soli Cedit" ("He never moves away from the sun"). Everything in building is ostentatious: the 428 sculptures which lead to the numerous apartments), the central dome, the **outbuildings★** (Karl von Gontard 1766-1769), which are probably the most successful part of the ensemble and form an exuberant festive setting intended to conceal an area of marshland. Oddly enough, these excessive decorations and over-abundance of sculpture create a fairy-tale atmosphere. **William II** and his court can be imagined parading round the castle, which he had landscaped (the lamp-posts and access roads date from that period); he also had electricity brought in to light up the stately and uncomfortable rooms. It was his favourite residence until 1918.

Tour ⊘ – *Only the north wing apartments on the ground floor and first floor can be visited.*
The **grotto** *(Muschelsaal)* offers a strange decor of walls inlaid with minerals, some of them semi-precious stones. Note, in the first-floor bedrooms (the castle contains four main staircases which lead to the numerous apartments), the bells used to ring the servants: *Bettfrau* (bed-attendant), *Kammerfrau* (chamber-maid), *Garderobefrau* (wardrobe attendant), *Schneiderin* (tailor). Two very fine children's portraits by Antoine Pesne decorate the Green Damask Room (Grüne Damas-tkammer): *Prince Augustus-Ferdinand of Prussia dressed like a Hussard* and *Prince Henry of Prussia*. The **Marble Hall** is amazing: the floor is made of inlaid marble as it is in the Grotto.
The **theatre**, built from a drawing by Knobelsdorff for a similar hall in the town castle, has charming white and gold decorations, with columns shaped like palm-trees. It can only be seen when there is a performance. Frederick II did not sit in a box, but in the third row of the stalls.
Beyond the Temple of Friendship *(Freundschaftstempel, 1768)* dedicated to Frederick II's beloved sister, Wilhelmina, the Margravine of Bayreuth, a path leads to Charlottenhof Castle. If you have some spare time, have a look at the charming racecourse, which offers a good view of Charlottenhof Palace, and at the nearby pheasantry, built in the style of an Italian villa.

Architecture suitable for parades: the New Palace

★**Schloß Charlottenhof** – *Guided tour; ticket office on the south side; the tour starts in the hall, on the west side.*

The small Neoclassical palace and its gardens are a complex, refined creation by **Schinkel** for the Crown Prince, the future Frederick-William IV, and his wife, a Bavarian princess. The purchase of the estate (1825), which was given to the prince as a Christmas present, made it possible to extend Sanssouci Park, which **P.J. Lenné** turned into a splendid landscape garden. There is a good view of the cupola of the New Palace and the park from the hemicycle, once clad with white and blue cloth (the Bavarian colours). An Italian style pergola links the hemicycle with the palace and runs alongside a garden.

Tour ⊘ – The interior, of moderate proportions, conceived after paintings from Pompeii, is exquisitely simple. The furniture was designed by Schinkel (armchairs, the crown princess's study, formal dining table in the dining-room). The **dining-room**, with its recesses painted red according to the prince's wishes, is the finest room in the palace, and the **"tent bedroom" (Zeltzimmer)**, reserved for courtesans, the most original.

Römische Bäder ⊘ – Set in harmonious grounds planted with various species of trees, this composite group, designed by **Schinkel** and built by his disciple Persius between 1829 and 1835, was never used as baths. Antique baths are blended with an Italian style villa surrounded by a garden: "various idyllic thoughts [...]were meant to mingle within a picturesque style and form a varied architectural ensemble which would blend harmoniously with the natural setting" (Schinkel). The **interior**★ is extremely refined: statues, caryatids, graceful metallic furniture, murals, openings through walls intended to create the same illusion as in the case of Roman architecture, green marble bath, cut with great skill. The pergola, decorated with hanging leafy vines, leads to the **tea-pavilion** shaped like a temple, which consists of a blue room, charmingly simple, overlooking the pond and the garden...

Ph. Gajic/MICHELIN

Chinese Tea House, group of figures making tea

★★**Chinesisches Teehaus** – Freshly gilt after its restoration, this "folly" in true 18C taste was modelled on a pavilion in Lunéville (now in the Lorraine region of France) and designed by Georg Büring, the architect behind the Painting Gallery. Charming closets give onto the circular room, decorated with "Chinese" paintings; various porcelain objects rest on console tables in rococo style. The ridge of the roof is surmounted by a mandarin under a parasol, but the most fascinating element of this extraordinary ensemble is the portico with palm-tree-shaped columns, near which are seated exotic life-size characters, who look as if they have been frozen in place.

★★**NEUER GARTEN** ETU

Time 2 1/2 hrs

Laid out round *Heiliger See*, at the end of the 18C, by Lenné for Frederick-William II, this garden became the personal domain of the crown prince and his wife Cecilia. The park is studded with various structures: the **Dutch buildings,** an **orangery,** concealed behind one of the Dutch houses (Damenhaus) and adjacent to a lovely garden *(walk straight on, keeping to the left as you skirt the building),* a **pyramid,** the **"Green House" (grünes Haus)**. The **Marble Palace★ (Marmorpalais)**, Frederick William II's summer residence, built by K. von Gontard and fitted by C.G. Langhans is being restored. From the "Green House", there is a view of the lake, the Marble Palace and St Nicholas's Church; north of the lake, the **view★★**, which conveys an impression of peace and beauty, extends from the square campanile of Sacrow Church, lost among the greenery, and the House of Cards on Peacock Island to Glienicke Park (the casino and bridge, *see WANNSEE)* and the Schäferberg telecommunications tower.

★ **Schloß Cecilienhof** ⊘ – The castle of the Crown Prince and his wife Cecilia, which looks rather like a huge cottage, has been turned into a luxury hotel, but it is still possible to visit the crown princess's **closet,** decorated like a ship's cabin, the Russian delegation's office, the white drawing room, the conference room (the table, which is *3.05m in diameter, was specially made in Moscow)* and the British and American delegations' rooms. *Explanations are in English, German and Russian.*

The Potsdam Conference

Prepared by the two preceding conferences of Teheran (1943) and Yalta (February 1945), the Potsdam Conference took place in the large reception room of Cecilienhof Castle between 17 July and 2 August 1945. **Winston Churchill** (replaced by Clement Attlee after the Labour election victory in England) and **Harry S. Truman** (Franklin D. Roosevelt had died in April that year) met in Potsdam on 15 July. Owing to a slight heart attack, **Joseph W. Stalin** arrived a day late. As he was afraid of flying, he travelled through East Germany in an armoured carriage; his itinerary was kept secret, but every kilometre of the route was guarded by troops! The head of the Kremlin could afford to be late. He was the only one of the three leaders present in Teheran and Yalta still in power: those facing him were not yet very experienced and they had agreed to leave the territories to the east of Germany (Thuringia, Saxony) which they had liberated, but which were part of the zone of Soviet occupation. Several questions were settled at the conference: the frontiers between Germany and Poland, the creation of a control commission and of an allied *Komandantur,* war damages and the trial of war criminals. The treaties were full of expressions such as "democratic", "peaceful", "lawfully", but the text was not particularly clear and left a number of ambiguities which were later exploited, as and when convenient, during the cold war.

Gotische Bibliothek – Built between 1792 and 1794, it is now being renovated

OTHER SIGHTS

★ **Russische Kolonie Alexandrowka** (DEU) – *No 92, 95* 🚊 *Puschkinallee.* Frederick William III had these charming carved-wood houses modelled on those of Russian military villages. The 12 remaining members of a military choir founded during the Napoleonic wars lived there. The **Alexander-Newski Chapel★** *(end of No 92* 🚊 *line climb to the top of the hill)* built at the top of Kapellenberg and dedicated to the memory of Tsar Alexander I, has been carefully restored.

Pfingstberg (ET) – *Follow the lane which skirts the Jewish cemetery on the right hand side (Puschkinallee 25), opposite the sign Russische Kolonie 14 and the path leading to Alexander-Newski Chapel.* Pentecost Hill was known as the Mount of the Jews *(Judenberg)* at the beginning of the 19C, because the Potsdam Jewish cemetery was situated there. Frederick-William II had plans to build a 45m-high neo-Gothic tower.

The **Belvedere** is still an overgrown ruin. It was designed by Frederick-William IV c1849 in order to offer visitors a good **view★★** of almost all the neighbouring parks as well as of the centre of Potsdam, dominated by the dome of St Nicholas's Church and surrounded by greenery. From the portico of the small **temple of Pomona** (1800) built by Schinkel at the age of 19 and situated slightly below, the view extends to the *Maschinenhaus* and the casino of Klein-Glienicke Park *(see WANNSEE).*

★ **Einsteinturm** (EV) ⊘ – *Go into "Wissenschaftspark A. Einstein" and apply to the keeper on duty inside the sentry-box. On the left, at the top; follow the signs "Einsteinturm". Several observation points. Allow 5 to 10 min walk.*
It is the work of Erich Mendelsohn (1920-24).

★ **Glienicker Brücke** (FU) – *No 93* 🚊 *Glienicker Brücke. See WANNSEE.*

SACROW *See map of Potsdam and surrounding areas* FT

See **HAVEL★★, WANNSEE★★**.

★BABELSBERG *See map of Potsdam and surrounding areas* FGUV

★★**Schloß Babelsberg** ⊘ – *See map of Potsdam and surrounding areas.* ⑤ *3, 7 Babelsberg, then* 🚌.
Princess Augusta, wife of Prince William (the future emporer), liked English castles. The first neo-Gothic building was designed by Schinkel in 1833 as a summer residence and later extended. The princess was keen on heavy ornamentation and disagreed with the architect who preferred light decoration such as that of the octagonal dining-room, which became the tea room. He was not present at the inauguration ceremony in 1835. The castle was extended after 1840 by another architect. The tour ends with the beautiful **ballroom** *(Tanzsaal)*.

★★**Park** – laid out by Lenné on a hillside, it is romantic, criss-crossed by winding lanes and studded with a variety of neo-Gothic *(Matrosenhaus)* or authentic medieval follies such as the law court gallery *(Gerichtslaube)*, built with stones from Berlin's former town hall and used as a tea room. There are pleasant views, from all angles, of the Havel and in particular **Glienicke Bridge**. The Glienicke Hunting Lodge *(Jagdschloß Glienicke, see WANNSEE)* can be seen in the distance. From the top of **Flatowturm**, an isolated keep, there is a view of Potsdam disfigured by the blocks of flats built by the GDR.

Studio Babelsberg (GV) – ⑤ *3, 7 Babelsberg, then (access from Großbeeren-straße)* 🚌 *Ahornstraße*.
Admission to **Filmpark Babelsberg** ⊘, set up on the site of the former UFA and DEFA studios *(see the INTRODUCTION, The Cinema)*, is very expensive. The stunt number is a kind of adaptation of *Mad Max*. The history of the studios is illustrated by a mediocre film fortunately preceded by two splendid advertisements! The *Caligari-halle*, which makes reference to the setting of R. Wiene's famous film, shows an extract from *Metropolis* and houses monsters and science-fiction characters. It will appeal to the fans of the master of special effects, **Ray Harryhausen**, who was responsible for the animated scenes of *Clash of the Titans (Kampf der Titanen)*, *Sindbad's Adventures* and *Jason and the Argonauts*. Note also that there is a room devoted to the **Sandman** *("Das Sandmännchen")*, after a fairy tale by Andersen, which was seen on GDR television in 1959. He used to throw a handful of sand at the end of each programme. All the children knew the "little chap with the pointed beard".

★★KLEIN-GLIENICKE

See **WANNSEE★★**.

Berlin's masterworks, a must for any visit to the city:

Reichtag Cupola (Sir Norman Foster, architect)

Practical
information

Before leaving

Formalities – A valid passport or identity card (if you come from the European Union) is all you will need to enter the Federal Republic of Germany.

Insurance – As countries of the European Union have reciprocal arrangements, ask for an **E111** form from your local post office before you leave for Germany. In exchange for this document, the **AOK**, German Health Insurance Service, will give the patient a form which entitles him or her to receive free health care. Payment is made directly to the doctor by the Health Insurance Service.
As the E111 does not cover all medical expenses, you are advised to also take out private insurance.

> **Some useful words:**
>
> **Bahnhof**: station.
>
> **Brücke**: bridge.
>
> **Platz**: square.
>
> **Straße**: street.
>
> **DM**: Deutsche Mark.
>
> The district (Charlottenburg, Mitte, Wilmersdorf, etc) is given in brackets for each address.

German Tourist Offices

London – German National Tourist Office, Nightingale House, 65 Curzon Street, London W1Y 8NE ; ☏ (0171) 495 00 81, fax: (0171) 495 61 29.

New York (Regional Management Nordamerika) – German National Tourist Office, 122 East 42nd Street, 52nd Floor, New York, N.Y. 10168-0072, USA ; ☏ (001212) 661 72 00, fax: (001212) 661 71 74.

Los Angeles – German National Tourist Office, 11766 Wiltshire Boulevard, Suite 750, Los Angeles, CA 90025, USA ; ☏ (001 310) 575 197 99, fax: (001 310) 575 15 65.

Canada – German National Tourist Office, 175 Bloor-street-East, North Tower, suite 604, Toronto, Ontario M4W3RS ; ☏ 416 968 15 70, fax: 416 968 19 86.

German cultural centres – These have libraries and offer language courses.

Goethe-Institut London – 50, Prince Gaio-Exhibition Rd., London, SW7 2PH ; ☏ (0171) 411 34 00, fax: (0171) 584 3180.

Goethe-Institut Dublin – German Institute, 37 Marrion Square, Dublin-2 ; ☏ (00 353 1) 661 11 55 or 661 11 56, fax: (00 353 1) 661 13 58.

Sprachabteilung – 62 Fitzwilliam Square, Dublin-2 ; ☏ (00 353 1) 661 85 06, fax: (00 353 1) 676 22 13.

Goethe-Institut New York – 1014 Fifth Avenue, New York, N.Y. 10028 ; ☏ (001 212) 439 87 00, fax: (001 212) 439 87 05.

Goethe-Institut Los Angeles – 57000 Wiltshire Boulevard, Suite 110, Los Angeles, California 90036 ; ☏ (001 213) 525 33 88, fax (001 213) 934 35 97.

Goethe-Institut Canada – 418. Sherbrook est. Montreal, PQ, H2L 1J6 ; ☏ (001) 514) 499 01 59, fax: (001 514) 499 09 05.

Goethe-Institut Sydney – 90 Ocean Street, P.O.B. 37, Woollahra, N.S.W. 2025 ; ☏ (0061-2) 328 74 11, fax: (0061-2) 326 13 23.

How to get there

BY CAR

Routes – To plan your itinerary across Europe, particularly if you wish to avoid toll motorways, use Michelin Map No 987 or the Michelin Route Planning Service on **Internet**: http://www.michelin-travel.com

Driving – The speed limit is 50km per hour in built-up areas and 100km per hour on main roads. There is no speed limit on motorways but you are advised not to exceed 130km per hour.
The wearing of **safety belts** is compulsory for both front and back seat passengers. You must carry an emergency triangle to warn other drivers if you have to stop at the side of the road.

Insurance – You must carry an international green card.

Roadside assistance – This is provided on motorways and main roads by the **ADAC** (Allgemeiner Deutscher Automobil-Club). Roadside repair is free; you pay only for spare parts.

ADAC Repair Centre – ☎ (01) 802 22 22 22. The Michelin *Deutschland* Red Guide gives the ADAC telephone numbers for main towns.

Fuel

Super Verbleit – 4-star petrol.

Super Bleifrei – unleaded petrol, 95 octane.

Super Plus Bleifrei – unleaded petrol, 98 octane.

Mitfahrzentrale
Private individuals offer their vehicles to one or more other people who share expenses.

City-netz – Kurfürstendamm 227, 3rd Floor of the Ku'Damm Eck (Charlottenburg); ☎ (030) 194 44; Ⓤ 9, 15 Kurfürstendamm.

Important Road Signs:

Anfang: start

Ausfahrt: way out

Baustelle: roadworks

Einbahnstraße: one way street

Ende: end

Einfahrt: way in

Gefährlich: dangerous

LKW: HGV

PKW: private car

Rechts einbiegen: turn right

Links einbiegen: turn left

Rollsplitt: loose chippings

Stau: traffic jam

Unfall: accident

Umleitung: diversion

Verengte Fahrbahn: road narrows

Vorfahrt: right of way

Vorsicht: caution

Mitfahrzentrale am Alex – Alexanderplatz U-Bahn station, on the concourse between lines 8 and 2 (Mitte); ☎ (030) 241 58 20; Ⓢ + Ⓤ Alexanderplatz.

Mensa (University Restaurant) – Hardenbergstraße. For students.

BY COACH

Zentraler Omnibusbahnhof (ZOB) – Masurenallee 4-6; Ⓢ 45, 46 Witzleben, Ⓤ 2 Kaiserdamm; ☎ (030) 301 80 28. Coach connections to large German cities and holiday destinations in the Hartz, Franken (in Bavaria) and the Black Forest.

Berlin Linien Bus – Mannheimer Straße 33-34 (Wilmersdorf); Ⓤ 1, 7 Fehrbelliner Platz; ☎ (030) 86 00 9 692.

BY TRAIN

You can travel on Eurostar from **London Waterloo International** to Brussels, then from **Bruxelles Midi** on a daily train to Berlin.

Deutsche Bahn AG passenger information service, ☎ 01 80 599 66 33.

Ph. Gajic/MICHELIN

The ICE high-speed train at Zoo station

Stations

Bahnhof Zoologischer Garten or **Bahnhof Zoo** (Charlottenburg) – Ⓢ + Ⓤ Zoologischer Garten; ☏ (030) 29 76 13 41; open every day from 5.30am to 11pm. Connections with the former *Länder* and western Europe; trains from the north also stop at Spandau station, those from the south and west at **Wannsee** station.

Ostbahnhof – Ⓢ + Ⓤ Ostbahnhof. Trains going to the new *Länder*, from Europe and the east (Budapest, Prague, Warsaw, Vienna) and from the CIS.

Bahnhof Lichtenberg – Ⓢ + Ⓤ Lichtenberg. Regional trains and trains to and from northern Europe.

Berlin-Airport connections

AIRPORTS

Since unification, the principal cities of Germany and Europe have direct connections with Berlin. **Lufthansa** and **British Airways** both have daily flights between Britain and Berlin.

British Airways information and reservations

London – 156 Regent Street, London, W1R 5TA; general reservations ☏ 0345 222 111.
Berlin – Europa Center, Budapester Straße, Berlin; ☏ (030) 69 10 21; and Flugbüro Arcadia, Poststraße 4/5, Nikolaiviertel, Berlin; ☏ (030) 247 36 80.

Lufthansa information and reservations

London – LH Sales Office, Lufthansa House, 10 Old Bond Street, London, W1X 4EN; ☏ (0181) 750 35 00.
New York – LH Sales Office, 680 Fifth Avenue, New York, N.Y. 10019-5429; ☏ (5212) 479 88 00.

Berlin-Tegel (TXL) – ☏ 01 805 000 186 (stops: Ⓢ + Ⓤ Zoologischer Garten, Ⓤ 9, 15 Kurfürstendamm, Ⓤ 7 Adenauerplatz, Ⓢ 3, 5, 7, 9, 75 Charlottenburg, Ⓤ 7 Jacob-Kaiser-Platz), 128 (stop: Ⓤ 9 Osloer Straße). A taxi ride between the city centre and the airport costs around **30 DM**.

Berlin-Tempelhof (THF) – ☏ 01 805 000 186; Ⓤ 6 Platz der Luftbrücke.

Berlin-Schönefeld (SXF) – ☏ 01 805 000 186; Ⓢ 9 (stops: Alexanderplatz, Friedrichstraße, Zoologischer Garten) and Ⓢ 45 Flughafen Berlin-Schönefeld (stop: Witzleben, near the Exhibition Park). Buses go between the Tegel and Schönefeld airports every 30 minutes. The taxi fare to the Zoo station is around 55 DM. There are railway connections within Germany and to Basle, Budapest, Prague and Vienna.

Airlines:

Air Canada (SXF) – ☏ Reservations (030) 882 58 79.

British Airways – Europa Center, Budapester Straße, Berlin; ☏ (030) 69 10 21.
Lufthansa City Center – Kurfürstendamm 220; ☏ Reservations (030) 88 75 88; ☏ TXL, SXF, THF (030) 88 75 63 33.
Sabena – ☏ THF (030) 69 51 38 50/51.

Animals

An anti-rabies vaccination certificate issued at least one month but no more than one year before, together with a health certificate issued in the last ten days (for European Countries) which must be accompanied by a certified German translation.

Accommodation

HOTELS

Hotels in Berlin are fairly expensive. The Michelin *Deutschland* Red Guide gives details of a selection of hotels and restaurants which have been visited and approved.

ADZ (Allgemeine Deutsche Zimmerreservierung) – Corneliusstraße 34, D-60 325 Frankfurt am Main; ☎ (069) 74 07 67, fax (069) 75 10 56. This German central booking office enables you easily to book any hotel, inn or guest house in Germany.

Hotel reservation service – Drususgasse 7 – 11. D-50667 Köln; ☎ (0221) 207 70, fax (0221) 207 76 66. English and French spoken. Immediate reservations.

Berlin Tourismus Marketing GmbH – Information and reservations ☎ (030) 25 00 25, fax (030) 25 00 24 24.

ACCOMMODATION FOR YOUNG PEOPLE

For a list of youth hostels, ask for the brochure *Preiswerte Pensionen, Jugendherbergen und Campingplätze in Berlin (Cheap hotels, youth hostels and campsites in Berlin)* from Tourist Offices. To obtain an international youth hostel card contact the **Deutsches Jugendherbergswerk**, Hauptverband; Bismarckstraße 8, D-32756 Detmold; ☎ (05231) 740 10.

Some useful addresses:

Jugendhotel Berlin – Kaiserdamm 3 (Charlottenburg); ☎ (030) 322 10 11, fax (030) 322 10 12.

Jugend- und Sporthotel Genslerstraße – Genslerstraße 18 (Hohenschönhausen); ☎ (030) 976 58 01, fax (030) 976 45 12.

Jugendgästehaus der Deutschen Schreberjugend – Franz-Künstler-Straße 4 (Kreuzberg); ☎ (030) 614 66 01.

Sportler-Übernachtsstätte Kreuzberg – Adalbertstraße 23b (Kreuzberg); ☎ (030) 25 88 24 47.

Internationales Jugendcamp Fließtal – Ziekowstraße 161 (Reinickendorf); ☎ (030) 791 30 40.

Jugendgästehaus Tegel – Ziekowstraße 161 (Reinickendorf); ☎ (030) 433 30 46.

Jugendherberge Ernst-Reuter – Hermsdorfer Damm 48-50 (Reinickendorf); ☎ (030) 262 30 24, fax (030) 262 95 29.

Jugendgästehaus Berlin – Kluckstraße 3 (Schöneberg); ☎ (030) 262 30 24, fax (030) 262 95 29

Jugendgästehaus Feurigstraße – Feurigstraße 63 (Schöneberg); ☎ (030) 781 52 11.

Studentenhotel – Meininger Straße 10 (Schöneberg); ☎ (030) 784 67 20.

Karl-Renner-Haus – Ringstraße 76 (Steglitz); ☎ (030) 833 50 29, fax (030) 833 91 57.

Touristenhaus Grünau – Dahmestraße (Treptow); ☎ (030) 679 92 30.

Jugendgästehaus Koloniestraße – Koloniestraße 23-24 (Wedding); ☎ (030) 439 50 75/76.

Jugendgästehaus Nordufer – Nordufer 28 (Wedding); ☎ (030) 451 70 30.

Haus Vier Jahreszeiten – Bundesallee 31a (Wilmersdorf); ☎ (030) 873 20 14, fax (030) 87 82 23.

Jugendgästehaus Central – Nikolsburger Straße 2-4 (Wilmersdorf); ☎ (030) 873 01 88, fax (030) 861 34 85.

Studentenwohnheim Hubertusallee (Wilmersdorf) – ☎ (030) 891 97 18.

Jugendgästehaus Am Wannsee – Badeweg 1 (Zehlendorf); ☎ (030) 262 30 24, fax (030) 262 95 29.

Campsite information:

Camping & Zeitplätze – ☎ (030) 218 60 71.

Getting around Berlin

ON FOOT

The **Falk Map (Falkplan**, 9.80 DM) is practical because its method of folding makes it easy to handle. A map is available for Berlin and Potsdam (13 DM). The layout of the streets and the U-Bahn and S-Bahn network are clearly shown; the bus system is less clear. The key to not getting lost in Berlin is the **Atlas** of the central area of Berlin (as far as Potsdam) published by the **BVG**. Although its format is not as practical as the *Falk plan*, this inexpensive Atlas (3.50 DM), gives the details of the streets together with an accurate presentation of public transport. The bus guide showing the location and name of the stations is very clear and will help you to get to any location no matter how isolated.

BY BICYCLE

See under the heading ON THE TOWN.

BY CAR

The location of the main car parks is given on the map of the centre of Berlin at the front of the guide. A list of hire firms is in the yellow pages of the phone book, under the heading *Autovermietung*. The **Michelin Deutschland Red Guide** gives a great deal of useful information: car parks, hire firms, garages, main service stations.

ADAC Berlin-Brandenburg – ADAC Haus, Bundesallee 29 (Wilmersdorf); ☏ information (030) 868 60, fax (030) 861 60 25.

If you break down:
ACE (Autoclub Europa) – ☏ (0 18 02) 34 35 36.
ADAC – ☏ (0 18 02) 22 22 22.

TAXIS

Taxi ranks:
Zoo Station, Hardenbergplatz (Charlottenburg).
Savignyplatz (Charlottenburg)
Although dispersed all over the western part of Berlin, in the east, taxi ranks are concentrated at Alexanderplatz, at the entrance to the S-Bahn station, in front of the *Palasthotel*, on Unter den Linden, to the south of the Weidendammerbrücke, on Rosenthaler Platz and near the Volksbühne.

Numbers to call:	☏ (030) 690 22	☏ (030) 21 01 01
	☏ (030) 691 50 59	☏ (030) 21 02 02
	☏ (030) 26 10 26	☏ (030) 96 44

Basic fare: 14 DM (+ 6 DM for a taxi called by telephone); many taxis accept credit cards.

PUBLIC TRANSPORT

The urban transport system is called **BVG** (Berliner Verkehrsbetriebe).

Information:

BVG-Pavillon Hardenbergplatz, in front of Zoo station – Open every day from 6.30am to 20.30. You can buy the BVG *Atlas* here (*see above*).

BVG Call Center – open 24h a day. Tel. (030) 194 49.

Women on their own and disabled people can call a taxi service from the U-Bahn stations in the evening after 8pm and until the trains stop running. Contact the station manager on the platform so that he can call and specify your destination and how you want to pay.

Fares

U-Bahn, S-Bahn, bus and tram are all covered by the same fare system. A single ticket is valid **for 2 hours** on all forms of transport.
You can buy a ticket in the yellow or orange automatic machines at the entrance of U-Bahn and S-Bahn stations. The machines accept uncreased notes and give change. The ticket has to be punched in the red box usually situated in front of the escalators and inside the buses. Tickets are frequently checked (by plain clothes inspectors), especially at weekends.
Single journey (*Normaltarif*) – 4 DM on the entire public transport system; valid for 2 hours.

Short journey *(Kurzstreckentarif)* – 2.50 DM; valid for three U-Bahn or S-Bahn stations and for six bus stations without changing lines.

Weekly pass *(Wochenkarte)* – 42 DM. This is the cheapest way to travel if you are going to be in Berlin for 4 or 5 days (don't forget that the transport system goes to Potsdam-Stadt).

The **Berlin Potsdam WelcomeCard** (32 DM) allows one adult and three children (up to 15 years) to use the entire public transport system in Berlin and Potsdam for two days. With this card you are also given numerous reductions, valid for three days, for museums, theatres and city excursions by coach. One-day pass – 8.70 DM, valid until 3 p.m. the following morning.

Car parks

Around the Kaiser-Wilhem-Gedächtniskirche (Memorial Church) (car parks open 24 hours a day):

Am Zoo – Budapester Straße 38; 305 spaces; 3 DM per hour.

Central-Garagen – Kantstraße 158; 600 spaces; 2.50 DM per hour.

Europa-Center – Nürnberger Straße 5-7; 910 spaces; 3 DM per hour.

Knesebeckstraße 72-73; 207 spaces; 2 DM.

Ku'damm Karree/Uhlandstraße – Uhlandstraße 30-32; 914 spaces; 3 DM per hour.

Los-Angeles-Platz – Augsburger Straße 30; 230 spaces; 2 DM per hour.

Meineckestraße 19 – 1010 spaces; 3 DM per hour (2.50 DM after two hours).

Uhlandtraße 190/Kantstraße/Fasanenstraße – 503 spaces; open 6am to midnight; 1.50 DM per hour.

In the historical centre, large hotel car parks open to the public:

Berlin Hilton – Mohrenstraße (Mitte); 387 spaces; open 6am to 11pm; 1 hour 3.50 DM, 2 hours 5 DM.

Forum Hotel Berlin – Alexanderplatz (Mitte); 186 spaces; open 24 hours a day; 1 hour 3 DM, 2 hours 5 DM.

Grand Hotel Esplanade – Lützowufer (Tiergarten); 125 spaces; open 24 hours a day; 1 hour 4 DM, 2 DM per additional hour.

Hotel Berlin – Kurfürstenstraße; 220 spaces; open 24 hours a day; 1 hour 4 DM, 3 DM per additional hour.

Maritim Grandhotel – Behrenstraße (Mitte); 476 spaces; open from 5am to 1am; 2 DM per hour.

Along the shopping streets, department store car parks:

Hertie – Turmstraße (Moabit); 115 spaces; open Monday to Friday, 9am to 7pm; 1 hour 3 DM, 2 hours 5 DM, 2 DM per additional hour.
Wilmersdorfer Straße (Charlottenburg); 260 spaces; open Monday to Friday 8am to 7pm; 3 DM per hour.
Karl-Marx-Straße (Neukölln) – 410 spaces; open Monday to Friday, 8.30am to 7pm; 3 DM per hour.

Leffers – Wilmersdorfer Straße (Charlottenburg); 304 spaces; open Monday to Friday, 8.30am to 7pm; 2 DM per hour.

Karstadt – Hermannplatz (Neukölln); 810 spaces; open Monday to Saturday after 8am; 3 DM per hour.

KaDeWe P1 and P2 – Passauer Straße; 893 spaces; open Monday to Friday,8.30am to 7pm; 3 DM per hour.

Where to park when you go to a concert or exhibition

Deutsche Oper – Bismarckstraße (Charlottenburg); 350 spaces; open 24 hours a day; free.

Martin-Gropius-Bau – Stresemannstraße (Kreuzberg); 230 spaces; open 24 hours a day; 2 DM per hour.

Philharmonie – Potsdamer Straße (Tiergarten); 103 spaces; open 24 hours a day; free.

S-Bahn station car parks:

🅄 8 **Gesundbrunnen** – 63 spaces. For visiting Wedding and the Humboldthain park.
🅄 7 **Rathaus Spandau** – 105 spaces. Just next to the old town of Spandau (Christmas market)
Ⓢ 1, 3, 7 **Wannsee** – 85 spaces. For bathing at the largest inland beach in Europe.
Ⓢ 1 + 🅄 9 **Rathaus Steglitz** – 264 spaces. Schloßstraße is a very busy shopping street.
Ⓢ 3 **Friedrichshagen** – 150 spaces. For visiting the hydro-electric power station.
🅄 6 **Alt-Tegel** – 290 spaces. A holiday spot from which you can take boat trips.
Ⓢ 1 **Frohnau** – 107 spaces. For visiting the garden town of Frohnau.

All these car parks are free.

U-Bahn

This is Berlin's underground. The stations are shown by a blue sign with a white "U". The network operates from shortly after 4am until midnight/1am. At weekends lines **U** 1, 15 and 9 run all night.

Some notable U-Bahn and S-Bahn stations

U 2 **Bülowstraße** (Schöneberg) – Elevated *Jugendstil* station which has lost much of its ironwork ornamentation.
U 1 **Dahlem-Dorf** (Zehlendorf) – Picturesque.
S 1 **Mexikoplatz** (Zehlendorf) – The most attractive *Art Nouveau* station in Berlin.
U 1, 3, 7 **Nikolasee** (Zehlendorf) – Gothic-style.
U 1, 12, 15 **Schlesisches Tor** (Kreuzberg) – Neo-Gothic style.
S 3, 7, **Wannsee** (Zehlendorf) – Expressionist-style.
U 1, 2, 12, 15 **Wittenbergplatz** (Charlottenburg) – The first underground station on the line which connected the Warsaw Bridge *(Warschauer Brücke)* with what is now Ernst-Reuter-Platz. Neoclassical in style (1911-13), it was a gateway to the new districts of the west.

S-Bahn
It is a regional express network. S-Bahn stations are indicated by a green sign with a white "S". The trains normally run every 10 minutes.

Regionalbahn
This network goes around the city of Berlin; a ticket is valid for 2 hours.

Bus
They operate between 4.30am and 1am. You enter at the front and descend from the middle of the bus. You can pay your fare to the driver (specifying if you want a single ticket) or at an orange or yellow automatic machine in the U-Bahn. There is a night bus on the major routes.

Tram
All the lines are in the east but may be extended to the western area of the city in the near future. The tram network, which only existed in the East a few years ago, has now been extended to the Western side of the city.

See Berlin by public transport !

The trip by **S-Bahn** between the Zoologischer Garten station and Alexanderplatz is practically equivalent to a city tour. The train goes along the Tiergarten to the north, providing a view of the modern buildings which border the Spree at Moabit, where they are building the Lehrte station and the huge construction site of the administrative district, the neo-Gothic wings of the Charité Hospital (which belonged to the eastern sector), the Reichstag (the Wall passed just behind), Friedrichstraße station, the island of Museums and the cathedral and Television Tower.

On the way back, the **100** bus takes you from Alexanderplatz and Zoologischer Garten station past a number of interesting sights: the cathedral and the Old Museum, Unter den Linden, the Brandenburg Gate, Bellevue castle, the Victory column and the Memorial Church. Two elevated trips on the **U-Bahn** are interesting: one is on **U** 1 or 15 between Gleisdreieck and Möckern-

Bus 100

brücke, which passes over the disused lines of the Anhalt station (at the same level as the Museum of Transport and Technology), and provides a view of the forest of cranes at the Potsdamer Platz construction site and the other on **U** 2 from Senefelderplatz.

Transport at night

The network operates between 1am and 4am. Buses and trams then have an **"N"** in front of their number. The fare is the same as during the day.

N 16 to Potsdam: every hour.

U 1 and **U 2**: on Friday and Saturday nights only.

S 3 to **10**: every hour.

N 11 and **N 41**: taxis provide a service at the normal fare.

General information

MONEY AND METHODS OF PAYMENT

The German currency is the **Deutsche Mark (DM)**, divided into 100 **Pfennig**. Transactions are usually cash (especially in the east), but you can also use Travellers' Cheques or **"Euro-cheques"**. Cheques issued by banks in the European Union and credit cards are not always accepted. Ensure you have enough cash with you, particularly for paying the hotel bill as you will quickly reach the card limit!

BANKS AND BUREAUX DE CHANGE

Banks are open from 8.30am to 12.30pm and from 2.30pm to 4pm (6pm on Thursdays). They are closed on Saturdays and Sundays. **Bureaux de change** generally offer better rates than the banks. Some stay open until late in the evening or during weekends.

American Express, Friedrichstraße 173; ☎ (030) 20 17 40 11 – Open Monday to Friday 9am to 5.30pm, Saturdays 10am to 1am.

Commerzbank

Kempi-Plaza, Uhlandstraße 181-183 – Open Monday to Thursday, 9am to 1.30pm, Tuesdays and Thursdays 3.30pm to 6.30pm, Fridays 9am to 1pm.

ATMs: Europa Center, Friedrichstraße 130, Kurfürstendamm 59 and 102.

Berliner Sparkasse

Alexanderplatz 2 – Open Monday to Friday 9am to 6pm, Saturdays 9am to 1pm.

On the corner of Kantstraße and Wilmersdorfer Straße – Open Monday to Friday 9am to 6pm.

ICC Berlin – Open Monday to Friday 9am to 6pm, Saturdays 9am to 1pm.

Rankestraße 33-34 – Open Monday to Friday 9am to 6pm, Saturdays 10am to 1pm.

Savignyplatz 9-10 – Open Monday to Friday 9am to 6pm.

Deutsche Bank

Otto-Suhr-Allee 6-16 – Open Monday to Wednesday 9am to 3.30pm, Tuesdays and Thursdays 9am to 6pm, Fridays 9am to 12.30pm.

ATMs: Alexanderplatz 6, Bismarckstraße 68, Hardenbergstraße 27 (Charlottenburg), Karl-Marx-Allee 60-62, Kurfürstendamm 28 and 182, Tauentzienstraße 1.

Deutsche Verkehrsbank

Wechseistube am Bahnhof Zoo – Open Monday to Saturday 7.30am to 10pm, Sundays and public holidays 8am to 7pm; ATM.

Wechselstube im Hauptbahnhof – Open Monday to Friday 7am to 10pm, Saturdays 7am to 6pm, Sundays 8am to 4pm.

POST AND TELEPHONE

Post offices are open Monday to Friday 8am to 6pm, Saturdays until 12 noon.

Post offices open late in the evening:

Postamt 120, at Zoologischer Garten station – Open Monday to Saturday, 8am to midnight, Saturdays and public holidays 10am to midnight (put *Hauptpostlagernd or Bahnhof-postlagernd* on your letters); ☎ (030) 311 00 20

Postamt 519, at Tegel airport – Open Monday to Friday 7am to 9pm, Saturdays, Sundays and public holidays 8am to 8pm; ☎ (030) 417 84 90.

Area code – The area code for Berlin is **030**. Do not dial the 0 when calling from abroad. To call Berlin from abroad dial the country code (49) + 30 + the number of the person you are calling.
To call the UK from Berlin dial 00 + the country code (44) + the area code + the number of the person you are calling.
To call the USA, Canada and Australia dial 00 + the country code + the area code + the number of the person you are calling.

TIME ZONE AND PUBLIC HOLIDAYS

Time zone – Berlin is one hour ahead of GMT and the same as British Summer Time.

Public holidays – 1 January, Good Friday, Easter Monday, 1 May, Ascension Day, Whit Monday, National Holiday (3 October, Unification Day), one Wednesday in November *(Buß- und Bettag*: day of Penitence and Prayer), 25 and 26 December.

DISABLED TRAVELLERS

Telebus-Zentrale – Esplanade 17 (Pankow); Ⓤ 2 Vinetastraße; ☎ (030) 47 88 20; open Monday to Friday 9am to 3pm. Special bus service for the disabled operating from 5am to 1am. Two weeks before setting off for Berlin contact the agency to obtain a pass.

Disabled information

Landesamt für Zentrale Soziale Aufgaben – W-1000 Berlin 31. Sächsische Straße 28-30; (030) 867 61 14.

Service-Ring Berlin e.V. – Information, advice, help. (030) 322 40 20.

Telebus – Participation in cultural activities. (030) 880 031 13.

Useful addresses

Useful numbers:

Mobile Accident Unit and Fire Brigade – ☎ 112.

Police – ☎ 110.

Medical emergencies – ☎ 1 00 31.

Poisoning – ☎ 192 40.

Information on pharmacies, dentists – ☎ 080 03 30 11 33; ☎ 42 21 14 37.

Telegrams by telephone – ☎ 0 11 31.

Information – ☎ (030) 011 88 33.

International information – ☎ (030) 0 01 18 34.

Lost and found (Fundbüro):

Zentrales Fundbüro – ☎ (030) 69 95.

BVG – Lorenzweg 5 (Tempelhof); ☎ (030) 751 80 21; Ⓤ 6 Ullsteinstraße; Open Mondays, Tuesdays, Thursdays 9am to 3pm, Wednesdays 9am to 6pm, Fridays 9am to 2pm.

Fundbüro der Polizei – Platz des Luftbrücke 6; ☎ (030) 69 90; Ⓤ 6 Platz der Luftbrücke.

Deutsche Bahn – ☎ (030) 29 72 96 12

Embassies:

United States of America – 4 Neustädtische Kirchstraße ☎ (030) 2 38 51 74

Canada – Friedrichstraße 95 ☎ (030) 261 11 61

United Kingdom – 32 Unter den Linden ☎ (030) 20 18 41 58

Australia – 181-183 Uhlandstraße ☎ (030) 8 80 08 80

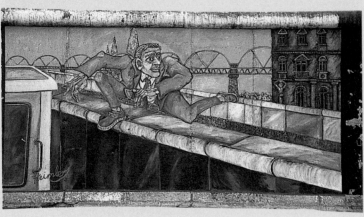

Admission times and charges

The times, charges and information indicating the days and periods when the sights described in this guide are closed apply to individual travellers not benefiting from concessionary rates. Ticket offices usually shut 30min before closing time. Many places offer special rates for group bookings and some have special times and rates for group visits. Large parties should apply in advance

Churches are usually closed when there is no religious service in progress.

Every sight for which times and charges are listed below is indicated by the symbol ⊘ after the title in the **Sights** section.

Public holidays – Telephone in advance to check whether the sight you wish to visit is open or not.

Guided tours – Theme visits are organised by the *Kulturbüro Berlin*; details are given in the **"Stadt(ver)führung"** pamphlet which is available in museums and cultural institutions *(commentaries are in German only)*.

A

ABGUSSSAMMLUNG ANTIKER PLASTIK

Open Thur-Sun 2-5pm; closed at Christmas. Free admission. ☎ (030) 342 40 54.

ÄGYPTISCHES MUSEUM

Open 10am-6pm; closed Mon. 8 DM; free admission the 1st Sun of the month. ☎ (030) 32 09 12 61.

ALTE NATIONALGALERIE

Closed for renovation work until 2001.

ALTES MUSEUM

Open 10am-6pm; closed Mon. 8 DM; free admission the 1st Sun of the month. ☎ (030) 20 90 55 66.

B

BAUHAUS ARCHIV

. Open 10am-5pm; closed Mon and 24 and 31 Dec. 5 DM. ☎ (030) 254 00 20.

BERLINER DOM

♿. Open 9am (noon on Sun) to 8pm (7pm Oct to Mar). 8 DM; free admission on religious holidays. ☎ (030) 20 26 91 52.

BERLINER KINOMUSEUM

Films on Tues, Wed, Fri and Sat at 5pm and 11pm.

BODEMUSEUM

Closed for renovation work. ☎ (030) 20 90 55 55.

BOTANISCHER GARTEN BERLIN-DAHLEM

♿. Open 9am, closing times vary according to the season (9pm May to July, 8pm Apr and Aug, 7pm Sept, 6pm Mar and Oct, 5pm Feb, 4pm Nov and Jan); closed 24 and 31 Dec. 8 DM. ☎ (030) 83 00 61 27.
Botanisches Museum – ♿. Open 10am-5pm; closed 24 and 31 Dec. 2 DM. ☎ (030) 83 00 61 27.

BRECHT-WEIGEL-GEDENKSTÄTTE

Guided tours (every 30min) Tues-Fri 10am-noon, 5-5pm Thur, 9.30am-2pm Sat, 11am-6pm Sun; closed public holidays. 6 DM. ☎ (030) 283 05 70 44.

BRÖHAN-MUSEUM

♿. Open 10am-6pm;
closed Mon and 24 and 31
Dec. 6 DM. ☎ (030) 32 69
06 00.

BRÜCKE-MUSEUM

♿. Open 11am-5pm;
closed Tues and 24 and
31 Dec. 7 DM.
☎ (030) 831 20 29.

BUDDHISTISCHES HAUS

Open in summer 8am-
8pm, winter 9am-6pm.
Free admission. ☎ (030)
401 55 80.

BRÖHAN MUSEUM

Bröhan Museum – Chandelier in art deco ironwork

C

Schloß CHARLOTTENBURG

Open 9am (10am Sat-Sun) to 5pm; closed Mon. 8 DM. ☎ (030) 32 09 12 75.

Historische Räume – Guided tours (every 45min) 9am (10am Sat-Sun) to 5pm (last admission: 4pm) ; closed Mon. 8 DM. ☎ (030) 32 09 12 75.

Schinkel-Pavillon – Open 10am-5pm; closed Mon. 4 DM. ☎ (030) 32 09 12 12.

Mausoleum – Open Apr to Oct 10am-5pm; closed Mon. 2 DM. ☎ (030) 32 09 12 80.

Belvedere – Open Apr to Oct Tues-Sun 10am-5pm, Nov to Mar Sat-Sun noon-4pm. 3 DM. ☎ (030) 32 09 12 85.

Knobelsdorff-Flügel – Open 10am (11am Sat-Sun) to 5pm; closed Mon. 5 DM. ☎ (030) 32 09 12 75.

Galerie der Romantik – Open 10am (11am Sat-Sun) to 6pm; closed Mon. 4 DM; free admission the 1st Sun of the month. ☎ (030) 32 09 11.

Museum für Vor- und Frühgeschichte – Open 10am (11am Sat-Sun) to 6pm; closed Mon. 4 DM; free admission the 1st Sun of the month. ☎ (030) 32 67 48 11.

D

Museums in DAHLEM

See MUSEUM DAHLEM

DEUTSCHER DOM

Open 10am-6pm (7pm June to Aug); closed Mon and 24 and 31Dec. Free admission.
☎ (030) 22 73 04 31.

DEUTSCHES HISTORISCHES MUSEUM

Closed until beginning 2002. ☎ (030) 20 30 40.

DEUTSCHES TECHNIKMUSEUM BERLIN

♿. Open Tues-Fri 9am-5.30pm, Sat-Sun 10am-6pm; closed 1 May, 24, 25 and 31 Dec. 5 DM. ☎ (030) 25 48 40.

DOMÄNE DAHLEM LANDGUT UND MUSEUM

Open 10am-6pm; closed Tues. 3 DM. ☎ (030) 832 50 00.

E - F

EPHRAIM-PALAIS (Collections from the city of Berlin museum)

Open 10am-6pm; closed Mon and 24 and 31 Dec. 4 DM; free admission Wed. ☎ (030) 24 00 20.

FERNSEHTURM

Floor with panoramic view open from May to Oct 9am-1 in the morning, Nov to Mar 10am-midnight. 10 DM. ☎ (030) 242 33 33.

FRANZÖSISCHER DOM

Open noon (11am Sun and public holidays) to 5pm; Closed Mon. ☎ (030) 204 15 07.

Hugenottenmuseum – Open noon (11am Sun and public holidays) 5pm; closed Mon. 3 DM. ☎ (030) 229 17 60.

Visit of the dome – 10am-5pm.
Bells – Ring every day 10am, noon and 2pm.

Schloß FRIEDRICHSFELDE

Open Mar tp Oct 10am-6pm, Nov to Feb 9am-5pm; closed Mon. ☎ (030) 513 81 41.

FRIEDRICHSWERDERSCHE KIRCHE

Open 10am-6pm; closed Mon. 4 DM; free admission the 1st Sun of the month. ☎ (030) 208 13 23.

FRISEUR MUSEUM

Open 10am-6pm; closed Mon. Free admission. ☎ (030) 541 02 31.

FUNKTURM

Floor with panoramic view accessible 10am-11pm (11am-9pm Mon); closed when outside temperatures are below zero. 6 DM. ☎ (030) 30 38 29 96.

G

GALERIE DER ROMANTIK

See Schloß CHARLOTTENBURG.

GEDENKSTÄTTE DEUTSCHER WIDERSTAND

Open 9am (10am Sat-Sun) to 6pm (8pm Thur); closed 1 Jan, 24, 25, 26 and 31 Dec. Free admission. ☎ (030) 26 99 50 00.

GEDENKSTÄTTE PLÖTZENSEE

&. Open 9am-5pm (4pm Nov to Feb); closed 1 Jan, 24, 25, 26, 31 Dec. Free admission. ☎ (030) 26 99 50 00.

GEMÄLDEGALERIE

Open 10am-6pm; (10pm Thur); closed Mon. 8 DM; free admission the 1st Sun of the month. ☎ (030) 266 20 01.

GEORG-KOLBE-MUSEUM

&. Open 10am-5pm; closed Good Fri and Easter Mon, 24 and 31 Dec. 8 DM. ☎ (030) 304 21 44.

GIPSFORMEREI STAATLICHE MUSEEN PREUSSISCHER KULTURBESITZ

Open 9am-4pm; closed Sat-Sun. Guided tours 1st Wed in the month. ☎ (030) 32 67 69 11.

Jagdschloß GRÜNEWALD

Open May to Oct 10am-5pm, closed Mon; Sat-Sun in Apr 10am-5pm, Sat-Sun Nov to Mar 10am 4pm. 4 DM. ☎ (03 31) 969 42 00.

GRÜNEWALDTURM (Kaiser-Wilhelm-Turm)

Open 10am-midnight (7pm Oct to Apr). 1.50 DM. ☎ (030) 300 07 30.

H

HAMBURGER BAHNHOF

Open 10am (11am Sat-Sun) to 6pm (10pm Thur); closed Mon. 8 DM; free admission the 1st Sun of the month. ☎ (030) 397 83 40.

HANDWERKMUSEUM

Open 10am-6pm; closed Mon. 4 DM; free admission Wed. ☎ (030) 541 02 31.

HAUS DER KULTUREN DER WELT

&. Open 10am-9pm; closed Mon. ☎ (030) 39 78 70.

HAUS DER WANNSEE KONFERENZ

&. Open 10am (2pm Sat-Sun) to 6pm; reference library and library closed Sat-Sun Free admission. ☎ (030) 805 00 10.

HEIMATMUSEEN

With reconstructed interiors (the Tempelhof), theme exhibitions (Mitte), photographs, press articles, plans, maps and models (Charlottenbourg), the following museums illustrate everyday life in the various districts of Berlin. Not all of them are described in the Sights section of the guide.

Heimatmuseum Charlottenburg

&. Open 10am (11am Sun and public holidays) to 5 pm; closed Mon and Sat, Aug, 1 Jan, 24 and 31 Dec. Free admission. ☎ (030) 34 30 32 01.

Heimatmuseum Friedrichshain

&. Open Tues, Thur and Sat 11am-6pm; closed public holidays. Free admission. ☎ (030) 249 68 75.

Bezirkskronik/Heimatmuseum Hellersdorf

Open 10am-6pm; closed Sat-Sun and public holidays. Free admission. ☎ (030) 99 20 41 71.

Heimatmuseum Hohenschönhausen

Open May to Sept Tues-Thur 10am-noon and 2-6pm, Sun 1-6pm; Oct to Apr Tues-Thur 9am-noon and 2-5pm, Sun 11am-4pm. Free admission. ☎ (030) 982 73 78.

Heimatmuseum Köpenick

&. Open Tues and Wed 10am-4pm, Thur 10am-6pm, Sat 2-6pm. Free admission. ☎ (030) 65 84 43 51.

Kreuzberg-Museum

Open Wed-Sun noon-6pm. Free admission. ☎ (030) 25 88 62 33.

Heimatmuseum Lichtenberg

Open Tues and Thur 11am-6pm, Wed 1-6pm, Sun 2-6pm; closed public holidays and Aug. ☎ (030) 57 79 46 53.

Heimatmuseum Marzahn

Open Tues to Thur 9am-5pm, Fri 9am-2pm, Sun 2-6pm. Free admission. ☎ (030) 540 07 75 22.

Heimatmuseum Neukölln

&. Open Wed-Fri 1-6pm, Sat-Sun noon-6pm. Free admission. ☎ (030) 68 09 25 35.

Heimatmuseum Pankow

Open Tues and Thur 10am-6pm, Sun 10am-5.30pm; closed public holidays and 3 or 4 weeks in Aug. Free admission. ☎ (030) 481 40 47.

Prenzlauer Berg Museum

Open Tues and Wed 1-6pm, Thur 3-8pm, Sun 1-6pm. Free admission. ☎ (030) 42 40 10 97.

Heimatmuseum Reinickendorf

&. Open Wed-Sun 10am-6pm; closed public holidays. Free admission. ☎ (030) 404 40 62.

Schöneberg Museum

Open Wed and Thur 3-6pm, Sun and public holidays 2-6pm; closed during summer holidays. Free admission. ☎ (030) 78 76 22 34.

Stadtgeschichtliches Museum Spandau

Open 9am (10am Sat-Sun) to 5pm; closed Mon and 3 Oct, 24, 25 and 31 Dec. 4 DM. ☎ (030) 354 94 42 00.

Museum und Archiv des Heimatvereins für den Bezirk Steglitz

Open Mon 4-7pm, Wed 3-6pm, Sun 2-5pm; closed summer and Christmas holidays. Free admission. ☎ (030) 78 33 21 09.

Heimatmuseum Tempelhof

Open Mon-Fri 9am-2pm, Sun 11am-3pm; closed public holidays. Free admission. ☎ (030) 75 60 74 65.

Heimatmuseum Tiergarten

&. Temporary exhibitions at varying times; visits of the city on foot are organised during the 1st week of the month. ☎ (030) 39 05 27 28.

Heimatmuseum Treptow

Open Thur-Sun 2-6pm. Free admission. ☎ (030) 53 31 56 29.

Heimatmuseum Wedding

Open Tues and Wed 10am-4pm, Thur 2-6pm, Sun and public holidays 11am-5pm; closed 1 Jan, 3 weeks in Aug and 24, 25 and 31 Dec. 3 DM. ☎ (030) 45 75 41 58.

Stadtgeschichtliches Museum Weißensee

&. Open Tues 10am-4pm, Wed and Thur noon-6pm, Sun 2-6pm. ☎ (030) 925 01 10 51.

Wilmersdorf Museum

Closed for renovation work. ☎ (030) 86 41 30 09.

Heimatmuseum Zehlendorf

Open Mon and Thur 4-7pm; closed during school and public holidays. Free admission. ☎ (030) 802 24 41.

HUGENOTTENMUSEUM

See FRANZÖSISCHE KIRCHE.

J – K

JÜDISCHES MUSEUM BERLIN

Closed until autumn 2001 ☎ (030) 28 39 74 44

KAISER-WILHELM-GEDÄCHTNIS-KIRCHE

Open 9am-7pm. ☎ (030) 218 50 23.

KÄTHE-KOLLWITZ-MUSEUM

Open 11am-6pm; closed Mon and 24 and 31 Dec. 8 DM. ☎ (030) 882 52 10.

KIRCHE AM HOHENZOLLERNPLATZ

Visiting times vary. For information call ☎ (030) 873 10 43.

KNOBLAUCHHAUS

Open 10am-6pm; closed Mon and 24 and 31 Dec. 3 DM; free admission Wed. ☎ (030) 24 00 20.

KPM (Königliche Porzellan Manufaktur)

Visiting times vary. For information call ☎ (030) 39 00 92.

KUNSTBIBLIOTHEK

Open Mon 2-8pm, Tues-Fri 9am-8pm. ☎ (030) 266 20 53.

KUNSTGEWERBEMUSEEN

Kulturforum – ♿. Open 10am (11am Sat-Sun) to 6pm; closed Mon. 4 DM; free admission the 1st Sun of the month. ☎ (030) 266 29 02.

Schloß Köpenick – Closed for restoration until 2002.

KÜNSTLERHAUS BETHANIEN

♿. Open 2-7pm; closed Mon and Tues. Free admission. ☎ (030) 616 90 30.

KUPFERSTISCHKABINETT

Open 10am (11am Sat-Sun) to 6pm; closed Mon. 4 DM. ☎ (030) 266 20 01.

L – M

LUISENKIRCHE

To visit, ask for the key at the vicarage, Gierkeplatz 4. ☎ (030) 341 90 61.

MARIA REGINA MARTYRUM

♿. Open 9-4pm (Sat 6pm, Sun and public holidays 2pm). If the church is closed, ask for the key at the monastery door. ☎ (030) 382 60 11.

MARIENKIRCHE

Open 10am (noon Sun and public holidays) to 4pm. ☎ (030) 242 44 67.

MÄRKISCHES MUSEUM

Open 10am-6pm; closed Mon and 24 and 31 Dec. 8 DM; free admission Wed. ☎ (030) 30 86 60.

MARTIN-GROPIUS-BAU

Visiting times vary. For information call ☎ (030) 25 48 60.

MUSEUM BERLIN-KARLSHORST

♿.Open from 10am-6pm; closed Mon. Free admission. ☎ (030) 50 15 08 10..

MUSEUM DAHLEM

Ethnologisches Museum – ♿. Open 10am (11am Sat-Sun) to 6pm; closed Mon. 4 DM; free admission the 1st Sun of the month. ☎ (030) 830 12 31.

Museum für Ostasiatische Kunst – Same times and charges than Ethnologisches Museum. ☎ (030) 830 13 81.

Museum für Indische Kunst – Same times and charges than Ethnologisches Museum. ☎ (030) 830 13 61.

Museum Europäischer Kulturen – Open 10am (11am Sat-Sun) to 6pm; closed Mon. 4 DM; free admission the 1st Sun of the month. ☎ (030) 83 90 12 87.

MUSEUM FÜR KOMMUNIKATION BERLIN

♿. Open Tues-Fri 9am-5pm, Sat-Sun 11am-7pm; closed 1 Jan, 24, 25 and 31 Dec. Free admission. ☎ (030) 20 29 40.

MUSEUM FÜR NATURKUNDE

♿.Open from 9am-5pm; closed Mon. 5 DM. ☎ (030) 20 93 85 91.

MUSEUM FÜR VOR– UND FRÜHGESCHICHTE

See SCHLOSS CHARLOTTENBURG.

MUSEUM HAUS AM CHECKPOINT CHARLIE

Open 9am-10pm. 8 DM. ☎ (030) 253 72 50.

MUSEUM IM WASSERWERK FRIEDRICHSHAGEN

Open Apr to Oct 10am-4pm (5pm Sat-Sun), Nov to Mar 10am-3pm; closed Mon and Tues, 1 Jan, 24, 25, 26 Dec. 4 DM. ☎ (030) 86 44 76 95.

MUSEUMSDORF DÜPPEL

&. Open Holy Week to mid-Oct Thur 3-6pm, Sun and public holidays 10am-4pm. 3 DM. ☎ (030) 802 66 71.

MUSIKINSTRUMENTEN-MUSEUM

&. Open 9am (10am Sat-Sun) to 5pm; closed Mon. 4 DM; free admission the 1st Sun of the month. ☎ (030) 25 48 11 78.

N – O – P

NEUE NATIONALGALERIE

Open 10am (11am Sat-Sun) to 6pm (10pm Thur); closed Mon. 8 DM; free admission the 1st Sun of the month. ☎ (030) 266 26 62.

"NEUE SYNAGOGE BERLIN" (Centrum Judaicum)

&. Open from 10am-5.30pm (1.30pm Fri); closed Sat, Jewish feast days and some public holidays. 5DM. ☎ (030) 88 02 83 16.

NIKOLAIKIRCHE

Open 10am-6pm; closed Mon and 24 and 31 Dec. 5 DM. ☎ (030) 24 00 21 82.

Peacock Island Castle– The tea rooms

OLYMPIASTADION

The stadium is closed to visitors until 2004.

Glockenturm – Open Apr to end Oct 9am-6pm. 4 DM. ☎ (030) 305 81 23.

PAROCHIALKIRCHE

Open 9am-7pm. (winter 5pm). ☎ (030) 247 59 50.

PERGAMONMUSEUM

Open 10am-6pm; (10pm Thur); closed Mon. 8 DM; free admission the 1st Sun of the month. ☎ (030) 20 90 55 66.

Schloß und Landschaftsgarten PFAUENINSEL

Guided tours (30min) Apr to Oct 10am-5pm; closed Mon. 4 DM. ☎ (03 31) 969 42 00.

PHILHARMONIE

&. Guided tours (1hr) by appointment. ☎ (030) 25 48 81 24.

POLIZEIHISTORISCHE SAMMLUNG

&. Open Mon-Wed 9am-3pm; closed public holidays. Free admission. ☎ (030) 69 93 50 50.

PUPPENTHEATER MUSEUM

Open 9am (11am Sun) to 4pm; closed Sat, 4 weeks in July and Aug and 24, 31 Dec. 5 DM. ☎ (030) 687 81 32.

R – S – T

REICHSTAG

&. Open 9am (10am Sat-Sun) to 4pm; closed 1 Jan, Good Friday, Easter Sunday, Palm Sunday, 24, 25, 26, 31 Dec and during certain parliamentary sessions. Free admission. ☎ (030) 22 73 21 52.

SAMMLUNG BERGGRUEN

Open 10am (11am Sat-Sun) to 6pm; closed Mon. 8 DM; free admission the 1st Sun of the month. ☎ (030) 326 95 80.

ST.-MATTHÄUS-KIRCHE

Open noon-6pm; closed Mon. Free admission; Access to the tower 1 DM. ☎ (030) 20 35 53 11.

ST.-NIKOLAI-KIRCHE

&. Open Apr to Oct Tues and Wed 10am-2pm, Thur 10am-5pm, Fri 10am-5pm, Sat 11am-3pm, Sun 2-4pm; Nov to Mar Sat-Sun only at the same times. ☎ (030) 333 56 39.

SIEGESSÄULE

Open 9.30am-6.30pm (7pm Fri-Sun, 5.30pm every day Oct to Mar); closed 24 Dec. 2 DM.

SOPHIEN KIRCHE

Open May to end Sept Wed 3-6pm, Sat 3-5pm, Sun 10am-1pm; closed 1 May and 3 Oct. ☎ (030) 308 79 20.

STAATSBIBLIOTHEK PREUßISCHER KULTURBESITZ

Haus 1 – Unter den Linden – &. Guided tours (1hr30min) 9am-9pm (5pm Sat); closed Sun and public holidays. 1 DM. ☎ (030) 266 13 69.

Haus 2 – Tiergarten (Kulturforum) – &. As for House 1.

Schloß TEGEL (Humboldtschloß)

Guided tours (45min) May to Sept Mon 10am, 11am, 3pm, 4pm; closed public holidays. 10 DM.

TIERPARK BERLIN-FRIEDRICHSFELDE

&. Open Apr to Sept 9am-7.30pm, Mar and Oct 9am-6.30pm, Nov to Feb 9am-5.30pm. 14 DM. ☎ (030) 51 53 10.

"TOPOGRAPHIE DES TERRORS"

Open 10am-8pm (5pm Oct to Apr); closed 24 and 31 Dec. Free admission. ☎ (030) 25 48 67 03..

Z

ZEISS-GROSSPLANETARIUM

&. Shows Mon-Fri 9.30am, 11.30am; additional sessions Wed 2pm, 3.30pm, 5pm, 8pm, Sat 2pm, 3.30pm, 5pm, 6.30pm, 8pm, Sun 2pm, 3.30pm, 5pm. 8 DM. ☎ (030) 42 18 45 12.

Ph. Gaïc/MICHELIN

Elephant's gate

ZOOLOGISCHER GARTEN

&. Open 9am-6.30pm (6pm 25 Sept to 30 Oct, 5.30pm 1-25 Mar, 5pm 30 Oct to Feb). 14 DM. ☎ (030) 25 40 10.

ZUCKERMUSEUM

Open Mon-Wed 9am-4.30pm, Sun 11am-6pm; closed 1 May, 24, 31 Dec. 4.50 DM. ☎ (030) 31 42 75 86.

POTSDAM

DAMPFMASCHINENHAUS

&. Guided tours (30min) mid-May to mid-Sept Sat-Sun 10am-5pm. 4 DM. ☎ (03 31) 969 42 00.

FILMMUSEUM POTSDAM

&. Open 10am-6pm; closed Mon. 4 DM. ☎ (03 31) 27 18 10.

FILMPARK BABELSBERG

&. Open Mar to Oct 10am-6pm. 29 DM. ☎ (018 05) 34 56 72.

Schloß und Park BABELSBERG

Open Apr to Oct 9am-5pm, Nov to Mar Sat-Sun only 9am-4pm. The park stays open till dusk. 4 DM. ☎ (03 31) 969 42 02.

Schloß und Park CECILIENHOF

&. Open 9am-5pm (4pm Nov to Mar); closed Mon and 25 Dec. 6 DM. ☎ (03 31) 969 42 44.

Schloß und Park SANSSOUCI

Schloß Sanssouci (Sanssouci Castle) – Guided tours (40min) 9am-5pm (4pm Nov to Mar); closed Mon. 10 DM. ☎ (03 31) 969 42 00.

Damenflügel (Wing reserved for the ladies-in-waiting) – Open mid-May to mid-Oct Sat-Sun 10am-5pm. 3 DM. ☎ (03 31) 969 42 00.

Bildergalerie (Picture gallery) – Open mid-May to mid-Oct 10am-5pm; closed Mon. 4 DM. ☎ (03 31) 969 42 00.

Neue Kammern (New rooms) – &. Open mid-May to mid-Oct 10am-5pm, Apr to mid-May and the second fortnight in Oct Sat-Sun only at the same time. 5 DM. ☎ (03 31) 969 42 00.

Neue Orangerie – &. Open mid-May to mid-Oct 10am-5pm; closed Mon. 5 DM. ☎ (03 31) 969 42 00.

Neues Palais (New Palace) – Guided tours (1hr) 9am-5pm (4pm Nov to Mar); closed Fri. 8 DM. ☎ (03 31) 969 42 00.

Römische Bäder (Roman baths) – Open mid-May to mid-Oct 10am-5pm; closed Mon. 3 DM. ☎ (03 31) 969 42 00.

Schloß Charlottenhof (Charlottenhof Castle) – Guided tours (45min) mid-May to mid-Oct 10am-5pm; closed Mon. 6 DM. ☎ (03 31) 969 42 00.

Ph. Gajic/MICHELIN

Trellis work pavilion on the terrace of Sans-souci Castle

Index